FOUR

REALISTIC

SAT®

PRACTICE

TESTS

Carefully Designed Tests for the New SAT, Written by Tutors
Who Take the Actual SAT and Score in the Top 1%

MARKS PREP

D1275239

Senior Editors: Dan Hertz, Anthony Celino, and Shaun Stiemsma

Preface

Dear Student and Parent,

Thank you for purchasing the third edition of this book, which provides you with four new, reliable, realistic and carefully designed SAT practice tests. After listening to popular demand, <u>we have added explanations for all four tests to this edition</u>. Please take a few minutes to read this Preface and the Introduction that follows. They contain helpful background information and practical advice on how to best use this book in conjunction with the free resources provided by the College Board.

Nitin Sawhney
Managing Director, Marks Prep

Why Is This Book Needed?

Since the SAT was redesigned in 2015, there has been a dearth of accurate and helpful preparation materials. As of the date of our publication, the College Board has only released eight official SATs to help students prepare for this entirely new test. They can be found on the Khan Academy website (www.khanacademy.org), along with other SAT preparation material.

Larger test preparation companies have prepared additional practice SAT tests. But, based on our review of many such tests, we believe they have been hurriedly produced. We have found errors on the tests. We've also identified Reading and Writing questions where strong test takers will disagree with the "correct" answers. It's questionable whether students taking these practice tests can rely on their results as an indicator of how well their preparation is going.

Thus far, the only good preparation tools, particularly for the Reading and Writing parts of the redesigned SAT, have been the eight College Board tests and the other material on the Khan Academy website.

Why Is It Important to Take More Practice Tests?

Marks Prep has produced this book of four practice tests because, based on our experience tutoring hundreds of SAT students each year, taking only eight practice tests provides insufficient practice, particularly if a student is aiming for scores in the 700s and/or large score improvements.

On average, each of our students takes many practice tests, including tests taken one section at a time and full-length practice tests. Our students start by doing a full, timed baseline test to evaluate weaknesses, and then, after reviewing weak areas, take timed practice test sections. Finally, they take full tests. Such repeated practice *on realistic tests* is essential for students to build confidence and to help overcome the anxiety of the full-length actual SAT.

The four tests in this book, as well as the explanations, were developed by our tutoring team with the initial aim of meeting the needs of Marks Prep students. The passages and questions that have made it onto each practice test have all been through hundreds of hours of review and editing. This is the only way to ensure error-free tests with non-ambiguous questions, particularly in the Reading and Writing parts of the redesigned SAT. We believe these tests are the best unofficial practice SATs available.

How to Use the Explanations?

We have put a lot of thought into writing explanations for all four tests in a way that mirrors the way we tutor – showing not only the solution for each question but also common traps that a test taker may fall into. In addition, we have suggested alternative strategies for solving challenging questions to give test takers multiple options.

Why Are We Publishing This Book?

We understand the issues of inequity in test preparation, and we work to correct them. Since I co-founded Marks Prep, every tutor has volunteered time to students in our non-profit partner Collegiate Directions (collegiatedirections.org).

Although we are in the tutoring business, we believe that it is possible for committed students to use excellent resources, such as the practice tests in this book, to study independently and do very well on standardized tests. These four practice tests and carefully written explanations provide additional practice on reliable, realistic, carefully designed tests. This practice can help dedicated students gain confidence and make large score improvements.

Why Not Simply Take the ACT?

Many students can do very well on the ACT and should consider that test. However, the ACT, which requires students to work very quickly, particularly on the Math, Reading, and Science sections, is not the best test for every test taker. The SAT, in contrast to the ACT, has more involved questions but also allows more time per question. Thus, it can be the better test for those who like to work carefully and not be rushed.

What Is Marks Prep?

Marks Prep is the test preparation and tutoring division of Marks Education, which provides tutoring, test preparation, and admissions counseling to students all over the world.

Each Marks Prep tutor is an experienced full-time educator and a top 1% test taker who sits for the SAT and other tests every year, in real test centers, along with our students. We use the knowledge gained from taking these tests and working with our students to write efficient strategies and materials for all the tests we tutor—from the SSAT and ISEE to the SAT, ACT, GRE, GMAT, MCAT, and LSAT.

The full-time tutors at Marks Prep have, for the past ten years, tutored hundreds of students each year across the United States and the world, via Skype and other platforms. Students who have worked with us for at least six sessions have, on average, improved their scores by 340 points on the (pre-2015, from baseline 10th grade PSATs). SAT and almost 7 points on the ACT. In contrast to many other firms, we use only actual College Board PSATs and real past ACTs for baseline tests. More specific score improvement data for all tests (including graduate school tests) are available on our website, www.marksprep.com.

Table of Contents

Practice Test Answer Keys

Introduction

How to Use This Book

You can use these tests either after using the practice tests on Khan Academy, or you can simply use these tests instead of those practice materials.

If you have already used the resources on Khan Academy, proceed with the steps below.

If not, you might consider using the tests on Khan Academy first and then using this book for additional practice.

1. Take Test 1 timed, in one sitting.
    1. Do not take breaks in the middle of a test section.
    2. Answer each question, even if you are not sure about the answer. There is no penalty for getting a question incorrect. Circle questions that you are not sure of, so you can review them later.
    3. Time your test carefully. It's a good idea to ask a parent or responsible sibling to time you.
    4. Please eat a full breakfast before the test, and do eat a snack during your breaks. Your brain needs glucose so you can think clearly.
    5. Total Testing Time: 3 hours 10 minutes

Section 1: Reading Test	65 minutes
Break	10 minutes
Section 2: Writing and Language Test	35 minutes
Section 3: Math Test – No Calculator	25 minutes
Break	5 minutes
Section 4: Math Test – Calculator	55 minutes

2. Score the test, and review errors on each section.
    1. Use the answer explanations to understand the problems that were incorrect and those you were not sure about. Also look at the alternative methods outlined for the other problems. Could you have done one of the questions more efficiently?

3. Address Careless Errors

1. You will probably find that on several problems you made careless errors. In other words, you knew how to solve the problem but did not get the right answer.

2. Use the following three-part strategy to eliminate careless errors:

   1. *Underline* (separately, not with one solid underline) what the question is telling you and *circle* what it's asking you.

   2. *Write* out all your work. Writing your work out is the fastest, most efficient way to solve questions. Many students who are strong in Math do problems "in their head". This almost always leads to more careless errors than writing out your work.
   We all have a finite amount of information we can hold in our short-term memory. When we are anxious, our short-term memory doesn't work as well. This is why students who don't write steps out make more avoidable errors on tests.
   Ever heard someone say: "I do fine when I practice at home, but I always do badly on full tests!"? Do you say that? Well, very possibly, it's because you don't write steps out as carefully as you should.

   3. *Double check* your work
   Verify that you have answered what the question is asking. *Follow this step immediately after you finish a problem.* It's far better to take an extra few seconds to double-check each problem than to finish with 5 minutes left and not know where you've made careless errors. It's almost impossible to find careless errors after you finish a test.

4. Complete all three remaining Marks Prep Tests.

Repeat Steps 1–3 above after each test.

SAT Practice Test 1

IMPORTANT REMINDERS

1

A No. 2 pencil is required for the test.
Do not use a mechanical pencil or pen.

2

Sharing any questions with anyone is a violation
of the Test Security and Fairness policies and
may result in your score being canceled.

This cover is representative of what you will see on the day of the SAT.

Reading Test

65 MINUTES, 52 QUESTIONS

Turn to Section 1 of your answer sheet to answer the questions in this section.

DIRECTIONS

Each passage or pair of passages below is followed by a number of questions. After reading each passage or pair, choose the best answer to each question based on what is stated or implied in the passage or passages and in any accompanying graphics (such as a table or graph).

Questions 1–10 are based on the following passage.

This passage is adapted from Jane Austen, *Northanger Abbey*, originally published in 1817. Here, Catherine Morland, Eleanor Tilney, and her brother, Henry Tilney, discuss the merits of different kinds of reading.

"But now really, do not you think *Udolpho*[1] the nicest book in the world?" asked Miss Morland.

"The nicest—by which I suppose you mean the neatest. That must depend upon the binding,"
5 replied Henry.

"Henry," said Miss Tilney, "you are very impertinent. Miss Morland, he is treating you exactly as he does his sister. He is forever finding fault with me, for some incorrectness of language, and now he
10 is taking the same liberty with you. The word 'nicest,' as you used it, did not suit him; and you had better change it as soon as you can, or we shall be overpowered with Johnson and Blair[2] all the rest of the way."

15 "I am sure," cried Catherine, "I did not mean to say anything wrong; but it is a nice book, and why should not I call it so?"

"Very true," said Henry, "and this is a very nice day, and we are taking a very nice walk, and you are
20 two very nice young ladies. Oh! It is a very nice word indeed! It does for everything. Originally perhaps it

---

[1] *The Mysteries of Udolpho*, a Gothic novel by Ann Radcliffe.

[2] Samuel Johnson wrote one of the first English dictionaries, and Hugh Blair was an influential writer and lecturer on rhetoric.

was applied only to express neatness, propriety, delicacy, or refinement—people were nice in their dress, in their sentiments, or their choice. But now
25 every commendation on every subject is comprised in that one word."

"While, in fact," cried his sister, "it ought only to be applied to you, without any commendation at all. You are more nice than wise. Come, Miss Morland,
30 let us leave him to meditate over our faults in the utmost propriety of diction, while we praise *Udolpho* in whatever terms we like best. It is a most interesting work. You are fond of that kind of reading?"

"To say the truth, I do not much like any other. I
35 can read poetry and plays, and things of that sort, and do not dislike travels. But history, real solemn history, I cannot be interested in. Can you?"

"Yes, I am fond of history."

"I wish I were too. I read it a little as a duty, but it
40 tells me nothing that does not either vex or weary me. The quarrels of popes and kings, with wars or pestilences, in every page; the men all so good for nothing, and hardly any women at all—it is very tiresome: and yet I often think it odd that it should be
45 so dull, for a great deal of it must be invention. The speeches that are put into the heroes' mouths, their thoughts and designs—the chief of all this must be invention, and invention is what delights me in other books."

50 "Historians, you think," said Miss Tilney, "display imagination without raising interest. I am fond of history—and am very well contented to take the false with the true. In the principal facts they have

CONTINUE ▶

1   1

sources of intelligence in former histories and
55 records, which may be as much depended on, I
conclude, as anything that does not actually pass
under one's own observation; and as for the little
embellishments you speak of, they are
embellishments, and I like them as such. If a speech
60 be well drawn up, I read it with pleasure, by
whomsoever it may be made—and probably with
much greater, if the production of Mr. Hume or Mr.
Robertson,[3] than if the genuine words of Caractacus,
Agricola, or Alfred the Great."[4]

1

Henry responds in lines 3–4 ("The nicest …
binding") to Catherine's claim about *Udolpho* by

A) expressing a deep-seated dislike of the novel.

B) inadvertently revealing his inability to
understand the meaning of her words.

C) deliberately misunderstanding her in order to
mock her word choice.

D) foolishly emphasizing the appearance of the
book instead of its content.

2

The phrase "taking the same liberty with you" in
line 10 most nearly means

A) espousing the same freedom for Catherine as a
natural right.

B) acting with similarly inappropriate romantic
license towards Catherine.

C) assuming an innate privilege common to all.

D) treating Catherine the same way without her
desiring it.

3

Miss Tilney mentions "Johnson and Blair" (line 13)
primarily to

A) make fun of her brother's tendency to be
pedantic.

B) prove that she is as well-read and knowledgeable
as her brother.

C) imply that her brother has excluded Catherine
from the conversation.

D) justify her disdain for definitions and grammar.

4

Henry repeatedly uses the word "nice" in lines 18–
20 primarily to

A) show his disapproval of the overuse and loss of
meaning of a common word.

B) mock Catherine's views, using irony to show his
disapproval of all the things he mentions.

C) endear himself to his audience, because he
knows he has upset them.

D) emphasize how pleased he is with their situation.

---

[3] David Hume and William Robertson were historians who
wrote during the 18th century.

[4] Caractacus, Agricola, and Alfred the Great were figures from
British and Roman history about whom history books were
written.

CONTINUE

1

1

5

Which choice provides the best evidence for the answer to the previous question?

A) Lines 7–8 ("Miss Morland … sister")

B) Lines 15–17 ("I am … call it so")

C) Lines 23–24 ("people were … their choice")

D) Lines 24–26 (But now … one word")

6

Based on her opinions expressed in the passage, which of the following would Catherine most enjoy reading?

A) A treatise on the causes of the fall of the Roman empire

B) An analysis of the accuracy of the speeches in Shakespeare's history plays

C) A novel about the romantic adventures of a knight under King Arthur

D) A philosophical dialogue regarding the impact of Marco Polo's journeys

7

The word "invention" as it is used in lines 45 and 48 most nearly means

A) something the author fabricated.

B) a newly developed technology.

C) an advancement in how people understand history.

D) something that is deceptive in order to make a point.

8

According to the passage, Miss Tilney believes that speeches recorded in history books are

A) not necessarily true, but much more useful for learning than fictional novels and plays.

B) inaccurate factually, but interesting and enjoyable anyway.

C) deliberately deceptive to give a biased impression of historical events and people.

D) as trustworthy as any other information that we must accept second hand.

9

Which choice provides the best evidence for the answer to the previous question?

A) Lines 45–49 ("The speeches … books")

B) Lines 50–51 ("Historians … interest")

C) Lines 53–57 ("In the … observation")

D) Lines 57–60 ("as for the … made")

10

Miss Tilney mentions Caractacus, Agricola, and Alfred the Great primarily to

A) suggest that their speeches were probably not as good as those written by contemporary historians.

B) emphasize the importance of accurately recording the genuine words of great men throughout history.

C) make fun of her brother's overly zealous reading of the works of historical leaders.

D) compare later rhetoricians to the great speakers of the past.

CONTINUE

1

Questions 11-20 are based on the following passage and supplemental material.

This passage is adapted from Mary Fisher's address to the 1992 Republican National Convention.

Tonight, I represent an AIDS community whose members have been reluctantly drafted from every segment of American society. Though I am white and a mother, I am one with a black infant struggling with
5 tubes in a Philadelphia hospital. Though I am female and contracted this disease in marriage and enjoy the warm support of my family, I am one with the lonely gay man sheltering a flickering candle from the cold wind of his family's rejection.
10 This is not a distant threat. It is a present danger. The rate of infection is increasing fastest among women and children. Largely unknown a decade ago, AIDS is the third leading killer of young adult Americans today. But it won't be third for long, because unlike other
15 diseases, this one travels. Adolescents don't give each other cancer or heart disease because they believe they are in love, but HIV is different; and we have helped it along. We have killed each other with our ignorance, our prejudice, and our silence.
20 We may take refuge in our stereotypes, but we cannot hide there long, because HIV asks only one thing of those it attacks. Are you human? And this is the right question. Are you human? Because people with HIV have not entered some alien state of being.
25 They are human. They have not earned cruelty, and they do not deserve meanness. They don't benefit from being isolated or treated as outcasts. Each of them is exactly what God made: a person; not evil, deserving of our judgment; not victims, longing for our pity—
30 people, ready for support and worthy of compassion.
My call to you, my Party, is to take a public stand, no less compassionate than that of the President and Mrs. Bush. They have embraced me and my family in memorable ways. In the place of judgment, they have
35 shown affection. In difficult moments, they have raised our spirits. In the darkest hours, I have seen them reaching not only to me, but also to my parents, armed with that stunning grief and special grace that comes only to parents who have themselves leaned too long
40 over the bedside of a dying child.
With the President's leadership, much good has been done. Much of the good has gone unheralded, and as the President has insisted, much remains to be done.

But we do the President's cause no good if we praise
45 the American family but ignore a virus that destroys it.
We must be consistent if we are to be believed. We cannot love justice and ignore prejudice, love our children and fear to teach them. Whatever our role as parent or policymaker, we must act as eloquently as we
50 speak—or we have no integrity. My call to the nation is a plea for awareness. If you believe you are safe, you are in danger. Because I was not hemophiliac, I was not at risk. Because I was not gay, I was not at risk. Because I did not inject drugs, I was not at risk.
55 My father has devoted much of his lifetime guarding against another holocaust. He is part of the generation who heard Pastor Niemoellor come out of the Nazi death camps to say:
"First they came for the Socialists, and I did not
60 speak out. Because I was not a Socialist. Then they came for the Trade Unionists, and I did not speak out. Because I was not a Trade Unionist. Then they came for the Jews, and I did not speak out. Because I was not a Jew. Then they came for me—and there was no one
65 left to speak for me."
The lesson history teaches is this: If you believe you are safe, you are at risk. If you do not see this killer stalking your children, look again. There is no family or community, no race or religion, no place left in America
70 that is safe. Until we genuinely embrace this message, we are a nation at risk.

AIDS Cases 1981–1991: Adult and Pediatric

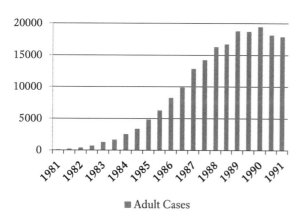

Adult Cases

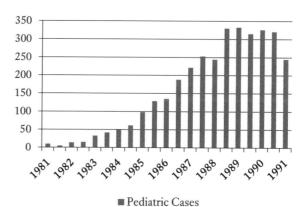

Pediatric Cases

Adapted from the Centers for Disease Control and Prevention website.

11

In response to the AIDS crisis, the author advocates most directly for

A) understanding and support for AIDS patients.

B) decreasing the rate of the spread of AIDS.

C) support for the President's AIDS initiatives.

D) heightened awareness of the behaviors that can lead to AIDS.

12

Which choice provides the best evidence for the answer to the previous question?

A) Lines 10–13 ("This is … today")

B) Lines 27–30 ("Each of … compassion")

C) Lines 33–36 ("They have … spirits")

D) Lines 51–54 ("If you … at risk")

13

In the first paragraph, the author most likely makes statements beginning with "though" in order to

A) separate herself from other AIDS patients.

B) highlight the role of race and sexuality in contracting AIDS.

C) draw attention to faulty stereotypes of AIDS patients.

D) emphasize her unique challenges as a white woman.

14

The author mentions an "alien state of being" in line 24 in order to

A) dehumanize AIDS patients.

B) compare physical differences between AIDS patients and healthy humans.

C) emphasize that the spread of AIDS has given people a new group identity.

D) belie the assumptions some people have made about AIDS patients.

1

1

15

The author emphasizes the ways that President Bush has responded to the AIDS crisis as a

A) compassionate personal friend.

B) bold leader creating legislation to address the issue.

C) nobly intentioned but insufficiently active politician.

D) sympathetic but ineffectual figurehead.

16

Which choice provides the best evidence for the answer to the previous question?

A) Lines 27–30 ("Each of … compassion")

B) Lines 36–40 ("I have … child")

C) Lines 42–43 ("Much of … be done")

D) Lines 44–45 ("But we … destroys it")

17

As used in line 50, "integrity" most nearly means

A) completeness.

B) purity.

C) consistency.

D) righteousness.

18

The author uses the terms "we" in line 46 and "you" in line 51 to refer to

A) completely different groups of people to suggest their opposition.

B) her own party as a whole and those within her party who don't wish to show compassion.

C) the American people as a whole and those who have not yet been personally affected by AIDS.

D) those who have AIDS and those who do not.

19

The primary rhetorical purpose of citing Pastor Niemoellor (lines 59–65) is to

A) compare the devastation caused by the AIDS epidemic to that of the Holocaust.

B) quote a religious source to support the legitimacy of the author's argument.

C) indicate that the public response to the AIDS crisis is analogous to public response to the Holocaust.

D) provide historical context for the proper response to the AIDS epidemic.

20

Based on the graphs of AIDS cases provided, it can be reasonably inferred that

A) pediatric cases were a much lower percent of the total number of children than adult cases were of the adult population.

B) pediatric cases made up a small proportion of all AIDS cases.

C) all cases increased over time, but pediatric cases increased at a much lower rate.

D) pediatric AIDS cases were more severe than adult AIDS cases.

Questions 21–30 are based on the following passage.

The following passage is from Dan Vergano, "Monkeys Steer Wheelchairs with Their Brains, Raising Hope for Paralyzed People." ©2014 by National Geographic.

Experimental wheelchairs and exoskeletons controlled by thought alone offer surprising insights into the brain, neuroscientists reported on Monday.

Best known for his experimental exoskeleton that
5 helped a paralyzed man kick the opening ball for June's World Cup in Brazil, Duke University neuroscientist Miguel Nicolelis presented the latest "brain-machine interface" findings from his team's "Walk Again Project" at the Society for
10 Neuroscience meeting.

"Some of our patients say they feel they are walking on sand," says Nicolelis, describing pilot research in which eight paralyzed patients walked using a robotic exoskeleton that moved in response to
15 readings of the patients' brain waves. "We are actually fooling the brain of patients to think it is not a machine carrying them, but they feel they are themselves walking forward."

Insights into the brains of paralyzed patients are
20 helping to drive the technology as well as leading to new discoveries, says neuroscientist Eberhard Fetz of the University of Washington in Seattle. Roughly 130,000 people yearly suffer spinal cord injuries worldwide, and for more than a decade, researchers
25 have sought to help these patients using robotic interfaces with the brain. After years of advances, efforts such as the exoskeleton are moving into the earliest stages of medical testing in patient volunteers.

30 "For patients, they are probably not coming fast enough," Fetz says. "But brain-machine interfaces are giving us results producing a basic understanding of neural mechanisms. That is going to happen in parallel with developing these as tools to benefit
35 patients."

Brain-machine interfaces have become a buzzword in recent years, triggering headlines when, for example, Brown University's John Donoghue's human patients drank coffee and picked up objects
40 with robotic arms controlled by brain-implanted electrodes.

At the meeting, Nicolelis also presented research on two rhesus monkeys that had electrodes implanted deep in their brains that, with training, allowed the
45 animals to steer a wheelchair using thought alone. The goal of that research is partly to help develop a "brain pacemaker" implant that would pick up clearer signals from thoughts to help control future robotic prosthetics.

50 Signals from deep in the brain are much easier for devices to read than ones picked up by electrical skin sensors on patient's skulls. Such implants made the monkeys relatively quick students at wheelchair driving. "They can reliably steer the wheelchair to
55 get a grape," Nicolelis said. "They like grapes."

Fetz and colleagues have similarly shown that brain interfaces in monkeys can "bridge" the damaged area in a spinal cord injury, allowing voluntary movement of muscles. "These efforts are
60 in fact coming along and offer a lot of promise," he says.

Training paralysis patients to walk with an experimental exoskeleton can have unexpected benefits too. The people in Nicolelis' study showed
65 improved muscle tone, heart health, and digestion over the last year, he says.

Most surprising has been the finding that the faster patients walk with the exoskeleton device—a skeletal frame equipped with 15 electrical motors
70 triggered by electroencephalogram readings—the more natural the walking feels to them.

Paralysis also cuts off sensation from the lower limbs, which can make standing upright feel alarming, as if one is simply hanging in air, Nicolelis
75 says. However, the brain's ability to manufacture "phantom" feeling, best known from amputees who report pain from phantom limbs they no longer possess, similarly kicks in for paralysis patients learning to walk in an exoskeleton.

80 If they walk slow, they feel that they are walking on sand; faster, that they are on grass, and fastest that they are walking on hot pavement."

Despite the excitement over brain-machine interfaces in recent years, a great deal of hard work
85 remains ahead for researchers and patients, cautions neuroscientist Daofen Chen of the National Institute of Neurological Disorders and Stroke, part of the federal National Institutes of Health.

"In my personal view, brain-machine interfaces are
90 offering important tools to understand the brain,"

1

Chen says. "We are far from understanding the brain well enough to expect them to serve as solutions."

Fetz, however, suggests that enough progress is being made to feel good about developing robotics
95 that might help patients, both in efforts such as the exoskeleton and other advances that might bridge spinal cord injuries to restore normal functions.

21

The overall structure of this text can be best described as

A) a detailed account of an experiment's scientific procedure followed by an analysis of its results.

B) a description of an innovative technological advancement and what scientists have learned from this invention.

C) a broad overview of a serious medical diagnosis and a digression into several avenues for treatment.

D) an explanation of a bold and impractical attempt at curing a medical condition that has proven incurable.

22

What is the author's main point?

A) Current brain-machine interfaces are intrinsically flawed and require further research to resolve specific defects.

B) Brain-machine interfaces are an excellent and promising cure for various causes of paralysis.

C) People suffering from paralysis suffer from a lack of effective treatment options and future research is necessary to find alternatives to current treatments.

D) Recent advances in brain-machine interfaces have promising applications in treatment of spinal cord injury.

23

As used in line 20, "drive" most nearly means

A) maneuver.

B) transport.

C) unveil.

D) stimulate.

24

According to Fetz, the relationship between brain-machine interface research and the development of related technology is

A) one-sided, because research provides an essential basis for the development of future technologies.

B) promising, but uncertain because so much more research must be completed for the technology to provide needed solutions.

C) interdependent, because technologies provide new insights and research enables new technologies.

D) deceptive, because, despite their apparent similarity, each has its own priorities and its own timetable.

25

Which choice provides the best evidence for the answer to the previous question?

A) Lines 15–18 ("We are ... forward")

B) Lines 31–35 ("But brain-machine ... patients")

C) Lines 56–59 ("Fetz and ... muscles")

D) Lines 89–92 ("In my personal ... solutions")

26

An advantage to using "electrodes implanted deep within" (lines 43–44) the brain is that they

A) function as a "brain pacemaker," which regulates brain activity.

B) are the best method to train monkeys to steer wheelchairs.

C) allow machines to receive clearer signals from the brain than skin sensors do.

D) are more reliable for use with wheelchairs than with exoskeletons.

27

Which choice provides the best evidence for the answer to the previous question?

A) Lines 42–45 ("At the ... alone")

B) Lines 50–52 ("Signals from ... skulls")

C) Lines 54–55 ("'They can ... like grapes'")

D) Lines 62–66 ("Training ... he says")

28

As used in line 77, "phantom" most nearly means

A) ghostly.

B) painful.

C) skeletal.

D) imagined.

29

In line 55, Nicolelis mentions that monkeys "like grapes" primarily to

A) provide an explanation for the monkeys' motivation to steer the wheelchairs.

B) indicate that the monkeys involved in the experiment were not mistreated.

C) challenge the assumption that monkeys are not able to complete tasks that benefit them.

D) offer a humorous detail that reveals his familiarity with the monkeys' habits.

30

Based on the passage as a whole, how does Fetz's attitude compare to Chen's?

A) Chen is more cautious whereas Fetz is more reckless.

B) Chen is more excited whereas Fetz is more reserved.

C) Chen and Fetz are both lukewarm.

D) Chen is more tentative whereas Fetz is more optimistic.

1

1

Questions 31–41 are based on the following passages.

The following passages are excerpted from the first Lincoln–Douglas debate on August 21, 1858 in Ottawa, Illinois. Passage 1 is adapted from Stephen Douglas's opening statement. Passage 2 is adapted from Abraham Lincoln's opening statement.

Passage 1

Mr. Lincoln, in the extract from which I have read, says that this Government cannot endure permanently in the same condition in which it was made by its framers—divided into free and slave
5 States. He says that it has existed for about seventy years thus divided, and yet he tells you that it cannot endure permanently on the same principles and in the same relative condition in which our fathers made it. Why can it not exist divided into free and slave
10 States? Washington, Jefferson, Franklin, Madison, Hamilton, Jay, and the great men of that day, made this Government divided into free States and slave States, and left each State perfectly free to do as it pleased on the subject of slavery. Why can it not exist
15 on the same principles on which our fathers made it? They knew when they framed the Constitution that in a country as wide and broad as this, with such a variety of climate, production and interest, the people necessarily required different laws and
20 institutions in different localities. They knew that the laws and regulations which would suit the granite hills of New Hampshire would be unsuited to the rice plantations of South Carolina, and they, therefore, provided that each State should retain its own
25 Legislature and its own sovereignty, with the full and complete power to do as it pleased within its own limits, in all that was local and not national. One of the reserved rights of the States, was the right to regulate the relations between Master and Servant,
30 on the slavery question. At the time the Constitution was framed, there were thirteen States in the Union, twelve of which were slaveholding States and one free State. Suppose this doctrine of uniformity preached by Mr. Lincoln, that the States should all be free or all
35 be slave had prevailed, and what would have been the result? Of course, the twelve slaveholding States would have overruled the one free State, and slavery would have been fastened by a Constitutional provision on every inch of the American Republic,
40 instead of being left as our fathers wisely left it, to

each State to decide for itself. Here I assert that uniformity in the local laws and institutions of the different States is neither possible nor desirable. If uniformity had been adopted when the Government
45 was established, it must inevitably have been the uniformity of slavery everywhere, or else the uniformity of negro citizenship and negro equality everywhere.

Passage 2

The great variety of the local institutions in the
50 States, springing from differences in the soil, differences in the face of the country, and in the climate, are bonds of Union. They do not make "a house divided against itself," but they make a house united. If they produce in one section of the country
55 what is called for by the wants of another section, and this other section can supply the wants of the first, they are not matters of discord but bonds of union, true bonds of union. But can this question of slavery be considered as among *these* varieties in the
60 institutions of the country? I leave it to you to say whether, in the history of our Government, this institution of slavery has not always failed to be a bond of union, and, on the contrary, been an apple of discord, and an element of division in the house. I ask
65 you to consider whether—so long as the moral constitution of men's minds shall continue to be the same, after this generation and assemblage shall sink into the grave, and another race shall arise, with the same moral and intellectual development we have—
70 whether, if that institution is standing in the same irritating position in which it now is, it will not continue an element of division? If so, then I have a right to say that, in regard to this question, the Union is a house divided against itself; and when the Judge
75 reminds me that I have often said to him that the institution of slavery has existed for eighty years in some States, and yet it does not exist in some others, I agree to the fact, and I account for it by looking at the position in which our fathers originally placed
80 it—restricting it from the new Territories where it had not gone, and legislating to cut off its source by the abrogation of the slave-trade thus putting the seal of legislation *against its spread*.

31

Based on his argument, the author of Passage 1 sees the founding fathers as

A) anachronisms.

B) paragons.

C) conservatives.

D) heroes.

32

Which choice provides the best evidence for the answer to the previous question?

A) Lines 1-9 ("Mr. Lincoln … made it")

B) Lines 9-15 ("Why can it … made it")

C) Lines 20-27 ("They knew … national")

D) Lines 33-41 ("Suppose … decide for itself")

33

In Passage 1, the author's underlying argument is that

A) each state should determine for itself whether to allow slavery, because each state has diverse needs.

B) a majority of states are slave states, so in order to unify the country slavery should be legal everywhere.

C) mandating universal citizenship is unlawful, because citizenship should be determined by individual state governments.

D) America should be divided on the issue of slavery because that is what the founding fathers wanted.

34

The author of Passage 1 describes the terrains of South Carolina and New Hampshire in lines 21-23 in order to

A) underscore the need for political similarities despite geographic differences.

B) accentuate the extreme and potentially irreconcilable differences between states.

C) argue that differences among the states require different laws and procedures.

D) imply that the Northern states have no need for slaves based on their economies.

35

Based on the views expressed in Passage 2, the author of Passage 2 most nearly views the institution of slavery as

A) acceptable eighty years ago, but now outdated.

B) an element of diversity that enhances America's union.

C) immoral and inconsistent with American values.

D) a source of long-lasting, divisive conflict.

36

The best evidence for the previous question is found in

A) lines 49-54 ("The great … united").

B) lines 60-64 ("I leave … the house").

C) lines 74-78 ("and when … the fact").

D) lines 78-83 ("I account … *spread*").

CONTINUE ➡

1

1

37

As used in line 66, "constitution" most nearly means

A) governing document.

B) authority.

C) composition.

D) rectitude.

38

In line 82, "abrogation" most nearly means

A) abolition.

B) increase.

C) reduction.

D) hiatus.

39

How do the authors of both passages interpret the founding fathers' approach to the legality of slavery?

A) Douglas argues that the founding fathers supported slavery federally, whereas Lincoln thinks they were opposed to slavery in all states.

B) Douglas and Lincoln both agree that the founding fathers fully supported the states' right to determine the legality of slavery.

C) Douglas claims that the founding fathers fully supported states' right to determine the status of slavery, whereas Lincoln argues that they wanted to restrict new states from legalizing slavery.

D) Douglas suggests that the founding fathers supported slave states permanently, whereas Lincoln indicates that they only supported slave states temporarily.

40

The authors of both passages most strongly agree that

A) America is comprised of diverse states.

B) slavery is a profitable institution for the South.

C) slavery is a divisive issue.

D) the founding fathers' principles must determine all laws.

41

Which choice provides the best evidence for the answer to the previous question?

A) Lines 1–9 ("Mr. Lincoln … made it") and lines 60–64 ("I leave … the house")

B) Lines 10–15 ("Washington … made it") and lines 78–83 ("I account … *spread*")

C) Lines 16–20 ("They knew … localities") and lines 49–54 ("The great … united")

D) Lines 27–30 ("One of … question") and lines 64–69 ("I ask … have")

CONTINUE

Questions 42–52 are based on the following passage and supplementary material.

This passage is adapted from Stephen Jay Gould, *The Panda's Thumb: More Reflections in Natural History.* ©1980 by W. W. Norton & Company.

The theory of plate tectonics has led us to reconstruct the history of our planet's surface. During the past 200 million years, our modern continents have fragmented and dispersed from a
5 single supercontinent, Pangaea, that coalesced from earlier continents 225 million years ago. If modern oddities are the signs of history, we should ask whether any peculiar things that animals do today might be rendered more sensible as adaptations to
10 previous continental positions. Among the greatest puzzles and wonders of natural history are the long and circuitous routes of migration followed by many animals. Some lengthy movements make sense as direct paths to favorable climates from season to
15 season; they are no more peculiar than the annual winter migration to Florida of large mammals inside metallic birds. But other animals migrate thousands of miles—from feeding to breeding grounds—with astounding precision when other appropriate spots
20 seem close at hand. Could any of these peculiar routes be rendered shorter and more sensible on a map of ancient continental positions? Archie Carr, world's expert on the migration of green turtles, has made such a proposal.
25 A population of the green turtle, *Chelonia mydas*, nests and breeds on the small and isolated central Atlantic island of Ascension. London soup chefs and victualing ships of Her Majesty's Navy found and exploited these turtles long ago. But they did not
30 suspect, as Carr discovered by tagging animals at Ascension and recovering them later at their feeding grounds, that *Chelonia* travels 2,000 miles from the coast of Brazil to feed on this "pinpoint of land hundreds of miles from other shores," this "barely
35 exposed spire in mid-ocean."
Turtles feed and breed on separate grounds for good reasons. They feed on sea grasses in protected, shallow-water pastures, but breed on exposed shores where sandy beaches develop—preferably, on islands
40 where predators are rare. But why travel 2,000 miles to the middle of an ocean when other, apparently appropriate breeding grounds are so much nearer?

(Another large population of the same species breeds on the Caribbean coast of Costa Rica.) As Carr
45 writes: "The difficulties facing such a voyage would seem insurmountable if it were not so clear that the turtles are somehow surmounting them."
Perhaps, Carr reasoned, this odyssey is a peculiar extension of something much more sensible, a
50 journey to an island in the middle of the Atlantic, when the Atlantic was little more than a puddle between two continents recently separated. South America and Africa parted company some 80 million years ago, when ancestors of the genus *Chelonia* were
55 already present in the area. Ascension is an island associated with the Mid-Atlantic Ridge, a linear belt where new sea floor wells up from the earth's interior. This upwelling material often piles itself high enough to form islands.
60 Iceland is the largest modern island formed by the Mid-Atlantic Ridge; Ascension is a smaller version of the same process. After islands form on one side of a ridge, they are pushed away by new material welling up and spreading out. Thus, islands tend to be older
65 as we move farther and farther from a ridge. But they also tend to get smaller and finally to erode away into underwater seamounts, for their supply of new material dries up once they drift away from an active ridge. Unless preserved and built up by a shield of
70 coral and other organisms, islands will eventually be eroded below sea level by waves. (They may also sink gradually from sight as they move downslope from an elevated ridge into the oceanic depths.)
Carr therefore proposed that the ancestors of
75 Ascension green turtles swam a short distance from Brazil to a "proto-Ascension" on the late Cretaceous Mid-Atlantic Ridge. As this island moved out and sank, a new one formed at the ridge and the turtles ventured a bit farther. This process continued until,
80 like the jogger who does a bit more each day and ends up a marathoner, turtles found themselves locked into a 2,000-mile journey.

Figure 1

Cretaceous Period, 65 million years ago

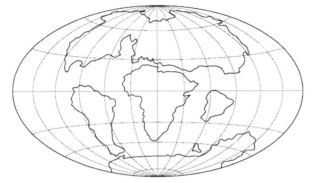

Adapted from PALEOMAP Project. © 2001 Christopher Scotese.

Figure 2

Present Day

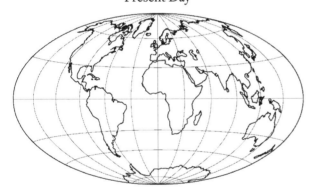

42

The author describes the turtles' journey primarily as

A) a curious phenomenon.

B) an impressive feat of memory.

C) an inexplicable outlier.

D) an unmatched instance of stamina.

43

Which choice provides the best evidence for the answer to the previous question?

A) Lines 13–18 ("Some lengthy ... birds")

B) Lines 25–35 ("A population ... mid-ocean''")

C) Lines 40–42 ("But why ... nearer?")

D) Lines 74–82 ("Carr therefore ... journey")

44

The overall structure of this text can be best described as

A) a chronological narrative of turtle migration beginning from 400 years ago until present day.

B) an argument advocating for a revolutionary theory of tectonic plate movement over time.

C) an interpretation of turtles' motives for journeying to Ascension and leaving their feeding grounds.

D) an explanation of a migratory pattern based on island formation in the Mid-Atlantic.

45

Which of the following would be most in conflict with the author's views expressed in lines 6–10 ("If modern ... continental positions")?

A) Researching the evolutionary development of tadpole metamorphosis without understanding all of its effects.

B) Failing to question whether birds actually do migrate seasonally, but simply trusting observable phenomena.

C) Neglecting to consider geological history in exploring evolutionary patterns in the human genome.

D) Ignoring a computer virus that has the potential to do serious damage.

46

In line 19, "astounding" most nearly means

A) horrifying.

B) superb.

C) astonishing.

D) alarming.

47

In lines 25–59, the author's primary purpose is to

A) explain why London soup chefs did not understand the origins of the turtles they fed to the Navy.

B) argue that the turtles' long migration is unnecessary and serves only to exhaust the turtles.

C) expose the historical human interventions that have lengthened turtle migration.

D) suggest the likely relationship between a current turtle migration pattern and past continental shifts.

48

Which choice provides the best evidence for the answer to the previous question?

A) Lines 27–29 ("London … long ago")

B) Lines 36–40 ("They feed … are rare")

C) Lines 44–47 ("As Carr … surmounting them'")

D) Lines 48–52 ("Perhaps … recently separated")

49

Based on lines 48–73 it can be reasonably inferred that

A) Africa and North America will drift back together over time just as they did during the time of Pangaea.

B) new islands may be formed on the Mid-Atlantic Ridge based on the welling up and spreading out of materials.

C) Ascension will erode into a seamount soon because it does not have a shield of coral to protect it.

D) Iceland will not be affected by the natural erosion process because it is surrounded by a shield of coral.

CONTINUE ➤

50

Carr's theory suggests that the distance of the turtles' migration has lengthened through time because

A) the island they have always swum to has moved farther and farther away as the continents have shifted.

B) the evolutionary adaptations of the turtles have made them better swimmers, able to seek better breeding grounds farther away.

C) the sea waves progressively eroded away their breeding islands, forcing them to move farther out to newly formed islands.

D) the Mid-Atlantic Ridge destroyed the island to which they originally migrated, forcing them to swim to more distant islands.

51

In lines 79–82 ("This process ... journey"), the author primarily employ which rhetorical device?

A) Repetition

B) Analogy

C) Metonymy

D) Hyperbole

52

Do the maps provide support for the author's claim that the turtles' journey to their breeding ground has lengthened over time?

A) Yes, because the maps provide evidence that various islands have been formed by the mid-Atlantic Ridge.

B) Yes, because the maps show that Africa and South America have grown further apart and the Atlantic Ocean has expanded.

C) No, because the maps do not indicate the original location of their breeding ground versus their contemporary breeding ground.

D) No, because the maps do not provide sufficient evidence of tectonic plate movement.

STOP

**If you finish before time is called, you may check your work on this section only.
Do not turn to any other section.**

Writing and Language Test
35 MINUTES, 44 QUESTIONS

Turn to Section 2 of your answer sheet to answer the questions in this section.

DIRECTIONS

Each passage below is accompanied by a number of questions. For some questions, you will consider how the passage might be revised to improve the expression of ideas. For other questions, you will consider how the passage might be edited to correct errors in sentence structure, usage, or punctuation. A passage or a question may be accompanied by one or more graphics (such as a table or graph) that you will consider as you make revising and editing decisions.

Some questions will direct you to an underlined portion of a passage. Other questions will direct you to a location in a passage or ask you to think about the passage as a whole.

After reading each passage, choose the answer to each question that most effectively improves the quality of writing in the passage or that makes the passage conform to the conventions of standard written English. Many questions include a "NO CHANGE" option. Choose that option if you think the best choice is to leave the relevant portion of the passage as it is.

Questions 1–11 are based on the following passage.

Iran's Independent Ulema

[1] From the late seventh century until around 1500 CE, Iran fulfilled this role by following a religious and economic path similar to that of the rest of the Islamic world. [2] However, under the Safavids, Iran's conversion to Shi'ism moved the Iranian people in a different direction. [3] In addition to this conversion, the changing role of Iran's ulema (religious scholars) pushed the Iranians on a path even further from that followed by

1

The author is considering adding the following phrase immediately after the underlined portion:

> in the early 16th century CE

Should the writer make that addition here?

A) Yes, because it provides context needed to understand the time period for the essay.

B) Yes, because it is an essential definition for understanding the paragraphs that follow.

C) No, because it diverges from the main point of the paragraph.

D) No, because it contradicts information elsewhere in the passage.

the rest of the Islamic world. [4] Since the Umayyad dynasty in 661 CE, Iran has played a role as an economic boon throughout the Islamic world. **2**

After the Safavids, the Iranian ulema divorced themselves from the secular political power, which changed the political trajectory of Iran for centuries to come. Under the Safavids, the ulema held positions in a state-controlled bureaucracy and expanded their power through acquiring soyurghal, land grants. With the fall of the central Safavid power in 1722 CE, the ulema lost their funding but successfully found new, independent sources of funding.

Now financially independent, the ulema **3** were no longer tied to a central political authority and gained autonomous power. The ulema deemed that they, as Islamic legal scholars, held utmost authority. **4** Under the Qajars, the ulema involved themselves in day to day affairs of the common people by **5** overseeing charities, marriages, funerals, and establishing justice.

2

For the sake of logic and clarity, sentence 4 should be placed
A) where it is now.
B) before sentence 1.
C) after sentence 1.
D) after sentence 2.

3

A) NO CHANGE
B) were not any longer tied to a central political authority and gained autonomous power.
C) were no longer tied to a central political authority and had gained autonomous power.
D) gained autonomous power.

4

Which choice provides the most specific chronological information?
A) NO CHANGE
B) Under the Qajars, who ruled Iran from 1785 to 1925,
C) Under the Qajars, who were also the rulers of Iran for over a century,
D) Under the Qajars, a Turkish tribe that ruled Iran through the entire 19th century,

5

A) NO CHANGE
B) overseeing charities, marriages, funerals, and justice.
C) overseeing charities, overseeing marriages, funerals, and establishing justice.
D) overseeing charities, marriages, overseeing funerals, and justice.

The ulema's independence impacted Iranian politics and distinguished Iran from its Ottoman neighbors. During the late 19th century and early 20th century both the Iranian Qajars and the Ottomans experienced constitutional [6] revolutions, however the ulema responded differently in each empire. In Iran the ulema supported a constitution because it limited the power of the state, a limitation they favored. In the Ottoman Empire, though, the ulema opposed a constitution and allied themselves with the state because the state financially supported the Ottoman ulema.

The ulema's competition for power against the state defined Iranian politics for the following centuries. Today, Iran's Ayatollah, the highest ranking of all Shi'a authorities, also [7] acts as a Supreme Leader and holds vast political control. Due to Iran's post-Safavid separation of the ulema from the state, the ulema grew more powerful and political in Iran than in anywhere else in the Middle East.

[8] Iran deviated from the rest of the Middle East beginning with the Safavid conversion in the 16th century, which resulted in its distinct religious and political demographics today. Separating from the state

[6]

A) NO CHANGE
B) revolutions, the
C) revolutions however
D) revolutions; however,

[7]

A) NO CHANGE
B) act as a Supreme Leader and holds
C) acts as a Supreme Leader and hold
D) act as a Supreme Leader and hold

[8]

A) NO CHANGE
B) However, Iran
C) Therefore, Iran
D) Finally, Iran

after the Safavid empire, [9] the ulema's power changed the political landscape of Iran and made it [10] unique of all Islamic countries. The ulema in Iran hold immense autonomous political and religious power in Iran's Islamic Republic today, whereas in the rest of the Middle East the ulema are civil servants. [11] The role of the ulema in Iran, so different from their role throughout the rest of the Ottoman world, impacted Iran's historical trajectory. It also continues to impact its contemporary politics up to today.

[9]

A) NO CHANGE
B) the ulemas power changed
C) the ulema used their power to change
D) the ulemas's used their power to change

[10]

A) NO CHANGE
B) unique among Islamic
C) unique to other Islamic
D) unique towards other Islamic

[11]

Which choice most effectively combines the two underlined sentences?

A) Their unique power in Iran has shaped not only Iran's historical trajectory but also its contemporary politics.

B) The role of the ulema in Iran, so different from their role throughout the rest of the Ottoman world, impacted Iran's historical trajectory, and it also continues to impact its contemporary politics up to today.

C) The role of the ulema in Iran, both impacting Iran's historical trajectory and continuing to impact its contemporary politics, is different than their role throughout the Ottoman world.

D) The role of the ulema in Iran, so different from their role throughout the rest of the Ottoman world, impacted Iran's historical trajectory; it also continues to impact its contemporary politics up to today.

Questions 12–22 are based on the following passage and supplementary material.

Are Professors an Endangered Species?

Higher education has long been a respected field as professors at universities and colleges throughout the United States have been seen [12] as essential contributors to the vast store of thought and knowledge in the sciences and humanities but also as indispensable mentors and educators to young people entering their specific fields. [13] Therefore, the reality of higher education in the 21st century has dramatically changed the position of "professor," and both students and professors are among those who suffer from the changing economics of higher education.

[14] Though some courses at large universities may be taught by graduate students, most "professors" in lower level courses are adjunct instructors, teachers hired part-time and typically paid by the course a semester at a time.

12

A) NO CHANGE
B) as helpful
C) not only as essential
D) DELETE the underlined portion.

13

A) NO CHANGE
B) However,
C) Thus,
D) Because,

14

At this point, the writer is considering adding the following sentence.

> In their first years at college, many students will never be taught by a full-time professor.

Should the writer make this addition here?

A) Yes, because it specifies which colleges and students are affected by the change discussed in the preceding paragraph.
B) Yes, because it provides a helpful context for understanding the importance of the following sentence.
C) No, because it distracts from the main idea of the passage.
D) No, because it conflicts with information that appears later in the same paragraph.

CONTINUE

From many local two-year community colleges to some exclusive liberal arts colleges, **15** these are often hired with little more than a perfunctory interview. Even if **16** he or she is well-qualified and excellent teachers, the lack of continuity from one semester to the next means that students will neither become connected to an academic department through their first courses nor develop relationships that might lead to a letter of recommendation or other advancement in their chosen field.

15
A) NO CHANGE
B) they
C) them
D) these instructors

16
A) NO CHANGE
B) they are well-qualified and an excellent teacher,
C) he or she is well-qualified and an excellent teacher,
D) they are well-qualified and excellent teachers,

Proportion of Instructors in Higher Education in Tenure Track Positions

1969

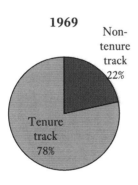

2009

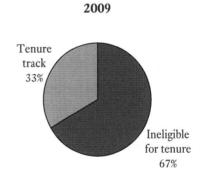

Adapted from the Association of Governing Boards of Universities and Colleges. ©2013.

This lack of continuity and depth of instruction is a relatively recent **17** thing. According to the Association of Governing Boards of Universities and Colleges, in 1969, full-time, tenure-track faculty made up nearly 80% of the instructors in all institutions of higher **18** learning but **19** tenured faculty made up only one third of all instructors twenty years later.

20 Why the change? Economic instability for higher education might account for some of the difference: tenured professors not only cost more each year, but also represent an economic obligation for many years into the future, so schools in immediate financial trouble may be unable to offer new tenure-track positions.

17

A) NO CHANGE
B) phenomenon.
C) event.
D) activity.

18

A) NO CHANGE
B) learning; whereas
C) learning, but
D) learning. Though

19

Which choice accurately reflects the information in the graph and supports the purpose of the sentence?

A) NO CHANGE
B) the group ineligible for tenure was down to below 70% by 2009.
C) tenure-track positions accounted for approximately one third of instructors by 2009.
D) the numbers of professors in all categories has risen considerably over the last 30 years.

20

Which choice best introduces this paragraph?

A) NO CHANGE
B) This is unfortunate.
C) At this rate, soon few if any full time faculty members will remain.
D) What can be done to fix this problem?

2 **2**

However, for most, it is more a question of priorities than of economic necessity. Since adjuncts receive minimal pay relative to the tuition and fees brought in by the students in their classes, the extensive use of adjuncts [21] are a natural choice when viewed in terms of immediate economic interest. Why pay more when the same job can be done for so much less?

A partial solution to these problems may be developing from the adjuncts themselves. Working together with groups like Adjunct Action, instructors have begun to put pressure on schools to offer better compensation and more benefits, with the goal of "creating better working conditions for themselves and better learning conditions for their students." Though the professor as a bespectacled sage in a padded jacket may be a thing of the past, such efforts may help to bring about more consistency and continuity in the classroom for both student and instructor.

Question 22 asks about the previous passage as a whole.

21

A) NO CHANGE
B) was
C) were
D) is

Think about the previous passage and included supplemental material as a whole as you answer question 22.

22

Which of the following best summarizes the data presented in the graph?

A) The number of tenure-track professors has decreased from 1969 to 2009.
B) The percentage of tenure-track professors has increased from 1969 to 2009.
C) The number of adjunct professors has increased from 1969 to 2009.
D) The percentage of non-tenure track professors has increased from 1969 to 2009.

2

2

Questions 23–33 are based on the following passage.

Shostakovich's Symphonic Statement

[23] Joseph Stalin's dictatorship in Soviet Russia during the 1930s and 1940s was founded upon Marxist theories of communism and characterized by terror. He involved himself with the music industry to ensure that all Soviet music [24] acted as propaganda and promoted his regime. Composers who did not conform to Stalin's standards were subject to public criticism, and many were exiled or persecuted. After the initial performance of his provocative Fourth Symphony, composer Dmitri Shostakovich faced harsh scrutiny from Stalin's government. As a means of survival, Shostakovich composed the final movement of his Fifth Symphony as an accurate representation of Soviet Marxist motifs.

23

The writer wants to craft a strong introductory sentence that moves clearly toward the main topic of the essay. Which choice best accomplishes this purpose?

A) NO CHANGE

B) Joseph Stalin's harsh dictatorship in Soviet Russia during the 1930s and 1940s was characterized by an attempt at totalitarian control of every aspect of his citizen's lives, even the music they listened to.

C) Joseph Stalin's rule of Soviet Russia in the 1930s and 1940s was so brutal that no other world leader came close to killing so many of his own people.

D) All composers have to work under difficult and pressured situations, and Dmitri Shostakovich was no exception, because of Joseph Stalin.

24

A) NO CHANGE

B) functioned as propaganda for his regime.

C) promoted his regime enthusiastically with nationalistic propaganda.

D) worked as propaganda to better the power of his regime.

CONTINUE

Some musicologists argue that Shostakovich's antagonistic feelings toward Stalin undermined Shostakovich's ability to accurately portray Soviet Marxist themes. In his memoir, *Testimony*, published in 1979 by Solomon Volkov, Shostakovich wrote, "I was a formalist, a representative of an antinational direction in music." By declaring himself a formalist, Shostakovich established himself as a direct ideological enemy of Stalin and the Soviet regime. Shostakovich's abhorrence of the regime was not only ideological but also personal. **25** His sister, brother in-law and uncle had all been exiled or arrested or even died under Stalin's regime. Based on Shostakovich's intense resentment of the regime, musicologists argue that he would have had no desire to **26** neither comply with the regime nor represent the Marxist Soviet themes it embodied.

25

Which choice most clearly describes the experience of specific members of Shostakovich's family under Stalin?

A) NO CHANGE

B) Several members of Shostakovich's family suffered while Stalin was in power, and the worst suffering was that they had done nothing wrong to deserve such treatment.

C) His sister was exiled to France, his mother-in-law and brother-in-law were arrested, and his uncle, despite his communist affiliation, was arrested and held until his death.

D) His family line was decimated by the actions of the government under Stalin.

26

A) NO CHANGE

B) comply with the regime nor

C) comply with the regime or to

D) either comply with the regime or to

Shostakovich's opposition to Stalin and Soviet Marxism is undeniable; however, his opposition negates neither his desire nor his ability to portray Soviet Marxist themes [27] accurately on a basic level: Shostakovich's depiction of these themes [28] lied in his desire for survival. He understood the grave danger he faced after his Fourth Symphony was censored and realized that he had to please the government to avoid persecution. On a deeper level, Shostakovich's negative feelings towards the regime actually propelled him to create this accurate portrayal of the themes the regime epitomized.

Often, the most powerfully satirical social protest manifests as an accurate portrayal of the flaws in society. [29] For example, Mark Twain was one of the most renowned satirists in American history, and his satire was comprised of exposing truths he saw around him. In its accuracy and adherence [30] of Soviet Marxist themes, Shostakovich's Fifth Symphony Finale paints a

[27]

A) NO CHANGE
B) accurately, on
C) accurately, and on
D) accurately. On

[28]

A) NO CHANGE
B) lies
C) lie
D) lay

[29]

The author is considering deleting the following sentence. Should the writer make this change?

A) Yes, because it does not logically follow from the previous sentence.
B) Yes, because it introduces information that is irrelevant at this point in the passage.
C) No, because it offers a generalization to support arguments made elsewhere in the passage.
D) No, because it provides a logical introduction to the rest of the paragraph.

[30]

A) NO CHANGE
B) to
C) with
D) among

raw satirical portrait of Stalin's regime. [31] The legacy of his composition verifies the potency of Shostakovich's [32] moving and satirical style as today [33] listeners around the world are taken aback by the horrors of Stalin's regime revived in the performance of Shostakovich's Fifth Symphony Finale.

31

At this point, the writer is considering adding the following sentence.

> For example, in its abbreviated sonata-allegro form, the timpani solo introduces a brief militaristic tonality into the finale of the movement.

Should the writer make this addition here?

A) Yes, because it provides information necessary to understand the preceding sentence.

B) Yes, because supports the conclusion contained in the following sentence.

C) No, because it merely restates information contained elsewhere in the essay.

D) No, because it is overly technical and does not assist in understanding the thesis of the paragraph.

32

A) NO CHANGE

B) interesting and specific

C) visceral and polemical

D) challenging and weird

33

A) NO CHANGE

B) every listener around the world is being

C) listeners around the world is

D) listener around the world are

Questions 34–44 are based on the following passage.

Can Genes Be Patented?

—1—

In 1990, geneticist Mark Skolnick founded Myriad Genetics Inc. to use Mormon family history to study genes linked to Hereditary Breast and Ovarian Cancer (HBOC). From 1994–1996, Skolnick's team from Myriad Genetics sequenced, published, and patented the BReast CAncer 1 (BRCA1) and BReast CAncer 2 (BRCA2) genes. [34] This began a quick race to isolate more HBOC genes. After sequencing the BRCA2 gene, Myriad developed BRCAnalysis, a DNA blood test that tests for BRCA1 and BRCA2 mutations and assesses HBOC risk. The Hospital at the University of Pennsylvania ran BRCA1 and BRCA2 tests in the Genetic Diagnostic Library until Myriad [35] told them it infringed upon their patent.

[34]

A) NO CHANGE
B) That began a quick race to isolate more HBOC genes.
C) This discovery led to the rapid beginning of a hectic race to isolate more genes linked to HBOC.
D) DELETE the underlined portion.

[35]

A) NO CHANGE
B) tells the hospital it was infringing upon its patent.
C) claimed doing so infringed upon its patent.
D) claimed they infringed upon its patent by it.

—2—

Many became very frustrated with Myriad's patent due to the high cost of HBOC testing. [36] Because the probability of developing breast cancer is nearly doubled for those with BRCA1 or 2, some felt that the prohibitive cost of testing violated the rights of patients. On May 12, 2009, the American Civil Liberties Union (ACLU) filed a suit against Myriad. [37] The case, heard by Judge Robert Sweet in the Southern District of New York court, ruling that genes are not patentable. Myriad appealed this ruling and the case was heard two years later by the US Court of Appeals for the Federal Circuit.

Breast and Ovarian Cancer Risk by Age 70

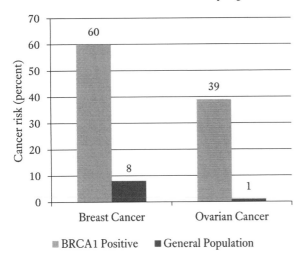

36

Which choice accurately reflects the data in the graph and best supports the point of the paragraph?

A) NO CHANGE

B) Because the likelihood of developing breast cancer is higher than that of ovarian cancer,

C) Although those with BRCA1 are somewhat more likely to develop breast cancer than members of the general population,

D) Because the lifetime risk of developing breast cancer risk is nearly eight times as great for those with BRCA1,

37

A) NO CHANGE

B) The case, heard in the Southern District of New York by Judge Robert Sweet, who ruled that genes are not patentable.

C) The case was heard in the Southern District of New York by Judge Robert Sweet, who ruled that genes are not patentable.

D) The case was heard by Judge Robert Sweet in the Southern District of New York court, he ruled that genes are not patentable.

—3—

[38] As a result, both the plaintiffs and defendants were dissatisfied with the US Court of Appeals' [39] ambiguous ruling, so they petitioned for a rehearing by the Supreme Court in August 2011. On February 17, 2012, the Supreme Court met to decide [40] whether to except the case, and on March 26, 2012, referred the decision back down to the US Court of Appeals. That August, the Court of Appeals upheld Myriad's claims to patent genes.

—4—

The plaintiffs were dissatisfied with the court's decision and realized they needed to present their case in a different light in order to get the Supreme Court to take it up after rejecting it the first time. On September 25, 2012, the ACLU and the Public Patent Foundation appealed to the Supreme Court and asked [41] them to evaluate as a larger landmark case: are genes patentable?

38

A) NO CHANGE
B) However,
C) Furthermore,
D) On the other hand,

39

The writer wants this sentence to clarify the reasons that both sides were not pleased with the finding of the court. Assuming that all of the following are true, which choice best accomplishes this?

A) NO CHANGE
B) ruling, which allowed the patenting of isolated genes but denied Myriad's right to patent the analytical process used to test for the genes, so both parties
C) unfavorable ruling that denied Myriad's right to claim copyright infringement regarding the analysis for testing the genes, so they
D) poor decision to allow patenting of isolated genes, which meant that Myriad would profit from human DNA, so the complainants and the accused

40

A) NO CHANGE
B) whether or not to except the case,
C) if they should accept the case or not,
D) whether to accept the case,

41

A) NO CHANGE
B) it
C) they
D) DELETE the underline portion

2   2

—5—

This case set a landmark precedent that genes themselves cannot be patented. [42] However, the court allowed that a lab that produces cDNA, a synthetic complement to the naturally occurring gene, can patent what it produces. Now that Myriad no longer holds patents on BRCA1 and BRCA2, other companies can use the genes to perform genetic screenings.

—6—

The Supreme Court agreed to take the case in November, heard arguments April 15, and ruled that claims on isolated DNA are invalid on June 13, 2013. Justice Clarence Thomas delivered the opinion [43] of the court: "For the reasons that follow, we hold that a naturally occurring DNA segment is a product of nature and not patent eligible merely because it has been isolated."

Question [44] asks about the previous passage as a whole.

[42]
A) NO CHANGE
B) However, cDNA, the complement of the naturally occurring template strand, can be synthetically produced in a lab and patented.
C) Unfortunately, the ruling still granted that cDNA, a complement of the naturally occurring template strand, can be produced synthetically in a lab and patented by the lab that was producing it.
D) Still, cDNA can be patented by labs.

[43]
A) NO CHANGE
B) from the court,
C) of the court,
D) of the court;

Think about the previous passage as a whole as you answer question 44.

[44]
To make the passage most logical, paragraph 5 should be placed
A) where it is now.
B) after paragraph 2.
C) after paragraph 3.
D) after paragraph 6.

STOP

**If you finish before time is called, you may check your work on this section only.
Do not turn to any other section.**

Math Test – No Calculator

25 MINUTES, 20 QUESTIONS

Turn to Section 3 of your answer sheet to answer the questions in this section.

DIRECTIONS

For questions 1–15, solve each problem, choose the best answer from the choices provided, and fill in the corresponding circle on your answer sheet. **For questions 16–20**, solve the problems and enter your answer in the grid on the answer sheet. Please refer to the directions before question 16 on how to enter your answers in the grid. You may use any available space in your test booklet for scratch work.

NOTES

1. The use of calculators **is not permitted**.

2. All variables and expressions used represent real numbers unless otherwise indicated.

3. Figures provided in this test are drawn to scale unless otherwise indicated.

4. All figures lie in a plane unless otherwise indicated.

5. Unless otherwise indicated, the domain of a given function f is the set of real numbers x for which $f(x)$ is a real number.

REFERENCE

   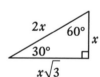

$A = \pi r^2$ $A = \ell w$ $A = \frac{1}{2}bh$ $c^2 = a^2 + b^2$ Special Right Triangles

$C = 2\pi r$

$V = \ell w h$ $V = \pi r^2 h$ $V = \frac{4}{3}\pi r^3$ $V = \frac{1}{3}\pi r^2 h$ $V = \frac{1}{3}\ell w h$

The number of degrees of arc in a circle is 360.
The number of radians of arc in a circle is 2π.
The sum of the measures in degrees of the angles in a triangle is 180.

CONTINUE

3

3

1

If $(x-1)(x+3) = k+2$ and $x = 2$, what is the value of k?

A) 0

B) 2

C) 3

D) 4

2

$$a - b = 12$$
$$2a - 5b = 3$$

Which of the following ordered pairs (a, b) satisfies the system of equations above?

A) $(19, 7)$

B) $(7, 20)$

C) $(17, 3)$

D) $(4, 9)$

3

Which of the following is equivalent $(3a^2 + 6b^2)^2$?

A) $3a^4 + 18a^2b^2 + 36b^4$

B) $2a^2 + 36a^2b + 36b^4$

C) $9a^4 + 36a^2b^2 + 36b^4$

D) $9a^4 + 18a^2b^2 + 36b^4$

4

To rent out the back room for a party, the amount a restaurant charges, in dollars, can be represented by the expression $35 + 8hn$, where h is the number of hours and n is the number of guests. Which of the following is the best interpretation of the number 8 in the expression?

A) There can be a maximum of 8 guests.

B) The restaurant charges $8 per hour per guest.

C) The flat rate of renting a room is $8.

D) For every additional guest, the price decreases by $8.

CONTINUE

5

$$\frac{\sqrt{x^2-9}}{a}=1$$

If $x < 0$ and $a = 4$, what is the value of $x - 5$?

A) −12

B) −10

C) −9

D) −3

6

Ryan has started a tutoring company. He charges clients a monthly flat rate, as well as a rate per session. The total amount paid by a client monthly, in dollars, is $24.45x + 10.50$, where x is the number of tutoring sessions. What is Ryan's rate per session?

A) $10.50

B) $15.05

C) $24.45

D) $35.45

7

$$h(x) = 3x^3 - ax$$

For the function $h(x)$ defined above, $h(2) = 20$. What is the value of $h(-1)$?

A) −5

B) −1

C) 1

D) 5

8

If $\dfrac{a^{2x^3}}{a^4} = a^{12}$, what is the value of 2^x?

A) 2

B) 4

C) 8

D) 16

CONTINUE

Questions 9 and 10 refer to the following information.

Monthly cell phone plans A and B can be described by the two following equations, where A is the price, in dollars, under plan A, and B is the price, in dollars, under plan B after m minutes of calling in a month.

$$A = 3.85 + 0.45m$$
$$B = 7.65 + 0.25m$$

9

After how many minutes of calling will the prices under each plan be equal?

A) 14

B) 16

C) 19

D) 23

10

Miranda uses cell phone plan A and paid $8.35 last month. How many minutes worth of calls did Miranda make?

A) 10

B) 13

C) 18

D) 20

11

If $i = \sqrt{-1}$, which of the following complex numbers is equivalent to $\dfrac{4 + 2i}{2 - i}$?

A) $\dfrac{6 + 8i}{5}$

B) $\dfrac{5 - 3i}{8}$

C) $\dfrac{4 - 2i}{7}$

D) $\dfrac{1 + 9i}{3}$

CONTINUE

12

A formula used for compound interest is

$A = P\left(1 + \dfrac{r}{n}\right)^{nt}$. Which of the following represents P in terms of A, n, and t?

A) $\dfrac{\left(1 + \dfrac{r}{n}\right)^{nt}}{A}$

B) $A\left(1 + \dfrac{r}{n}\right)^{nt}$

C) $\dfrac{A}{\left(1 + \dfrac{r}{n}\right)^{nt}}$

D) $\dfrac{1}{A\left(1 + \dfrac{r}{n}\right)^{nt}}$

13

The graph of line q has a slope of -2 and contains the point $(0, 8)$. Line p contains the points $(2, 7)$ and $(0, 5)$. If p and q intersect at the point (a, b), what is the value of $a - b$?

A) -5

B) 1

C) 5

D) 6

14

Which of the following is equivalent to $\dfrac{1}{x + 2} - \dfrac{1}{x - 3}$?

A) $\dfrac{2x - 1}{x^2 - x - 6}$

B) $\dfrac{2x - 5}{x^2 - x - 6}$

C) $\dfrac{2x}{x^2 - x - 6}$

D) $\dfrac{-5}{x^2 - x - 6}$

15

If, for all values of x, $(3x + a)(2x + b) = 6x^2 + cx + 6$ and $4a + 6b = 12$, what is the value of c?

A) 24

B) 18

C) 12

D) 6

DIRECTIONS

For questions 16–20, solve the problem and enter your answer in the grid, as described below, on the answer sheet.

1. Although not required, it is suggested that you write your answer in the boxes at the top of the columns to help you fill in the circles accurately. You will receive credit only if the circles are filled in correctly.
2. Mark no more than one circle in any column.
3. No question has a negative answer.
4. Some problems may have more than one correct answer. In such cases, grid only one answer.

5. **Mixed numbers** such as $3\frac{1}{2}$ must be be gridded as 3.5 or 7/2. If $\boxed{3\,1/2}$ is entered into the grid, it will be interpreted as $\frac{31}{2}$, not $3\frac{1}{2}$.)

6. **Decimal answers:** If you obtain a decimal answer with more digits than the grid can accommodate, it may be either rounded or truncated, but it must fill the entire grid.

Answer: $\frac{7}{13}$

Answer: 2.5

Write answer in boxes →

Grid in result

← Fraction line

← Decimal Point

Acceptable ways to grid $\frac{2}{3}$ are:

Answer: 210 – either position is correct

NOTE: You may start your answers in any column, space permitting. Columns you don't need to use should be left blank.

CONTINUE

16

A history quiz consists of 60 points and contains questions that are either True/False or multiple-choice. If a True/False question is worth 3 points and a multiple-choice question is worth 8 points, and the quiz has at least one question of each type, what is a possible number of multiple-choice questions on the quiz?

17

If $2b^2 - 12 = 60$ and $b > 0$, what is the value of b?

18

An angle opposite a leg of a right triangle measures $w°$, and $\tan(w°) = \dfrac{3}{4}$. What is $\sin(90° - w°)$?

CONTINUE

19

$$ax + by = 16$$
$$3x + 2y = 64$$

In the system of equations above, a and b are constants. If the system has infinitely many solutions, what is the value of ab?

20

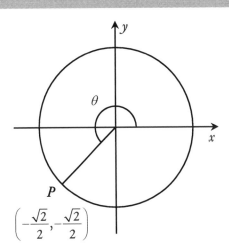

The angle θ on the unit circle (shown above), formed

when the segment that connects the origin to point

$P\left(-\frac{\sqrt{2}}{2}, -\frac{\sqrt{2}}{2}\right)$ meets the positive x-axis, can be

written as $\frac{10\pi}{a}$ radians. What is the value of a?

STOP

If you finish before time is called, you may check your work on this section only.
Do not turn to any other section.

4 **4**

Math Test – Calculator
55 MINUTES, 38 QUESTIONS

Turn to Section 4 of your answer sheet to answer the questions in this section.

DIRECTIONS

For questions 1–30, solve each problem, choose the best answer from the choices provided, and fill in the corresponding circle on your answer sheet. **For questions 31–38**, solve the problems and enter your answer in the grid on the answer sheet. Please refer to the directions before question 31 on how to enter your answers in the grid. You may use any available space in your test booklet for scratch work.

NOTES

1. The use of calculators is **permitted**.

2. All variables and expressions used represent real numbers unless otherwise indicated.

3. Figures provided in this test are drawn to scale unless otherwise indicated.

4. All figures lie in a plane unless otherwise indicated.

5. Unless otherwise indicated, the domain of a given function f is the set of real numbers x for which $f(x)$ is a real number.

REFERENCE

$A = \pi r^2$　　　　$A = \ell w$　　　　$A = \dfrac{1}{2}bh$　　　$c^2 = a^2 + b^2$　　Special Right Triangles

$C = 2\pi r$

$V = \ell w h$　　　　$V = \pi r^2 h$　　　　$V = \dfrac{4}{3}\pi r^3$　　　$V = \dfrac{1}{3}\pi r^2 h$　　　$V = \dfrac{1}{3}\ell w h$

The number of degrees of arc in a circle is 360.
The number of radians of arc in a circle is 2π.
The sum of the measures in degrees of the angles in a triangle is 180.

CONTINUE ▶

4 **4**

1

A lemonade stand sells small and large cups. Small cups are sold for $2.25 and large cups are sold for $3.50. Which of the following represents the amount of money the stand makes if they sell s small cups and l large cups?

A) $2.25s - 3.50l$

B) $2.25s + 3.50l$

C) $3.50s + 2.25l$

D) $(3.50 + 2.25)(s + l)$

2

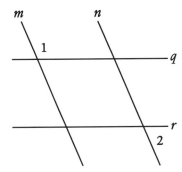

In the figure above, lines q and r and lines m and n are parallel. If the measure of angle 1 is 130 degrees, what is the measure, in degrees, of angle 2?

A) 130

B) 65

C) 50

D) 40

3

If $3a + 17$ is 6 less than 50, then what is the value of $9a$?

A) 117

B) 81

C) 27

D) 9

CONTINUE

4 **4**

Questions 4 and 5 refer to the following information.

The density of a gas is inversely proportional to its volume, assuming that the mass of the gas is constant. A gas with a density of 0.50 kilograms per cubic meter has a volume of 4 cubic meters.

4

What would the density of the gas be if it filled a volume of 10 cubic meters?

A) 0.20 kg/m^3

B) 0.45 kg/m^3

C) 0.80 kg/m^3

D) 1.25 kg/m^3

5

As part of a science experiment, the volume of the gas when its density is 0.50 kg/m^3 is decreased 30 percent. What is its density after the decrease, rounded to the nearest hundredth?

A) 0.15 kg/m^3

B) 0.35 kg/m^3

C) 0.71 kg/m^3

D) 1.67 kg/m^3

6

1 dekaliter = 10 liters
1,000 milliliters = 1 liter

A car has a 6 dekaliter gas tank. Based on the information above, how many milliliters of gas can the car's gas tank hold?

A)   0.0006

B)   60

C)   6,000

D)   60,000

7

$$y = 2x^2 - 8x - 20$$

The equation above defines the graph of a parabola. Which of the following equations is equivalent to the equation above and shows the coordinates of the vertex of the parabola as constants?

A) $y = 2x(x - 4) - 10$

B) $y = 2(x - 2)^2 - 28$

C) $y = 2(x^2 - 4x - 5)$

D) $y = 2(x - 5)(x + 1)$

CONTINUE

4

4

8

Number of Apartment Buildings in 4 Cities

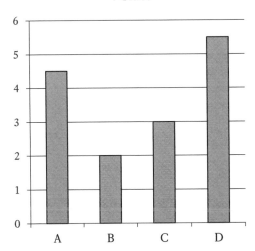

The number of apartment buildings in four different cities is shown in the graph above. If the total number of apartment buildings represented in the graph is 15,000, what are the increments of the vertical axis?

A) Tens

B) Hundreds

C) Thousands

D) Tens of thousands

9

A snack company is determining how to package a new line of chips. Bags will contain three different types of chips, identically shaped. One type has 10 calories per chip, one has 12, and one has 14. The bag can have up to 65 chips, but it must have exactly 700 calories in it. Let a represent the number of 10 calorie chips, b the number of 12 calorie chips, and c the number of 14 calorie chips. Which of the following represents this relationship?

A)
$$\frac{a}{10} + \frac{b}{12} + \frac{c}{14} = 700$$
$$a + b + c \le 65$$

B)
$$10a + 12b + 14c \le 700$$
$$a + b + c \le 65$$

C)
$$a + b + c \le 700$$
$$10a + 12b + 14c = 65$$

D)
$$10a + 12b + 14c = 700$$
$$a + b + c \le 65$$

CONTINUE

Questions 10 and 11 refer to the following information.

$$d = 171.3 + 55t$$

The equation above models a family's distance from home during the second day of a road trip, where d represents distance in miles and t represents time, in hours, after they began driving on the second day.

10

Which of the following shows the time traveled by the family on the second day in terms of their distance from home?

A) $t = \dfrac{d - 171.3}{55}$

B) $t = \dfrac{55}{d - 171.3}$

C) $t = \dfrac{d + 171.3}{55}$

D) $t = \dfrac{d}{55} - 171.3$

11

After how many hours of driving on the second day will the family's distance from home be about 400 miles?

A) 10.39 hours

B)   5.14 hours

C)   5.08 hours

D)   4.16 hours

12

Number of printers	50
Hours the printers run per day	10
Number of days the printers are used per week	7
Number of sheets required to make the book	300
Number of sheets a printer can print per minute	50
Number of workers working the printers	4

A publishing company is printing copies of a new book. The initial print run of the book will be 10,000 copies. Based on the information above pertaining to the printers available to the company to print the book, how many days will it take for the initial print run to be run off?

A)   2

B)   20

C)   100

D)   120

CONTINUE

4   **4**

Questions 13 and 14 refer to the following information.

Cost of Pizza by Toppings

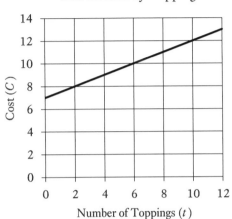

The graph above shows the cost C of a pizza as determined by the number of toppings t.

13

What does the C-intercept represent in the graph?

A) The total number of toppings on the pizza.

B) The total number of pizzas bought.

C) The cost of each additional topping.

D) The price of a pizza with no toppings.

14

Which of the following shows the relationship between C and t?

A) $C = 7t$

B) $C = t + 0.5$

C) $C = 0.5t + 7$

D) $C = t + 7$

15

A family's home pool has a capacity of 9,500 gallons. There are 3,250 gallons of water in it already. The family's hose sprays 25 gallons of water per minute. Let x represent the number of minutes that the hose is left running into the pool. Which of the following represents the set of all times that the hose is left running at which the pool will be full or overflowing?

A) $25x \geq 9,500$

B) $9,500 - 3,250 \leq x$

C) $3,250 + 25x \geq 9,500$

D) $6,250 \leq x + 3,250$

16

	Mac	PC	Total
Female	45	29	74
Male	48	30	78
Total	93	59	152

People on the street were randomly selected and asked whether they preferred to use Macs or PCs. Which of the following comprised approximately 32 percent of the total group?

A) Males who prefer Macs

B) Females who prefer Macs

C) People who prefer PCs

D) Males who prefer PCs

17

Jupiter travels a distance of approximately 4.9 billion kilometers during its orbit around the Sun. Jupiter completes an orbit in about 12 Earth years. Which of the following is closest to the number of kilometers Jupiter travels in one hour?

A)   47

B)   1,100

C)   47,000

D) 560,000

18

A survey counted the number of flowers on the bushes in a park. The average number of flowers was 34 while the median was 45. What factor most likely would account for the difference between average and median?

A) There were some bushes with extremely few flowers.

B) The mode of the data was a number greater than 34.

C) Many bushes had between 34 and 45 flowers.

D) There is little variance in the number of flowers on the bushes.

CONTINUE

4 **4**

19

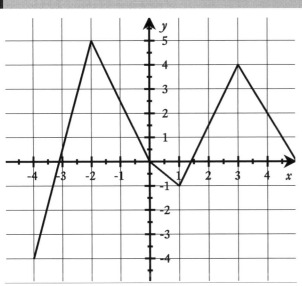

The complete graph of $f(x)$ is shown above. For which of the following values of x is $f(x)$ at its maximum?

A) −4

B) −2

C) 3

D) 5

20

A parking garage charges $11 on weekdays and $15 on weekends. If the garage brought in $53,234 in one week and a total of 4,122 people used the garage, how many people used the garage during the weekend?

A) 304

B) 1,973

C) 2,149

D) 3,549

Questions 21 and 22 refer to the following information.

A high school asked 200 underclassmen and 200 upperclassmen how many hours they spent on homework the previous night. There are 680 underclassmen and 600 upperclassmen in the school.

Hours spent on homework	Underclassmen	Upperclassmen
1	20	10
2	70	50
3	80	90
4	20	40
5	10	10

21

What is the median number of hours spent on homework by those students surveyed?

A) 2

B) 3

C) 4

D) Cannot be determined from the information given

22

Based on this data, which of the following most accurately describes the expected total numbers of students who spent 5 hours on homework last night?

A) 10 underclassmen and 10 upperclassmen spent 5 hours on homework.

B) 4 more underclassmen than upperclassmen spent 5 hours on homework.

C) 4 more upperclassmen than underclassmen spent 5 hours on homework.

D) 80 more underclassmen than upperclassmen spent 5 hours on homework.

CONTINUE

4 **4**

23

Harold prepared a sample of bacteria. A strain of virus killed 30 percent of the bacteria, but within a week the surviving population had grown 47 percent. Which of the following represents the value of the original population in terms of the current population p?

A) $\dfrac{p}{1.17}$

B) $1.17p$

C) $\dfrac{p}{(0.7)(1.47)}$

D) $(0.7)(1.47)p$

24

$$x^2 + y^2 - 10y = 9$$

The equation above defines a circle in the coordinate plane. Which of the following is the length of the circle's radius?

A) 3

B) $\sqrt{10}$

C) 5

D) $\sqrt{34}$

Questions 25 and 26 refer to the following information.

$$T = 2\pi\sqrt{\dfrac{m}{k}}$$

The equation above describes the period T of an oscillating object attached to a spring in terms of its mass m and spring constant k.

25

Which of the following expresses the object's mass in terms of the period T and the spring constant k?

A) $m = \dfrac{T^2 k}{2\pi}$

B) $m = \dfrac{T^2 k}{2\pi^2}$

C) $m = \dfrac{T^2 k}{4\pi^2}$

D) $m = \dfrac{T k}{2\pi}$

26

For two systems with the same spring constant, object 1 has a mass 25 times that of object 2. What fraction of the period of object 1 is that of object 2?

A) $\dfrac{1}{10}$

B) $\dfrac{1}{5}$

C) $\dfrac{1}{25}$

D) $\dfrac{1}{125}$

CONTINUE

4 **4**

27

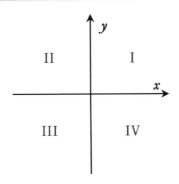

If the system of inequalities $y \le \frac{1}{3}x + 2$ and

$y > \frac{1}{2}x + 4$ were graphed on the xy-plane shown

above, which of the following quadrants would contain

at least one solution to the system?

A) Quadrant II

B) Quadrant III

C) Quadrant IV

D) None of the above

28

Clara received a score on a test that was 5 percent higher than the class average for the test. If Clara's score was 85 percent, what was the class average, rounded to the nearest whole number?

A) 78

B) 80

C) 81

D) 89

29

Emily's home library is composed of 9 identical bookshelves. Each bookshelf has 12 shelves within it, each of which contains approximately the same number of books. To find a rough estimate of the number of books in her library, Emily counted the number of books on one shelf in each bookshelf. The results are shown below.

104	92	113
93	89	101
74	97	85

Approximately how many books does Emily have in her entire collection?

A)   850

B)   7,600

C)   10,200

D)   91,600

30

For a polynomial $h(t)$, $h(3) = 7$. Which of the following must be true about $h(t)$?

A) $(t + 3)$ is a factor of $h(t)$.

B) $(t - 3)$ is a factor of $h(t)$.

C) The remainder when $h(t)$ is divided by $(t - 3)$ is 7.

D) The remainder when $h(t)$ is divided by 3 is 7.

CONTINUE ➡

DIRECTIONS

For questions **31–38**, solve the problem and enter your answer in the grid, as described below, on the answer sheet.

1. Although not required, it is suggested that you write your answer in the boxes at the top of the columns to help you fill in the circles accurately. You will receive credit only if the circles are filled in correctly.
2. Mark no more than one circle in any column.
3. No question has a negative answer.
4. Some problems may have more than one correct answer. In such cases, grid only one answer.

5. **Mixed numbers** such as $3\frac{1}{2}$ must be be gridded as 3.5 or 7/2. If $\boxed{3\,1\,/\,2}$ is entered into the grid, it will be interpreted as $\frac{31}{2}$, not $3\frac{1}{2}$.)

6. **Decimal answers:** If you obtain a decimal answer with more digits than the grid can accommodate, it may be either rounded or truncated, but it must fill the entire grid.

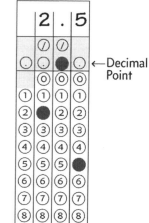

Acceptable ways to grid $\frac{2}{3}$ are:

Answer: 210 – either position is correct

NOTE: You may start your answers in any column, space permitting. Columns you don't need to use should be left blank.

CONTINUE

4 **4**

31

Stan's plant grows 2.5 inches per week. It is 15 inches tall now. In how many weeks will the plant be 42.5 inches tall?

32

In the xy-coordinate plane, the point $(3, 8)$ lies on the graph of the function $f(x) = x^3 - bx^2 - x + 2$. What is the value of b?

33

Joe can read at least 32 pages and as many as 40 pages per hour. Given this, what is a possible amount of time, in hours, it could take Joe to read 200 pages?

CONTINUE

34

Number of Books Read over the
Summer by High School Students

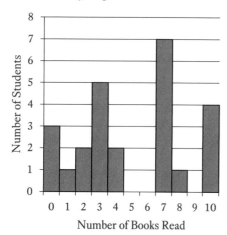

The histogram above shows the number of books read
by a class of high school students over the summer.
What is the average number of books read by each
student?

35

Herman was away from home on vacation for exactly
d days and 6 hours, for a total of 174 hours. For how
many full days was he away?

36

A store brand cereal has 40 percent fewer calories than
does the name brand cereal. The name brand has 150
calories per serving. How many calories per serving
does the store brand have?

$$(2x+3)^2 - (4x-7) = ax^2 + bx + c$$

In the equation above, a, b, and c are constants. If the equation is true for all values of x, what is the value of ac ?

Darin uses an empty rubber cone to block off traffic. The cone has a volume of 810π in^3. If the cone is 30 inches high, what is its <u>diameter</u> in <u>feet</u>?

STOP

**If you finish before time is called, you may check your work on this section only.
Do not turn to any other section.**

This page left intentionally blank

SAT Practice Test 2

IMPORTANT REMINDERS

1

A No. 2 pencil is required for the test.
Do not use a mechanical pencil or pen.

2

Sharing any questions with anyone is a violation
of the Test Security and Fairness policies and
may result in your score being canceled.

This cover is representative of what you will see on the day of the SAT.

1

1

Reading Test

65 MINUTES, 52 QUESTIONS

Turn to Section 1 of yourA answer sheet to answer the questions in this section.

DIRECTIONS

Each passage or pair of passages below is followed by a number of questions. After reading each passage or pair, choose the best answer to each question based on what is stated or implied in the passage or passages and in any accompanying graphics (such as a table or graph).

Questions 1–10 are based on the following passage.

This passage is from Oscar Wilde, "The Canterville Ghost." Originally published in 1887. Here, Mr. Otis, who is the United States Minister to Britain, and his family deal with an unexpected tenant in their new lodgings.

The next morning, when the Otis family met at breakfast, they discussed the ghost at some length. The United States Minister was naturally a little annoyed to find that his present had not been
5 accepted. "I have no wish," he said, "to do the ghost any personal injury, and I must say that, considering the length of time he has been in the house, I don't think it is at all polite to throw pillows at him,"—a very just remark, at which, I am sorry to say, the
10 twins burst into shouts of laughter. "Upon the other hand," he continued, "if he really declines to use the Rising Sun Lubricator, we shall have to take his chains from him. It would be quite impossible to sleep, with such a noise going on outside the
15 bedrooms."

For the rest of the week, however, they were undisturbed, the only thing that excited any attention being the continual renewal of the blood-stain on the library floor. This certainly was very strange, as the
20 door was always locked at night by Mr. Otis, and the windows kept closely barred. The chameleon-like colour, also, of the stain excited a good deal of comment. Some mornings it was a dull (almost Indian) red, then it would be vermilion, then a rich
25 purple, and once when they came down for family prayers, according to the simple rites of the Free American Reformed Episcopalian Church, they found it a bright emerald-green. These kaleidoscopic changes naturally amused the party very much, and
30 bets on the subject were freely made every evening. The only person who did not enter into the joke was little Virginia, who, for some unexplained reason, was always a good deal distressed at the sight of the blood-stain, and very nearly cried the morning it was
35 emerald-green.

The second appearance of the ghost was on Sunday night. Shortly after they had gone to bed they were suddenly alarmed by a fearful crash in the hall. Rushing down-stairs, they found that a large suit of
40 old armour had become detached from its stand, and had fallen on the stone floor, while seated in a high-backed chair was the Canterville ghost, rubbing his knees with an expression of acute agony on his face. The twins, having brought their pea-shooters with
45 them, at once discharged two pellets on him, with that accuracy of aim which can only be attained by long and careful practice on a writing-master, while the United States Minister covered him with his revolver, and called upon him, in accordance with
50 Californian etiquette, to hold up his hands! The ghost started up with a wild shriek of rage, and swept through them like a mist, extinguishing Washington Otis's candle as he passed, and so leaving them all in total darkness. On reaching the top of the staircase he
55 recovered himself, and determined to give his celebrated peal of demoniac laughter. This he had on more than one occasion found extremely useful. It was said to have turned Lord Raker's wig grey in a

CONTINUE ▶

1

single night, and had certainly made three of Lady
60 Canterville's French governesses give warning before
their month was up. He accordingly laughed his most
horrible laugh, till the old vaulted roof rang and rang
again, but hardly had the fearful echo died away when
a door opened, and Mrs. Otis came out in a light blue
65 dressing-gown. "I am afraid you are far from well,"
she said, "and have brought you a bottle of Doctor
Dobell's tincture. If it is indigestion, you will find it a
most excellent remedy." The ghost glared at her in
fury, and began at once to make preparations for
70 turning himself into a large black dog, an
accomplishment for which he was justly renowned,
and to which the family doctor always attributed the
permanent idiocy of Lord Canterville's uncle, the
Hon. Thomas Horton. The sound of approaching
75 footsteps, however, made him hesitate in his fell
purpose, so he contented himself with becoming
faintly phosphorescent and vanished with a deep
churchyard groan, just as the twins had come up to
him.

1

As the passage opens, it can be inferred that the
United States Minister has just given the ghost a gift
because

A) he wants to be friendly to his host.

B) he is afraid and wants to avoid upsetting the
ghost.

C) it is expected of him as an ambassador.

D) he hopes the ghost will use the gift and be less
noisy.

2

Which choice provides the best evidence for the
answer to the previous question?

A) Lines 3-5 ("The United … accepted")

B) Lines 5-8 ("I have … at him")

C) Lines 11-15 ("if he … bedrooms")

D) Lines 19-21 ("This certainly … barred")

3

Based on lines 8-10 ("a very just … laughter") the
narrator is best described as

A) the story's protagonist.

B) an inept observer.

C) a wry commentator.

D) a circumspect apologist.

4

The tone of the narrator in lines 31-35 ("The only
… emerald-green") is best described as

A) harshly judgmental.

B) foolishly oblivious.

C) warmly compassionate.

D) subtly ironic.

CONTINUE

5

The author's purpose in referring to "Californian etiquette" in line 50 is

A) nationalistic: it emphasizes that the Minister's polite behavior is due to his American identity.

B) satirical: it characterizes the response of the United States Minister as more appropriate to the Wild West than to his own home.

C) derisive: it mocks the United States Minister's attempts to be courteous to a ghost who desires to frighten him.

D) illustrative: it contrasts American notions of acceptable domestic behavior with proper British rules for household manners.

6

As used in line 48, "covered" most nearly means

A) protected.

B) hid from.

C) aimed at.

D) put on.

7

The author mentions "Lord Raker's wig" (line 58) and "Lady Canterville's French governesses" (lines 59–60) primarily to

A) suggest that the ghost has been more successful at scaring people in the past.

B) account for the diversity of people that have visited the house.

C) provide background needed to understand the ghost's origin.

D) compare the ghost's laugh with other frightening occurrences.

8

In line 75, "fell" most nearly means

A) failed.

B) lowered.

C) evil.

D) vain.

9

As a whole, the attitude of most members of the family to their situation is

A) guileless because they have been placed in a frightening situation.

B) cruel and unusual due to their aggressive and uncharitable nature.

C) culpably ignorant, given the foreshadowing of impending disaster.

D) oddly audacious, given the apparently alarming situation they encounter.

10

Which choice provides the best evidence for the answer to the previous question?

A) Lines 16–21 ("For the ... barred")

B) Lines 28–30 ("These ... evening ")

C) Lines 36–43 ("The second ... face")

D) Lines 68–74 ("The ghost ... Horton")

CONTINUE

1

1

Questions 11–20 are based on the following passage and supplementary material.

The passage is adapted from Susan Daugherty, "Entrepreneur Changes Life in Uganda by Turning Waste Into Fuel." ©2014 by National Geographic.

Sanga Moses grew up barefoot in a small Ugandan village of thatched roof dwellings that lacked electricity. Yet he became his clan's first college graduate and took a bank job in Kampala.

5 Returning home for a visit from the Ugandan capital in 2009, he met his 12-year-old sister on the road. "She stood there crying, with a heavy bundle of wood on her head," Moses remembers. "She was upset because, like most rural girls, she missed days

10 of school each week searching for fuel wood."

"My sister… was losing the only opportunity she had to make her life better—education."

It wasn't the only change Moses noticed in his hometown. "When I was young, our home was

15 surrounded by national forests," he says. "Now all those trees are gone, and children must walk longer and longer distances to gather wood."

Searching for a solution to problems born of burning wood, Moses quit his job and began learning

20 everything he could about renewable resources. Eventually he came across the increasingly popular practice of turning organic waste into fuel.

"I looked out my window and saw a huge pile of sugar cane debris," he says. "Uganda is primarily

25 agricultural, but farm waste is just abandoned."

So Moses began working with engineering students to design kilns and briquetting machines.

Four years later, 2,500 farmers use his kilns to turn farm waste—coffee husks and waste from sugar cane

30 and rice—into charcoal. A company that Moses founded, called Eco-Fuel Africa, buys the char and turns it into briquettes for cooking that burn cleaner and cost less than wood.

The company takes those briquettes to market,

35 providing fuel for more than 19,000 Ugandan families. "Burning fuel wood not only destroys Uganda's trees," Moses says, but it also affects "the health and educational opportunities of our poorest people.

40 "We're giving them an alternative."

The problems that wood burning created for Moses' family and in his hometown can be seen across sub-Saharan Africa. Eight in ten people in the region depend on wood to cook and to heat their

45 homes. As more forests are destroyed to feed that demand—in Uganda, 70 percent of protected forests are gone—families must walk more miles every day to buy increasingly scarce and costly wood.

Families in the developing world spend up to 40

50 percent of their income on cooking fuel. Besides leaving children with less time for education, it means that poor farmers are less able to afford fertilizer, causing harvests to suffer and malnutrition to rise.

55 And wood burning takes a huge toll on human health, creating smoky indoor air that leads to respiratory diseases that kill more women and children each year than HIV/AIDS.

Moses' cleaner-burning green charcoal reduces

60 indoor air pollution and has already saved more than three million dollars in energy-related expenses for Ugandans. "Families use that money to pay school fees for their children, afford three meals a day, and finance new income-generating activities," he says.

65 Indeed, farmers who work with Eco-Fuel Africa have tripled their incomes by selling char from kilns. The coarser, leftover char is used as fertilizer, which can increase harvests by more than 50 percent and create surplus crops to sell at market.

70 Moses' group also battles deforestation, investing profits into planting 12,000 new trees and partnering with local schools to make reforestation part of environmental education.

"Today young people who graduate from college

75 come to us and say, 'I don't care how much you pay me; I want to join you because I believe so strongly in what you do,' " Moses says.

Eco-Fuel Africa also looks for employees among Uganda's widows and single mothers, who often

80 struggle after husbands die of HIV/AIDS.

"They value the opportunity to become machine operators and retailers," Moses says, "bringing unbelievable commitment, dedication, and hard work to our project." "Many times when I visit villages,"

85 he continues, "a woman will grab my hand and say, 'Six months ago I could barely feed my family. Now I've been able to enroll my daughter in school and buy a solar panel and mobile phone.' "

Funding from National Geographic recently

90 helped the organization develop a briquette-making

machine that can run without electricity, so it's workable in remote rural areas.

"Now we can micro-franchise in villages far off the power grid," Moses says. "We identify
95 entrepreneurs, supply training and support, and provide technology on a credit basis so they can start sustainable businesses, create jobs, and meet local energy needs."

All while improving Ugandans' health—and
100 saving their forests.

Forest Data: Uganda from 1990–2005
(measured in hectares*)

	1990	2000	2005
Rain Forest	4,924,000	4,059,000	3,627,000
Other Wooded Areas	1,404,000	1,235,000	1,150,000
Plantations	33,000	35,000	36,000
Total Wooded Land (Forest area+ Wooded area – Plantations)	6,295,000	5,259,000	4,741,000

* 1 hectare = 10,000 square meters

Adapted from Mongabay website.

11

The second and third paragraphs (lines 5–12) mention Moses' meeting his sister primarily to

A) contrast Moses' own opportunities with those available to females from his own clan.

B) characterize Moses as compassionate in showing brotherly love.

C) illustrate one of the many negative effects of families burning wood for fuel.

D) provide a reference point to reveal the impact of Moses' education on his whole family.

12

Based on the passage as a whole, the author's attitude toward Moses' project could be best described as

A) somewhat conflicted.

B) cautious endorsement.

C) constructively critical.

D) optimistic approval.

13

Lines 26–27 serve primarily to

A) transition from a narrative about the past to a project in the present.

B) introduce the problem which the remainder of the article addresses.

C) redirect readers from the sociological impact of wood burning to its environmental impact.

D) present new ideas about how to restore the wood needed for burning.

14

One of the serious problems associated with burning wood is that

A) many people develop fatal diseases from smoke inhalation.

B) families have to spend over 40 percent of their income on wood, which inhibits overall economic success.

C) forests are protected, and so families cannot get enough wood.

D) it takes away jobs from those who most need them.

CONTINUE ▶

15

Which choice provides the best evidence for the answer to the previous question?

A) Lines 41–45 ("The problems … homes")

B) Lines 55–58 ("And wood … HIV/AIDS")

C) Lines 59–62 ("Moses' cleaner-burning … Ugandans")

D) Lines 70–73 ("Moses' group … education")

16

The unsold char left over from burning in the kilns has provided farmers with

A) triple their income.

B) harvests double their former yield.

C) fertilizer for their fields.

D) reforestation initiatives.

17

Which choice provides the best evidence for the answer to the previous question?

A) Lines 62–64 ("Families … says")

B) Lines 65–67 ("Indeed, farmers … kilns")

C) Lines 67–69 ("The coarser … market")

D) Lines 84–88 ("Many … phone")

18

As it is used in line 81, the word "value" most nearly means

A) appreciate.

B) enjoy.

C) determine the cost of.

D) save.

19

As it is used in line 96, the word "credit" most nearly means

A) beneficial to both parties.

B) freely given due to need.

C) belief in improvement.

D) promise of later payment.

20

The data in the included table indicate that

A) the author has exaggerated about the severity of deforestation in Uganda because some types of wooded areas are better maintained than others.

B) Moses' attempt to counteract deforestation by planting 12,000 trees has been successful because wooded areas are steadily increasing.

C) Eco-Fuel Africa's goal to reduce use of firewood is important because the amount of forested land has reduced dramatically since 1990.

D) trees are more spread out now which forces children to walk further distances to collect wood.

Questions 21–31 are based on the following passage and supplementary material.

This passage is adapted from Jingwen Zhang "Twenty-first Century Genetics: Power and Responsibility." ©2013 National High School Journal of Science.

Of the relatively recent, notable advancements in the fields of medicine and biotechnology, many are connected to the study of genetics and genomics. Following Watson and Crick's discovery of the DNA
5   double helix, research on DNA and its implications in genetics and life escalated through the 1980s and 1990s to the epic, groundbreaking work of the Human Genome Project in 2003. Today, ten years later, genetic information plays a significant part in
10   public health and medicine. Along with the unveiling of genetics as an integral factor in the 21st-century world comes the realization of responsibilities and future complications that cloud its newfound role.

The expanding field of molecular biology has
15   already translated notable scientific progress from the lab bench to the clinics. For example, thorough exploration and experimentation with the ApoE and BRCA1/BRCA2 genes—associated with Alzheimer's disease and breast cancer, respectively—have allowed
20   specialists to identify high risk patients before the onset of any symptoms. Before the days of targeting the known genes, breast cancer was usually only detected by physical examinations and mammograms, and Alzheimer's went unnoticed until
25   memory loss actually began. Individuals now have the option to take a proactive, rather than reactive, stance in their medical future. Genetics is used to assess football players' (and other high-impact sports athletes') risks of getting Alzheimer's, and to
30   determine the appropriateness and effectiveness of certain medical procedures such as mastectomies. Unfortunately, the absence of the above mutations is not evidence that an individual is not at risk for breast cancer or Alzheimer's disease, since those mutations
35   are found only in a small subset of patients diagnosed clinically. Both diseases are simply too complex and can arise via multiple mechanisms.

Biotechnological advancements have also kept pace with the recently expanding role of genetics in
40   everyday life. With improvements in rapid whole-genome sequencing, companies such as 23 and Me allow the public to see some of what might come in

their future based on their unique genes. Non-invasive whole genome sequencing for fetuses, a way
45   to use maternal plasma to explore the fetal genetic information, was successfully developed in 2012 and has been seen as a large step toward improving neonatal and pediatric treatments with a genetic approach.

50   With these drastic medical advances made in part due to the advent of genetic studies, it becomes very easy to overstate the importance of genetics in changing the course of personalized medicine and in determining an individual's future. The world may
55   seem to believe that genes are all-important: information regarding genetics can be found in almost every hospital, news headlines frequently report how diseases are connected to our genes, public figures like actress Angelina Jolie—who, after
60   learning she had the breast cancer-associated version of the BRCA1 gene, had a preventive double mastectomy—advocate for preventative measures largely based on genetic tests.

These events are certainly not bad in themselves;
65   the problem arises when the public is led to believe that DNA is destiny, when the truth is that singular genetic makeup is only one of many factors contributing to disease development. In addition, although genetic information, hailed as the
70   "language" or "blueprint" of life, can seem very scientifically straightforward with little room for error or doubt, genetics itself is in fact far from an exact science. Much of the human genome has not been studied in depth yet, as it had previously been
75   thought to be "junk" DNA; it has only recently been found to be vital to the expression of exons, the coding regions. Scientists have also discovered that variants in certain genes do not result in the predicted phenotype or condition for every
80   individual, which further complicates the use of genetic information as guides to personal health forecasts. Furthermore, diseases can arise via multiple mechanisms: for example the BRCA1 and BRCA2 genes are found to be mutated only in
85   approximately 10% of patients diagnosed with breast cancer. Advancements in genetics can be extremely helpful in developing future medical treatments, but putting too much stock into it certainly can be harmful. Environmental factors—maternal smoking
90   and drinking, folic acid intake, diet and exercise,

CONTINUE

1

1

etc.—play a significant and often deciding role as well, yet their importance is not accentuated appropriately. Using genomic information, personalized medicine may allow patients to take
95 more control of their own treatments, but if non-genetic factors are not viewed crucial as well, patients may lose some of the power they have over their health.

Lifetime Breast Cancer Risk

Group	Lifetime Breast Cancer Risk	Median Age of Breast Cancer Onset
General Population	11%	61
BRCA 1	65%	43
BRCA 2	45%	41

Adapted from K. Metcalfe and S. Narod, "Breast Cancer Prevention in Women with a BRCA1 or BRCA2 Mutation." © 2007 Bentham Open.

21

The primary purpose of the first paragraph is to

A) establish the basis for a spurious claim in order to challenge it.

B) provide the reader with the context needed for discussion which follows.

C) enumerate the limitless possibilities and the inherent risks of a scientific development.

D) argue for the significance of specific developments in genetic research.

22

As used in line 13, the word "cloud" most nearly means

A) limit.

B) darken.

C) obscure.

D) hamper.

23

According to the passage, one of the primary medical benefits to individuals which has come from genetic research is that

A) certain health risks can be identified in advance and addressed before problems develop.

B) average people now have learned enough about their own DNA to accurately predict their future health.

C) the behaviors that tend to promote the development of certain health issues can be identified and eliminated.

D) doctors now fully understand the causes of diseases and can correct genetic problems in their patients.

24

Which choice provides the best evidence for the answer to the previous question?

A) Lines 1–8 ("Of the … in 2003")

B) Lines 14–16 ("The expanding … clinics")

C) Lines 25–31 ("Individuals … mastectomies")

D) Lines 86–93 ("Advancements … appropriately")

25

The primary purpose of the fourth paragraph (lines 50–63) is to

A) discuss the problems caused by the apparent advancements in genetic research.

B) transition from a discussion of advancements in genetic research to possible concerns.

C) warn readers against accepting medical information determined through genetic advancements.

D) provide a specific, relatable example to illustrate the usefulness of genetic research.

26

The author's tone regarding the idea that "DNA is destiny" (line 66) is best described as

A) disinterested.

B) optimistic.

C) cynical.

D) cautionary.

27

The author most likely uses quotation marks around the word "junk" (line 75) in order to

A) mock a widely held idea.

B) clarify which words are borrowed from another source.

C) suggest that the label is now seen as ironically inaccurate.

D) emphasize the importance of the term.

28

In order to limit an overemphasis upon genetic research as the key to solving concerns regarding certain diseases, the author

A) reminds readers that genetic research has only proven significant in dealing with Alzheimer's and breast cancer.

B) warns doctors that failure to consider non-genetic factors will lead to misdiagnosis and ineffective treatment.

C) dismisses the advancements in genetic research regarding diseases as essentially unfruitful.

D) insists upon the vital role of environmental factors in understanding and treating diseases.

29

Which choice provides the best evidence for the answer to the previous question?

A) Lines 16–21 ("For example … symptoms")

B) Lines 50–54 ("With these … future")

C) Lines 68–73 ("In addition … science")

D) Lines 89–98 (Environmental … health")

30

As used in line 88, the word "stock" most nearly means

A) inventory.

B) confidence.

C) judgment.

D) investment.

31

Based on the data in the article and the table, one can determine

A) the percentage of the total cases of breast cancer attributable to genetic causes alone.

B) the total number of cases of breast cancer linked to each genetic marker.

C) the average age of breast cancer onset for the entire population.

D) that the vast majority of cases of breast cancer develop in a population that has less than an 11 percent chance of developing the disease.

CONTINUE ➤

Questions 32–42 are based on the following passages.

In passage 1, Edmund Burke discusses Marie Antoinette in his book Reflections on the Revolution in France, *published in 1790. Passage 2 is an excerpt from* The Rights of Man, *1791, in which Thomas Paine responds to Burke's book.*

Passage 1

It is now sixteen or seventeen years since I saw the Queen of France, then the Dauphiness,[1] at Versailles; and surely never lighted on this orb, which she hardly seemed to touch, a more delightful vision.
5 I saw her just above the horizon, decorating and cheering the elevated sphere she had just begun to move in, glittering like the morning star full of life and splendor and joy.

Oh, what a revolution! and what a heart must I
10 have, to contemplate without emotion that elevation and that fall! Little did I dream, when she added titles of veneration to those of enthusiastic, distant, respectful love, that she should ever be obliged to carry the sharp antidote against disgrace concealed in
15 that bosom; little did I dream that I should have lived to see such disasters fallen upon her, in a nation of gallant men, in a nation of men of honor, and of cavaliers! I thought ten thousand swords must have leaped from their scabbards, to avenge even a look
20 that threatened her with insult.

But the age of chivalry is gone; that of sophisters, economists, and calculators has succeeded, and the glory of Europe is extinguished forever. Never, never more, shall we behold that generous loyalty to rank
25 and sex, that proud submission, that dignified obedience, that subordination of the heart, which kept alive, even in servitude itself, the spirit of an exalted freedom! The unbought grace of life, the cheap defense of nations, the nurse of manly
30 sentiment and heroic enterprise is gone. It is gone, that sensibility of principle, that chastity of honor, which felt a stain like a wound, which inspired courage whilst it mitigated ferocity, which ennobled whatever it touched, and under which vice itself lost
35 half its evil, by losing all its grossness.

---

[1] The wife of the Dauphin, who is the eldest son of the King of France.

Passage 2

As to the tragic paintings by which Mr. Burke has outraged his own imagination, and seeks to work upon that of his readers, they are very well calculated for theatrical representation, where facts are
40 manufactured for the sake of show, and accommodated to produce, through the weakness of sympathy, a weeping effect. But Mr. Burke should recollect that he is writing history, and not plays, and that his readers will expect truth, and not the
45 spouting rant of high-toned exclamation…

Not one glance of compassion, not one commiserating reflection that I can find throughout his book, has he bestowed on those who lingered out the most wretched of lives, a life without hope in the
50 most miserable of prisons.[2] It is painful to behold a man employing his talents to corrupt himself. Nature has been kinder to Mr. Burke than he is to her. He is not affected by the reality of distress touching his heart, but by the showy resemblance of it striking his
55 imagination. He pities the plumage, but forgets the dying bird. Accustomed to kiss the aristocratical hand that hath purloined him from himself, he degenerates into a composition of art, and the genuine soul of nature forsakes him. His hero or his heroine must be
60 a tragedy-victim expiring in show, and not the real prisoner of misery, sliding into death in the silence of a dungeon.

32

In Passage 1, the author's initial assessment of Marie Antoinette is characterized by

A) enthusiastic admiration of her beauty and vivacious personality.

B) hesitant endorsement of her right to rule.

C) amorous infatuation with details of her physical body.

D) a desire to protect her from the coming tragedy.

---

[2] The Bastille, a prison Revolutionaries in France overthrew in order to free the prisoners held there.

CONTINUE ▶

33

Which choice provides the best evidence for the answer to the previous question?

A) Lines 1–2 ("It is now … Versailles")

B) Lines 4–8 ("I saw her … joy")

C) Lines 11–15 ("Little did I … bosom")

D) Lines 18–20 ("I thought … insult")

34

The author of Passage 1 repeats the phrase "little did I dream" (lines 11 and 15) in order to

A) emphasize the limits of his own ability to imagine.

B) mock the ways in which Marie Antoinette has changed because of the Revolution.

C) accentuate how unimaginable the changes which took place in France were.

D) reference the dream-like state his idolization of Marie Antoinette puts him in.

35

The author of Passage 1 characterizes "the age of chivalry" (line 21) primarily as

A) acceptable in its own time, but now superseded by a better age.

B) overly permissive of certain evils.

C) a lost ideal of honor.

D) oppressive to those of lower classes.

36

The word "grossness" as used in line 35 most nearly means

A) dirtiness of appearance.

B) disgust in reaction.

C) coarseness of manner.

D) largess of nature.

37

The most prevalent rhetorical strategy used in Passage 2 is

A) establishing an analogy between the writing of Passage 1 and drama.

B) personal attack against the character of those discussed by the author of Passage 1.

C) systematically developing a parallel point to each point in Passage 1.

D) attempting to control the emotions of the audience through theatrical effects.

38

As it is used in line 57, the word "purloined" most nearly means

A) stolen.

B) elevated.

C) hidden.

D) abstracted.

CONTINUE ➡

1   1

39

In Passage 2, the author claims "He pities the plumage, but forgets the dying bird" (lines 55–56) to suggest that the author of Passage 1 is

A) forgetting that birds are more valuable for the meaning of their death than for their outer beauty.

B) too enamored of the external appearance of honor to notice the damage it does.

C) limited in his approach, because he is unable to respond emotionally to the events he describes.

D) incomplete in his historical methods, but still trying to be honest in his emotions.

40

The two passages relate to each other primarily by

A) discussing the same events from the perspective of very different times and places.

B) sympathizing with different sides of the same conflict.

C) emphasizing different aspects of an event to reach the same conclusion.

D) struggling toward common ground from which to discuss their common values.

41

The author of Passage 2 would respond to the claim in Passage 1 regarding "the spirit of an exalted freedom" (lines 27–28) of those "in servitude" (line 27) by

A) denying their freedom existed because some of them were forced to live in terrible conditions in prison.

B) acknowledging the importance of liberty, but suggesting that it comes from nature rather than the monarch.

C) suggesting that their freedom is only outward, but not true freedom, because they merely act out a part.

D) finding their freedom to be tragic, whereas they think of it as liberating and ennobling.

42

Which choice provides the best evidence for the answer to the previous question?

A) Lines 39–42 ("where facts … effect")

B) Lines 48–50 ("those who … prisons")

C) Lines 51–52 ("Nature has … to her")

D) Lines 59–60 ("His hero … in show")

Questions 43–52 are based on the following passage.

The following passage is adapted from An Urchin in the Storm, *published in 1987, in which Stephen Jay Gould reviews* The Evolution of Culture in Animals, *by John Tyler Bonner, and* Man, the Promising Primate, *by Peter J. Wilson.*

The female mason wasp, *Monobia quadridens*, excavates a broad chamber by digging a long tube into the pith of trees and stems. She deposits a series of eggs in the tube, starting at the bottom and separating
5 each egg from the next by a curved mud partition. The partitions are shaped with their rough and convex side toward daylight and their smooth and concave side toward the cul de sac at the blind end of the chamber. The larvae feed and pupate within their
10 chambers, which the mother has provisioned with food. When the young adults emerge, they crawl toward freedom by chewing through the rough, convex sides of the partitions. If the partitions are experimentally reversed, so that the rough and
15 convex sides now point toward the cul de sac, the emerging adults cut their way into the stem, pile up at the blind end of the tube, and eventually die. Apparently, the mason wasp has evolved a rigidly programmed rule of behavior: cut through the rough
20 and convex side of the partition. In nature, obedience to this rule always leads to daylight. If a human experimenter intervenes to reverse the partitions, the wasp cannot accommodate and digs to its own death, steadfastly obeying its unbreakable rule.
25 What the wasps lack—and what human beings possess in unparalleled abundance—is the common theme of both books: flexibility in behavior response. Bonner defines culture as "the transfer of information by behavioral means," and structures his
30 fascinating book as a survey of culture in the animal kingdom, marching up the venerable chain of being toward bigger brains, increasing behavioral complexity, and freedom from rigid genetic programs specifying "single response behaviors." Wilson
35 identifies flexibility—that is, freedom from genetic programming of specific behaviors—as the key to our evolutionary promise; he traces the origins of human culture to the structural and nongenetic (but biologically based) rules that we follow in establishing
40 systems of kinship.

Human flexibility has at least three complex and interrelated sources. First, we possess a brain much

larger, in proper relation to the size of our bodies, than any other animal (except the bottle-nosed
45 dolphin). More circuitry increases (indeed explodes) at a far faster rate than the growth of its material substrate. A simple machine can handle tic-tac-toe; complex computers may soon be giving chess grand masters a run for it. The metaphor may be somewhat
50 mixed, but it is an arresting thought nonetheless that our brains contain more information, in an engineer's technical sense, than all the DNA in our genes.

Second, we have evolved our massive brains largely by the evolutionary process of neoteny: the
55 slowing down of developmental rates and the consequent retention to adulthood of traits that mark the *juvenile* stages of our ancestors. We retain the rapid fetal growth rate of neurons well beyond birth (when the brain of most mammals is nearly
60 complete), and end our growth with the bulbous cranium and relatively large brain so characteristic of juvenile primates. Neoteny also slows down our maturation and gives us a long period of flexible childhood learning. I believe that the analogy
65 between childhood wonder and adult creativity is good biology, not metaphor.

Third, as primates we belong to one of the few groups of mammals sufficiently unspecialized in bodily form to retain the morphological capacity for
70 exploiting a broad range of environments and modes of life. A bat has committed its forelimbs to flight, a horse to running, and a whale to balancing and paddling. Culture and intelligence at a human level have required the evolution of a free forelimb and a
75 generalized hand endowed with the capacity to manufacture and manipulate tools (both from *manus* = hand). Only the morphologically unspecialized among mammals have not made inflexible commitments to particular modes of life
80 that preclude this prerequisite to intelligence.

CONTINUE

1   **1**

43

The purpose of the first paragraph (lines 1–24) in terms of the passage as a whole is to

A) offer evidence to support the passage's endorsement of biological determinism.

B) illustrate the cruelty of human experimenters in working with other forms of biological life.

C) provide a negative example to contrast with the remainder of the passage.

D) argue for genetic modification needed to allow Mason wasps to thrive.

44

Which choice provides the best evidence for the answer to the previous question?

A) Lines 18–21 ("Apparently … daylight")

B) Lines 21–24 ("If a human … rule")

C) Lines 25–27 ("What wasps … response")

D) Lines 41–42 ("Human … sources")

45

Based on the first paragraph, which of the following is NOT characteristic of a natural wasp lifecycle?

A) Larvae share chambers with siblings in order to maximize their potential success as adults.

B) Larvae develop from eggs into pupae in their chambers and only leave their chambers as young adults.

C) The *Monobia quadridens* is responsible for creating chambers in the pith of trees and providing her offspring with food.

D) As young adults in nature, wasps chew through the convex side of the partition and never through the concave side.

46

As used in line 24, "steadfastly" most nearly means

A) bravely.

B) unequivocally.

C) unfortunately.

D) assiduously.

47

Which of the following gives the best explanation of the relationship between Bonner and Wilson as expressed in the passage?

A) Wilson disagrees with Bonner by believing that flexibility is genetic whereas Wilson thinks genetics are not involved.

B) Bonner builds on Wilson's ideas by providing evidence for Wilson's novel theories of human flexibility.

C) Bonner and Wilson are in agreement in stating that genetic flexibility is key in determining brain size.

D) Wilson discusses in greater detail one of the ideas in Bonner's book by examining the biological causes of human flexibility.

48

Bonner's concept of "culture" (line 28) is related to Wilson's notion of "flexibility" (line 35) in that

A) both are exclusively traits of humans.

B) both suggest aspects of animal behavior that are not genetically determined.

C) both are determined by the size of any animal's brain.

D) neither is known to have an impact on biological success.

49

According to the passage, which of the following is most analogous to the benefit of a large brain size?

A) A larger basement provides more storage space.

B) A country with more laws is more obedient and orderly.

C) A larger puppet can have more strings, which allow for more movement.

D) A more viscous substance is more fluid.

50

Which choice provides the best evidence for the answer to the previous question?

A) Line 42–45 ("First, we ... dolphin")

B) Line 45–47 ("More circuitry ... substrate")

C) Line 49–52 ("The metaphor ... genes")

D) Line 53–57 (Second, we ... ancestors")

51

Which of the following would be in most conflict with the author's description of neoteny in lines 53–66?

A) Neoteny is a biological characteristic of humans.

B) Neoteny slows down human brains.

C) Adult humans are more creative because of neoteny.

D) Children are biologically better suited to learn than adults.

52

As used in line 71, "committed" most nearly means

A) perpetrated.

B) dedicated.

C) achieved.

D) lost.

STOP

**If you finish before time is called, you may check your work on this section only.
Do not turn to any other section.**

CONTINUE

No Test Material On This Page

Writing and Language Test

35 MINUTES, 44 QUESTIONS

Turn to Section 2 of your answer sheet to answer the questions in this section.

DIRECTIONS

Each passage below is accompanied by a number of questions. For some questions, you will consider how the passage might be revised to improve the expression of ideas. For other questions, you will consider how the passage might be edited to correct errors in sentence structure, usage, or punctuation. A passage or a question may be accompanied by one or more graphics (such as a table or graph) that you will consider as you make revising and editing decisions.

Some questions will direct you to an underlined portion of a passage. Other questions will direct you to a location in a passage or ask you to think about the passage as a whole.

After reading each passage, choose the answer to each question that most effectively improves the quality of writing in the passage or that makes the passage conform to the conventions of standard written English. Many questions include a "NO CHANGE" option. Choose that option if you think the best choice is to leave the relevant portion of the passage as it is.

Questions 1–11 are based on the following passage.

On the Campaign Trail

[1] In my senior year of high school when I started working on campaigns as a **1** volunteer; I was immediately attracted to the energy of campaigning, thus I joined a campaign as an intern the following summer. [2] Even though doing a task like this could be exhausting and repetitive, everyone in the office was excited to contribute to the effort. [3] Upon joining the campaign, I was asked to help with **2** compiling our financial records, volunteers, and our press releases.

1

A) NO CHANGE

B) volunteer, I was immediately attracted to the energy of campaigning, so

C) volunteer I was immediately attracted to the energy of campaigning, so that

D) volunteer, I was immediately attracted to the energy of campaigning; so,

2

A) NO CHANGE

B) compiling our financial records and press releases as well as supervising volunteers.

C) compiling our financial records, coordinating our press releases, as well as supervising volunteers.

D) compiling our financial records, and press releases; and supervising volunteers.

2

2

[4] Tedious tasks were not reserved for [3] volunteers; my campaign manager and I spent several hours [4] watching the World Cup and stuffing envelopes for our major mailing campaign as well. [5] Working on a campaign requires that everyone helps and that no task is "beneath" anyone. [5]

3

A) NO CHANGE
B) volunteers—and my
C) volunteers, my
D) volunteers: while my

4

The writer is considering deleting the underlined portion. Should the author make this change?

A) Yes, because this detail is irrelevant to the purpose of describing working on a campaign.
B) Yes, because this detail makes the writer's experience seem like fun.
C) No, because this detail adds necessary humor to lighten up this otherwise somber passage.
D) No, because this detail adds an example needed to understand working on a campaign.

5

To make the paragraph most coherent and logical, sentence 2 should be placed

A) where it is now.
B) before sentence 1.
C) after sentence 3.
D) after sentence 4.

CONTINUE ➡

I spent most of my weekends on the campaign canvassing, which [6] involve walking around a neighborhood and knocking on doors to persuade people to vote for a candidate. Although it sounds outdated, canvassing is actually one of the most effective ways to secure votes [7]. [8] While canvassing, many voters got the opportunity to learn more about the candidate and his policies. Some people were not receptive and slammed the door in my face, but most people were friendly and interested in hearing about the candidate.

[6]

A) NO CHANGE
B) had involved
C) involves
D) has involved

[7]

The writer is considering adding the following clause here:

> because it provides the voter with a much more personal interaction than the standard automated phone call

Assuming punctuation was adjusted, should the author make this change?

A) Yes, because this clause emphasizes the ineffectiveness of auto dialers.
B) Yes, because this clause clarifies why canvassing is still an effective mode of campaigning.
C) No, because this clause provides information that the reader can clearly infer from the context.
D) No, because this clause does not provide sufficient detail on canvassing strategies.

[8]

A) NO CHANGE
B) My canvassing provided many voters with
C) During canvassing, they all got
D) While I was canvassing the voters, got

2   2

[9] The week leading up to Election Day required a massive "Get Out the Vote" effort involving many volunteers, hundreds of phone calls, hours of canvassing, and many boxes of stale pizza. Each night, I made over 100 phone calls to remind voters about Election Day and to try to persuade them to vote for my candidate. In all our calls, we only successfully reached a voter 10 percent of the time because people did not pick up the phone or we had an outdated number on file. **[10]** Nonetheless, we were desperate to secure votes in that last week, so we did all we could and worked tirelessly around the clock. Even if we reached only a few people, we believed that our efforts would have a positive impact on both the election and the democratic process as a whole.

Nothing was more exciting than the victory party on Tuesday night after the polls closed. I rushed from my designated polling station to join my fellow workers as we watched the election results. **[11]** We have been running a clever, effective, and well-organized campaign, so it was exciting to see our hard work pay off. After working on this campaign, I realized the importance of being involved in our country's political process and have committed myself to continuing political engagement.

9

Which choice most vividly depicts the author's experience during the "Get Out the Vote" week?

A) NO CHANGE

B) The week leading up to Election Day required us to do a "Get Out the Vote" effort.

C) We recruited a lot of volunteers for a massive "Get Out the Vote" effort during the week leading up to Election Day.

D) "Get Out the Vote" was a big effort we led during the week leading up to Election Day with lots of volunteers working around the clock.

10

A) NO CHANGE

B) Consequently,

C) Therefore,

D) Unfortunately,

11

A) NO CHANGE

B) We have run

C) We had run

D) We are running

Questions 12–22 are based on the following passage and supplemental material.

A Waste of Nuclear Energy?

The world's rapidly growing population has demanded ever-increasing supplies of energy from a variety of sources. During the Industrial Revolution, handmade production methods gave way to mass production in coal-powered factories. In the late nineteenth century, Thomas Edison spurred the spread of electric power to run his newly invented [12] lightbulbs, and the automobile created a new and still booming market for oil. After harnessing atomic energy during the Second World War, scientists in the mid-twentieth century began applying nuclear power to civilian energy projects.

Proponents of harnessing nuclear power cite several benefits, many [13] of them seem to make it superior to other possible sources of energy. Because nuclear power reduces dependence on fossil fuels, such as oil and coal, its widespread use could lower greenhouse gas emissions caused by burning carbon-based fuels. Thus, it is an energy option that may slow devastating climate change. In addition, nuclear power plants have demonstrated the capacity to generate the large [14] numbers of power needed to meet industrial needs and the energy demands of large, urban populations. And finally, it is efficient: nuclear power yields a large energy output from a

12

A) NO CHANGE
B) lightbulbs and
C) lightbulbs; and
D) lightbulbs: and

13

A) NO CHANGE
B) of whom
C) of which
D) of these benefits

14

A) NO CHANGE
B) totals
C) aggregates
D) quantities

relatively small amount of fuel. This saves not only on direct fuel costs but also on the cost and environmental effects of transporting raw materials.

Critics of nuclear power, however, cite environmental and human health concerns about the development of nuclear power. **15** Nuclear power plants generate plenty of energy but also waste. Radioactivity levels in the waste remaining high for hundreds of thousands of years. Because radiation has been demonstrated to cause genetic mutations and cancer, it is essential to store nuclear waste safely. However, the cost both to build and to maintain secure storage of radioactive byproducts is high.

In 1986, a major disaster at a civilian nuclear plant in Chernobyl, Ukraine, highlighted for the world the potential danger of nuclear power development. **16** The long-term effects of this disaster are still being studied. The United Nations estimates the number of probable

15

Which choice most effectively combines the underlined sentences?

A) Radioactivity in nuclear waste remains high for hundreds of thousands of years; nevertheless, nuclear power plants generate plenty of energy.

B) Even though nuclear power plants generate plenty of energy, they have downsides that create concerns: radioactivity levels in the waste remain high for hundreds of thousands of years.

C) Though nuclear power plants produce plenty of energy, they also generate waste that remains highly radioactive for hundreds of thousands of years.

D) Generating plenty of energy, nuclear power plants also generate waste; this waste remains with high levels of radioactivity for hundreds of thousands of years.

16

At this point, the writer is considering adding the following sentence:

> This facility suffered a meltdown due to human error wherein tons of radioactive materials were released into the surrounding environment.

Should the writer make this addition here?

A) Yes, because without the knowledge that the damage was caused by human error, readers might assume that radioactive material itself is unsafe.

B) Yes, because it provides helpful information to understand the main point of the paragraph.

C) No, because the information contained in the sentence can be inferred from the rest of the paragraph.

D) No, because it distracts readers from the main topic of the paragraph.

deaths associated with the disaster at around 4,000. [17] Instead, a new book by former Soviet government scientists [18] reveal that almost a million deaths, most due to cancer, may be attributable to the accident at Chernobyl.

As human beings continue to debate options for developing energy [19] sources—whether conventional, renewable, or nuclear—to meet the demands of a growing population, the importance of energy conservation should be central to the discussion. An easy way to reduce our energy consumption is to scale back our use of energy for nonessential activities. No energy source capable of [20] endowing the needs of a large population will be entirely safe and free of destructive consequences. As citizens of the world, we need to be mindful of the

17
A) NO CHANGE
B) Moreover,
C) However,
D) Regardless,

18
A) NO CHANGE
B) reveals
C) is revealing
D) would reveal

19
A) NO CHANGE
B) sources—whether conventional, renewable, or nuclear,
C) sources, whether conventional, renewable, or nuclear;
D) sources: whether conventional, renewable, or nuclear,

20
A) NO CHANGE
B) supplying
C) giving
D) donating

[21] affects of our actions and strive to reduce our energy footprint. Wherever our energy comes from, we must learn to preserve our resources by using them wisely.

Question [22] asks about the previous passage as a whole.

21

A) NO CHANGE
B) affects for
C) effects of
D) effects for

Think about the previous passage and included supplemental material as a whole as you answer question 22.

22

Which statement most accurately interprets the data presented in the graph about energy consumption in the United States in 2005?

A) The amount of energy consumed from petroleum was almost twice the amount of energy consumed from coal and natural gas combined.

B) The US consumed more energy from hydro-electric power than from wood, waste, and alcohol fuels.

C) A total of 1 million Btu of geothermal, solar, and wind energy were consumed.

D) Nuclear power provided less than 10 percent of the total energy consumed.

US Energy Consumption by Source (2005)

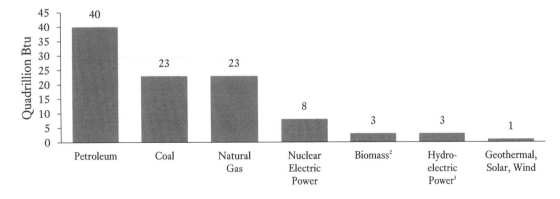

[1] Conventional Hydro-electric power. [2] Wood, waste, and alcohol fuels.

Adapted from Energy Information Administration, *Annual Energy Review 2005.* © 2006

CONTINUE

2

2

Questions 23-33 are based on the following passage.

Shakespeare's Forerunner

Christopher Marlowe may be literature's best-known second place finisher. Doomed always to stand in the shadow of Shakespeare, [23] Marlowe's work is still widely read and performed today, but his true significance as an innovator is underappreciated. Critics commonly assert that Marlowe preceded Shakespeare in writing serious tragedy for the English stage, but [24] Marlowe also kept up with Shakespeare in the development of the history play, the form most commonly associated with Shakespeare.

Shakespeare, who was then considered an undereducated upstart, wrote the three parts of *Henry VI*, [25] the second of which was originally titled *The Contention of the Noble and Illustrious Houses of York and Lancaster*, in the late 1580s, while Marlowe's *Edward II* was likely first staged in 1593. However, despite some interesting characters and powerful lines, Shakespeare's

[23]

A) NO CHANGE
B) Marlowe's position is assured because his plays are
C) Marlowe wrote plays that are
D) DELETE the underlined portion

[24]

Which choice most clearly emphasizes the point that Marlowe was an influence on Shakespeare's history plays?

A) NO CHANGE
B) Shakespeare was most commonly associated with history plays, though Marlowe also wrote one of the earlier history plays.
C) Marlowe also wrote a single English history play, and its effect on Shakespeare's later history plays is clear.
D) Shakespeare influenced Marlowe to write his first and only history play.

[25]

The writer is considering deleting the underlined portion, adjusting the punctuation appropriately. Should the writer make this change?

A) Yes, because the full title of Shakespeare's play is clear from the context.
B) Yes, because the phrase adds an unnecessary detail to the paragraph.
C) No, because the information is needed to make sense of the rest of the paragraph.
D) No, because the phrase provides context that readers will need to understand the main point of the essay.

CONTINUE

Henry VI plays **26** are unstructured: they seem to exist merely to portray a loosely connected series of events but without dramatic unity. It wasn't until Marlowe, who was then regarded as the premiere playwright for the London stage, made his first foray into English history that the history **27** play became its own form of cohesive art.

[1] In telling the story of Edward **28** II, whom was a weak and failed monarch, Marlowe **29** combined: elements of a morality play and classical tragedy. [2] In the play, history was not a collection of events but a narrative corresponding to recognizable types, a true work of art. [3] Like a character in a morality play, Marlowe's Edward is **30** shrouded by a corrupting influence, that of Gaveston, a self-indulgent flatterer who

26
A) NO CHANGE
B) lack structure, portraying loosely connected events without unity or purpose, dramatically speaking.
C) lack dramatic unity, presenting history only as a loosely connected series of events.
D) are less structured than his later plays, such as *Hamlet* and *King Lear*, which is also about English history.

27
A) NO CHANGE
B) plays become their own
C) play becomes its own
D) play, becoming a

28
A) NO CHANGE
B) II, who
C) II whom
D) II who

29
A) NO CHANGE
B) combined a morality play, with tragic aspects.
C) combined elements from both a morality play and a classical tragedy.
D) combined a morality play—together with tragic elements.

30
A) NO CHANGE
B) inundated
C) drowned
D) overcome

has stolen the heart of the king. [4] [31] <u>Unlike a character in</u> a morality play, Edward has no "good angels" to help him become a better ruler, for the king's counselors murder Gaveston only to increase their own power. [5] Then, when Edward's wife and several nobles turn against him, the audience sympathizes with the king as he loses his power and is eventually killed, turning him from a pathetic character to one who arouses the pity and fear that Aristotle claimed tragedy required. [6] Shakespeare's later history plays show evidence that he learned a great deal from Marlowe's play: aspects of classical tragedy and English morality are clear in many of Shakespeare's best historical dramas of the mid-to-late 1590s. [32]

Marlowe cannot compete with Shakespeare: he died too young, never having reached the level of subtlety and sophistication Shakespeare attained in his career. However, Marlowe should not be considered a second-place finisher to Shakespeare. It is more accurate to characterize him as the first to arrive at the finish line, whereas Shakespeare reached that line and found that he [33] <u>had just begun to race at the point where Marlowe finished.</u>

[31]

A) NO CHANGE
B) As opposed to
C) However, not like
D) Moreover, in the opposite way of

[32]

To make the paragraph most coherent and logical, sentence 6 should be placed

A) where it is now.
B) before sentence 1.
C) after sentence 3.
D) after sentence 4.

[33]

A) NO CHANGE
B) had only begun racing where Marlowe had stopped.
C) had enough energy to continue racing from that point on.
D) had merely begun to race.

2

2

Questions 34–44 are based on the following passage.

GM Crops: Are they really safe?

Genetically modified food has become prevalent in the United States since the commercialization of genetic engineering in 1976. Over the past decade, the use of GM crops has become [34] increasingly more and more popular and now [35] accounts for roughly 94 percent of the acreage of soybeans and 93 percent of that of corn in the US. However, as GM crops have increased in [36] prevalence they have also become more controversial, and many believe that not enough long-term research has been done to ensure that they are safe for consumption.

34

A) NO CHANGE
B) more widespread
C) appallingly ubiquitous
D) the popular thing to do

35

Which of the following provides specific support for the main idea of this paragraph?

A) NO CHANGE
B) is used in many places.
C) makes growing and protecting crops much easier for farmers.
D) helps ease the burden of producing the food needed to meet the demand of the US and the world.

36

A) NO CHANGE
B) prevalence—they
C) prevalence, they
D) prevalence, and they

[37] Nonetheless, in 2012, French scientist Eric-Gilles Seralini conducted an experiment that has since become very controversial. [38] They wanted to test the toxicity of [39] Monsanto's genetically modified NK603 corn. Monsanto's NK603 corn is genetically modified to resist RoundUp, a commonly used herbicide. The experimenters tested 200 Sprague-Dawley rats in groups of 10 and fed them variations of genetically modified RoundUp-resistant corn, water with RoundUp, or unmodified corn and water. Seralini's team monitored the rats over the course of two years and observed that the rats that were fed GM corn died sooner than those fed the unmodified corn.

37

A) NO CHANGE
B) Shockingly, in 2012,
C) As a consequence, in 2012,
D) In 2012,

38

A) NO CHANGE
B) He
C) It
D) His experiment

39

Which of the following choices provides the best way to combine these two sentences?

A) Monsanto's NK603 corn, which is genetically modified to resist RoundUp, which is an herbicide commonly used.

B) Monsanto's, genetically modified to resist RoundUp, a commonly used herbicide, corn called NK603.

C) Monsanto's NK603 corn, which is genetically modified to resist the common herbicide RoundUp.

D) Monsanto's genetically modified NK603 corn: this type of corn is genetically modified to resist RoundUp, which is a commonly used herbicide.

2

2

[1] Seralini then held a press conference and published startling results with pictures of experimental rats with huge and alarming tumors. [2] Many news sources and social media sites caused an international outrage and widespread fear of genetically modified crops by reporting that GM corn caused tumors. [3] In reaction, some countries, such as Russia, banned GM corn entirely. [4] **40** On the other hand, some biology and bioethics organizations criticized the study for practicing poor science. [5] The scientists at these institutions pointed out that Seralini's sample size of 200 rats in groups of 10 **41** was far too small for an experiment lasting two years: the Organization for Economic Co-operation and Development recommends groups of at least 20 for toxicity and at least 50 for carcinogenicity tests of this length. [6] Furthermore, these rats are extremely susceptible to spontaneous tumors, making Seralini's claims about tumors particularly suspect. **42**

40

Which of the following is LEAST acceptable?
A) NO CHANGE
B) However, some
C) Though some
D) Unconvinced, other

41

A) NO CHANGE
B) were too small by far
C) is far to small
D) were far too small

42

Where is the most logical place in this paragraph to insert the following sentence?

> Another concern was that the time span was too long, because the average Sprague-Dawley rat's lifespan is less than two years.

A) After sentence 2
B) After sentence 3
C) After sentence 4
D) After sentence 5

Nonetheless, the results of **43** Seralini's experiment are undoubtedly cause for concern because GM corn is so common in our diets. However, the experimental design was flawed in many ways, and Seralini has been criticized for having an anti-GM agenda, a bias that makes his results less credible. Are GM crops safe? **44** Many scientists believe that they pose no harm, but perhaps more rigorous and accurate research could be done to make sure.

43

A) NO CHANGE
B) Seralini and his teams'
C) Seralinis'
D) Seralini's teams

44

The writer wants the last sentence to emphasize that the answer to the question "Are GM crops safe?" is both uncertain and essential to determine. Which choice best accomplishes this intention?

A) NO CHANGE
B) Though some scientists believe they are safe to consume, more rigorous long-term research must be done to ensure public health.
C) Seralini's flawed methods have not helped us to know for certain, and so we cannot really know.
D) Despite the problems with Seralini's experiment, the problems it found make it clear that GM foods are not safe to eat.

STOP

**If you finish before time is called, you may check your work on this section only.
Do not turn to any other section.**

No Test Material On This Page

Math Test – No Calculator

25 MINUTES, 20 QUESTIONS

Turn to Section 3 of your answer sheet to answer the questions in this section.

DIRECTIONS

For questions 1–15, solve each problem, choose the best answer from the choices provided, and fill in the corresponding circle on your answer sheet. For questions 16–20, solve the problems and enter your answer in the grid on the answer sheet. Please refer to the directions before question 16 on how to enter your answers in the grid. You may use any available space in your test booklet for scratch work.

NOTES

The use of calculators **is not permitted**.

All variables and expressions used represent real numbers unless otherwise indicated.

Figures provided in this test are drawn to scale unless otherwise indicated.

All figures lie in a plane unless otherwise indicated.

Unless otherwise indicated, the domain of a given function f is the set of real numbers x for which $f(x)$ is a real number.

REFERENCE

$A = \pi r^2$
$C = 2\pi r$

$A = \ell w$

$A = \dfrac{1}{2}bh$

$c^2 = a^2 + b^2$

Special Right Triangles

$V = \ell w h$

$V = \pi r^2 h$

$V = \dfrac{4}{3}\pi r^3$

$V = \dfrac{1}{3}\pi r^2 h$

$V = \dfrac{1}{3}\ell w h$

The number of degrees of arc in a circle is 360.
The number of radians of arc in a circle is 2π.
The sum of the measures in degrees of the angles in a triangle is 180.

CONTINUE

1

A commercial pilot flies a Cessna 182 for private passengers wishing to take trips from small airports. The total expenses for a flight can be represented by the expression $tgX + C$, where t is the number of hours travelled, g is gallons of fuel used per hour, X is a constant with units of dollars per gallon, and C is the total cost of plane inspection, parts, servicing, and hangar rental. If the price of fuel rises by 5 percent, which of the factors in the expense expression would change?

A) t

B) X

C) g

D) C

2

For $i = \sqrt{-1}$, what is the value of $3(4 - 3i) + 2i$?

A) $12 + 7i$

B) $12 - 11i$

C) $12 + 11i$

D) $12 - 7i$

3

Which of the following is equivalent to $x^{\frac{3}{4}}$ for all values of x ?

A) $\sqrt[3]{x^{\frac{1}{4}}}$

B) $\sqrt[3]{x^4}$

C) $\sqrt[4]{x^{\frac{1}{3}}}$

D) $\sqrt[4]{x^3}$

4

A group of friends is eating at a diner. Each entree costs $5.25, and each soda costs $1.50. If d people order an entree and p people order a soda, which of the following expressions represents the total number of dollars paid by the group?

A) $5.25p + 1.5d$

B) $6.75d$

C) $5.25d + 1.5p$

D) $5.25d - 1.5p$

CONTINUE

5

$$4x^4 + 20x^2 y + 25y^2$$

Which of the following is equivalent to the expression above?

A) $(4x^2 + 5y^2)^2$

B) $(4x^2 + 10y^2)^2$

C) $(2x^2 + 5y^2)^2$

D) $(2x^2 + 5y)^2$

6

$$3a - 4b = -14$$
$$4a - 3b = -7$$

Given the system of equations above, what is the value of $a - b$?

A) -7

B) -3

C) 7

D) 10

7

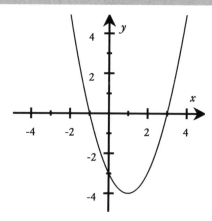

Given the function $f(x)$ shown in the graph above, which of the following must be a factor of $f(x)$?

A) $x - 1$

B) $x - 2$

C) $x - 3$

D) $x - 4$

8

If $\dfrac{p}{q} = \dfrac{4}{3}$, what is the value of $\dfrac{12q}{p}$?

A) 6

B) 8

C) 9

D) 16

3 **3**

9

Which of the following inequalities has a graph in the xy-plane for which y is always less than -4?

A) $y < (x-4)^2$

B) $y \le (x+4)^2$

C) $y < -(x^2 + 4)$

D) $y \ge |x-4|$

10

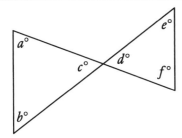

Note: Figure not drawn to scale

In the figure above, the sum of b and c is equal to the sum of f and d. Which of the following must be true?

     I. $b = f$
    II. $e = b$
   III. $a = e$

A) I only

B) III only

C) I, II, and III

D) I and III only

11

A line in the xy-plane contains the point $(3, -5)$ and has a slope of $\frac{4}{3}$. Which of the following points lies on the line?

A) $(0, -9)$

B) $(-3, 2)$

C) $(4, -5)$

D) $(3, -6)$

12

What is the sum of all values of b that satisfy $3b^2 - 2b - 4 = 0$?

A) $\frac{2}{3}$

B) $\frac{3}{2}$

C) $\frac{\sqrt{13}}{2}$

D) $2\sqrt{13}$

CONTINUE

13

$$\frac{16x^2 + 28x - 19}{nx - 5} = -4x - 2 - \frac{29}{nx - 5}$$

Given the equation above, in which n is a constant and $x \neq \dfrac{5}{n}$, what is the value of n?

A) −8

B) −4

C) 4

D) 8

14

If $(5^b)^{3a} = 25$, what is the value of $36ab$?

A) 24

B) 12

C) 4

D) 3

15

$$J = -\frac{3}{7}(A + 78)$$

On the planet Sandor, the number of Jagons (J) and Ambloos (A) are related by the relationship given in the equation above. Based on the equation, which of the following must be true?

   I. A decrease of 1 Ambloo is equivalent to an increase of $\dfrac{3}{7}$ of a Jagon.

   II. An increase of 1 Ambloo is equivalent to a decrease of $\dfrac{3}{7}$ of a Jagon.

   III. A decrease of $\dfrac{7}{3}$ Ambloos is equivalent to an increase of 1 Jagon.

A) I and II only

B) I and III only

C) II and III only

D) I, II, and III

CONTINUE

3   3

DIRECTIONS

For questions 16–20, solve the problem and enter your answer in the grid, as described below, on the answer sheet.

1. Although not required, it is suggested that you write your answer in the boxes at the top of the columns to help you fill in the circles accurately. You will receive credit only if the circles are filled in correctly.
2. Mark no more than one circle in any column.
3. No question has a negative answer.
4. Some problems may have more than one correct answer. In such cases, grid only one answer.
5. **Mixed numbers** such as $3\frac{1}{2}$ must be be gridded as 3.5 or 7/2. If ³¹⁄₂ is entered into the grid, it will be interpreted as $\frac{31}{2}$, not $3\frac{1}{2}$.)
6. **Decimal answers:** If you obtain a decimal answer with more digits than the grid can accommodate, it may be either rounded or truncated, but it must fill the entire grid.

Answer: $\frac{7}{13}$

Write answer in boxes →

←Fraction line

Grid in result

Answer: 2.5

←Decimal Point

Acceptable ways to grid $\frac{2}{3}$ are:

Answer: 210 – either position is correct

NOTE: You may start your answers in any column, space permitting. Columns you don't need to use should be left blank.

3   **3**

16

$$x^3(x^2 - 10) = -9x$$

What is a solution to the above equation if $x > 0$?

17

$$w + x - y = 4$$
$$x - w + y = 6$$
$$3x - w = 8$$

In the system of equations above, what is the value of y?

18

$$\frac{11}{15}x - \frac{8}{15}x = \frac{1}{6} + \frac{1}{12}$$

What value of x satisfies the equation shown above?

CONTINUE ➤

19

At a sports memorabilia store, each football jersey costs \$40 more than each hockey jersey. If 2 hockey jerseys and 4 football jerseys cost \$1,000, how much does one hockey jersey cost? (Note: Disregard the \$ sign when gridding your answer.)

20

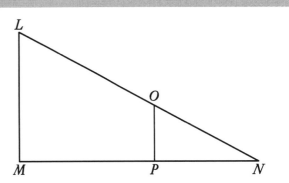

Note: Figure not drawn to scale

In the figure above, $\triangle LMN$ and $\triangle OPN$ are similar. The angles $\angle LMP$ and $\angle OPN$ are both right angles, and $LM = 9$, $OP = 6$, and $PN = 8$. What is the value of $\cos L$?

STOP

**If you finish before time is called, you may check your work on this section only.
Do not turn to any other section.**

4 **4**

Math Test – Calculator

55 MINUTES, 38 QUESTIONS

Turn to Section 4 of your answer sheet to answer the questions in this section.

DIRECTIONS

For questions 1–30, solve each problem, choose the best answer from the choices provided, and fill in the corresponding circle on your answer sheet. **For questions 31–38**, solve the problems and enter your answer in the grid on the answer sheet. Please refer to the directions before question 31 on how to enter your answers in the grid. You may use any available space in your test booklet for scratch work.

NOTES

1. The use of calculators **is permitted**.

2. All variables and expressions used represent real numbers unless otherwise indicated.

3. Figures provided in this test are drawn to scale unless otherwise indicated.

4. All figures lie in a plane unless otherwise indicated.

5. Unless otherwise indicated, the domain of a given function f is the set of real numbers x for which $f(x)$ is a real number.

REFERENCE

$A = \pi r^2$
$C = 2\pi r$

$A = \ell w$

$A = \frac{1}{2}bh$

$c^2 = a^2 + b^2$

Special Right Triangles

$V = \ell w h$

$V = \pi r^2 h$

$V = \frac{4}{3}\pi r^3$

$V = \frac{1}{3}\pi r^2 h$

$V = \frac{1}{3}\ell w h$

The number of degrees of arc in a circle is 360.
The number of radians of arc in a circle is 2π.
The sum of the measures in degrees of the angles in a triangle is 180.

CONTINUE ➡

4 **4**

1

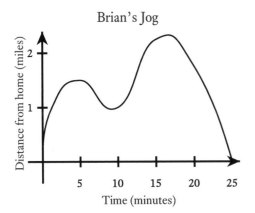

Brian's Jog

The graph above shows Brian's distance from his home during a 25-minute jog. He was feeling tired and was on his way home when he changed his mind and decided to run farther. Approximately how many minutes into his jog did Brian turn around to run farther?

A)   5 minutes

B)   9 minutes

C)   15 minutes

D)   20 minutes

2

The equation for momentum is $p = mv$, where p is momentum in kilogram meters per second, m is the mass of an object in kilograms, and v is the object's velocity in meters per second. If an object's momentum is 4 kg·m/s when its velocity is 12 m/s, what is its momentum when its velocity is 27 m/s, assuming the mass is constant?

A)   81 kg·m/s

B)   19 kg·m/s

C)   12 kg·m/s

D)   9 kg·m/s

3

Two out of every 45 people in line for a video game release are randomly chosen to receive a special prize. If there are 675 people in the line, how many will get a prize?

A) 54

B) 45

C) 30

D) 15

4

	Cream	No Cream	Total
Sugar	4	7	11
No Sugar	15	1	16
Total	19	8	27

The table above shows the distribution of coffee preferences among the members of the DC Book Club. If a club member is to be selected at random, what is the probability that the member will prefer his or her coffee with both sugar and cream or with no sugar and no cream?

A) $\frac{5}{27}$

B) $\frac{1}{4}$

C) $\frac{16}{27}$

D) $\frac{19}{27}$

CONTINUE

5

$$v_f = 6 + 2t$$

A biker has an initial velocity of 6 m/s (meters per second) before beginning to accelerate at a constant rate of 2 m/s² (meters per second squared). The equation above models the biker's final velocity v_f, in meters per second, in terms of the time t, in seconds, since the biker began accelerating. If the biker's velocity is 13 m/s, how many seconds has he been accelerating?

A)   3.5

B)   7

C)   9.5

D)   34

6

At Big Bob's Tackle shop, approximately 12 percent of shoppers are club members and 8 percent of shoppers are premium members. If there is no overlap between club and premium members and there were a total of 730 purchases made last week at Big Bob's, which of the following is most likely closest to the total number of club and premium members who made purchases last week?

A)   58

B)   88

C)   146

D)   584

7

$$R = 5x^2 - 13x + 2$$
$$S = -2x^2 + 2x + 7$$

Which of the following is equal to $R - S$?

A) $3x^2 + 15x - 5$

B) $3x^2 - 11x + 9$

C) $7x^2 - 15x - 5$

D) $7x^2 + 15x + 9$

8

The value of Carlos' car can be modeled by the equation $y = -3,046x + 24,000$, where x represents the number of years since he purchased the car, and y represents the value of the car. Which of the following best describes the meaning of the number 3,046 in the equation above?

A)   The initial value of the car when Carlos purchased it

B)   The estimated decrease in the value of the car per year

C)   The value of the car x years after it was purchased

D)   The amount that Carlos still owes on his car

4   **4**

9

For the function $C(x)$, $C(34) = 21$ and $C(53) = 44$.
For the function $R(x)$, $R(44) = 31$ and $R(23) = 21$.
What is $R(C(53))$?

A) 21

B) 31

C) 53

D) 94

▼

Questions 10 and 11 refer to the following information.

Car Model	Fuel Economy (miles/gallon)
Kia Soul Hybrid	105
Chevrolet Volt	93
Toyota Prius Hybrid	56
Ford Fusion	47
Honda Insight	42
Ford Mustang	26
Dodge Viper	16

The chart above shows approximations of the fuel

economy in miles per gallon for seven popular cars in

2015. The cost of gas for driving a car can be found by

using the formula $C = \dfrac{mg}{f}$, where C is the amount of

money expended on gas, m is the number of miles the

car is driven, g is the price of gas per gallon, and f is

the fuel efficiency of the car measured in miles per

gallon.

10

US Route 550 stretches 305 miles from Bernalillo,
New Mexico to Montrose, Colorado. If gas costs $2.50
per gallon, how much must be spent on gas for a Kia
Soul Hybrid to drive the entire length of US
Route 550?

A) $0.86

B) $1.16

C) $4.49

D) $7.26

11

Gas prices fluctuate based on supply and demand. If a
Ford Fusion can drive the length of Route 48 for only
$12.97, how much would it cost a Ford Mustang to
make the same drive at the same gas price?

A) $16.22

B) $23.45

C) $29.32

D) $46.92

▲

CONTINUE ▶

12

For what value of x is $|x+2|+1=0$ true?

A) −3

B) −1

C) 0

D) For no value of x

13

$$\frac{1}{d_o} + \frac{1}{d_i} = \frac{1}{f}$$

The equation above is used to find the focal length f of a thin lens. When an object is placed at a distance d_o from a thin lens, it produces an image at a distance d_i from that lens. Which of the following gives d_i in terms of d_o and f?

A) $f - d_o$

B) $\dfrac{1}{f - d_o}$

C) $\dfrac{f d_o}{d_o - f}$

D) $\dfrac{f - d_o}{f d_o}$

14

	Roast Beef	Turkey	Peanut Butter and Jelly	Total
Male	48	33	78	159
Female	51	40	50	141
Total	99	73	128	300

All of the students at a high school lunch were asked what their preferred sandwich was among roast beef, turkey, and peanut butter and jelly. Which of the following comprised 26 percent of those surveyed?

A) Males who prefer roast beef

B) People who prefer turkey

C) Females who prefer peanut butter and jelly

D) Males who prefer peanut butter and jelly

15

The Leghorn is a breed of chicken originating in Italy. It is a good layer of white eggs, laying an average of 280 eggs per year. Which of the following equations represents n, the average number of <u>dozens</u> of eggs produced by a Leghorn chicken in m <u>months</u>?

A) $n = \dfrac{280m}{(12)(12)}$

B) $n = \dfrac{280m}{12}$

C) $n = 12m + 280$

D) $n = 280m$

CONTINUE

Questions 16 and 17 refer to the following information.

	Education	Environment & Recreation	Health Care	Human Services	Infrastructure, Housing & Economic Development	Law & Public Safety
FY16	7,718,943	211,233	18,608,181	4,103,619	2,284,184	2,620,984
FY15	7,478,954	197,421	17,616,167	3,956,955	2,201,409	2,644,481
FY14	7,284,482	188,161	16,284,388	3,696,711	2,114,165	2,566,129
FY13	6,933,564	176,208	14,956,428	3,502,458	1,765,973	2,451,851

Adapted from Massachusetts Budget and Policy Center website.

The table above lists the Massachusetts budgets (in thousands of dollars) for some government programs during several fiscal years.

16

Which of the following best approximates the average rate of change in the yearly budget for education during the fiscal years shown?

A) $200 million

B) $260 million

C) $350 million

D) $790 million

17

Which ratio is closest to that of the budget for Human Services in FY15 to that of FY14?

A) Law & Public Safety FY15 to FY14

B) Environment & Recreation FY16 to FY15

C) Health Care FY15 to FY14

D) Infrastructure, Housing & Economic Development FY14 to FY13

CONTINUE

4   **4**

18

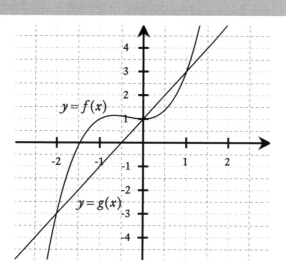

Graphs of the functions f and g are shown in the xy-plane above. For how many of the values of x in the domain pictured above does $f(x) + g(x) = 2f(x)$?

A) 0

B) 1

C) 2

D) 3

19

	Spent under $100	Spent $100 or more
Shopped online	19	56
Shopped at the mall	36	39

A survey was done of people who spent an hour shopping in a mall and online, recording whether they spent more or less than $100. The results are shown above. If one of those who spent under $100 were randomly selected for further questioning, what is the probability that they shopped at the mall?

A) $\dfrac{39}{95}$

B) $\dfrac{36}{75}$

C) $\dfrac{36}{55}$

D) $\dfrac{19}{75}$

4 **4**

Questions 20 and 21 refer to the following information.

Perry is selling lemonade at the county fair, and his profit $P(n)$, in dollars, can be modeled by the equation $P(n) = \frac{5}{2}n - 12$, where n equals the number of cups he sells. His sister Jasmine is selling orange juice at the same fair, and her profit $J(n)$, in dollars, can be modeled by the equation $J(n) = 4n - 30$, where n equals the number of cups she sells.

20

By how many dollars does each cup of orange juice sold affect the profit that Jasmine makes?

A)   4

B) $\frac{5}{2}$

C) -12

D) -30

21

In the morning, Perry and Jasmine each manage to sell 32 cups of juice. Which of the following describes their relative profits as n increases?

A) Initially Perry had a greater profit, but after they had each sold 12 cups of juice Jasmine had the greater profit.

B) Initially Jasmine had a greater profit, but after they had each sold 12 cups of juice Perry had the greater profit.

C) Initially Perry had a greater profit, but after they had each sold 18 cups of juice Jasmine had a greater profit.

D) Initially Jasmine had a greater profit, but after they had each sold 18 cups of juice Perry had a greater profit.

22

Which of the following is the equation for a circle with a diameter whose endpoints are at $(-2, 6)$ and $(6, 0)$?

A) $(x-4)^2 + (y-3)^2 = 13$

B) $(x-2)^2 + (y-3)^2 = 25$

C) $(x-2)^2 + (y-3)^2 = 100$

D) $(x-6)^2 + y^2 = 100$

CONTINUE

23

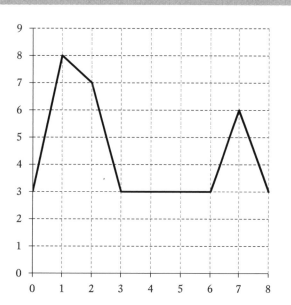

The graph above is that of the function $g(x)$. Which of the following is equal to 3?

      I. $g(0)$

      I. $g(3)$

      II. $g\left(\dfrac{11}{2}\right)$

A) I and II

B) II only

C) I, II, and III

D) None of the above

24

$$h = -4.9t^2 + 14t + 2$$

David found a stone on the beach. He threw the stone upward with an initial velocity of 14 meters per second from 2 meters in the air. The stone is caught by David's friend at the same height at which David released it. The equation above models the height h, in meters, of the stone in terms of the time t, in seconds. After approximately how many seconds does David's friend catch the stone?

A) 0.4

B) 2.9

C) 3.0

D) 4.9

25

Jane thinks her homework will take x hours, where x is greater than 3. She tells her friend that the amount of time her homework actually takes will be within 15 minutes of her estimate. If what Jane tells her friend is true, and it takes her y hours to finish her homework, then which of the following accurately describes the relationship between Jane's estimate and the actual result?

A) $|y - x| = 15$

B) $|y - x| < 15$

C) $-0.25 < y - x < 0.25$

D) $y - x < 2.75$

26

In order to determine if generic cold medicine is as effective in remedying the symptoms of a cold as name-brand cold medicine, a research study was conducted. From a large population of people, 200 people with colds were randomly selected. Half of the participants chose to receive the name-brand medicine, and half chose to receive the generic medicine. The resulting data showed that participants who received name-brand cold medicine had significantly improved cold symptoms as compared to those who received the generic medicine. Based on the design and results of the study, which of the following is the best conclusion?

A) The results prove that name-brand medicine can improve cold symptoms better than generic medicine.

B) The results prove that generic medicine is not effective in treating cold symptoms.

C) The results are questionable because of how participants were assigned to their groups.

D) The results are questionable because the experiment needs to be repeated with more participants.

27

	Regular Sales	3D Sales	Total Sales
Space Battles			$3,040
Servitors			$1,272

The table above shows the sales for a Monday matinee at Bob's Movie Barn. Regular tickets cost $10 and 3D tickets cost $14. If *Space Battles* sold twice as many 3D tickets as regular, and if *Servitors* sold 25 percent more regular tickets than 3D tickets, which of the following is closest to the percent of the revenue from ticket sales that were from 3D shows?

A) 52%

B) 53%

C) 68%

D) 74%

CONTINUE

28

During a road trip, George drove 35 percent more miles today than he did yesterday. If he drove 428 miles today, how many miles did he drive yesterday (rounded to the nearest whole mile)?

A) 317

B) 349

C) 393

D) 578

29

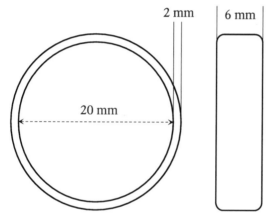

The above diagram shows the design for a simple gold wedding band. Which of the following is closest to the volume of gold necessary to make this wedding band?

A)   830 mm^3

B)   1440 mm^3

C)   1580 mm^3

D)   3320 mm^3

30

A line given by the equation $y = mx$ passes through the points $(27, k)$ and $(k, 48)$. What is the value of m?

A) $\dfrac{3}{4}$

B) $\dfrac{9}{16}$

C) $\dfrac{4}{3}$

D) $\dfrac{16}{9}$

CONTINUE

4 4

DIRECTIONS

For questions 31–38, solve the problem and enter your answer in the grid, as described below, on the answer sheet.

1. Although not required, it is suggested that you write your answer in the boxes at the top of the columns to help you fill in the circles accurately. You will receive credit only if the circles are filled in correctly.

2. Mark no more than one circle in any column.

3. No question has a negative answer.

4. Some problems may have more than one correct answer. In such cases, grid only one answer.

5. **Mixed numbers** such as $3\frac{1}{2}$ must be be gridded as 3.5 or 7/2. If ⟨3 1 / 2⟩ is entered into the grid, it will be interpreted as $\frac{31}{2}$, not $3\frac{1}{2}$.)

6. **Decimal answers:** If you obtain a decimal answer with more digits than the grid can accommodate, it may be either rounded or truncated, but it must fill the entire grid.

Answer: $\frac{7}{13}$

Write answer → in boxes

← Fraction line

Grid in result

Answer: 2.5

← Decimal Point

Acceptable ways to grid $\frac{2}{3}$ are:

Answer: 210 – either position is correct

NOTE: You may start your answers in any column, space permitting. Columns you don't need to use should be left blank.

CONTINUE

31

Year	Number of Gold Medals
1984	83
1988	36
1992	37
1996	44
2000	40
2004	35
2008	36
2012	46

The table above shows the number of Gold Medals won by the United States during each Summer Olympics since 1984. What is the difference between the median and the mode of the number of gold medals won?

32

In a board game, each player starts with a certain number of points. The goal is to get rid of all of the chips one has. For every chip a player has at the end of the game, the player loses 3 points. At the end of the game, one of the players had 50 points and had 50 chips. How many points did the player start with?

33

$$-x(2x+1)+x(7+x)$$

If the expression above is rewritten in the form $ax^2 + bx + c$, where a, b, and c are constants, what is the value of $a+b$?

CONTINUE

34

Hours Slept by High School Students

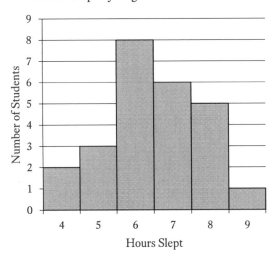

The histogram above shows the number of hours slept the previous night by a group of teenagers. Based on the histogram, what was the average number of hours slept, rounded to the nearest hundredth?

35

Brian has a square-shaped patio. He decides to extend the length so that it will be 5 feet shorter than 5 times the width. If the final area of the patio will be 1,050 square feet, what is the length, in feet, of one side of the patio before the extension?

36

Ignacio sells refurbished guitars. In order to maintain his profit margin, Ignacio must sell his guitars for an average price of $500. This month he's already sold 11 guitars for $425 each and 3 guitars for $475 each. If Ignacio has 6 more guitars to sell, what must be the average price of these last guitars in order to maintain his profit margin? (Note: Disregard the $ sign when gridding your answer.)

4 **4**

Questions 37 and 38 refer to the following information.

Supercomputer *LEP*, at a military base, can do 2 million calculations in one second. Moore's Law says that computer chip performance doubles every 2 years. The military base always uses the most current technology to upgrade its supercomputers, so in 4 years, supercomputer *LEP* will do 8 million calculations in one second according to Moore's Law.

37

A military spy camera with a 3.2 gigapixel lens requires a computer that can do 1.92 billion calculations per <u>minute</u>. In how many years will supercomputer *LEP* be able to power the spy camera?

38

How many times more powerful, in calculations per second, is supercomputer *LEP* now than it was 20 years ago?

STOP

If you finish before time is called, you may check your work on this section only.
Do not turn to any other section.

SAT Practice Test 3

IMPORTANT REMINDERS

1

A No. 2 pencil is required for the test.
Do not use a mechanical pencil or pen.

2

Sharing any questions with anyone is a violation
of the Test Security and Fairness policies and
may result in your score being canceled.

This cover is representative of what you will see on the day of the SAT.

Reading Test

65 MINUTES, 52 QUESTIONS

Turn to Section 1 of your answer sheet to answer the questions in this section.

DIRECTIONS

Each passage or pair of passages below is followed by a number of questions. After reading each passage or pair, choose the best answer to each question based on what is stated or implied in the passage or passages and in any accompanying graphics (such as a table or graph).

Questions 1–10 are based on the following passage.

This passage is adapted from Charles Dickens, *Hard Times*, originally published in 1854.

Thomas Gradgrind, sir. A man of realities. A man of facts and calculations. A man who proceeds upon the principle that two and two are four, and nothing over, and who is not to be talked into allowing for
5 anything over. Thomas Gradgrind, sir—peremptorily Thomas—Thomas Gradgrind. With a rule and a pair of scales, and the multiplication table always in his pocket, sir, ready to weigh and measure any parcel of human nature, and tell you exactly what it comes to.
10 It is a mere question of figures, a case of simple arithmetic. You might hope to get some other nonsensical belief into the head of George Gradgrind, or Augustus Gradgrind, or John Gradgrind, or Joseph Gradgrind (all supposititious, non-existent persons),
15 but into the head of Thomas Gradgrind—no, sir!

In such terms Mr. Gradgrind always mentally introduced himself, whether to his private circle of acquaintance, or to the public in general. In such terms, no doubt, substituting the words "boys and
20 girls," for "sir," Thomas Gradgrind now presented Thomas Gradgrind to the little pitchers before him, who were to be filled so full of facts.

Indeed, as he eagerly sparkled at them from the cellarage before mentioned, he seemed a kind of
25 cannon loaded to the muzzle with facts, and prepared to blow them clean out of the regions of childhood at one discharge. He seemed a galvanizing apparatus, too, charged with a grim mechanical substitute for

the tender young imaginations that were to be
30 stormed away.

"Girl number twenty," said Mr. Gradgrind, squarely pointing with his square forefinger, "I don't know that girl. Who is that girl?"

"Sissy Jupe, sir," explained number twenty,
35 blushing, standing up, and curtseying.

"Sissy is not a name," said Mr. Gradgrind. "Don't call yourself Sissy. Call yourself Cecilia."

"It's father as calls me Sissy, sir," returned the young girl in a trembling voice, and with another
40 curtsey.

"Then he has no business to do it," said Mr. Gradgrind. "Tell him he mustn't. Cecilia Jupe. Let me see. What is your father?"

"He belongs to the horse-riding, if you please,
45 sir."

Mr. Gradgrind frowned, and waved off the objectionable calling with his hand.

"We don't want to know anything about that, here. You mustn't tell us about that, here. Your father
50 breaks horses, don't he?"

"If you please, sir, when they can get any to break, they do break horses in the ring, sir."

"You mustn't tell us about the ring, here. Very well, then. Describe your father as a horsebreaker. He
55 doctors sick horses, I dare say?"

"Oh yes, sir."

"Very well, then. He is a veterinary surgeon, a farrier, and horsebreaker. Give me your definition of a horse."

CONTINUE →

1

1

60 (Sissy Jupe thrown into the greatest alarm by this demand.)

"Girl number twenty unable to define a horse!" said Mr. Gradgrind, for the general behoof of all the little pitchers. "Girl number twenty possessed of no
65 facts, in reference to one of the commonest of animals! Some boy's definition of a horse. Bitzer, yours."

The square finger, moving here and there, lighted suddenly on Bitzer, perhaps because he chanced to sit
70 in the same ray of sunlight which, darting in at one of the bare windows of the intensely white-washed room, irradiated Sissy. His cold eyes would hardly have been eyes, but for the short ends of lashes which, by bringing them into immediate contrast with
75 something paler than themselves, expressed their form. His short-cropped hair might have been a mere continuation of the sandy freckles on his forehead and face. His skin was so unwholesomely deficient in the natural tinge, that he looked as though, if he were
80 cut, he would bleed white.

"Bitzer," said Thomas Gradgrind. "Your definition of a horse."

"Quadruped. Graminivorous. Forty teeth, namely twenty-four grinders, four eye-teeth, and twelve
85 incisive. Sheds coat in the spring; in marshy countries, sheds hoofs, too. Hoofs hard, but requiring to be shod with iron. Age known by marks in mouth." Thus (and much more) Bitzer.

"Now girl number twenty," said Mr. Gradgrind.
90 "You know what a horse is."

1

The first paragraph (lines 1–15) primarily serves to

A) describe a character's habitual activities, personal interests, and passionately held beliefs.

B) characterize the seriousness of one man's approach to life.

C) introduce the ways in which a certain teacher is different from his students.

D) clarify to readers that they should not suppose Gradgrind will be like his relatives.

2

The author refers to the students as "little pitchers" (lines 21 and 63) in order to

A) hint at their tendency to misbehave and cause disruptions.

B) reveal how insignificant their ideas are relative to those of their teacher.

C) use a metaphor to indicate their desire for greater knowledge.

D) show that Gradgrind views them as merely vessels to be filled with facts.

3

Based on the descriptions in the passage, Thomas Gradgrind views his task with his pupils primarily as

A) solving a problem using the methods and tools of modern science.

B) sternly reprimanding students so that they will be more obedient to him.

C) violently replacing ignorance and imagination with accurate information.

D) personally mentoring them as they move from childhood to maturity.

4

Which choice provides the best evidence for the answer to the previous question?

A) Lines 2–11 ("A man ... arithmetic")

B) Lines 24–30 ("he seemed ... away")

C) Lines 67–75 ("The square ... form")

D) Lines 82–87 ("Quadruped ... Bitzer")

1   **1**

5

In line 27, the word "discharge" most nearly means

A) emancipation.

B) shot.

C) excrescence.

D) lesson.

6

In line 62, the word "behoof" most nearly means

A) putting on of horseshoes.

B) taking away of difficulties.

C) mockery.

D) benefit.

7

The narrator suggests that Mr. Gradgrind may have called upon Bitzer because of

A) Bitzer's physical location relative to Sissy.

B) Gradgrind's confidence in Bitzer's superior knowledge of horses.

C) Bitzer's clipped way of providing accurate, factual information in response to questions.

D) Gradgrind's own lack of certainty about the answer.

8

Which choice provides the best evidence for the answer to the previous question?

A) Lines 61–66 ("Girl ... yours")

B) Lines 67–71 ("The square ... Sissy")

C) Lines 71–77 ("His cold ... face")

D) Lines 82–87 ("Quadruped ... Bitzer")

9

Bitzer's definition of a horse is

A) personal, being based on his own experiences with his father.

B) impertinent, for he has shown himself to be too pedantic in his explanation.

C) incorrect in context but accurate based on his own limited understanding.

D) accurate insofar as it relays many factual details about the animal.

10

The tone of Mr. Gradgrind's words to Sissy (lines 88–89) after hearing Bitzer's definition is

A) ironic: Sissy already knew what a horse was, and thus did not need the definition.

B) mocking: Bitzer's definition was foolish, and now he must provide a better definition for both of them.

C) gloating: Bitzer's answer evinced the success of his method in its thorough-going attention to specific detail.

D) relieved: he no longer has to explain things to Sissy, whose ignorance annoys him.

CONTINUE →

Questions 11–20 are based on the following passage.

This passage is adapted from President Ronald Reagan's speech to a joint session of Congress on the Program for Economic Recovery, April 28, 1981.

It's been half a year since the election that charged all of us in this government with the task of restoring our economy. And where have we come in these six months? Inflation, as measured by the Consumer
5   Price Index, has continued at a double-digit rate. Mortgage interest rates have averaged almost 15 percent for these six months, preventing families across America from buying homes. There are still almost eight million unemployed. The average
10 worker's hourly earnings after adjusting for inflation are lower today than they were six months ago, and there have been over 6,000 business failures.

Six months is long enough. The American people now want us to act and not in half-measures. They
15 demand and they've earned a full and comprehensive effort to clean up our economic mess. Because of the extent of our economy's sickness, we know that the cure will not come quickly and that even with our package, progress will come in inches and feet, not in
20 miles. But to fail to act will delay even longer and more painfully the cure which must come. And that cure begins with the federal budget. And the budgetary actions taken by the Congress over the next few days will determine how we respond to the
25 message of last November 4th. That message was very simple. Our government is too big, and it spends too much.

For the last few months, you and I have enjoyed a relationship based on extraordinary cooperation.
30 Because of this cooperation we've come a long distance in less than three months. I want to thank the leadership of the Congress for helping in setting a fair timetable for consideration of our recommendations. And committee chairmen on both
35 sides of the aisle have called prompt and thorough hearings. We have also communicated in a spirit of candor, openness, and mutual respect. Tonight, as our decision day nears and as the House of Representatives weighs its alternatives, I wish to
40 address you in that same spirit.

The Senate Budget Committee, under the leadership of Pete Domenici, has just today voted out a budget resolution supported by Democrats and

Republicans alike that is in all major respects
45 consistent with the program that we have proposed. Now we look forward to favorable action on the Senate floor, but an equally crucial test involves the House of Representatives. The House will soon be choosing between two different versions or measures
50 to deal with the economy. One is the measure offered by the House Budget Committee. The other is a bipartisan measure, a substitute introduced by Congressmen Phil Gramm of Texas and Del Latta of Ohio.
55   On behalf of the Administration, let me say that we embrace and fully support that bipartisan substitute. It will achieve all the essential aims of controlling government spending, reducing the tax burden, building a national defense second to none,
60 and stimulating economic growth and creating millions of new jobs. At the same time, however, I must state our opposition to the measure offered by the House Budget Committee. It may appear that we have two alternatives. In reality, however, there are
65 no more alternatives left.

The committee measure quite simply falls far too short of the essential actions that we must take. For example, in the next three years, the committee measure projects spending $141 billion more than
70 does the bipartisan substitute. It regrettably cuts over $14 billion in essential defense spending, funding required to restore America's national security. It adheres to the failed policy of trying to balance the budget on the taxpayer's back. It would increase tax
75 payments over a third, adding up to a staggering quarter of a trillion dollars. Federal taxes would increase 12 percent each year. Taxpayers would be paying a larger share of their income to the government in 1984 than they do at present. In short,
80 that measure reflects an echo of the past rather than a benchmark for the future. High taxes and excess spending growth created our present economic mess; more of the same will not cure the hardship, anxiety, and discouragement it has imposed on the American
85 people.

Let us cut through the fog for a moment. The answer to a government that's too big is to stop feeding its growth. Government spending has been growing faster than the economy itself. The massive
90 national debt which we accumulated is the result of

CONTINUE ➜

the government's high spending diet. Well, it's time to change the diet and to change it in the right way.

Inflation Rates in America 1975–1985
as of January 1

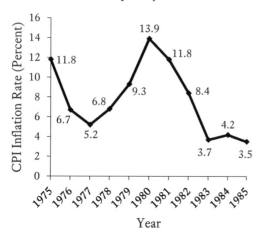

Adapted from the US Bureau of Labor and Statistics website.

From this passage it can be inferred that Reagan's primary goal is to

A) reduce inflation and mortgage interest rates expediently because they are damaging the economy.

B) work with Congress to create more job opportunities with higher wages to help those who are unemployed.

C) introduce a stimulus package in Congress because increasing government spending will fuel economic recovery.

D) encourage Congress to pass a bipartisan measure that will control government spending.

12

The primary purpose of the first paragraph (lines 1–12) is to

A) portray the American economy in a state of irreparable disaster.

B) highlight the failures of Congress in the past six months.

C) provide significant context for the need to restore the economy.

D) show several conflicting metrics for measuring the state of the economy.

Which of the following suggestions conflicts most with Reagan's views in lines 13–27?

A) Congress must increase government spending on infrastructure to help the economy improve gradually.

B) Congress must implement comprehensive measures because the economy is in a state of disrepair and needs drastic change.

C) Congress must act swiftly and decisively because the American people are frustrated and demand action.

D) Congress must shrink the size of the federal budget because the government is recklessly spending too much money.

In line 37, "candor" most nearly means

A) sincere obfuscation.

B) careful reverence.

C) impartial honesty.

D) cloaked partisanship.

1   1

15

Which of the following is a specific reason Reagan recommends rejecting the House Budget Committee's measure?

A) It was not introduced by the Senate Budget Committee and thus is not bipartisan in its origins.

B) It cuts spending on the development of necessary weapons for national defense.

C) It does not go far enough to reduce government spending.

D) It would raise taxes on too many Americans for the benefit of too few.

16

Which choice provides the best evidence for the answer to the previous question?

A) Lines 61-63 ("At the same ... Committee")

B) Lines 66-70 ("The committee ... substitute")

C) Lines 79-81 ("In short ... future")

D) Lines 83-85 ("more of ... people")

17

In line 86, "cut through the fog" most nearly means

A) deeply contemplate the issue.

B) clarify what has been obscured.

C) attack the problem.

D) identify what is clouding the issue.

18

An economist claims that inflation rates had already begun to fall prior to the implementation of the proposals discussed in this passage. Does evidence from the passage or the graph support this claim?

A) No; lines 3-5 ("And where ... rate") prove that the rate was still rising.

B) No; the graph shows that inflation rates reached their height during 1981.

C) Yes; lines 57-61 ("It will ... jobs") suggest what has already been accomplished.

D) Yes; the graph shows that inflation rates were lower by the start of 1981.

19

The graph shows that, prior to "the election that charged all of us in this government with the task of restoring our economy" (lines 1-3), inflation rates had

A) consistently increased for over a decade.

B) more than doubled since 1977.

C) not directly impacted overall economic growth.

D) outpaced mortgage interest rates.

20

Based on the graph one can infer that 1977-1983 was a period of

A) economic stability.

B) economic expansion.

C) economic recession.

D) economic change.

CONTINUE

Questions 21–31 are based on the following passages.

The following passages discuss explanations for the variety and similarity among biological species. Passage 1 is adapted from Robert Chambers, *Vestiges of the Natural History of Creation*, first published in 1844. Passage 2 is adapted from Charles Darwin, *On the Origin of Species*, first published in 1859.

Passage 1

Confining our attention, in the meantime, to the animal kingdom—it does not appear that this gradation passes along one line, on which every form of animal life can be, as it were, strung; there may be
5   branching or double lines at some places; or the whole may be in a circle composed of minor circles, as has been recently suggested. But still it is incontestable that there are general appearances of a scale beginning with the simple and advancing to the
10 complicated. The animal kingdom was divided by Cuvier into four sub-kingdoms, or divisions, and these exhibit an unequivocal gradation in the order in which they are here enumerated: Radiata (polypes), mollusca (pulpy animals), articulate (jointed
15 animals), vertebrate (animals with internal skeleton). The gradation can, in like manner, be clearly traced in the classes into which the sub-kingdoms are Subdivided, as, for instance, when we take those of the vertebrate in this order—reptiles, fishes, birds,
20 mammals.
      While the external forms of all these various animals are so different, it is very remarkable that the whole are, after all, variations of a fundamental plan, which can be traced as a basis throughout the whole,
25 the variations being merely modifications of that plan to suit the particular conditions in which each particular animal has been designed to live. Starting from the primeval germ, which, as we have seen, is the *representative* of a particular order of full-grown
30 animals, we find all others to be merely advances from that type, with the extension of endowments and modification of forms which are required in each particular case; each form, also, retaining a strong affinity to that which precedes it, and tending to
35 impress its own features on that which succeeds.

Passage 2

In considering the Origin of Species, it is quite conceivable that a naturalist, reflecting on the mutual affinities of organic beings, on their embryological relations, their geographical distribution, geological
40 succession, and other such facts, might come to the conclusion that each species had not been independently created, but had descended, like varieties, from other species. Nevertheless, such a conclusion, even if well founded, would be
45 unsatisfactory, until it could be shown how the innumerable species inhabiting this world have been modified so as to acquire that perfection of structure and co-adaptation which most justly excites our admiration. Naturalists continually refer to external
50 conditions, such as climate, food, etc., as the only possible cause of variation. In one very limited sense, as we shall hereafter see, this may be true; but it is preposterous to attribute to mere external conditions, the structure, for instance, of the woodpecker, with
55 its feet, tail, beak, and tongue, so admirably adapted to catch insects under the bark of trees. In the case of the mistletoe, which draws its nourishment from certain trees, which has seeds that must be transported by certain birds, and which has flowers
60 with separate sexes absolutely requiring the agency of certain insects to bring pollen from one flower to the other, it is equally preposterous to account for the structure of this parasite, with its relations to several distinct organic beings, by the effects of external
65 conditions, or of habit, or of the volition of the plant itself.
      The author of the "Vestiges of Creation" would, I presume, say that, after a certain unknown number of generations, some bird had given birth to a
70 woodpecker, and some plant to the mistletoe, and that these had been produced perfect as we now see them; but this assumption seems to me to be no explanation, for it leaves the cause of the coadaptations of organic beings to each other and to
75 their physical conditions of life, untouched and unexplained.
      It is, therefore, of the highest importance to gain a clear insight into the means of modification and coadaptation. As many more individuals of each
80 species are born than can possibly survive; and as, consequently, there is a frequently recurring struggle

1 **1**

for existence, it follows that any being, if it vary
however slightly in any manner profitable to itself,
under the complex and sometimes varying conditions
85 of life, will have a better chance of surviving, and
thus be naturally selected. From the strong principle
of inheritance, any selected variety will tend to
propagate its new and modified form.

21

In listing the sub-kingdoms of animals in lines 13–15,
the author intends to arrange them from

A) most complicated to least sophisticated.

B) least similar to humans to most similar to
humans.

C) smallest to largest.

D) simplest to most complex.

22

In contrasting the analogy of "gradation ... along one
line" (line 3) with that of "a circle composed of
minor circles" (line 6), the author shows

A) that biological life varies in complexity based on
simple, predictable steps.

B) that the variations among biological life-forms
are more complex than a single line can
illustrate.

C) how the varied shapes of life-forms indicate their
position in the gradation of kingdoms.

D) the inaccuracy of Cuvier's model of kingdoms
and sub-kingdoms of life.

23

In line 35, the word "impress" most nearly means

A) influence.

B) amaze.

C) infer.

D) imprint.

24

In passage 1, the author's use of the words
"fundamental plan" (line 23) and "designed" (line
27) suggest

A) that variations in animal species are present
according to a deliberate intention.

B) the relationship of specific instances of
biological diversity to the overall pattern.

C) the method by which specific variations of life
that exist in nature came to be.

D) an ironic mockery of the ideas to which the
author is fundamentally opposed.

25

In lines 37–38, the phrase "mutual affinities" most
nearly means

A) shared values.

B) united affections.

C) shared similarities.

D) visible attributes.

26

The author of passage 2 suggests that the specific
variations evident in living things are best accounted
for by

A) a new form of life being brought forth from an
existing form spontaneously.

B) existing forms of life choosing to alter specific
attributes as an act of their own will.

C) attributes that increase the likelihood of survival
naturally predominating in the inheritance of
characteristics.

D) each form of life being designed specifically to
suit its climate, geography, and purpose.

CONTINUE

27

Which choice provides the best evidence for the answer to the previous question?

A) lines 36–43 ("it … species")

B) lines 56–66 ("In … itself")

C) lines 68–76 ("after … unexplained")

D) lines 79–88 ("As … form")

28

The repeated use of the word "preposterous" (lines 53 and 62) in passage 2 serves primarily to

A) reveal the significance and novelty of the author's findings.

B) mock the unscientific methods that others have used to draw their conclusions.

C) remind the audience that theories are not untrue simply because they are improbable.

D) emphasize the absurdity of a particular explanation when carried to its logical conclusion.

29

The second passage responds to the first by

A) making use of its most important data and its biological perspective but disagreeing with its fundamental conclusions.

B) agreeing with its central observations but offering an explanation for the mechanism behind the phenomena discussed.

C) describing as foolish and misguided methodologies employed by the author of passage 1.

D) concurring with its author's final conclusions but quibbling with the logical structure of the argument.

30

The author of passage 2 would respond to the explanation given in lines 27–35 ("Starting … succeeds") by

A) criticizing the author for failing to explain how these advancements took place.

B) denying the possible existence of a primeval germ, making the conclusion specious.

C) agreeing with the specific observation but limiting the scope of the conclusions that can be drawn from it.

D) pointing out the lack of verifiable evidence to support the specific conclusion drawn.

31

Which choice provides the best evidence for the answer to the previous question?

A) lines 67–70 ("The author … mistletoe")

B) lines 72–76 ("but … unexplained")

C) lines 77–79 ("It is … coadaptation")

D) lines 86–88 ("From … form")

1

1

Questions 32–42 are based on the following passage.

The following passage is adapted from Nelson Mandela, "I Am Prepared to Die," originally delivered on April 20, 1964. Mandela gave this speech as the opening statement of his defense case in the Rivonia Trial in Pretoria, South Africa.

The lack of human dignity experienced by Africans is the direct result of the policy of white supremacy. White supremacy implies black inferiority. Legislation designed to preserve white
5   supremacy entrenches this notion. Menial tasks in South Africa are invariably performed by Africans. When anything has to be carried or cleaned the white man will look around for an African to do it for him, whether the African is employed by him or not.
10 Because of this sort of attitude, whites tend to regard Africans as a separate breed. They do not look upon them as people with families of their own; they do not realize that they have emotions—that they fall in love like white people do; that they want to be with
15 their wives and children like white people want to be with theirs; that they want to earn enough money to support their families properly, to feed and clothe them and send them to school. And what "house-boy" or "garden-boy" or laborer can ever hope to do
20 this?

Pass laws, which to the Africans are among the most hated bits of legislation in South Africa, render any African liable to police surveillance at any time. I doubt whether there is a single African male in South
25 Africa who has not at some stage had a brush with the police over his pass. Hundreds and thousands of Africans are thrown into jail each year under pass laws. Even worse than this is the fact that pass laws keep husband and wife apart and lead to the
30 breakdown of family life.

Poverty and the breakdown of family life have secondary effects. Children wander about the streets of the townships because they have no schools to go to, or no money to enable them to go to school, or no
35 parents at home to see that they go to school, because both parents (if there be two) have to work to keep the family alive. This leads to a breakdown in moral standards, to an alarming rise in illegitimacy, and to growing violence which erupts everywhere. Life in
40 the townships is dangerous. There is not a day that goes by without somebody being stabbed or assaulted. And violence is carried out of the

townships into the white living areas. People are afraid to walk alone in the streets after dark.
45 Housebreakings and robberies are increasing, despite the fact that the death sentence can now be imposed for such offences. Death sentences cannot cure the festering sore.

The only cure is to alter the conditions under
50 which Africans are forced to live and to meet their legitimate grievances. Africans want to be paid a living wage. Africans want to perform work which they are capable of doing, and not work which the Government declares them to be capable of. Africans
55 want to be allowed to live where they obtain work, and not be endorsed out of an area because they were not born there. Africans want to be allowed to own land in places where they work, and not to be obliged to live in rented houses which they can never call
60 their own. Africans want to be part of the general population, and not confined to living in their own ghettoes. African men want to have their wives and children live with them where they work, and not be forced into an unnatural existence in men's hostels.
65 African women want to be with their menfolk and not be left permanently widowed in the Reserves. Africans want to be allowed out after eleven o'clock at night and not to be confined to their rooms like little children. Africans want to be allowed to travel in
70 their own country and to seek work where they want to and not where the Labor Bureau tells them to. Africans want a just share in the whole of South Africa; they want security and a stake in society.

Above all, we want equal political rights, because
75 without them our disabilities will be permanent. I know this sounds revolutionary to the whites in this country, because the majority of voters will be Africans. This makes the white man fear democracy.

But this fear cannot be allowed to stand in the way
80 of the only solution which will guarantee racial harmony and freedom for all. It is not true that the enfranchisement of all will result in racial domination. Political division, based on color, is entirely artificial and, when it disappears, so will the
85 domination of one color group by another.

During my lifetime, I have cherished the ideal of a democratic and free society in which all persons live together in harmony and with equal opportunities. It is an ideal which I hope to live for and to achieve. But
90 if needs be, it is an ideal for which I am prepared to die.

32

Based on the passage as a whole, what is the author's main point?

A) Africans need political power so that they will be able to control the government since they are the majority.

B) White people in South Africa are racist in both their official policies and personal attitudes towards Africans.

C) Africans need equal rights, in part because of the social problems created by inequality.

D) The standard of living for Africans is appalling, and policies have to be put in place to provide assistance to them.

33

In line 5, "menial" most nearly means

A) lowly.

B) manual.

C) easy.

D) sycophantic.

34

Which of the following best reflects how the author suggests whites view Africans?

A) Africans cannot be trusted to work in areas where whites are the dominant race.

B) Africans exist to serve whites by doing things that they consider beneath them.

C) Africans deserve basic human rights, but should be kept separate, maintaining Apartheid.

D) Africans are inherently inferior to whites morally, physically, and mentally.

35

Which choice provides the best evidence for the answer to the previous question?

A) Lines 1–5 ("The lack ... notion")

B) Lines 5–9 ("Menial ... not")

C) Lines 37–40 ("This ... dangerous")

D) Lines 45–48 ("Housebreakings ... sore")

36

In terms of the argument as a whole, the primary function of the third paragraph (lines 31–48) is to

A) enumerate unintended consequences of a discriminatory policy referenced in the previous paragraph.

B) contrast the list of the benefits of a law explained earlier in the passage by examining its societal costs.

C) explain ways in which Africans have changed in order to show that they haven't always been dangerous.

D) provide an example of a rule that is based on the assumption of white supremacy mentioned at the beginning of the passage.

37

As it is used in line 50, the word "meet" most nearly means

A) come together with.

B) deal with.

C) match up with.

D) coincide with.

CONTINUE ▶

38

The author uses a repetitive sentence structure in the fourth paragraph (lines 49–73) in order to

A) criticize the government for its failure to enforce regulations, which has allowed poor conditions to become so widespread.

B) stress the importance of the restrictions on Africans but show that they do not go far enough to address the real problem.

C) emphasize the distance between what Africans want and what their government allows them to do.

D) reveal the value of reasonable aspirations and contrast them with the poor outcomes of those desires.

39

Based on the author's views, what is the main reason white South Africans resist granting equal rights to Africans?

A) They worry that they will no longer have social inferiors to do tasks they prefer not to themselves.

B) They believe that equality will enable Africans to continue their criminal behavior and make society less safe as a whole.

C) They fear it would result in the overturning of pass laws, which protect white people from African crime.

D) They are concerned that African political power will be too great if they represent a majority of voters.

40

Which choice provides the best evidence for the answer to the previous question?

A) Lines 21–23 ("Pass … time")

B) Lines 45–48 ("Housebreakings … sore")

C) Lines 75–78 ("I know … democracy")

D) Lines 81–85 ("It is … another")

41

The author repeats the word "ideal" several times in the final paragraph (lines 86–91) primarily to

A) highlight the impracticality of his dream.

B) juxtapose his goals with the reality of his situation.

C) emphasize his longing for something better.

D) set a clear, achievable goal for himself and his society.

42

Based on the passage as a whole, the author believes that "pass laws" (line 21) are

A) salutary in their immediate impact on individuals but deleterious in their effect on families.

B) designed for the maintenance of a stable society but harmful in some of their unintended effects.

C) responsible for many Africans being illegally arrested and for the breakdown of familial relationships.

D) unfair in subjecting Africans to police harassment and detrimental to the unity of African families.

Questions 43–52 are based on the following passage.

This passage is adapted from S. Galinez et al., "Stroke: Historical Review and Innovative Treatments." ©2014 by the National High School Journal of Science.

The medical knowledge of strokes has progressed significantly from ancient understandings of the brain and nervous system to modern technological advances in both treatment and prevention. The first
5 historical reference to the nervous system was found in ancient Egyptian records dating back to 3500 BCE, when Papyrus described the brain and the fluids that covered the brain.

Hippocrates, in 400 BCE, first described paralysis
10 and convulsion or seizures that resulted after brain injuries, along with the observation that paralysis to the opposite side of the body resulted when a section from one half of the brain was injured. In the 17th century, Thomas Willis conducted a detailed study of
15 the brain and nervous system at Oxford University. Willis did experiments on cadavers and discovered that dye injected into one carotid artery would be expelled from the opposing carotid artery. He classified the nerves of the brain and described the
20 communication of the arteries at the base of the brain that we now call the Circle of Willis. He also recognized that lesions in a specific part of the brain led to weakness in an associated part of the body.

In the 1800s carotid surgery became a more
25 prevalent procedure and reports of successful closures of injuries to the carotid arteries were documented. The first documented case of successful carotid artery surgery in the United States was performed by Dr. Amos Twitchell in New
30 Hampshire on October 18, 1807. Another milestone came in 1927 when Egas Moniz of Portugal successfully performed cerebral arteriograms for the study of cerebral tumors.

Despite these advances, there were actually very
35 few effective treatments for an acute stroke. In the early 1900s most of the treatments for stroke patients were limited to rehabilitation after an acute stroke, and most patients were usually left with permanent and severe deficits. In the 1950s it was recognized
40 that disease in the carotid arteries could also cause transient ischemic attacks resulting in temporary weakness or blindness that resolved within a few hours, and that these attacks could be warning signs

for future strokes. Doppler ultrasound studies were
45 first used to identify plaque and disease in the carotid arteries, and aggressive treatment of high blood pressure also was found to be very important.

In the 1960s carotid endarterectomy was greatly improved but this procedure was used mostly for
50 stroke prevention and there was still no effective treatment after an acute stroke. The invention of the computed tomography scan (CT scan) greatly assisted in the diagnosis of stroke, and it became widely used in the United States to help distinguish
55 between the different types of stroke. In the 1970s aspirin was found to be very effective in stroke prevention. In the 1980s another breakthrough was the discovery that cigarette smoking was a definite risk factor for stroke; after this, smoking cessation
60 programs became very important. A major breakthrough came in 1996 when the FDA approved stroke treatment using tissue plasminogen activator, a protein that is now widely used to break down blood clots. Soon rapid diagnosis became crucial for
65 immediate treatment, whereas in the past rehabilitation was the most common response and doctors often waited 12–24 hours before giving a diagnosis of acute stroke.

As advances continue in the future, strokes may
70 become a temporary illness for which rapid and minimally invasive treatments allow for maximum recovery. Such treatments would be coupled with an emphasis on healthy lifestyles and prevention. For immediate improvement in blood flow to the area of
75 the stroke, we suggest an ultrasound device that allows delivery of Vascular Endothelial Growth Factor (VEGF) directly into the affected tissue with minimal risk to the patient. A specialized minute pellet provides a dual mechanism of releasing
80 medication into the affected tissue: Fifty percent is processed onto a porous scaffold and immediately released, and the remaining fifty percent is processed into specialized glycolide spheres with semipermeable membranes to provide additional
85 sustained release of the medication into the affected tissue. The pellet thus provides both immediate and sustained gradual delivery of VEGF to provide immediate and sustained neovascularization. We propose that VEGF administered directly into acute
90 ischemic tissue will lead to dramatic advances in the treatment of stroke.

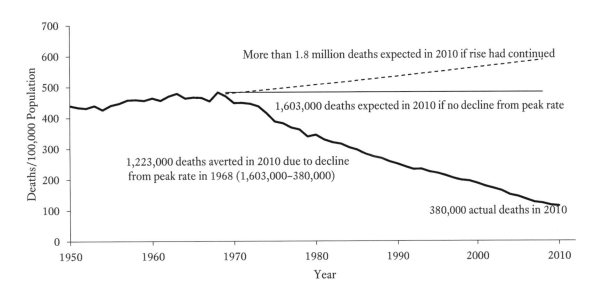

Adapted from the National Heart, Lung, and Blood Institute, National Institutes of Health website.

43

The authors' primary intention in the passage is to

A) debunk Hippocrates' observations on the brain because they are outdated and modern research has provided better answers.

B) argue that a stroke is now easily curable with a simple rehabilitation effort if it is caught in the preliminary phases.

C) convey the severity of acute stroke and the long term effects it has on a person's longevity, memory, and quality of life.

D) provide a brief history of stroke research and delineate contemporary technological advancements.

44

The tone of the passage is best described as

A) critical but constructive.

B) rhetorical and pedantic.

C) measured and inquisitive.

D) informative and optimistic.

1   1

45

Based on the passage, in relation to the work of Hippocrates, Willis' research

A) repudiates some of the findings of Hippocrates by discovering alternate causes of paralysis and brain injury.

B) confirms all of Hippocrates' claims by using dye stain experiments to reaffirm Hippocrates' hypotheses on paralysis.

C) builds on Hippocrates' earlier findings by studying certain arteries in the brain and describing communication between them.

D) is unrelated to that of Hippocrates, because Willis studied arteries which do not pertain to brain injuries.

46

According to the passage, why is the study of the carotid artery important for an understanding of strokes?

A) A faulty carotid artery causes cerebral arteriograms.

B) Diseased carotid arteries can lead to stroke.

C) A stroke causes damage to the carotid artery.

D) Willis discovered the carotid artery.

47

Which choice provides the best evidence for the answer to the previous question?

A) Line 16–20 ("Willis … brain")

B) Line 24–30 ("In the 1800s … 1807")

C) Line 30–35 ("Another … stroke")

D) Line 39–44 ("In the 1950s … strokes")

48

In line 78, "minute" most nearly means

A) condensed.

B) very small.

C) very brief.

D) insignificant.

49

In line 90, "dramatic" most nearly means

A) unbelievable.

B) theatrical.

C) impressive.

D) drastic.

CONTINUE

50

According to the authors, which of the following actions would minimize the likelihood of permanent damage from a stroke for some individuals?

A) Making a specific lifestyle change in order to reduce the complications that result from stroke

B) Using aspirin before and immediately after a stroke to prevent the escalation of symptoms

C) Using Doppler ultrasounds to detect high blood pressure and treating high blood pressure prior to suffering a stroke

D) Diagnosing an acute stroke quickly and beginning treatment immediately

51

Which choice provides the best evidence for the answer to the previous question?

A) Lines 44–47 ("Doppler … important")

B) Lines 55–57 ("In the … prevention")

C) Lines 57–60 ("In the … important")

D) Lines 64–68 ("Soon … stroke")

52

Based on the graph, if the number of deaths from strokes had continued to rise at the rate it rose from 1950 to 1970, roughly how many deaths per 100,000 would have been expected for 2010?

A) 1,800,000

B) 1,223,000

C)   590

D)   475

STOP

If you finish before time is called, you may check your work on this section only.
Do not turn to any other section.

2   2

Writing and Language Test

35 MINUTES, 44 QUESTIONS

Turn to Section 2 of your answer sheet to answer the questions in this section.

DIRECTIONS

Each passage below is accompanied by a number of questions. For some questions, you will consider how the passage might be revised to improve the expression of ideas. For other questions, you will consider how the passage might be edited to correct errors in sentence structure, usage, or punctuation. A passage or a question may be accompanied by one or more graphics (such as a table or graph) that you will consider as you make revising and editing decisions.

Some questions will direct you to an underlined portion of a passage. Other questions will direct you to a location in a passage or ask you to think about the passage as a whole.

After reading each passage, choose the answer to each question that most effectively improves the quality of writing in the passage or that makes the passage conform to the conventions of standard written English. Many questions include a "NO CHANGE" option. Choose that option if you think the best choice is to leave the relevant portion of the passage as it is.

Questions 1–11 are based on the following passage and supplementary material.

Immunizations and Global Health

[1] Immunization the process of inoculation and vaccination through the artificial introduction of infectious material, has been a tremendous boon for world

A) NO CHANGE
B) Immunization, the process of inoculation and vaccination through the artificial introduction of infectious material has
C) Immunization, the process of inoculation and vaccination through the artificial introduction of infectious material, has
D) Immunization: the process of inoculation and vaccination through the artificial introduction of infectious material, has

CONTINUE ➡

2

2

health. However, in recent years [2] it has unfairly come under attack. [3] It is necessary that we must understand immunization properly because it is essential for public health. With population density increasing, the prevention of the spread of infectious diseases is growing in importance.

A clear example of the importance of immunization is the successful vaccination effort against paralytic poliomyelitis, commonly known as [4] polio, a helpful disease to study to learn more about immunization. Until the mid-twentieth century, polio was a serious public health concern in the United States. In the twenty states that kept track of the spread of polio, nearly 58,000 cases were reported in 1952, with over 3,000 people dying and nearly 22,000 left with mild to disabling paralysis.

[5] Therefore, Jonas Salk began testing the first vaccine for polio in 1952. By 1955, it was determined that the vaccine was [6] safe and affective. In the years since, polio has effectively been eradicated in the industrialized world.

2

A) NO CHANGE
B) they have attacked immunization unfairly.
C) its unfairly come under attack.
D) immunization has unfairly come under attack.

3

A) NO CHANGE
B) It is absolutely requisite for us that immunization must be understood properly
C) It is very important for us that we must understand immunization properly
D) Immunization must be understood properly

4

A) NO CHANGE
B) polio, a virus through which one can become more knowledgeable of immunization.
C) polio, through which one can better comprehend immunization.
D) polio.

5

A) NO CHANGE
B) Also in 1952,
C) In response to these outbreaks,
D) However, in another development,

6

A) NO CHANGE
B) safe, and effective.
C) safe and effective.
D) safe, and affective.

CONTINUE

However, for much of the world, particularly developing countries, polio is still a serious concern; with the high level of interaction between members of nearly all societies, it could certainly [7] reemerge in the industrial world. In 2014, the World Health Organization said the international spread of polio "constitutes an extraordinary event and a public health risk to other countries for which a coordinated international response is essential." In some war-torn countries, children have not had the opportunity to be vaccinated. Afghanistan, Cameroon, Equatorial Guinea, Ethiopia, Iraq, Nigeria, Pakistan, and Syria [8] are all currently experiencing polio patients and also have relatively low rates of vaccination.

Unfortunately, vaccination is also becoming a concern in some industrialized nations for entirely different reasons. [9] Its' use have been opposed by some concerned parents in America, the UK, and Ireland in recent years. Most of these parents' concerns stem from a 1998 article [10] made specious claims establishing a link between MMR (measles, mumps, and rubella) vaccines and autism. Though the lead author of that paper was discredited and the article itself retracted, a number of celebrity supporters have promulgated these faulty findings, creating an irrational fear of vaccines in some people and decreasing vaccination rates in some areas.

7

A) NO CHANGE
B) happen again
C) bounce back
D) exist more

8

Assuming that each is true, which of the following best suggests a link between low rates of vaccination and higher rates of infection?

A) NO CHANGE
B) are all currently suffering from serious outbreaks of polio and have some of the lowest vaccination rates in the world.
C) are countries that have low vaccination rates right now and have some problems with polio as well.
D) currently have problems with vaccinating for polio.

9

A) NO CHANGE
B) It's use has
C) Its use having
D) Its use has

10

A) NO CHANGE
B) that made specious claims establishing a link
C) had made specious claims establishing a link
D) which was making specious claims establishing a link

This decrease has allowed a resurgence of previously controlled diseases even in places where levels of infection were at or near zero for some time.

So, what is to be done? Perhaps an educational campaign to inform people about what vaccines are, how they work, how safe they are, and why they are so important to public health is the best place to start.

Question **11** asks about the previous passage as a whole.

Think about the previous passage and included supplemental material as a whole as you answer question 11.

11

Which choice best reflects the information presented in the graph and the passage?

A) Since the introduction of the polio vaccine in 1955, the average yearly number of reported polio infections in the United States has dramatically decreased until it reached zero.

B) Since 1955, the average yearly number of reported polio infections in the United States has only decreased after fluctuating in previous years.

C) Since 1955, the average yearly number of reported polio infections in the United States has fluctuated, sometimes reaching levels close to pre-1955, but the overall trend is a decrease.

D) Since the introduction of the polio vaccine in 1955, the average yearly number of reported polio infections in the United States has fluctuated, but a small decrease may be attributable to vaccination.

Paralytic Poliomyelitis: Number of cases reported in United States, 1950–2010

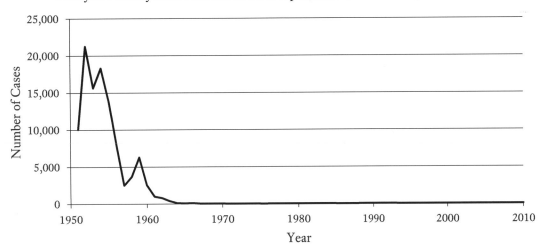

Adapted from the Centers for Disease Control and Prevention website.

CONTINUE

2

2

Questions 12–22 are based on the following passage.

An Artist's Home

—1—

When I was growing up in China during the Cultural Revolution, artistic creativity was stifled. Art exhibits were shut down by the police, and **12** various artistic techniques were forbidden. **13** The only art that was endorsed by the government was political propaganda. It represented the ideas of the ruling political party. Many artists were sentenced to years in labor camps and prisons. My philosophy differed from that of the government. I believed that art should be a personal expression of inner thoughts and beliefs rather than a tool of external control.

—2—

In my free time I used to visit my local library. **14** There I explored a world that I was eager to learn about, that of traditional Chinese art. The library became a place of comfort for me, whereas in school I was never the kind of student that teachers liked and did not fit in with my classmates. The pursuit of a formal education seemed unnecessary to me because the material I was told to study in school did not seem relevant to my life. However, I never gave up expressing myself artistically.

12

Which choice most clearly specifies some of the artistic techniques that were banned?

A) NO CHANGE

B) some techniques employed by artists

C) artistic techniques such as woodcuts and splashing ink

D) many different kinds of artistic techniques

13

Which choice most effectively combines the underlined sentences?

A) The only art that was endorsed by the government was political propaganda; this propaganda represented the ideas of the ruling political party.

B) The government endorsed only art that was essentially propaganda for the ruling political party.

C) The political propaganda that the government endorsed was the only art that represented the ideas of the ruling political party.

D) The art that represented the ideas of the ruling political party was the only political propaganda endorsed by the government.

14

A) NO CHANGE

B) When I was there, visiting the library,

C) While visiting the library,

D) Meanwhile,

CONTINUE

2
2

—3—

When the government threatened to arrest me for my artistic views, I moved to the United [15] States and studied fine art at a college in New York. There I learned in an unfamiliar setting the history and techniques of the great painters of many traditions. [16] My education changed the way in which I viewed myself as a person and, as a result, the way in which I viewed art.

—4—

Many years after the Cultural Revolution, I returned to my home town to display my artworks in an [17] exhibit titled: "Words and Scenes: Modern Chinese Paintings." My artwork, including some works that formerly would have been prohibited, [18] was displayed with that of other contemporary painters.

15

A) NO CHANGE
B) States, and studied
C) States; and studied
D) States and studied,

16

The author is considering adding the following sentence at this point:

> I also learned a lot about American culture, from movies to fast food.

Should the author make this addition?

A) Yes, because it provides a broader view of the author's American experience.
B) Yes, because the following sentence is unclear without this context.
C) No, because it is irrelevant to the main idea of the paragraph.
D) No, because the information is easily assumed by readers.

17

A) NO CHANGE
B) exhibit, titled, "Words
C) exhibit titled "Words
D) exhibit titled, "Words

18

A) NO CHANGE
B) were displayed
C) displayed
D) displaying

—5—

After completing university and obtaining my PhD in Fine Arts and Art History, I began working as a professor of Chinese art, specializing in calligraphy. My friends and I formed **19** a cluster of Chinese artistic intellectualism and were able to explore new avenues of cultural expression without the constraints we had felt in our home country. However, my distance from the epicenter of my native culture created within me a nostalgia for my childhood home, an urge to see the rolling hills of the Chinese countryside, **20** and a desire to further my understanding of Chinese culture.

—6—

For three weeks, I met with **21** locals, old friends, idealistic art students, and reporters from around the world. My visit was short, but it was meaningful to me to return to the land of my first home and to no longer feel constrained artistically.

Question 22 asks about the previous passage as a whole.

19
A) NO CHANGE
B) an enclave
C) a bunch
D) an arrangement

20
A) NO CHANGE
B) and desired
C) and desiring
D) desiring

21
A) NO CHANGE
B) locals—old friends, idealistic art students, and reporters from around the world.
C) local's, old friends; idealistic, art students; and reporters from around the world.
D) local's friends, idealistic students and reporters from around the world.

Think about the previous passage as a whole as you answer question 22.

22
To make this passage most logical, paragraph 4 should be placed
A) where it is now.
B) after paragraph 1.
C) after paragraph 3.
D) after paragraph 5.

CONTINUE

2

2

Questions 23–33 are based on the following passage.

Designing Board Games

Designing board games for a living is an interesting—though not a particularly lucrative—job. I have to [23] craft a theme, develop rules, supervise artists, coordinate test groups, organize marketing, supply chain management, and often finance the entire project while still making enough money so that I can eat every day and live indoors.

The first step in my process is to come up with an idea: it may be a theme, like intergalactic trading among alien races, or a mechanism, like rolling a unique kind of die. Often, even when I feel like I have a great idea, I find out that someone else has already done something similar, and I have to go back to the drawing board.

After I decide on a concept for my game, the next step is determining a design. This is the most intellectually challenging part of the enterprise. I have to make sure that every mechanism, rule, and accompanying piece of text makes sense in the context of the whole game, a task that [24] is like brain surgery and rocket science combined.

23

A) NO CHANGE

B) craft a theme, develop rules, supervise artists, coordinate test groups, organize marketing, and supply chain management,

C) craft a theme, develop rules, supervise artists, marketing, supply chain management,

D) craft a theme, develop rules, supervise artists, coordinate test groups, organize marketing, manage the supply chain,

24

Which choice provides a conclusion for the sentence that is most consistent with writer's tone and the main idea of this paragraph?

A) NO CHANGE

B) is really super confusing and hard to do.

C) requires both attention to detail and systematic thinking.

D) requires impossible to obtain skills that no one has.

CONTINUE ▶

2

2

During the design process, I refine the rules with help from others who playtest my prototype. Playtesting helps **25** ensure that my ideas make sense to someone other than just me. I usually will play the game I'm working on hundreds of times before I can finalize the rules.

While I am designing rules, I also work with a contract artist to produce relevant and affordable illustrations to go along with the game. Usually, most of this work goes into the game **26** itself; but some of it gets saved for publicity materials.

Once a game is nearly ready, I can begin exploring publishing options. One possibility is to contract with a known publisher to manage the printing, marketing, and distribution of my game. This is the lowest-risk option but also the least financially rewarding. **27** Another possibility, which comes with a higher risk of failure but also sometimes leads to the biggest profits, **28** are to self-publish.

25
A) NO CHANGE
B) insure that
C) unsure that
D) DELETE the underlined portion

26
A) NO CHANGE
B) themselves, but
C) themselves; but
D) itself, but

27
Which choice most logically follows the previous sentence?
A) Professional board game publishers retain most of the profits of the games that they sell.
B) Professional board game publishers often have in-house art staff.
C) Professional board game publishers rarely market games until development is nearly completed.
D) Professional board game publishers can be organized as partnerships or corporations.

28
A) NO CHANGE
B) will be
C) is
D) that is

CONTINUE

I have many more funding options now than I did a decade ago thanks to crowd funding websites. 29 Previously, I would pay for not only the development but 30 also for the manufacture and distribution of a game. Now that I can use the internet to gather support to cover these costs prior to incurring them, the potential for losing money beyond my initial investment is greatly reduced.

29

The writer is considering adding the following sentence here.

> These websites allow potential buyers to pool their money so that designers know they will sell enough units to make manufacturing a game profitable.

Should the writer make this change?

A) Yes, because it clarifies a potentially unfamiliar term.

B) Yes, because it provides a specific example that supports the preceding sentence.

C) No, because it is unrelated to the subject matter of the paragraph.

D) No, because it was previously explained in the passage.

30

A) NO CHANGE

B) also, the manufacturing and distribution.

C) the manufacture and distribution as well, of a game.

D) also the manufacture and distribution of a game.

2   2

[1] Although there are fewer financial risks than in the past, it remains difficult to make large profits by selling board games. [2] Thus, success is a relative term: a game is considered successful if 10,000 copies are sold in a year. [3] Further, my new games face a lot of competition because there are many other games on the market, and older, established games tend to sell the most copies. **31**

32 To wrap things up, the profit margin for board games is also extremely thin. On average, a game that I design costs between four and ten dollars per unit to manufacture. Then it costs about that much again in shipping to get each unit to the United States. If I sell the copies myself, I have to keep thousands of them in my garage for years as they **33** slowly trickle away. If, on the other hand, I sell a game through a distribution company, that company will take half the profits from each sale. After paying the artist, manufacturing company, and distributor, I'm lucky if I make much more than minimum wage on the time I spend on the entire endeavor.

31

To improve the cohesion and flow of this paragraph, the writer wants to add the following sentence.

> The primary reason for this difficulty is that most board games don't sell many copies.

The sentence would most logically be placed

A) before sentence 1.

B) after sentence 1.

C) after sentence 2.

D) after sentence 3.

32

What choice provides the best introduction to the paragraph?

A) NO CHANGE

B) Conclusively,

C) To summarize,

D) DELETE the underlined portion (and adjust capitalization appropriately).

33

A) NO CHANGE

B) eventually fall to the wayside.

C) are gradually purchased.

D) gently fade into nothingness.

2   2

Questions 34–44 are based on the following passage.

Charles Dickens—Medical Expert?

When celebrated author Charles Dickens died, his life was commemorated in many newspapers of his day. An obituary for the author also appeared, perhaps [34] surprisingly in another publication—the *British Medical Journal*. This probably seems curious to many modern readers. [35] Why, one might ask, would an author noted for his fictional writings be honored by an obituary in a leading medical journal?

The field of medicine has long paid tribute to [36] Dickens' keen eye about subtle detail and his description of the physiology and presentation of illnesses. Indeed, it has been hypothesized that his descriptions of the physical attributes and behaviors of his characters are so specific that one can diagnose from them a variety of diseases such as tuberculosis, Tourette's syndrome, and supranuclear palsy. For his time, Dickens had a remarkably [37] modern, medical approach, to describing illness. He had the eye of a clinician and recorded symptoms like a trained physician.

[34]

A) NO CHANGE
B) surprisingly, in another publication the
C) surprisingly—in another publication—the
D) surprisingly, in another publication: the

[35]

The author wants to revise this sentence so that, instead of asking a question, it clearly expresses the main idea of the passage as a whole. Which of the following choices best accomplishes this?

A) Although he is best known today as a novelist, Charles Dickens deserves to be recognized for his scientific acumen and contributions to the medical field as well.
B) Charles Dickens was one of the foremost men of his day, and so he deserved to be remembered by all people in all fields.
C) Charles Dickens wrote many novels, and his ideas in those novels made a deep impact in many fields of study.
D) Despite having made several contributions to medical science, Charles Dickens is much more important as a novelist than a scientist.

[36]

A) NO CHANGE
B) Dicken's keen eye for
C) Dickens keen eye about
D) Dickens' keen eye for

[37]

A) NO CHANGE
B) modern, medical approach
C) modern medical approach
D) modern—medical approach—

[1] One medical field that Dickens has played a notable part in is that of sleep disorders. [2] One hundred twenty years after the *Pickwick Papers* was written, one of the work's characters, Joe the Fat Boy, [38] inspired the research of Sydney Burwell and his colleagues. [3] Although their claims were later shown to be inaccurate, their conclusions laid the groundwork for further study of the causes of Pickwickian Syndrome. [4] Joe is described by Dickens as an obese boy with a ruddy face and gluttonous tendencies [39] that are consistently either sleeping or extremely drowsy. [5] The researchers used the name Pickwickian Syndrome to describe a condition presented by one of their patients, who bore a resemblance, in appearance and behavior, to the character Joe. [6] The researchers concluded that their patient's somnolence was due to an excess of carbon dioxide caused by heavy breathing during sleep. [40]

In addition to his contributions through his careful description of the symptoms of his characters, Dickens also inspired interest in developing fields of medical study further. In his famous novel *A Christmas Carol*, for example, Dickens arouses sympathy for the crippled Tiny Tim, and this portrayal, together with those of other Dickensian characters, [41] have led to developments in

38
A) NO CHANGE
B) challenged
C) started
D) fired up

39
A) NO CHANGE
B) whom is
C) which are
D) who is

40
To make this paragraph most logical, sentence 3 should be placed
A) where it is now.
B) after sentence 1.
C) after sentence 4.
D) after sentence 6.

41
A) NO CHANGE
B) have lead
C) has led
D) had lead

the fields of orthopedics and pediatrics and contributed to the emerging cultural understanding of the importance of compassionate care for those with various kinds of disabilities. Dickens also exposed the unsanitary conditions of urban life in many of his novels, creating an awareness of a developing health crisis caused by the rapid industrialization of his time. [42] He showed that his dedication to this cause in London went beyond fiction. He was also a leader in making public demands for the establishment of a London Department of Health. [43] Dickens wrote his novels with an observant eye and a compassionate heart.

42

The writer wants to combine the following two underlined sentences to show the relationship between them. Which choice best accomplishes this?

A) Because he was leading public demands for the establishment of a London Department of Health, Dickens was clearly showing his dedication to this cause in London.

B) He showed that his dedication to this cause in London went beyond fiction, and he was also a leader demanding the establishment of a London Department of Health.

C) By leading public demands for the establishment of a London Department of Health, Dickens showed that his dedication to this cause went beyond fiction.

D) Dickens, as the leader of public demands for the establishment of a London Department of Health, showed that his dedication to this cause in London went beyond fiction.

43

The author is considering deleting the underlined sentence. Should the author make this change?

A) Yes, because it contradicts the rest of the passage as a whole.

B) Yes, because it does not support the main point of the paragraph.

C) No, because it is needed to understand the following paragraph.

D) No, because it provides a new example to support the main idea.

Although Charles Dickens was a prolific author—he wrote fifteen novels and many short stories—his works hold an importance beyond their literary value. Although his influence on the world of literature is certainly what he is best remembered for, Charles Dickens made significant contributions to the field of medicine as well. **44** He also made contributions to many other fields unrelated to literature.

44

Which choice concludes the essay with a final, vivid example to illustrate the point of the essay as a whole?

A) NO CHANGE

B) By carefully describing characters like Old Bill Barley the gout sufferer in *Great Expectations*, Dickens has helped the world better understand many maladies and their symptoms.

C) He will always be remembered as both a great writer and a humanitarian who showed philanthropy whenever possible, which is a legacy that any novelist should envy.

D) Many of Dickens' contemporaries wrote more novels than Charles Dickens, and their works should be explored to consider how they might contribute to our understanding of medical practice and research.

STOP

If you finish before time is called, you may check your work on this section only.
Do not turn to any other section.

No Test Material On This Page

Math Test – No Calculator
25 MINUTES, 20 QUESTIONS

Turn to Section 3 of your answer sheet to answer the questions in this section.

DIRECTIONS

For questions 1–15, solve each problem, choose the best answer from the choices provided, and fill in the corresponding circle on your answer sheet. **For questions 16–20,** solve the problems and enter your answer in the grid on the answer sheet. Please refer to the directions before question 16 on how to enter your answers in the grid. You may use any available space in your test booklet for scratch work.

NOTES

The use of calculators **is not permitted.**

All variables and expressions used represent real numbers unless otherwise indicated.

Figures provided in this test are drawn to scale unless otherwise indicated.

All figures lie in a plane unless otherwise indicated.

Unless otherwise indicated, the domain of a given function f is the set of real numbers x for which $f(x)$ is a real number.

REFERENCE

$A = \pi r^2$
$C = 2\pi r$

$A = \ell w$

$A = \frac{1}{2}bh$

$c^2 = a^2 + b^2$

Special Right Triangles

$V = \ell w h$

$V = \pi r^2 h$

$V = \frac{4}{3}\pi r^3$

$V = \frac{1}{3}\pi r^2 h$

$V = \frac{1}{3}\ell w h$

The number of degrees of arc in a circle is 360.
The number of radians of arc in a circle is 2π.
The sum of the measures in degrees of the angles in a triangle is 180.

CONTINUE ➡

3 **3**

1

If $3x + 12 = 21$, what is the value of $2x + 8$?

A) 16

B) 14

C) 7

D) 3

2

Which of the following expressions can equal -1 for some value of a?

A) $|a - 3| + 2$

B) $|a - 2| + 1$

C) $|a - 1|$

D) $|a - 2| - 2$

3

$$f(x) = \frac{c}{3}x + 2$$

In the function given above, c is a constant. If $f(6) = -6$, what is the value of $f(-9)$?

A) -10

B) -4

C) -2

D) 14

4

The number of auto workers that joined a particular union between 1960 and 1985 is three times the number of auto workers that joined between 1986 and 2010. If 9,600 workers joined the union between 1960 and 1985 and n workers joined between 1986 and 2010, which of the following equations is true?

A) $9600n = 3$

B) $9600 = 3n$

C) $\frac{n}{3} = 9600$

D) $n + 3 = 9600$

CONTINUE

3   **3**

5

Which of the following expressions is equivalent to $2(3x-1)(-x+4)$?

A) $-3x^2+13x-4$

B) $-6x^2-8$

C) $-6x^2+26x-8$

D) $-12x^2+52x-16$

6

$$2x-3y=9$$
$$ax-5y=3$$

What value of a will result in the above system of equations having no solutions?

A) $\dfrac{10}{3}$

B) $\dfrac{2}{3}$

C) $-\dfrac{2}{3}$

D) $-\dfrac{10}{3}$

7

In a project for business class, Bobby launched a website with humor and pop culture content and aimed to get as many visitors to the website as possible. On day 6 there were 20 visitors to the website, and on day 18 there were 320 visitors. Which of the following best describes the average change in visitors to the website over the given period?

A)   The number of visitors to the website increased by an average of 18.25 visitors per day.

B)   The number of visitors to the website increased by an average of 25 visitors per day.

C)   The number of visitors to the website increased by an average of 69 visitors per day.

D)   The number of visitors to the website increased by an average of 71 visitors per day.

8

$$6x-4y=14$$
$$2x-3y=3$$

According to the system of equations above, what is $x+y$?

A) -3

B) 1

C) 4

D) 8

3 **3**

9

The graph of $y = (x+7)^2$ intersects the line $y = 16$ at the two points M and N. What is the length of $\overline{MN}$?

A) 6

B) 8

C) 10

D) 12

10

$$nA = 360$$

The above equation shows the relationship between the measure A, in degrees, of an exterior angle of a regular polygon and n, the number of sides of the polygon. If a regular polygon's exterior angle is greater than 80 degrees, what is the greatest number of sides it can have?

A) 4

B) 5

C) 6

D) 8

11

Amanda, Jesse, and Liana buy three gifts for a baby shower and split the cost evenly. Two of the gifts cost d dollars each, the third gift costs $6 less than each of the other two, and there is 10 percent tax on the total purchase. What is the amount paid by each of the gift givers, in dollars?

A) $d - 2$

B) $2d - 6$

C) $1.1d - 2.2$

D) $3.3d - 6.6$

12

$$x = 6 - 5i$$
$$y = 2 + i$$

If $i = \sqrt{-1}$, what is the value of b in the quotient $\dfrac{x}{y}$ when written in the form $a + bi$ (where a and b are real numbers)?

A) $-\dfrac{16}{3}$

B) $-\dfrac{16}{5}$

C) $\dfrac{7}{5}$

D) $\dfrac{16}{5}$

CONTINUE

13

$$y = a(x+3)(x-5)$$

The equation above represents a quadratic function with a as a non-zero constant and vertex of (m, n). Which of the following is equal to n?

A) -8

B) $-4a$

C) $-12a$

D) $-16a$

14

In 2015, it was estimated that a town of 43,560 had an annual population increase of 15.5%. At this rate of growth, which of the following functions models how many people live in the town t years after 2015?

A) $P(t) = 43,560(15.5)^t$

B) $P(t) = 43,560(1.155)^t$

C) $P(t) = 15.5(43,560)^t$

D) $P(t) = 43,560(0.155)^t$

15

Which of the following is equivalent to $\dfrac{8x+2}{3x-1}$?

A) $2 + \dfrac{2x+4}{3x-1}$

B) $6x - 2$

C) $3x + \dfrac{1}{2x+4}$

D) $2 - \dfrac{3x+5}{3x-1}$

CONTINUE

DIRECTIONS

For questions 16–20, solve the problem and enter your answer in the grid, as described below, on the answer sheet.

1. Although not required, it is suggested that you write your answer in the boxes at the top of the columns to help you fill in the circles accurately. You will receive credit only if the circles are filled in correctly.
2. Mark no more than one circle in any column.
3. No question has a negative answer.
4. Some problems may have more than one correct answer. In such cases, grid only one answer.

5. **Mixed numbers** such as $3\frac{1}{2}$ must be be gridded as 3.5 or 7/2. If $\boxed{3\,1\,/\,2}$ is entered into the grid, it will be interpreted as $\frac{31}{2}$, not $3\frac{1}{2}$.)

6. **Decimal answers:** If you obtain a decimal answer with more digits than the grid can accommodate, it may be either rounded or truncated, but it must fill the entire grid.

Answer: $\frac{7}{13}$

Write answer → 7 / 1 3
in boxes

← Fraction line

Grid in result

Answer: 2.5

2 . 5

← Decimal Point

Acceptable ways to grid $\frac{2}{3}$ are:

2 / 3

.666

.667

Answer: 210 – either position is correct

2 1 0

2 1 0

NOTE: You may start your answers in any column, space permitting. Columns you don't need to use should be left blank.

CONTINUE

16

$$2a + 4b = 12$$
$$5a - 2b = 30$$

Given the system of equations above, if (a, b) is a solution, what is the value of b ?

17

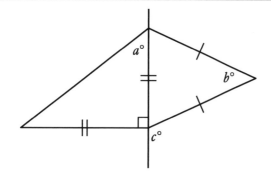

Note: Figure not drawn to scale

Two isosceles triangles are shown in the figure above. If $b = \frac{2}{3}a$, what is the value of c ?

18

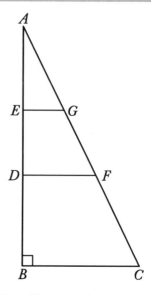

Note: Figure not drawn to scale

In the figure above, $AB = 8$ and $BC = 6$. If D is the midpoint of $\overline{AB}$, E is the midpoint of $\overline{AD}$, $\overline{AB} \perp \overline{BC}$, and $\overline{EG} \parallel \overline{DF} \parallel \overline{BC}$, what is the length of $\overline{FG}$?

19

If $w = 12\sqrt{2}$ and $\frac{1}{4}w = \sqrt{2x}$, what is the value of x ?

20

If $x^3 - 7x^2 + 3x - 21 = 0$, what is a real number solution for x ?

STOP

If you finish before time is called, you may check your work on this section only.
Do not turn to any other section.

Math Test – Calculator

55 MINUTES, 38 QUESTIONS

Turn to Section 4 of your answer sheet to answer the questions in this section.

DIRECTIONS

For questions 1–30, solve each problem, choose the best answer from the choices provided, and fill in the corresponding circle on your answer sheet. **For questions 31–38**, solve the problems and enter your answer in the grid on the answer sheet. Please refer to the directions before question 31 on how to enter your answers in the grid. You may use any available space in your test booklet for scratch work.

NOTES

1. The use of calculators **is permitted**.

All variables and expressions used represent real numbers unless otherwise indicated.

Figures provided in this test are drawn to scale unless otherwise indicated.

All figures lie in a plane unless otherwise indicated.

Unless otherwise indicated, the domain of a given function f is the set of real numbers x for which $f(x)$ is a real number.

REFERENCE

$A = \pi r^2$
$C = 2\pi r$

$A = \ell w$

$A = \frac{1}{2} bh$

$c^2 = a^2 + b^2$

Special Right Triangles

$V = \ell w h$

$V = \pi r^2 h$

$V = \frac{4}{3} \pi r^3$

$V = \frac{1}{3} \pi r^2 h$

$V = \frac{1}{3} \ell w h$

The number of degrees of arc in a circle is 360.
The number of radians of arc in a circle is 2π.
The sum of the measures in degrees of the angles in a triangle is 180.

CONTINUE ➡

4 **4**

1

Flannery is a cab driver. She will start tomorrow's shift with $300 and will make an average of $45 an hour throughout the day. In order to rent, fuel, and insure her cab, Flannery must pay a cab fee of $150 when she returns her cab at the end of each day. If Flannery's goal is to leave work with $420 tomorrow, which of the following expressions could be used to find the number of hours Flannery must work to reach her goal?

A) $45n - 150 = 120$

B) $45n - 150 = 420$

C) $45n + 150 = 120$

D) $45n - 150 = 270$

2

a	3	6	9	12
$f(a)$	−2	−1	0	1

The table above shows some values of the linear function f. Which of the following defines f?

A) $f(a) = \dfrac{1}{3}a - 3$

B) $f(a) = -\dfrac{1}{3}a - 1$

C) $f(a) = a - 5$

D) $f(a) = 2a - 8$

3

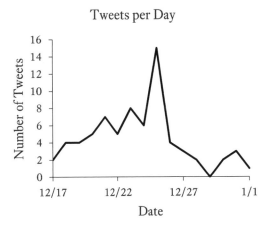

Tweets per Day

The graph above shows the number of Tweets produced by a pop star in the two weeks from December 17th through January 1st . Based on the graph, which of the following best describes the general trend in her tweets from December 17th to January 1st?

A) Tweets generally increased each day after December 17th.

B) Tweets generally decreased each day after December 17th.

C) Tweets reached a maximum on December 31st.

D) Tweets generally increased until December 25th and then generally decreased.

4

Tires are tested by sampling 24 tires from each batch of 600. If 87.5 percent of the tires in a sample pass inspection, how many tires in the batch would most likely pass inspection?

A) 525

B) 550

C) 575

A) 579

CONTINUE

4 **4**

5

When 4 times some integer z is subtracted from 12, the result is 32. What is the result when 3 times z is added to 7?

A)　22

B)　−5

C)　−8

D)　−48

6

Population of Five Countries

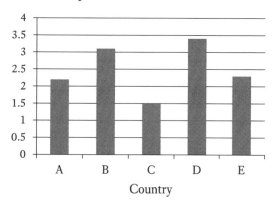

Country

The populations of five different countries are shown in the graph above. If the total population of the countries is 1.25 million people, which of the following is an appropriate title for the vertical axis?

A) Population (in thousands)

B) Population (in hundreds of thousands)

C) Population (in millions)

D) Population (in hundreds of millions)

7

The graph of the function $g(x)$ is a line that contains points in quadrants I, II, and III. The graph of the function $g(x) - 2$ is a line that contains points in quadrants I, III, and IV. Which of the following statements about the function $g(x)$ is true?

A) It has a y-intercept between $(0, 2)$ and the origin.

B) It has a y-intercept between $(0, -2)$ and the origin.

C) It has a negative slope.

D) It has a slope of zero.

8

Laura can read 2 pages of her favorite book in 75 seconds. If she reads at this same rate, which of the following is closest to the number of pages she can read in 1 hour?

A)　24

B)　48

C)　96

D)　192

CONTINUE

9

Smoking Status (Determined number of cigarettes per day)	Weight Status			Total
	Normal	Overweight	Underweight	
Non-smoker	543	1,903	53	2,499
Light (1–5)	171	375	32	578
Moderate (6–15)	234	306	35	575
Heavy (16–25)	381	618	47	1046
Very Heavy (> 25)	133	325	11	469
Total	1,462	3,527	178	5,167

The table above shows the results of a study that examined the relationship between cigarette smoking and weight. Based on the table, if a participant who smoked between 6 and 25 cigarettes per day were selected at random, which of the following is closest to the probability that the participant was underweight?

A) 0.016

B) 0.045

C) 0.051

D) 0.061

Questions 10 and 11 refer to the following information.

The graph below shows both the height and reach (measured from the left middle fingertip to the right middle fingertip when arms are spread) of the 10 gold medalists for boxing in the 2012 Summer Olympic Games.

Height and Reach of 2012 Olympic Boxing Gold Medalists

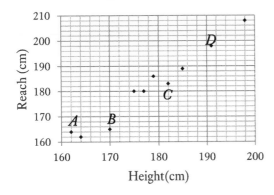

10

What is the height of the shortest boxer with a reach of at least 184 cm?

A) 162 cm

B) 164 cm

C) 179 cm

D) 185 cm

11

Of the labeled boxers, who has the smallest ratio of height to reach?

A) *A*

B) *B*

C) *C*

D) *D*

CONTINUE

12

Which of the following is <u>not</u> a solution to the inequality $4x - 3 \geq 2x + 7$?

A) 3

B) 5

C) 7

D) 9

13

Age of Sample (Years)	Number of Carbon-14 atoms
0	3.2×10^{12}
5,730	1.6×10^{12}
11,460	8.0×10^{11}
17,190	4.0×10^{11}
22,920	2.0×10^{11}
28,650	1.0×10^{11}

The table above shows the estimated number of Carbon-14 atoms in a sample over the course of five half lives. Which of the following describes the relationship between the age of the sample and the estimated number of Carbon-14 atoms?

A) Decreasing linear

B) Increasing linear

C) Exponential growth

D) Exponential decay

Questions 14 and 15 refer to the following information.

The graph below models the total monthly cost C, in dollars, of using a gym u times.

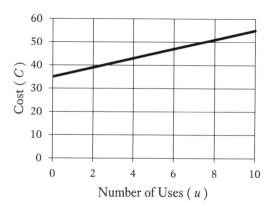

14

What does the C-intercept represent in the graph?

A) The minimum number of monthly uses

B) The base cost of a gym membership each month

C) The cost of the first use of the gym

D) The total cost of using the gym per month

15

Which of the following represents the relationship between number of uses and cost?

A) $C = 2u$

B) $C = \frac{1}{2}u + 35$

C) $C = 2u + 35$

D) $C = \frac{1}{2}u$

4 **4**

16

Stories					
5	5	5	6	6	6
6	7	7	7	9	9
10	11	12	14	15	25

The table above shows the number of stories in each of the apartment buildings on Elm Street. The 25 story building is an outlier. If that building is removed from the set, which of the following will change the most?

A) Mean

B) Median

C) Range

D) All change by the same amount

17

A professional football team practices 6 days a week. A water boy for the team knows that the players drink about 200 gallons of water during each day of practice. If the water filter in the utility room pours water at a rate of 9 gallons per minute, how many hours a week does the water boy spend filling water containers?

A) $\dfrac{20}{9}$

B) 3

C) 5

D) 6

18

If $14p - 22 \ge -10$, what is the maximum possible value of $11 - 7p$?

A) −5

B) 0.86

C) 2.29

D) 5

19

	Pizza	Chinese	Burgers	Total
Lunch	71	32	47	150
Dinner	52	45	53	150
Total	123	77	100	300

A mall food court has three options: pizza, Chinese food, and burgers. People were surveyed on their choices at lunchtime and at dinnertime to see if there were noticeable differences in preferences for each meal. The results are shown above. Based on the data, what is the probability that someone who had dinner at the food court did <u>not</u> eat Chinese food?

A) $\dfrac{45}{150}$

B) $\dfrac{77}{150}$

C) $\dfrac{105}{150}$

D) $\dfrac{118}{150}$

Questions 20 and 21 refer to the following information.

Company	Rental Insurance I (in dollars)	Reservation Fee R (in dollars)	Truck Rental T (in dollars per mile)	Gas Expenses G (in dollars per mile)
A	35	20	0.60	0.10
B	25	40	0.75	0.12
C	0	50	0.75	0.15

The total cost, $c(x)$, for renting a truck for a day in terms of the number of miles driven, x, is given by $c(x) = (T+G)x + I + R$.

20

For what range of miles will the total cost of renting a truck from company A be greater than or equal to the total cost of renting a truck from company C?

A) $x \le 25$

B) $x \ge 0$

C) $x \ge 500$

D) Company C's trucks are never less expensive than company A's

21

If the relationship between the total cost, $c(x)$, of renting a truck from any of the companies for x miles were graphed in the xy-plane, what would the slope of the line represent?

A) The total cost of gas

B) The cost of reservation

C) The total cost of renting the truck

D) The cost of per-mile expenses

CONTINUE

22

Jerry opens a savings account with $200. If the bank account is supposed to grow at an exponential rate, which of the following could represent Jerry's bank account balance at the end of each year for four consecutive years?

A) $210, $220, $230, $240

B) $310.10, $420.20, $530.30, $640.40

C) $210, $220.50, $231.53, $243.10

D) $300, $400, $500, $600

23

A linear function has distinct intercepts at $(h, 0)$ and $(0, k)$. If $h - k = 0$, which of the following can be concluded about the slope of the line?

A) It is zero.

B) It is positive.

C) It is negative.

D) Nothing can be determined about the slope from this information.

24

If $g(b) = 20b^3 - 15b^2 + 25b$ and $f(b) = 4b^2 - 3b + 5$, then what is the value of $\dfrac{f(b) - g(b)}{5b - 1}$?

A) $f(b)$

B) $-f(b)$

C) $g(b)$

D) $-b \cdot g(b)$

25

The Florida Aquarium is going to increase the volume of its cylindrical tank by 50 percent. If the radius is increased by 18 percent, the height of the tank would have to be increased by what percent (rounded to the nearest tenth of a percent)?

A) 27.1%

B) 12.0%

C) 7.7%

D) 2.0%

CONTINUE

26

Dependency Ratio in Japan

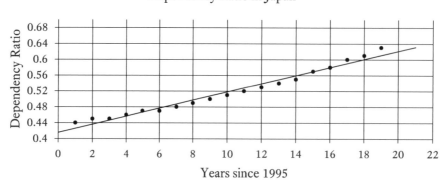

Years since 1995

In economics, the dependency ratio is an age-population ratio of those typically not in the labor force to those typically in the labor force. More specifically, the dependency ratio is defined as

$$\text{Dependency Ratio} = \frac{\text{Number of people under age 15 or over age 65}}{\text{Number of people aged 16–65}}.$$

The scatterplot above shows the dependency ratio for Japan for each year since 1995. The line of best fit is also shown and has the equation $y = 0.103x + 0.416$. Which of the following statements about the above data is true?

A) In 1995, the dependency ratio for Japan was between 0.42 and 0.41.

B) In 2005, the number of people of working age in Japan was 51 percent of those whose ages were below 15 or above 65.

C) The dependency ratio for Japan increases by a value of 0.103 each year.

D) In 2002, Japan had 48 people that were not of working age for every 100 working-age people.

27

A line segment in the coordinate plane has endpoints $A\,(1, 3)$ and $B\,(5, 1)$. Which of the following is the equation of a line perpendicular to segment $\overline{AB}$ intersecting $\overline{AB}$ at its midpoint?

A) $y = \dfrac{1}{2}x + \dfrac{1}{2}$

B) $y = \dfrac{1}{2}x + \dfrac{5}{2}$

C) $y = 2x - 1$

D) $y = 2x - 4$

28

The population of mosquitos in a biology laboratory can increase by 50 percent every 2 weeks. If a population started with 200 mosquitos, which expression gives the number of mosquitos after d days?

A) $200(0.5)^{\frac{d}{14}}$

B) $200(1.5)^{\frac{d}{14}}$

C) $200(0.5)^{14d}$

D) $200(1.5)^{14d}$

CONTINUE

29

The function $f(x)$ is a quadratic function such that $f(x) + 5 = 0$ yields exactly one real solution. Which of the following could be $f(x)$?

A) $f(x) = x^2 + 10x + 20$

B) $f(x) = (x - 5)^2$

C) $f(x) = (x + 5)^2 + 5$

D) $f(x) = x^2 + 10x - 5$

30

$$R = 16(2)^A$$
$$P = 4(2)^B - 5$$

In the equations above, A and B are constants. If B is two less than A, then what is the value of P in terms of R?

A) $P = \dfrac{R}{16} + 5$

B) $P = \dfrac{R}{16} - 5$

C) $P = \dfrac{R}{4}$

D) $P = 4R - 5$

CONTINUE

4 **4**

DIRECTIONS

For questions 31–38, solve the problem and enter your answer in the grid, as described below, on the answer sheet.

1. Although not required, it is suggested that you write your answer in the boxes at the top of the columns to help you fill in the circles accurately. You will receive credit only if the circles are filled in correctly.
2. Mark no more than one circle in any column.
3. No question has a negative answer.
4. Some problems may have more than one correct answer. In such cases, grid only one answer.

5. **Mixed numbers** such as $3\frac{1}{2}$ must be be gridded as 3.5 or 7/2. If $3|1|/|2$ is entered into the grid, it will be interpreted as $\frac{31}{2}$, not $3\frac{1}{2}$.)

6. **Decimal answers:** If you obtain a decimal answer with more digits than the grid can accommodate, it may be either rounded or truncated, but it must fill the entire grid.

Answer: $\frac{7}{13}$

Write answer in boxes →

← Fraction line

Grid in result

Answer: 2.5

← Decimal Point

Acceptable ways to grid $\frac{2}{3}$ are:

Answer: 210 – either position is correct

NOTE: You may start your answers in any column, space permitting. Columns you don't need to use should be left blank.

CONTINUE

4 **4**

31

Allie can type between 30 and 45 words per minute. Given this, what is a possible number of <u>hours</u> it might take Allie to type 5,400 words?

32

Last month Genie and Sarah sold a total of 299 sunglasses. If Genie sold 67 fewer sunglasses than Sarah, how many sunglasses did Sarah sell?

33

The acre is a unit of area that can be calculated by multiplying one chain (a unit of length) by one furlong (another unit of length). One chain is 66 feet and one furlong is 660 feet. How many acres are there in a plot of land that has an area of 87,120 square feet?

34

If a circle has a radius of 12 units, what is the measure, in degrees, of the central angle that subtends an arc with a length of 8π ?

CONTINUE

35

240 boys and 100 girls have been accepted to Buzz Cut Military College. If the college wants to cap male acceptances to 60 percent of the total acceptances, and is prepared to not accept any more boys, then how many additional girls should it admit?

36

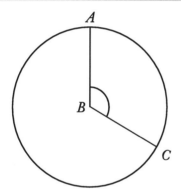

In the figure above, the circle centered at B has a diameter of 10 units. If the area of the smaller sector ABC is between 24 and 25 square units, then what is one possible value of the measure, in degrees (rounded to the nearest degree), of $\angle ABC$?

Questions 37 and 38 refer to the following information.

A study shows that after the average man turns 40, he begins to lose height at the rate of approximately 0.1% each year. Mr. Celio is exactly 40 years old and 76 inches tall, and he uses the equation $H = 76v^{t}$ to measure his height at any age t years in the future.

37

What value should Mr. Celio use for v ?

38

To the nearest tenth of an inch, what does Mr. Celio expect his height to be when he turns 70?

STOP

If you finish before time is called, you may check your work on this section only.
Do not turn to any other section.

SAT Practice Test 4

IMPORTANT REMINDERS

1

A No. 2 pencil is required for the test.
Do not use a mechanical pencil or pen.

2

Sharing any questions with anyone is a violation
of the Test Security and Fairness policies and
may result in your score being canceled.

This cover is representative of what you will see on the day of the SAT.

1

1

Reading Test

65 MINUTES, 52 QUESTIONS

Turn to Section 1 of your answer sheet to answer the questions in this section.

DIRECTIONS

Each passage or pair of passages below is followed by a number of questions. After reading each passage or pair, choose the best answer to each question based on what is stated or implied in the passage or passages and in any accompanying graphics (such as a table or graph).

Questions 1-10 are based on the following passage.

This passage is adapted from Stephen Crane, *Maggie, A Girl of the Streets*. Originally published in 1893.

A very little boy stood upon a heap of gravel for the honor of Rum Alley. He was throwing stones at howling urchins from Devil's Row who were circling madly about the heap and pelting at him.

5   His infantile countenance was livid with fury. His small body was writhing in the delivery of great, crimson oaths.

"Run, Jimmie, run! Dey'll get yehs," screamed a retreating Rum Alley child.

10   "Naw," responded Jimmie with a valiant roar, "dese fellas can't make me run."

Howls of renewed wrath went up from Devil's Row throats. Tattered gamins on the right made a furious assault on the gravel heap. On their small,

15   convulsed faces there shone the grins of true assassins. As they charged, they threw stones and cursed in shrill chorus.

The little champion of Rum Alley stumbled precipitately down the other side. His coat had been

20   torn to shreds in a scuffle, and his hat was gone. He had bruises on twenty parts of his body, and blood was dripping from a cut in his head. His wan features wore a look of a tiny, insane demon.

On the ground, children from Devil's Row closed

25   in on their antagonist. He crooked his left arm defensively about his head and fought with cursing fury. The little boys ran to and fro, dodging, hurling stones and swearing in barbaric trebles.

From a window of an apartment house that

30   upreared its form from amid squat, ignorant stables, there leaned a curious woman. Some laborers, unloading a scow at a dock at the river, paused for a moment and regarded the fight. The engineer of a passive tugboat hung lazily to a railing and watched.

35   Over on the Island, a worm of yellow convicts came from the shadow of a building and crawled slowly along the river's bank.

A stone had smashed into Jimmie's mouth. Blood was bubbling over his chin and down upon his ragged

40   shirt. Tears made furrows on his dirt-stained cheeks. His thin legs had begun to tremble and turn weak, causing his small body to reel. His roaring curses of the first part of the fight had changed to a blasphemous chatter.

45   In the yells of the whirling mob of Devil's Row children there were notes of joy like songs of triumphant savagery. The little boys seemed to leer gloatingly at the blood upon the other child's face.

Down the avenue came boastfully sauntering a lad

50   of sixteen years, although the chronic sneer of an ideal manhood already sat upon his lips. His hat was tipped with an air of challenge over his eye. Between his teeth, a cigar stump was tilted at the angle of defiance. He walked with a certain swing of the

55   shoulders which appalled the timid. He glanced over into the vacant lot in which the little raving boys from Devil's Row seethed about the shrieking and tearful child from Rum Alley.

"Gee!" he murmured with interest. "A scrap.

60   Gee!"

CONTINUE ➡

1

He strode over to the cursing circle, swinging his shoulders in a manner which denoted that he held victory in his fists. He approached at the back of one of the most deeply engaged of the Devil's Row
65 children.

"Ah, what deh heck," he said, and smote the deeply-engaged one on the back of the head. The little boy fell to the ground and gave a hoarse, tremendous howl. He scrambled to his feet, and
70 perceiving, evidently, the size of his assailant, ran quickly off, shouting alarms. The entire Devil's Row party followed him. They came to a stand a short distance away and yelled taunting oaths at the boy with the chronic sneer. The latter, momentarily, paid
75 no attention to them.

"What deh heck, Jimmie?" he asked of the small champion.

Jimmie wiped his blood-wet features with his sleeve.
80 "Well, it was dis way, Pete, see! I was goin' teh lick dat Riley kid and dey all pitched on me."

Some Rum Alley children now came forward. The party stood for a moment exchanging vainglorious remarks with Devil's Row. A few stones were thrown
85 at long distances, and words of challenge passed between small warriors. Then the Rum Alley contingent turned slowly in the direction of their home street. They began to give, each to each, distorted versions of the fight. Causes of retreat in
90 particular cases were magnified. Blows dealt in the fight were enlarged to catapultian power, and stones thrown were alleged to have hurtled with infinite accuracy.

1

Throughout the passage, the author is primarily concerned with

A) clearly assigning guilt to the parties responsible for the instigation of a deplorably violent incident.

B) carefully reporting an incident of violence as clearly as possible.

C) overtly mocking the ignorance and brutality of the people involved in a conflict.

D) subtly providing readers with a reason to take action against the unjust actions he portrays.

2

According to Jimmie, the incident began because

A) he was defending his home neighborhood in Devil's Row when the local boys ganged up on him.

B) he would not leave when the local boys found him in Devil's Row and tried to chase him away.

C) he first threw stones at the boys from Devil's Row and they then threw stones back at him.

D) he was fighting one of the boys from Devil's Row and the rest of the boys joined the fight.

3

Which choice provides the best evidence for the answer to the previous question?

A) Lines 1–4 ("A very … him")

B) Lines 8–13 ("Run … throats")

C) Lines 76–81 ("What … me")

D) Lines 89–93 ("Causes … accuracy")

CONTINUE

4

The description of Jimmie in lines 18–23 ("The little … demon") most strongly characterizes him as

A) poor but noble.

B) foolish and ignorant.

C) pitiable though fierce.

D) aggressive and arrogant.

5

The primary purpose of lines 29–34 ("From a … watched") is to

A) provide a broader spectrum of the social issues that underlie the conflict presented.

B) reveal the indifference of those who observe the violence occurring.

C) suggest that the conflict is insignificant and uninteresting to any outside observers.

D) create a contrast between the problems of the boys and the purposeful labor of those around them.

6

The boys from Devil's Row retreat from the conflict primarily because of

A) the irenic presence of an adult who has become aware of the situation.

B) their inability to match the anger and vehemence of Jimmie.

C) their sense of fairness and sympathy in response to Jimmie's helplessness.

D) the involvement of a large defender of the Rum Alley boy.

7

Which choice provides the best evidence for the answer to the previous question?

A) Lines 29–31 ("From … woman")

B) Lines 38–44 ("A stone … chatter")

C) Lines 66–72 ("Ah … him")

D) Lines 82–88 ("The party … street")

8

As it is used in lines 18 and 77, the word "champion" most nearly means one who

A) defends someone or something.

B) has won a competition.

C) is superior to others in the same field.

D) is to be congratulated.

9

As it is used in line 87, the word "contingent" most nearly means

A) depending upon.

B) group.

C) unforeseen element.

D) challenger.

10

In lines 89–93 ("Causes … accuracy"), the author indicates

A) the kinds of distortions that the boys create in retelling the story of the fight.

B) the scale and significance of the scuffle between the two parties as well as its likely outcomes.

C) the kinds of misunderstandings that have arisen regarding the conflict since its resolution.

D) that the reality of the past is never as good as it seems to be in the recollections of those who experienced it.

1

1

Questions 11–20 are based on the following passage and supplementary material.

This passage is adapted from Ralph Calel, "The Founding Fathers v. The Climate Change Skeptics." ©2014 by The Public Domain Review.

The United States has in recent years become a stronghold for climate change skepticism, especially since the country's declaration in 2001 that it would not participate in the Kyoto Protocol. Far from the
5 ambivalence of the American response to modern theories, the country's founders were vocal proponents of early theories of man-made climate change. The country's founders were keen observers of climatic trends and might even be counted among
10 the first climate change advocates. They wrote extensively in favor of the idea that settlement was improving the continent's climate, and their efforts helped to lay the foundation of modern meteorology.

From the start, the project to colonize North
15 America had proceeded on the understanding that climate followed latitude; so dependent was climate on the angle of the sun to the earth's surface, it was believed, that the word 'climate' was defined in terms of parallels of latitude. New England was expected to
20 be as mild as England, and Virginia as hot as Italy and Spain. Surprised by harsh conditions in the New World, however, a great number of the early settlers did not outlast their first winter in the colonies.

A view formed in Europe that the New World was
25 inferior to the Old. In particular, medical lore still held that climate lay behind the characteristic balance of the Hippocratic humors—it explained why Spaniards were temperamental and Englishmen reserved—and it was believed that the climate of the
30 colonies caused physical and mental degeneration. The respected French naturalist Georges-Louis Leclerc explained in his encyclopedia of natural history that "all animals of the New World were much smaller than those of the Old. This great
35 diminution in size, whatever may be the cause, is a primary kind of degeneration." He speculated that the difference in climate might be the cause. Swedish explorer Pehr Kalm observed in his travel diary that the climate of the New World caused life—plants and
40 animals, including humans—to possess less stamina, stature, and longevity than in Europe.

In the New World, refuting such theories became a matter of patriotism. The colonists set about arguing that their settlement was causing a gradual
45 increase in temperatures and improvement of the flora and fauna of North America. Benjamin Rush, physician and signatory of the Declaration of Independence, speculated that, if cultivation kept pace with clearing of new lands, climate change
50 might even reduce the incidence of fevers and disease. Thomas Jefferson was especially eager to rebut the proponents of the theory of climatic degeneracy. He expended substantial efforts to this effect with page after page of animal measurements
55 showing that the American animals were not inferior to their European counterparts. He also had help from James Madison, who shared his own measurements and urged Jefferson to use them in his arguments.

60 The Founders did not settle for mere advocacy: they wanted more and better evidence. On the question of whether the winters were getting milder, Ben Franklin encouraged the president of Yale University to make steady wintertime observations in
65 different parts of the country. Madison made regular observations at his estate, which he assiduously entered into his meteorological journals. Jefferson, too, kept meticulous records, and encouraged his friends and colleagues to submit their measurements
70 to the American Philosophical Society to show the effect of clearing and culture towards the changes of climate. Jefferson himself made significant contributions to the development of modern meteorology, promoting methodological
75 standardization and expansion of geographical coverage and calling for the establishment a national meteorological service.

Modern reconstructions show that although there was a brief warming period in New England during
80 the late 1700s, Jefferson's measurements predate any actual man-made climate change. The theories of Jefferson and his contemporaries could not consider the modern understanding of the greenhouse effect. Their theories led to a belief that a changing climate
85 would necessarily be beneficial, whereas today there is an awareness of the dangers of climate change.

Yet one should not belittle the efforts of these early climate change advocates. Their search for evidence resulted in substantial contributions to

CONTINUE ▶

90 zoology and was instrumental to the foundation of
modern meteorology and climatology. Far from a
stronghold of climate change skepticism, as the
United States is sometimes seen today, the country's
founders were vocal proponents of early theories of
95 man-made climate change, writing extensively in
favor of the theory that settlement was improving the
continent's climate. Today's climate change

advocates may recognize in themselves some of the
overzealousness of the Founding Fathers and
100 therefore better guard against potential fallacies.
Skeptics may recognize in themselves the often anti-
scientific spirit of the degeneracy-theorists and thus
make greater efforts to engage constructively in the
scientific enterprise today.

US Temperature (Annual Mean) 1880–2015

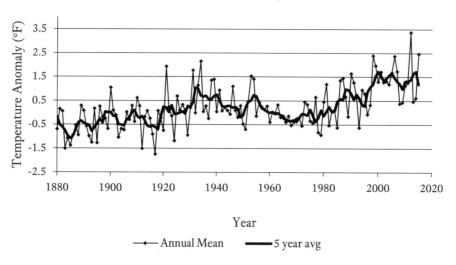

Adapted from NASA Goddard Institute for Space Studies website. © 2016

11

The main point of the passage is that

A) the founding fathers believed in global warming,
so Americans today should follow their lead and
take action on climate change.

B) understanding the history, science, and politics
of climate change in the time of the founding
fathers may help people approach these issues
today.

C) climate change skepticism and advocacy both
have a long history in the United States.

D) man-made climate change was not achieved
during the time of the founding fathers and thus
is not likely to be possible today.

12

As it is used in line 5, "ambivalence" most nearly
means

A) apathy.

B) uncertainty.

C) neutrality.

D) negativity.

CONTINUE

1　　　　　　　　　　　　　　　　　　　　　　　**1**

13

Based on the passage, at least some of the founding fathers believed that man-made climate change was

A) a myth since all climate change is based on world-wide weather patterns and changes.

B) possible to achieve through the actions of colonizing and likely to bring about positive effects.

C) desirable as a means of creating conditions for humans to have a greater biological advantage over other species.

D) a falsehood spread by the prejudices of those who viewed Europe as superior to the Americas.

14

Which choice provides the best evidence for the answer to the previous question?

A) Lines 36–37 ("He … cause")

B) Lines 42–43 ("In the New … patriotism")

C) Lines 43–46 ("The colonists … America")

D) Lines 51–56 ("Thomas … counterparts")

15

The author of the passage mentions Georges-Louis Leclerc's and Pehr Kalm's ideas primarily to

A) suggest that modern notions regarding climate change have their origins in the thought of respected European thinkers.

B) offer examples of scientists whose ideas support the beliefs of the founding fathers.

C) mock them as foolish compared to current views and the notions of early colonists.

D) explain the founding fathers' interest in studying and even trying to impact the climate of the United States.

16

As it is used in line 51, the word "eager" most nearly means

A) restless.

B) nervous.

C) keen.

D) prepared.

17

The passage suggests that the historical example discussed is applicable to modern climate concerns in that

A) the mistakes of the founders can help people today to be more careful about inaccurate assumptions in their own thinking.

B) the arguments the founders made are directly applicable to the central questions regarding climate change today.

C) the past beliefs illuminate the foolishness of the still-prevalent belief that man-made climate change is a positive force.

D) the anti-scientific thinking that spurred Jefferson and others is the basis of the views of those who deny man-made climate change.

18

Which choice provides the best evidence for the answer to the previous question?

A) Lines 4–8 ("Far … change")

B) Lines 60–61 ("The Founders … evidence")

C) Lines 97–100 ("Today's … fallacies")

D) Lines 101–104 ("Skeptics … today")

CONTINUE ➤

19

Which of the following gives the best summary of the information provided in the graph?

A) Average temperatures in the United States have steadily increased since the time of the founding fathers.

B) Average temperatures in the United States have fluctuated over the past 130 years, but never more than ±1 °F.

C) After a century of fluctuation above and below long-term averages, the past thirty years show a trend of increasing average temperatures.

D) The temperature fluctuations that Jefferson measured were more significant than the changes measured over the past 130 years.

20

The information provided in the graph suggests that the variation in average temperatures from year to year

A) is greater than the mean variation over a five-year period.

B) is insufficient to indicate a measurable difference over greater periods of time.

C) is decreasing while overall temperatures are increasing.

D) never changes more than 0.1 °F.

CONTINUE

1

1

Questions 21–30 are based on the following passage.

This passage is adapted from Lydia Pyne, "Neanderthals in 3D: L'Homme de La Chapelle." ©2015 by The Public Domain Review. Here, Pyne considers the significance of a landmark publication in paleoanthropology.

On August 3, 1908, French prehistorian Jean Bouyssonie, his brother, Amédée Bouyssonie, and their colleague Louis Bardon found a Neanderthal skeleton in a system of caves near La Chapelle-aux-
5 Saints in south-central France. The discovery was exciting for the newly-emerging field of paleoanthropology because the Neanderthal was found in its original, undisturbed archaeological context—in situ—and excavations of the skeleton
10 revealed that it was more complete than anything else in the fossil record. La Chapelle quickly became an iconic fossil within scientific and popular circles and went on to inspire everything from dioramas at the Field Museum of Natural History to science fiction's
15 *A Guerre du Feu* (Quest for Fire.)

After the skeleton was excavated, the Bouyssonies sent the remains to the eminent Marcellin Boule, the Director of the Laboratory of Palaeontology at the prestigious Musée d'Histoire Naturelle in Paris.
20 Boule conducted a two-year detailed anatomical study of the fossil that culminated in a hefty monograph, *L'Homme Fossile de La Chapelle-aux-Saints*, published in 1911. *L'Homme* was the first and most comprehensive publication of Neanderthal
25 skeletal anatomy in scientific literature, establishing the La Chapelle skeleton as the most complete fossil reference for early paleo-studies. Boule's detailed anatomical description of the skeleton provided a framework for any new Neanderthal fossils
30 discovered, and the 1911 reconstructions of La Chapelle became the basis for all subsequent Neanderthal research. The book is filled with chapters of anatomical descriptions, careful measurements, photographs of the skeleton in the
35 ground, prior to excavation, as well as sketches of geomorphic cross-sections from the cave. In addition to the tables of metrics and photographs of the La Chapelle fossil, Boule included another type of medium that gave readers of *L'Homme* a way to
40 interact with the fossil for themselves. At the back of the book, Boule included six stereoscopic plates of the Neanderthal skull.

By the time *L'Homme* was published, the stereoscope would have been a familiar object, one of
45 the many optical toys—along with kaleidoscopes, zoetropes and cameras—through which the nineteenth-century eye had peered in wonder. The stereoscope's particular trick was to give a two-dimensional image an illusion of depth. Gazing
50 through its viewfinder, the two slightly offset images of the stereoscopic plate, or stereogram, positioned in front would combine to create an illusion of three dimensions.

The device, however, was much more than just a
55 toy or illustrative distraction—it developed into an important tool for laboratory and scientific work in the late nineteenth and early twentieth centuries. Just as telescopes and microscopes expanded what is visible, the stereoscope expanded how researchers
60 were able to see different specimens.

As fossils were themselves too rare and important to send between researchers, proxies—casts, measurements, sketches, photographs, and highly detailed descriptions—were needed to provide
65 accurate and sufficient information. Drawing from a tradition of stereoscopic anatomical atlases, the La Chapelle-aux-Saints Neanderthal plates gave the reader a first-person experience of interacting with the fossil in three dimensions.

70 The stereo cards of the Neanderthal skull gave readers of the *L'Homme Fossile de La Chapelle-aux-Saints* the opportunity to see for themselves the complexity of the Neanderthal cranium. This added dimensionality of the stereo cards helped bring the
75 La Chapelle skeleton to the forefront of paleoanthropological research in the early twentieth century—the stereo plates deepened viewers' connections to the fossil. (*L'Homme's* beautifully detailed stereoscopic prints of each bone from the
80 skeleton were the 1911 version of data sharing.) While it is easy to think of 3D rendering of fossils as a recent technological phenomenon, stereograms offer a glimpse at the explanatory power of stereoscopic images and highlight the connections three-
85 dimensional viewing made between viewer and object. Boule's inclusion of stereoscopic images of the La Chapelle Neanderthal helped solidify the fossil's iconic status in the early-twentieth-century paleoanthropology.

CONTINUE

21

Based on the passage, what can be reasonably inferred about the La Chapelle skeleton?

A) The La Chapelle skeleton is the only Neanderthal that has ever been discovered.

B) The fossil remains that were found were unusually complete.

C) Scientists were initially ignorant of the scientific value of the La Chapelle skeleton.

D) The skull of the La Chapelle skeleton was never found.

22

As it is used in line 9, "in situ" most nearly means

A) in a seated position.

B) into an underground location.

C) in its original setting.

D) in a place set aside for a purpose.

23

It can be inferred from the passage that the Bouyssonnie brothers sent the La Chapelle skeletal remains to Marcellin Boule in order to

A) encourage him to make stereoscopic plates of the Neanderthal skull.

B) allow him to distribute the fossils to other researchers.

C) enable him to conduct a complete anatomical study.

D) prove to Boule that the skeleton they found was iconic.

24

As it is used in line 17, "eminent" most nearly means

A) distinguished.

B) conspicuous.

C) grandiose.

D) noble.

25

The primary purpose of the second paragraph (lines 16-42) is to shift the focus of the passage from the discovery of the fossil to

A) an explanation of the fossil's achievement of iconic status and its impact on modern science.

B) an analysis of the influence of a scientist's contributions to a particular field of study.

C) biographical information of an important scientist and a summary of his anatomical study.

D) a detailed description of a scientific publication about the fossil which included an example of an important optical technology.

26

Which choice provides the best evidence for the answer to the previous question?

A) Lines 16–19 ("After…Paris")

B) Lines 23–27 ("L'Homme … studies")

C) Lines 27–32 ("Boule's…research")

D) Lines 36–42 ("In addition…skull")

27

According to the passage, one difference between a stereoscope and a kaleidoscope is

A) the stereoscope created an illusion of three dimensions.

B) the stereoscope was a familiar object to people in the nineteenth century.

C) the kaleidoscope was an optical toy and the stereoscope was not.

D) the kaleidoscope was more similar to zoetropes and cameras than the stereoscope was.

28

In lines 78–80 ("L'Homme's...sharing") the author includes a comparison between stereoscopic prints and modern data sharing in order to

A) provide the reader with a metaphor for envisioning what stereoscopic prints look like.

B) give the reader a better understanding of the purpose and impact of Boule's inclusion of stereoscopic images in his book.

C) describe in modern terms how Boule made the stereoscopic images that he included in his book.

D) emphasize the significant differences between a method of data sharing in 1911 and the modern technology used today.

29

It can be reasonably inferred that the reaction of Boule's colleagues to the stereograms in his book would most likely have been

A) bewildered confusion: the stereoscope was an unusual object and viewed as a distraction at the turn of the century.

B) sincere appreciation: they provided a first-person experience of an important discovery.

C) grudging acceptance: in 1911 stereograms weren't as useful for presenting images as photographs.

D) surprised delight: stereoscopic images had never been used in a scientific publication before.

30

Which choice provides the best evidence to the previous question?

A) Lines 54–57 ("The device ... centuries")

B) Lines 61–65 ("As ... information")

C) Lines 73–78 ("This ... fossil")

D) Lines 86–89 ("Boule's ... paleoanthropology")

CONTINUE

Questions 31–41 are based on the following passage and supplementary material.

This passage is Susan B. Anthony's speech "Women's Rights to Suffrage." She delivered the speech in 1873 after she was fined for illegally attempting to vote.

Friends and Fellow Citizens: I stand before you tonight under indictment for the alleged crime of having voted at the last presidential election, without having a lawful right to vote. It shall be my work this
5   evening to prove to you that in thus voting, I not only committed no crime, but, instead, simply exercised my citizen's rights, guaranteed to me and all United States citizens by the National Constitution, beyond the power of any State to deny.
10 The preamble of the Federal Constitution says: "We, the people of the United States, in order to form a more perfect union, establish justice, insure domestic tranquility, provide for the common defense, promote the general welfare, and secure the
15 blessings of liberty to ourselves and our posterity, do ordain and establish this Constitution for the United States of America."
It was we, the people; not we, the white male citizens; nor yet we, the male citizens; but we, the
20 whole people, who formed the Union. And we formed it, not to give the blessings of liberty, but to secure them; not to the half of ourselves and the half of our posterity, but to the whole people—women as well as men. And it is a downright mockery to talk to
25 women of their enjoyment of the blessings of liberty while they are denied the use of the only means of securing them provided by this democratic-republican government—the ballot.
For any State to make sex a qualification that must
30 ever result in the disfranchisement of one entire half of the people is to pass a bill of attainder, or an ex post facto law, and is therefore a violation of the supreme law of the land. By it the blessings of liberty are forever withheld from women and their female
35 posterity. To them this government has no just powers derived from the consent of the governed.
To them this government is not a democracy. It is not a republic. It is an odious aristocracy; a hateful oligarchy of sex; the most hateful aristocracy ever
40 established on the face of the globe; an oligarchy of wealth, where the rich govern the poor, an oligarchy of learning, where the educated govern the ignorant,

or even an oligarchy of race, where the Saxon rules the African, might be endured; but this oligarchy of
45 sex, which makes father, brothers, husband, sons, the oligarchs over the mother and sisters, the wife and daughters of every household—which ordains all men sovereigns, all women subjects, carries dissension, discord and rebellion into every home of
50 the nation.
Webster, Worcester and Bouvier all define a citizen to be a person in the United States, entitled to vote and hold office.
The only question left to be settled now is: Are
55 women persons? And I hardly believe any of our opponents will have the hardihood to say they are not. Being persons, then, women are citizens; and no State has a right to make any law, or to enforce any old law, that shall abridge their privileges or
60 immunities. Hence, every discrimination against women in the constitutions and laws of the several States is today null and void, precisely as is every one against Negroes.

Impact of Women's Suffrage on Voter Turnout
(averaged across all states)

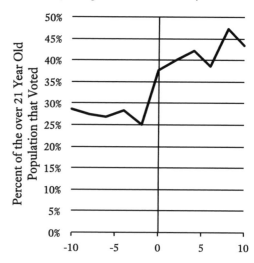

The horizontal axis shows the years before and after women were given the right to vote in different states: Year zero is the first year in which women were allowed to vote in different states.

Adapted from John R. Lott Jr. and Lawrence W. Kenny, "Did Women's Suffrage Change the Size and Scope of Government?" ©1999 by The University of Chicago.

CONTINUE

1

1

31

The author constructs an argument in favor of women's suffrage by

A) claiming that women in America worked to earn the right to vote.

B) comparing it to Negro emancipation.

C) quoting established laws that explicitly support women's suffrage.

D) showing that disenfranchisement of women is unconstitutional.

32

Which choice provides the best evidence for the answer to the previous question?

A) Lines 11–17 ("We the people … America")

B) Lines 18–24 ("It was we … men")

C) Lines 29–33 ("For any … the land")

D) Lines 54–57 ("The only … not")

33

Throughout the passage, the speaker's tone is best described as

A) forceful.

B) pedantic.

C) irate.

D) despondent.

34

The author quotes the preamble of the Constitution lines 11–17 ("We the people…America") in order to

A) mimic its rhetorical strategies to enhance the legitimacy of her argument.

B) analyze it to further advance her primary argument.

C) suggest, by way of inference and direct argument, that it is outmoded.

D) suggest an alteration by way of amendment to the US Constitution.

35

In line 33, "supreme" most nearly means

A) unquestionable.

B) perfect.

C) highest.

D) rare.

36

Based on lines 33–38 ("By it … aristocracy"), which of the following can be inferred as a larger consequence of female disenfranchisement?

A) It undermines true democracy.

B) Women's voices and those of their posterity will forever be silenced.

C) Women's issues will be neglected.

D) Only white males have the blessing of liberty.

CONTINUE ▶

37

How does the author distinguish between the oligarchies mentioned in lines 40–44 ("an oligarchy … might be endured") and the oligarchy of sex mentioned in lines 44–50 ("but this oligarchy … home of the nation")?

A) Other oligarchies are more short term.

B) The oligarchy of sex pertains to everyone.

C) The oligarchy of sex is more damaging to those it harms.

D) Other oligarchies are more politically charged.

38

In line 60, "immunities" most nearly means

A) pardons.

B) exceptions.

C) protections.

D) inoculations.

39

The author draws a link between women and Negroes to suggest that

A) both need to be enfranchised because of the ways they have been mistreated by oppressive rulers.

B) the two groups need to collaborate for civil rights activism because their goals are the same.

C) women should be sympathetic to Negroes, and vice versa, because both have struggled through the same challenges.

D) the same reasoning that makes discrimination against Negroes unconstitutional also makes discrimination against women unconstitutional.

40

Which choice provides the best evidence for the answer to the previous question?

A) Lines 18–20 ("It was we…the Union")

B) Lines 37–41 ("To them…the poor")

C) Lines 43–47 ("even an oligarchy… household")

D) Lines 60–63 ("Hence…against Negroes")

41

The graph most strongly suggests that women's suffrage resulted in

A) no discernible impact upon on the outcomes of specific elections or the participation of specific individuals.

B) no change in the trend for voter participation prior to suffrage.

C) an immediate increase in voter participation and a maintaining of at least a 10 percent total increase for ten years.

D) a doubling of total voter participation due to both genders being allowed to vote followed by a slow return to previous percentages.

CONTINUE

1   1

Questions 42–52 are based on the following passages.

Passage 1 is adapted from a 1913 translation of J.H. Fabre's *The Life of the Fly*. Passage 2 is adapted from Stephen Jay Gould's 1982 essay "Nonmoral Nature."

Passage 1

The considerations which I have set forth seem to me strictly logical: the Anthrax,[1] owing to the very fact that he is free to take his nourishment where he pleases on the body of the fostering larva, must, for
5 his own protection, be made incapable of opening his victim's body. I am so utterly convinced of this harmonious relation between the eater and the eaten that I do not hesitate to set it up as a principle. I will therefore say this: whenever the egg of any kind of
10 insect is not fastened to the larva destined for its food, the young grub, free to select the attacking point and to change it at will, is as it were muzzled and consumes its provisions by a sort of suction, without inflicting any appreciable wound. This
15 restriction is essential to the maintenance of the victuals in good condition. My principle is already supported by examples many and various, whose depositions are all to the same effect. All insects— flies, ichneumon flies and beetles—scrupulously
20 spare their foster mother; they are careful not to tear her skin, so that the vessel may keep its liquid good to the last.

The wholesomeness of the victuals is not the only condition imposed: I find a second, which is no less
25 essential. The substance of the fostering larva must be sufficiently fluid to ooze through the unbroken skin under the action of the sucker. The necessary fluidity is realized as the time of the metamorphosis draws near. When they wished Medea to restore
30 Pelias to the vigor of youth, his daughters cut the old king's body to pieces and boiled it in a cauldron, for there can be no new existence without a prior dissolution. We must pull down before we can rebuild; the analysis of death is the first step towards
35 the synthesis of life. The substance of the grub that is to be transformed into a bee begins, therefore, by disintegrating and dissolving into a fluid broth. The materials of the future insect are obtained by a general recasting. Even as the founder puts his old
40 bronzes into the melting pot in order afterwards to

---

[1] The Anthrax is a type of bee fly.

cast them in a mold whence the metal will issue in a different shape, so life liquefies the grub, a mere digesting machine, now thrown aside, and out of its running matter produces the perfect insect, bee,
45 butterfly or beetle, the final manifestation of the living creature.

Passage 2

As I read through the nineteenth- and twentieth-century literature on ichneumons, nothing amused me more than the tension between an intellectual
50 knowledge that wasps should not be described in human terms and a literary or emotional inability to avoid the familiar categories of epic and narrative, pain and destruction, victim and vanquisher. We seem to be caught in the mythic structures of our
55 own cultural sagas, quite unable, even in our basic descriptions, to use any other language than the metaphors of battle and conquest. We cannot render this corner of natural history as anything but story, combining the themes of grim horror and fascination
60 and usually ending not so much with pity for the caterpillar as with admiration for the efficiency of the ichneumon.

I detect two basic themes in most epic descriptions: the struggles of prey and the ruthless
65 efficiency of parasites. Although we acknowledge that we may be witnessing little more than automatic instinct or physiological reaction, still we describe the defenses of hosts as though they represented conscious struggles. Thus, aphids kick and
70 caterpillars may wriggle violently as wasps attempt to insert their ovipositors. The pupa of the tortoiseshell butterfly (usually considered an inert creature silently awaiting its conversion from duckling to swan) may contort its abdominal region so sharply that attacking
75 wasps are thrown into the air. The caterpillars of *Hapalia*, when attacked by the wasp *Apanteles machaeralis*, drop suddenly from their leaves and suspend themselves in air by a silken thread. But the wasp may run down the thread and insert its eggs
80 nonetheless. Some hosts can encapsulate the injected egg with blood cells that aggregate and harden, thus suffocating the parasite.

CONTINUE

42

The author of Passage 1 refers to a "harmonious relation between the eater and the eaten" in line 7 to suggest that

A) insects are as comfortable in the role of predator as of prey.

B) the particular characteristics of each are best suited to enact their roles.

C) the symbiotic relationship between the two is mutually beneficial.

D) the euphonious sound produced by the two is compelling to the author.

43

In the first paragraph of Passage 1 (lines 1–22), the terms "victuals," "foster mother," and "vessel" refer to

A) the larva being devoured.

B) the maternal care given to insects.

C) nature's providential arrangements.

D) the Anthrax as it nourishes itself.

44

The author of Passage 1 mentions the "founder" and the "melting pot" (lines 39–40) primarily to

A) provide support for his claims regarding the nature of insect hierarchy.

B) suggest the infinite variety of actions within every area of insect life.

C) show one application of insect life to human affairs.

D) compare the insect transformation to a more familiar image.

45

As it is used in line 15, "restriction" most nearly means

A) conscious restraint.

B) necessary limitation.

C) surprising constriction.

D) unavoidable choice.

46

The best evidence for the validity of the claim in lines 48–53 ("nothing … vanquisher") is found in

A) Lines 1–2 ("The considerations … logical")

B) Lines 8–11 ("I will … food")

C) Lines 25–29 ("The substance … near")

D) Lines 29–33 ("When … dissolution")

47

The primary point of the first paragraph of Passage 2 (lines 47–62) is to

A) point out a problem many scientists have in writing about nature.

B) introduce a common misconception about the nature of insect life and suggest a method to correct it.

C) deride the writings of naturalists of the past in order to assert the superiority of collecting data to offering explanations.

D) insist upon the impossibility of true objectivity in scientific studies by exploring past examples.

1   **1**

48

The author of Passage 2 would most likely respond to the statement made in lines 33–35 ("We … life") of Passage 1 by

A) accepting the evidence behind the claim but offering a contradictory interpretation of that evidence.

B) agreeing that life and death are undeniably and irrevocably linked and suggesting further proofs of the linkage.

C) denying that such themes about the nature of human life and death can be drawn from the world of insects.

D) quibbling over the specific words but valuing the effort to convey the truths of life through the study of insects.

49

Which choice provides the best evidence for the answer to the previous question?

A) Lines 49–55 ("the tension …sagas")

B) Lines 59–62 ("combining … ichneumon")

C) Lines 63–65 ("I detect … parasites")

D) Lines 75–82 ("The caterpillars … parasite")

50

The author of Passage 2 presents the relationship between "automatic instinct" and "conscious struggles" as contrasting

A) basic needs and loftier goals.

B) lower and higher forms of life.

C) scientific fact and human interpretation.

D) nonmoral and immoral actions.

51

The two passages relate to each other in that

A) Passage 2 criticizes aspects of Passage 1's research methodology.

B) Passage 1 is an example of the trend Passage 2 examines.

C) Passage 1 raises a concern that Passage 2 resolves.

D) Passage 2 concurs with the conclusions drawn in Passage 1 using new data.

52

The author provides the references in lines 69–82 ("Thus … parasite") primarily to

A) provide more accurate descriptions of insect behavior than those he criticizes.

B) reveal the inefficient nature of actual relations in the natural world.

C) mock the methods of observation most common in earlier naturalists.

D) suggest the faulty kinds of descriptions given in previous works on insect behavior.

STOP

If you finish before time is called, you may check your work on this section only.
Do not turn to any other section.

2

2

Writing and Language Test

35 MINUTES, 44 QUESTIONS

Turn to Section 2 of your answer sheet to answer the questions in this section.

DIRECTIONS

Each passage below is accompanied by a number of questions. For some questions, you will consider how the passage might be revised to improve the expression of ideas. For other questions, you will consider how the passage might be edited to correct errors in sentence structure, usage, or punctuation. A passage or a question may be accompanied by one or more graphics (such as a table or graph) that you will consider as you make revising and editing decisions.

Some questions will direct you to an underlined portion of a passage. Other questions will direct you to a location in a passage or ask you to think about the passage as a whole.

After reading each passage, choose the answer to each question that most effectively improves the quality of writing in the passage or that makes the passage conform to the conventions of standard written English. Many questions include a "NO CHANGE" option. Choose that option if you think the best choice is to leave the relevant portion of the passage as it is.

Questions 1–11 are based on the following passage.

Dylan Goes Electric

—1—

In the summer of 1965, folk music was flourishing, both gaining a wider audience and spreading political messages through the medium of song. Perhaps the best known figure to emerge from this movement in the early 1960s was Bob **1** Dylan, whose songs were often political protests disguised as simple folk ballads. [A] His **2** songs, "Masters of War" and "Blowin' in the Wind" railed against war profiteers and the purposeless destruction of war, and songs like "The Times They Are A-Changin'" and "A Hard Rain's A-Gonna Fall" were

1

A) NO CHANGE
B) Dylan's
C) Dylan, who's
D) Dylan, his

2

A) NO CHANGE
B) songs "Masters of War," and "Blowin' in the Wind,"
C) songs "Masters of War" and "Blowin' in the Wind"
D) songs, "Masters of War," and "Blowin' in the Wind,"

CONTINUE

seen as prophecies of a coming revolution of peace, freedom, and equality.

—2—

Thus, when Dylan came to play the Newport Folk [3] Festival for the third year in a row in July 1965, promoters and fans were ready for another set of his familiar acoustic guitar and harmonica arrangements and excited to hear the "voice of a generation" continue to lead the call for political change in the form of folk music. What Dylan did instead [4] lead to immediate controversy, even [5] bitter anger. Apparently irritated by criticism that the Paul Butterfield Blues Band had received for playing electric blues, Dylan shocked his audience by performing with a full electric rock [6] band, and played new songs without political themes, such as

[3]

The author would like to revise this sentence to clarify the context of the performance in terms of the main idea of this paragraph. Which choice best accomplishes this?

A) Festival, a yearly folk festival held at Newport, RI,

B) Festival, the premier traditional folk music event at the time,

C) Festival, a precursor to later concerts like Bonnaroo, Coachella, and Lollapalooza,

D) Festival, a great opportunity for any new artist to make a mark on the world of folk music,

[4]

A) NO CHANGE

B) leads

C) led

D) has lead

[5]

A) NO CHANGE

B) sardonic vitriol.

C) depressed dejection.

D) unhappiness in some folks.

[6]

A) NO CHANGE

B) band and playing

C) band playing

D) band, they played

his now-classic "Like a Rolling Stone," ⑦ a song which would later be named the greatest rock song of all time by *Rolling Stone* magazine. [B]

—3—

But many people did not approve of this development. The response of the Newport audience was mixed, with both boos and cheers audible between songs in the recording; however many key figures in the folk movement were incredibly upset by his decision. [C] Listening to Dylan's performance at Newport, folk singer Pete Seeger allegedly threatened to cut the power cables with an ax, though he later claimed he did so because he was concerned that the audience could not understand Dylan's lyrics rather than offended at his electrically amplified sound. [D] Soon after, Joan Baez, who had often performed with Dylan, penned a song "To Bobby," imploring him to write folk songs of political protest again. **8** Universally, both Dylan's new sound and new themes were seen by some as failures to live up to his artistic duty.

7

The writer is considering deleting the underlined portion and changing the preceding comma to a period. Should the writer make this change?

A) Yes, because it adds information that is not relevant to the point of the sentence.

B) Yes, because it contradicts the rest of the sentence.

C) No, because it is needed to understand the main idea of the sentence.

D) No, because it provides a connection necessary to understand the next paragraph.

8

A) NO CHANGE

B) Furthermore, both

C) Conversely, both

D) Thus, both

CONTINUE ▶

—4—

Dylan's 1965 Newport performance has been re-examined to determine just how negative the initial [9] reaction was, Dylan saw the performance as an opportunity to take a new direction as an artist. In his view, the audience that made him popular had no more right to restrict his themes or control his choices as an artist than the government they wanted him to agitate against. [10]

Question [11] asks about the previous passage as a whole.

[9]

A) NO CHANGE
B) reactions were, Dylan
C) reaction was, but Dylan
D) reactions were, though Dylan

[10]

The author wants to add a sentence that effectively concludes the story by reiterating its main ideas and considering its relevance today. Which choice best accomplishes this?

A) Dylan has remained a popular and idiosyncratic artist, one of America's treasures as a songwriter, performer, and icon.

B) Dylan has continued to defy expectations in his long and successful career, changing his sound and themes freely to express his artistic independence.

C) Interestingly, Dylan later went on to record multiple acoustic folk records and wrote many more songs of political protest, so his change was short-lived.

D) Surprisingly, many of his fans from back in 1965 have since changed their minds about Dylan's decision, and they now can download the whole concert!

Think about the previous passage as a whole as you answer question 11.

[11]

The author wants to add the following sentence to the essay:

Dylan claims he didn't necessarily mean to offend: he saw changing his sound and themes as a natural part of his development as an artist.

Where should this addition be made?

A) Point A in Paragraph 1.
B) Point B in Paragraph 2.
C) Point C in Paragraph 3.
D) Point D in Paragraph 3.

CONTINUE ▶

2

2

Questions 12–22 are based on the following passage and supplementary material.

Exercise: It Does a Brain Good

—1—

For many years, there has been an overwhelming amount of research supporting the health and fitness benefits of regular exercise. However, recent research suggests that exercise may promote positive outcomes not only for the body but also for the mind. Studies indicate that aerobic exercise may have surprising effects on mental well-being, including **12** unexpected short-term psychological benefits and long-term cognitive benefits.

—2—

13 In addition to these immediate psychological benefits of exercise, consistent exercise has been shown to have more long-term mental benefits, as well. A recent study suggests that regular aerobic exercise can improve long-term cognitive functioning. The University of Minnesota study conducted in 2014 by Dr. David R. Jacobs and his **14** colleagues' testing the cardiorespiratory fitness (CRF) of healthy young people

12

A) NO CHANGE
B) unforeseen
C) inexplicable
D) DELETE the underlined portion.

13

Which of the following best combines the two underlined sentences?

A) A recent study suggests that regular aerobic exercise not only provides immediate psychological benefits but also improves long-term cognitive functioning.

B) A recent study suggests that regular aerobic exercise can improve long-term cognitive functioning in addition to its providing immediate psychological benefits from regular aerobic exercise.

C) On top of these immediate psychological benefits of exercise, consistent exercise has been shown to have more long-term mental benefits, as well; for example, a recent study suggests that regular aerobic exercise can improve long-term cognitive functioning.

D) In addition to these immediate psychological benefits of exercise, more long-term mental benefits of consistent exercise have been shown, and a study has suggested that regular aerobic exercise can improve long-term cognitive functioning.

14

A) NO CHANGE
B) colleague's tested
C) colleagues tests
D) colleagues tested

2   2

with an average age of 25. Jacobs and his team then re-tested as many of the same individuals as possible 25 years later. [15] Its results serve as a reminder of the importance of not only exercising while young, but also maintaining a consistent exercise program into middle age. First, those who showed greater CRF when first tested showed higher cognitive abilities across the [16] board, particularly for verbal memory. Second, those whose CRF decreased less between the initial test and the follow-up over two decades later showed better executive functioning—one of the key elements of effective mental activity—than those whose CRF had deteriorated more over the time between tests, indicating a less active lifestyle in the intervening years.

—3—

First, many studies in recent years have suggested that aerobic exercise [17] —even just ten minutes of brisk walking—can reduce symptoms for those who suffer from [18] anxiety or depression symptoms. Further, many psychologists and doctors recommend regular exercise [19] as apart of a program, together with medication and

---

15

A) NO CHANGE
B) Their results serve
C) Its result serves
D) Their results has served

16

A) NO CHANGE
B) board; particularly
C) board—particular
D) board: in particularly

17

The writer is considering deleting the underlined portion. Should the writer make this change?

A) Yes, because it contradicts the paragraph's emphasis on exercising more.
B) Yes, because it is already implied by the beginning of the sentence.
C) No, because it gives a detail that may help readers understand the point.
D) No, because it defines the unfamiliar term "aerobic exercise."

18

A) NO CHANGE
B) symptoms of anxiety or depression.
C) anxiety or depression.
D) anxiety symptoms or depression symptoms.

19

A) NO CHANGE
B) as apart in
C) as a part about
D) as a part of

therapy, to treat symptoms of these disorders. [20] Even those without a diagnosed anxiety or depression disorder, regular exercise has been shown to increase mental functioning and reduce stress.

—4—

These studies are just two recent pieces of evidence that add to our understanding of the many ways in which exercise benefits us—ways that go beyond physical fitness. [21] Most people, when asked about the benefits of exercise, don't think of mental and psychological aspects. Perhaps as these kinds of benefits become more widely proven and known, more people will be willing to take the time to reap the many benefits of exercise.

Responses to the Request to "State a Benefit of Exercise"

Benefit of Exercise	Number of Respondents	Percent of Respondents
Increased physical fitness	206	45.9
Control of chronic diseases	99	22
Prevention of chronic diseases	91	20.3
Mental well being	44	9.8
Other	9	2

Adapted from TJR Babwah and P. Nunes, "Exercise Habits in Trinidad: motivating forces and barriers." ©2010 by The University of the West Indies.

Question [22] asks about the previous passage as a whole.

[20]

A) NO CHANGE
B) Even for those
C) Even they
D) Even for them

[21]

The writer would like to revise this sentence to add specific data from the table to support the main point of the paragraph. Which choice best accomplishes this intention?

A) According to a recent survey, most people see the benefits of exercise as related primarily to long-term physical health, with very few citing cognitive or psychological benefits.

B) According to a recent survey, less than 10 percent of respondents cited mental well-being as a benefit of exercise.

C) Surprisingly, over 45 percent of people in a recent survey claimed that physical fitness was a benefit of exercise.

D) Physical fitness is still the main benefit of exercise that the majority of people think of, according to a recent survey, though other kinds of benefits are also cited.

Think about the previous passage as a whole as you answer question 22.

[22]

In order for the passage to be most logical, paragraph 3 should be placed

A) where it is now.
B) before paragraph 1.
C) after paragraph 1.
D) after paragraph 4.

CONTINUE

Questions 23–33 are based on the following passage and supplementary material.

Napping on the Job

The Centers for Disease Control and Prevention (CDC) consider lack of sleep to be a public health concern. According to a recent poll, **23** almost 30 percent of American adults reported sleeping six hours or less per night, which is not enough sleep. **24** It has become common knowledge—lack of sleep is associated with serious health **25** problems, such as, heart disease, high blood pressure, diabetes, and stroke. Adults who sleep poorly at night often report having trouble performing daily tasks. Even small sleep deficits have

Sleep Duration of U.S. Adults Aged 20+
(according to CDC survey)

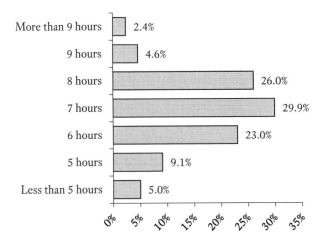

Adapted from CDC. ©2011 by the Centers for Disease Control and Prevention.

23

The writer wants to use the specific data in the graph to show how widespread the problem of insufficient sleep is. Which choice best accomplishes this?

A) NO CHANGE

B) many American adults sleep less than 5 hours per night, which is dangerously less than the recommended 7–9 hours per night.

C) only 3 percent of American adults get more than 10 hours of sleep each night, and only 7–9 hours are recommended.

D) over 35 percent of American adults reported sleeping 6 hours or less per night, well below the 7–9 hours recommended for adults.

24

The writer would like to change the beginning of this sentence to indicate that the majority of Americans are unaware of the health risks associated with a lack of sleep. Which choice best accomplishes this goal?

A) Some consequences of insufficient sleep may be temporary, but others are chronic and life threatening;

B) Both epidemiological and sleep deprivation studies support an alarming conclusion:

C) The CDC has partnered with other organizations in a widespread campaign to alert the public to a growing concern among health professionals:

D) A popular magazine recently published several articles discussing illnesses stemming from sleep deprivation—

25

A) NO CHANGE

B) problems such as:

C) problems; such as

D) problems, such as

noticeable impacts on coordination, alertness, and concentration. [26]

In the workplace, these deficits add up to decreased productivity, accidents, and lost revenue. An overtired [27] <u>workforce many</u> researchers have found, is less active and therefore less productive. By some estimates, the loss of productivity due to sleepiness among workers costs US businesses $63 billion dollars annually, and preventable workplace accidents cost businesses $31 billion dollars. The health of both workers and businesses depends on finding a way for employees to meet their sleep requirements.

One solution to daytime sleepiness comes from the National Aeronautics and Space Administration (NASA). In the eighties and nineties, NASA conducted field experiments in an effort to improve alertness and responsiveness among pilots. Reviewing the results, [28] <u>pilot error was reduced significantly and performance was boosted by as much as 100 percent by taking short naps while on duty.</u>

[26]

The writer is considering adding the following sentence:

> Sleep deprivation also affects teenagers: 70 percent of high-school students report sleeping fewer than the recommended number of hours a night.

Should the writer make this addition here?

A) Yes, because it introduces the central topic of the following paragraph.

B) Yes, because it allows the reader to compare the reported sleep statistics of workers to those of students.

C) No, because it contradicts evidence provided earlier in the paragraph.

D) No, because it focuses on data that is not directly related to the main point of the passage.

[27]

A) NO CHANGE

B) workforce: many

C) workforce, many

D) workforce—many

[28]

A) NO CHANGE

B) short naps were discovered while on duty by researchers to reduce pilot error significantly and boost performance by as much as 100 percent.

C) researchers discovered that short naps while on duty reduced pilot error significantly and boosted performance by as much as 100 percent.

D) a discovery was made that short naps while on duty reduced pilot error and boosted performance by as much as 100 percent.

Inspired by such studies, a growing number of employers have implemented nap-friendly policies in the workplace. Businesses from Ben and Jerry's to the New York Times have installed nap stations where tired workers can lie down to [29] reserve mentally and physically.

Experts recommend including several features in the development of a napping-friendly workplace environment. Employers should clearly designate the area in which employees can rest. It is important for workers to have a separate, dedicated space for napping because it reminds them that napping is a break from the regular work routine. In order to maximize rest time, napping should occur in a cool, dark, and quiet place.

[30] Ideally, the formulation of napping policies should be part of a discussion about how to create a workplace culture that is safe, healthy, and productive. Additionally, overtired workers should be evaluated for potential health problems contributing to [31] there fatigue. Proponents of workplace naps point out that employees are allowed to eat and exercise on breaks. Sleep, they argue, is a biological necessity and needs to be

29
A) NO CHANGE
B) recharge
C) resurrect
D) enliven

30
A) NO CHANGE
B) Nevertheless, the
C) Consequently, the
D) Alternatively, the

31
A) NO CHANGE
B) their
C) one's
D) his or her

accommodated by employers as well. That an increasing number of employers are supportive of napping practices [32] which is encouraging to sleep activists. [33] Soon, predicts author and sleep activist Arianna Huffington, nap rooms will be "as common as conference rooms."

32

A) NO CHANGE

B) that

C) and

D) DELETE the underlined portion.

33

The writer would like to conclude the paragraph with a sentence indicating that accommodating workplace napping is a trend among employers that will continue to increase in popularity. Which choice best accomplishes this goal?

A) NO CHANGE

B) Increasingly, their message is spreading to colleges and universities, and nap centers are springing up in campus libraries across the country to provide hard-working students a reprieve during study sessions.

C) Napping at work has proven beneficial, and in the future, more employees might sleep during work hours.

D) Employers continue to cite improved employee health, increased productivity, and reduced turnover rates as incentives for implementing napping policies.

CONTINUE

2

Questions 34–44 are based on the following passage.

Public Transportation

Ever since Henry Ford popularized the automobile in the early 20th century, the United States [34] had been a nation of cars. In 1956, President Eisenhower signed the Federal-Aid Highway [35] Act, which funded a 41,000 mile national system of interstate highways. The new highway system unified the country, [36] making it possible to travel by car throughout almost every state. Nonetheless, in the past decade more Americans have depended less on their cars, and the use of public transportation has increased by more than 20 percent in response to economic, health, and environmental concerns related to automobile use. In 2014, Americans took 10.8 billion trips on public transportation, the greatest number of trips in a single year in nearly 60 years. Responding to increased demand, many communities are investing in infrastructure for public transport.

Public transit is a key component of the economy in many regions. For those workers who use it, public transit provides an efficient and reliable method of travel. In fact, the majority of trips on public transportation are to and from the workplace. [37] However, public transit can also financially benefit individuals. For some, using public transportation is a logical response to high gas prices, and public transportation may even eliminate the need to have a car altogether.

34

A) NO CHANGE
B) has been
C) is
D) was

35

A) NO CHANGE
B) Act; and it funded
C) Act: funding
D) Act, which was funding

36

The author would like to conclude the sentence by indicating that the car became symbolic of American values. Which choice best accomplishes this goal?

A) NO CHANGE
B) allowing Americans to commute to work and encouraging the expansion of suburbs.
C) and the car became synonymous in the public imagination with American independence and individuality.
D) and within a decade, the number of car sales increased by more than 50 percent.

37

A) NO CHANGE
B) Moreover,
C) Even so,
D) Regardless,

CONTINUE

Driving is not only an economic burden but also a public health concern. Vehicle crashes are a significant cause of death in the United States: [38] in 2014, over 35,000 deaths resulted from almost 30,000 fatal crashes. The act of operating a vehicle itself creates stress, which adversely affects the health of drivers. Consistently, drivers who experience the longest commutes to work report the lowest sense of well-being and mood. Additionally, vehicle emissions contribute to the poor air quality that is linked to a variety of [39] ailments: including asthma, chronic bronchitis, and heart disease.

Using public transportation reduces the emissions [40] engaged in poor air quality, ozone depletion, and global climate change by as many as 37 million metric tons of carbon dioxide annually. Public transit also uses [41] as much energy per passenger as private vehicles, which saves the US more than 11 million gallons of

[38]

Which statement best supports the claim made previously in the sentence?

A) NO CHANGE

B) the number of licensed drivers increased from 163 million in 1988 to 210 million in 2010.

C) according to a recent survey, American drivers were ranked as the seventh worst in the world.

D) in 2010, the rate of alcohol impairment among drivers involved in fatal crashes was four times higher at night than during the day.

[39]

A) NO CHANGE

B) ailments—including

C) ailments, including

D) ailments; including

[40]

A) NO CHANGE

B) available

C) developed

D) implicated

[41]

Which choice results in a logical introduction to the second part of the sentence?

A) NO CHANGE

B) less energy per passenger than private vehicles,

C) more energy per passenger than private vehicles,

D) an unmeasurable amount of energy per passenger,

CONTINUE

gasoline each day. Environmental advocates cite these and other reasons [42] for use of and investment in public transit infrastructure.

[43] The development and expansion of public transit systems positively impacts local communities. The construction of infrastructure projects creates green jobs and extends subway lines and bus routes to new areas. Since 45 percent of Americans have no access to any mode of public transportation, expanding the country's transit systems would benefit millions of Americans, allowing [44] these to benefit from the modes of transportation vital to healthy communities. Although cars continue to remain the transportation mode of choice for most Americans, transportation researchers expect that growing energy and car ownership costs, an awareness of public and personal health risks, environmental concerns, and improved access will continue to increase the use of public transportation throughout the country.

42

A) NO CHANGE
B) for use of and investing in
C) for using and to invest in
D) for use and investing in

43

The writer is considering deleting this sentence. Should the writer make this change?

A) Yes, because it contradicts the paragraph's claim that some communities currently are not served by any form of public transportation.
B) Yes, because it doesn't include any statistics to support its assertion that expanding public transit provides benefits to local communities.
C) No, because it provides a logical introduction to the paragraph and sets up the information that follows.
D) No, because it provides an example of the impact of public transportation.

44

A) NO CHANGE
B) whom
C) those
D) them

STOP

**If you finish before time is called, you may check your work on this section only.
Do not turn to any other section.**

Math Test – No Calculator

25 MINUTES, 20 QUESTIONS

Turn to Section 3 of your answer sheet to answer the questions in this section.

DIRECTIONS

For questions 1–15, solve each problem, choose the best answer from the choices provided, and fill in the corresponding circle on your answer sheet. **For questions 16–20**, solve the problems and enter your answer in the grid on the answer sheet. Please refer to the directions before question 16 on how to enter your answers in the grid. You may use any available space in your test booklet for scratch work.

NOTES

1. The use of calculators **is not permitted**.

2. All variables and expressions used represent real numbers unless otherwise indicated.

3. Figures provided in this test are drawn to scale unless otherwise indicated.

4. All figures lie in a plane unless otherwise indicated.

5. Unless otherwise indicated, the domain of a given function f is the set of real numbers x for which $f(x)$ is a real number.

REFERENCE

$A = \pi r^2$
$C = 2\pi r$

$A = \ell w$

$A = \frac{1}{2}bh$

$c^2 = a^2 + b^2$

Special Right Triangles

$V = \ell wh$

$V = \pi r^2 h$

$V = \frac{4}{3}\pi r^3$

$V = \frac{1}{3}\pi r^2 h$

$V = \frac{1}{3}\ell wh$

The number of degrees of arc in a circle is 360.
The number of radians of arc in a circle is 2π.
The sum of the measures in degrees of the angles in a triangle is 180.

CONTINUE

3 **3**

1

What is the value of $8a + 5$ if $4a = 24$?

A) 6

B) 29

C) 48

D) 53

2

Given the function $f(x) = 3x^2 - 4x$, which of the following is equal to $f(2x)$?

A) $6x^2 - 4x$

B) $12x^2 - 8x$

C) $18x^3 - 6x^2$

D) $36x^2 - 8x$

3

What is the value of $5x$ if $\dfrac{3}{x} = \dfrac{21}{x+12}$?

A) 15

B) 10

C) 5

D) 2

4

$$\frac{m}{n} = 3$$
$$6(n-4) = m$$

Given the system of equations above, what is the value of n?

A) 4

B) 8

C) 16

D) 24

CONTINUE

5

If $\dfrac{y+2x}{x} = \dfrac{10}{3}$, which of the following must also be true?

A) $\dfrac{x}{y} = \dfrac{3}{16}$

B) $\dfrac{x}{y} = \dfrac{3}{4}$

C) $\dfrac{y+x}{y} = \dfrac{3}{4}$

D) $\dfrac{y-2x}{y} = -\dfrac{3}{8}$

6

The point (p, q), where p and q are positive integers, lies on the line given by the equation $y = mx + 3$, where m is a constant. What is the slope of the line in terms of p and q?

A) $\dfrac{q-3}{p}$

B) $\dfrac{p-3}{q}$

C) $\dfrac{3-q}{p}$

D) $\dfrac{3-p}{q}$

7

If $x - 3 = \sqrt{p(x-3)}$, where $p = 2$, what are the possible values of x?

A) 3 and 5

B) 3 only

C) 5 only

D) 1 and 5

8

Which of the following equations represents a line that is perpendicular to the line with the equation $6x + 2y = 9$?

A) $y = -3x + 4$

B) $y = -\dfrac{1}{3}x - 5$

C) $y = \dfrac{1}{3}x + 2$

D) $y = 3x - 3$

CONTINUE

9

Katie is an English tutor. The amount of money, p, Katie profits in dollars can be modeled by the equation $44.50h = p + 2.20h,$ where h represents the number of hours spent tutoring and $2.20 is an average per-student travel expense. What does 44.50 represent in this equation?

A) The total amount of money charged by Katie after working h hours

B) The amount of money Katie charges per hour

C) The number of students whom Katie has tutored

D) The total amount of money paid by a student after h hours

10

In a table tennis tournament that begins with a draw of 64 people, half of the players are eliminated each round. Which of the following functions represents the number of people left in the tournament after r rounds?

A) $f(r) = 64(2)^r$

B) $f(r) = \dfrac{1}{2}(64)^r$

C) $f(r) = 64\left(\dfrac{1}{2}\right)^r$

D) $f(r) = 2\left(\frac{1}{2}\right)^{-r}$

11

Which of the following complex numbers is equivalent to $\dfrac{6+3i}{2-5i}$? (Note: $i = \sqrt{-1}$)

A) $\dfrac{-3-15i}{25}$

B) $\dfrac{12+5i}{16}$

C) $\dfrac{-3+36i}{29}$

D) $\dfrac{-5-5i}{21}$

12

$$A = 14.6 + 2.35d$$
$$B = 6.9 + 3.45d$$

In the equations above, A and B represent the heights, in centimeters, of two plants d days after a starting date. For what value of d will the plants have equal heights?

A) 11

B) 9

C) 7

D) 6

CONTINUE

13

If for all x, $(ax+4)(3x+b)=18x^2+cx+12$, what is the value of c ?

A) 30

B) 24

C) 18

D) 15

14

Given the equations $3x+4y=20$ and $y=x(-x-4)$, how many solutions (x, y) exist for the system?

A) 0

B) 1

C) 2

D) Cannot be determined

15

If $4a-2b=10$, what is the value of $\dfrac{9^a}{3^b}$?

A) 9^2

B) 3^{10}

C) 3^5

D) 3^2

CONTINUE

3 3

DIRECTIONS

For questions 16–20, solve the problem and enter your answer in the grid, as described below, on the answer sheet.

1. Although not required, it is suggested that you write your answer in the boxes at the top of the columns to help you fill in the circles accurately. You will receive credit only if the circles are filled in correctly.
2. Mark no more than one circle in any column.
3. No question has a negative answer.
4. Some problems may have more than one correct answer. In such cases, grid only one answer.

5. **Mixed numbers** such as $3\frac{1}{2}$ must be be gridded as 3.5 or 7/2. If $\boxed{3\,1/2}$ is entered into the grid, it will be interpreted as $\frac{31}{2}$, not $3\frac{1}{2}$.)

6. **Decimal answers:** If you obtain a decimal answer with more digits than the grid can accommodate, it may be either rounded or truncated, but it must fill the entire grid.

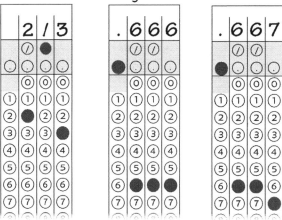

Answer: $\frac{7}{13}$ Answer: 2.5

Write answer in boxes →

← Fraction line

Grid in result

← Decimal Point

Acceptable ways to grid $\frac{2}{3}$ are:

Answer: 210 – either position is correct

NOTE: You may start your answers in any column, space permitting. Columns you don't need to use should be left blank.

16

If $k > 0$ and $k^4 + 5 = 21$, what is the value of k ?

17

$$3j - k = -4$$
$$2j + 5k = 3$$

According to the system of equations above, what is the value of $j + k$?

18

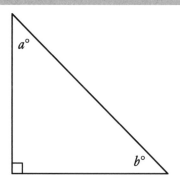

Note: Figure not drawn to scale

In the triangle above, the cosine of $b°$ is equal to 0.8. What is the value of the sine of $a°$?

CONTINUE

19

As a probe descends to the Kuril Trench in the Pacific Ocean, it records the amount of dissolved oxygen in the water in units of parts per million (ppm). At depths below 2,000 meters, the dissolved oxygen drops at a constant rate of d ppm for every change in depth of 100 meters, until it reaches zero. At a depth of 2,530 meters, the dissolved oxygen is measured to be 205 ppm. At a depth of 3,030 meters, the dissolved oxygen is measured to be 65 ppm. What is the value of d ?

20

If $b = 3\sqrt{5}$ and $4b = \sqrt{5x}$, what is the value of x ?

STOP

If you finish before time is called, you may check your work on this section only.
Do not turn to any other section.

Math Test – Calculator

55 MINUTES, 38 QUESTIONS

Turn to Section 4 of your answer sheet to answer the questions in this section.

DIRECTIONS

For questions 1–30, solve each problem, choose the best answer from the choices provided, and fill in the corresponding circle on your answer sheet. **For questions 31–38,** solve the problems and enter your answer in the grid on the answer sheet. Please refer to the directions before question 31 on how to enter your answers in the grid. You may use any available space in your test booklet for scratch work.

NOTES

1. The use of calculators is **permitted**.

2. All variables and expressions used represent real numbers unless otherwise indicated.

3. Figures provided in this test are drawn to scale unless otherwise indicated.

4. All figures lie in a plane unless otherwise indicated.

5. Unless otherwise indicated, the domain of a given function f is the set of real numbers x for which $f(x)$ is a real number.

REFERENCE

$A = \pi r^2$
$C = 2\pi r$

$A = \ell w$

$A = \frac{1}{2}bh$

$c^2 = a^2 + b^2$

Special Right Triangles

$V = \ell w h$

$V = \pi r^2 h$

$V = \frac{4}{3}\pi r^3$

$V = \frac{1}{3}\pi r^2 h$

$V = \frac{1}{3}\ell w h$

The number of degrees of arc in a circle is 360.
The number of radians of arc in a circle is 2π.
The sum of the measures in degrees of the angles in a triangle is 180.

CONTINUE ➡

4 **4**

1

Luis is having carpeting installed in his living room. Each square yard of carpeting costs $50, and the labor for the installation costs $160. If Luis spends $710 to carpet his living room, what is the area of Luis' living room in square yards?

A) 11

B) 13

C) 14

D) 15

2

Given that 1 lb of coffee beans can make 40 cups of coffee, how many cups of coffee can be made from 20 oz of coffee beans (1 lb = 16 oz)?

A)   8

B)   44

C)   50

D)   86

3

A museum sells three types of tickets: child, adult, and senior. Child tickets cost $10, adult tickets cost $15, and senior tickets cost $12. Which of the following represents the amount of money the museum makes if they sell c child tickets, a adult tickets, and s senior tickets?

A) $10a + 12s + 15c$

B) $10c + 12s - 15a$

C) $10c + 12s + 15a$

D) $(10 + 12 + 15)(c + s + a)$

4

$$v = 27 + 6t$$

A car drives at an initial velocity of 27 miles per hour before accelerating at a constant rate of 6 miles per hour per second in order to get on the highway. The equation above models the car's velocity v, in miles per hour, in terms of the time t, in seconds, that the car has been accelerating. If the car's velocity is 66 miles per hour, how many seconds has it been accelerating?

A)   6.5

B)   11

C)   15.5

D)   33

5

If $\dfrac{28}{9}z = \dfrac{35}{3}$, what is the value of z ?

A) $\dfrac{15}{4}$

B) $\dfrac{5}{4}$

C) $\dfrac{4}{5}$

D) $\dfrac{4}{15}$

6

| 1 dekaliter = 10 liters |
| 1,000 milliliters = 1 liter |

A juice company ships its product in boxes each containing 3 dekaliters of juice. Based on the information above, how many milliliters are there in each box?

A)   0.0003

B)   30

C)   300

D) 30,000

7

Electronics City Computer Sales				
	April	May	June	Total
Vishal	10	11	7	28
Josh	4	8	6	18
Sonny	12	14	14	40
Gigi	9	8	6	23
Total	35	41	33	109

The table above shows the number of computers sold over a three-month period by each member of the sales staff at Electronics City. Sonny's May and June computer sales together make up what fraction of all computers sold in the three-month period?

A) $\dfrac{28}{40}$

B) $\dfrac{14}{40}$

C) $\dfrac{40}{109}$

D) $\dfrac{28}{109}$

Questions 8 and 9 refer to the following information.

Assuming its mass is constant, an object's momentum is directly proportional to its velocity. A bowling ball rolling with a velocity of 2 meters per second has a momentum of 12 kilogram-meters per second.

8

What will be the ball's momentum if it has a velocity of 10 meters per second?

A) $2.4 \text{ kg} \cdot \text{m/s}$

B) $20 \text{ kg} \cdot \text{m/s}$

C) $60 \text{ kg} \cdot \text{m/s}$

D) $240 \text{ kg} \cdot \text{m/s}$

9

The bowling ball starts out with a velocity of 4 meters per second but by the time it hits the pins its speed has decreased 27 percent. What is its momentum when it hits the pins?

A) $6.48 \text{ kg} \cdot \text{m/s}$

B) $17.52 \text{ kg} \cdot \text{m/s}$

C) $27.00 \text{ kg} \cdot \text{m/s}$

D) $70.08 \text{ kg} \cdot \text{m/s}$

10

The function $f(x)$ has zeros (roots) at $x = 5$, $x = 2$, and $x = -3$. Which of the following could be the function $f(x)$?

A) $(x^2 - 2x - 15)(x - 2)$

B) $(x^2 - 2x - 15)(x + 2)$

C) $(x^2 - 2x + 15)(x - 2)$

D) $(x^2 + 2x + 15)(x - 2)$

11

Eddy surveyed 50 students who were waiting in line to buy lunch in his school's cafeteria. Since 45 of the 50 students surveyed said they preferred the school lunch to the local fast food restaurant, Eddy concluded that exactly 90 percent of the entire school's 330 students would prefer the school lunch to the fast food restaurant. His friends had the following criticisms of Eddy's conclusion:

Kate said one cannot make conclusions about an exact percentage of a population based on a sample of it.

Elizabeth said that Eddy's conclusions are unreliable because of a bias in his chosen sample.

Ian said that there is no whole number, and thus no appropriate number of people, that is exactly 90 percent of 330.

Which of Eddy's friends is/are correct?

A) Kate only

B) Kate and Elizabeth only

C) Elizabeth and Ian only

D) All three are correct

12

Scores							
35	71	72	75	77	85	87	87
87	87	87	88	88	88	90	91
92	93	93	93	95	96	100	100

The table above shows the scores that students in a biology class received on their final exam. The score of 35 is an outlier. If that score were removed from the set, which of the following would change by the greatest amount?

A) Mean

B) Median

C) Range

D) Mode

13

$$h(t) = 80,000\left(1 - \frac{12}{100}\right)^t$$

Leonardo just bought a new boat whose value depreciates at a rate of 12 percent per year. The expression above gives the value of his boat, in dollars, after t years has passed. Which of the following expressions could be used to determine the number of years it would take for the value of his boat to decrease by 25 percent?

A) $20,000 = 80,000\left(1 - \dfrac{12}{100}\right)^t$

B) $20,000 = 80,000\left(1 - \dfrac{25}{100}\right)^t$

C) $60,000 = 80,000\left(1 - \dfrac{12}{100}\right)^t$

D) $60,000 = 80,000\left(1 - \dfrac{12}{100}\right)^{4t}$

CONTINUE

14

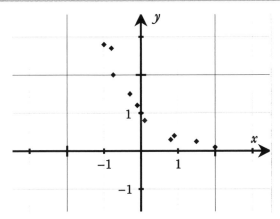

The above scatterplot shows a relationship that can be approximately modeled by which of the following equations if $0 < m < 1$?

A) $y = m^x$

B) $y = x^m$

C) $y = -mx$

D) $y = \dfrac{x}{m}$

15

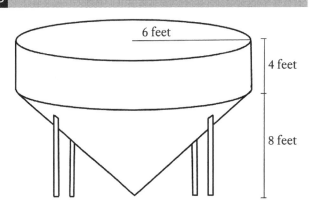

Vladimir owns a food company that sells blueberry jam in 18 in³ jars. He makes his jam in large vats as shown above, composed of a cone base and a shorter cylindrical body. If a batch of jam fills the vat to the very top, approximately how many jars can he fill from one vat of blueberry jam (12 in = 1 ft)?

A) 14,000

B) 25,000

C) 42,000

D) 72,000

CONTINUE

4   **4**

16

A large group of students took a test. The median score was 75 while the average score was 81. Which factor would, if true, best account for the difference between the average and median scores?

A) Most of the students scored in the C range (71–80).

B) No students failed the test (scored below 65).

C) No students scored higher than 90.

D) A few students scored much higher than the rest of the class.

17

Mario is cutting a pipe that is 66 inches long into three pieces. The second piece is 50 percent longer than the first, and the third piece is twice as long as the second. How long, in inches, is the longest piece?

A) 12

B) 18

C) 24

D) 36

18

Sheila had a bag of small candies, of which she gave away 70 percent. Her friend returned to Sheila a quantity of candy that equaled 20 percent of the amount Sheila had remaining after giving away the 70 percent. What is the original amount of candy in the bag in terms of the amount, x, that Sheila has now?

A) $(0.3)(1.2)x$

B) $\dfrac{x}{(0.3)(1.2)}$

C) $0.5x$

D) $2x$

19

Mrs. Brennan wants to buy x computers for her company and has a budget of B dollars. If she buys x computers today, they will cost \$1,000 each, and she will need to raise an additional \$2,000, but if she waits two months, the computers will cost \$900 each and she will have \$400 left over. What is the value of B?

A) \$24,000

B) \$22,000

C) \$21,600

D) \$20,000

4 **4**

Questions 20–22 refer to the following information.

The table below shows the number of international tourists visiting 10 countries over a three-year period.

International Tourism: Number of Arrivals per Year			
Country Name	2011	2012	2013
France	81,550,000	83,051,000	84,726,000
United States	62,821,000	66,657,000	69,768,000
Spain	56,177,000	57,464,000	60,661,000
China	57,581,000	57,725,000	55,686,000
Italy	46,119,000	46,360,000	47,704,000
Turkey	34,654,000	35,698,000	37,795,000
Germany	28,374,000	30,411,000	31,545,000
United Kingdom	29,306,000	29,282,000	31,169,000
Russian Federation	24,932,000	28,177,000	30,792,000
Thailand	19,230,000	22,354,000	26,547,000
Total	440,744,000	457,179,000	476,393,000

20

If the figures for the international tourists in 2012 were represented in a pie chart, what would be the best approximation for the measurement of the central angle for the portion of the pie chart representing the number of international tourists visiting the United States?

A) 37°

B) 46°

C) 52°

D) 74°

21

Which of the following best approximates the percent increase from 2012 to 2013 in the number of international tourists visiting Thailand?

A) 16%

B) 19%

C) 28%

D) 38%

22

The average increase, per year, for international tourists going to Germany between 2011 and 2013 is closest to that of which other country?

A) United Kingdom

B) China

C) France

D) Spain

CONTINUE

23

Vocabulary Quiz Scores	
Test Score	Number of Students
100	1
90	5
80	10
70	8
60	2

The table above shows the distribution of test scores in Mrs. Keaton's English class. Which of the following sets of test scores, if added, would change the standard deviation of the distribution the least?

A) 90, 90, 90

B) 70, 80, 85

C) 100, 100, 60

D) 60, 60, 60

---▼---

Questions 24 and 25 refer to the following information.

$$F = \frac{Gm_1m_2}{r^2}$$

The equation above defines the force, in newtons, of gravity between two objects in terms of the masses of the two objects m_1 and m_2 and the distance between the two objects r. G is the universal gravitational constant, equaling approximately 6.674×10^{-11}.

24

Which of the following expresses the square of the distance between two objects as defined by the masses of the two objects and the force of gravity between them?

A) $r^2 = \dfrac{m_1m_2}{GF}$

B) $r^2 = \dfrac{Gm_1m_2}{F}$

C) $r^2 = \dfrac{F}{Gm_1m_2}$

D) $r^2 = FGm_1m_2$

25

The Planet Quenya's elliptical orbit around its star is shaped such that the farthest distance away from the star (at the aphelion) is three times the nearest distance (at the perihelion). If the gravitational attraction between the planet and its star is called g, then what is the ratio of g at the aphelion to g at the perihelion?

A) $\dfrac{1}{3}$

B) $\dfrac{1}{9}$

C) $\dfrac{1}{27}$

D) $\dfrac{1}{81}$

---▲---

CONTINUE

4 **4**

26

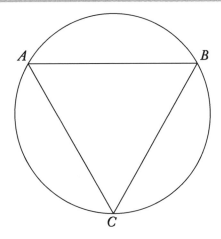

If $\triangle ABC$ is equilateral and the length of $\overset{\frown}{ABC}$ is 18π, what is the radius of the circle?

A)   6

B)   9

C)   13.5

D)   18

27

In order to ride the Kiddie Coaster at the local amusement park, a child must be at least 34 inches tall and no taller than 56 inches. Which of the following expressions can be used to determine whether a child h inches tall can ride the coaster?

I. $34 \geq h \geq 56$

II. $|h - 45| \leq 11$

III. $56 - h > 22$

A) I only

B) II only

C) I and III only

D) I, II, and III

CONTINUE

28

The population of an ant colony is expected to increase by 34 percent from one month to the next over the course of a year. What type of relationship should be expected between the age of the colony, in months, and its population over that year?

A) A linear relationship whose graph has a positive slope

B) A linear relationship whose graph has a negative slope

C) An exponential relationship in which higher populations correspond to higher ages of the colony

D) A quadratic relationship in which higher populations correspond to higher ages of the colony

29

For a polynomial $f(x)$, $f(4) = 5$. Which of the following must therefore be true about $f(x)$?

A) The leading coefficient of $f(x)$ is 4.

B) The remainder when $f(x)$ is divided by $(x-4)$ is 5.

C) $(x-4)$ is a factor of $f(x)$.

D) $(x-5)$ is a factor of $f(x)$.

30

	Less than 3 hours	3 to 6 hours	More than 6 hours	Total
Class 1	6	19	5	30
Class 2	8	15	7	30
Total	14	34	12	60

A teacher asked the students in two of his classes how many hours they had spent studying for their recent midterm. The results are shown in the table above. If a student is chosen from those that studied at most 6 hours, what is the probability the student is from Class 1?

A) $\dfrac{5}{30}$

B) $\dfrac{5}{12}$

C) $\dfrac{25}{48}$

D) $\dfrac{25}{30}$

CONTINUE

DIRECTIONS

For questions 31–38, solve the problem and enter your answer in the grid, as described below, on the answer sheet.

1. Although not required, it is suggested that you write your answer in the boxes at the top of the columns to help you fill in the circles accurately. You will receive credit only if the circles are filled in correctly.
2. Mark no more than one circle in any column.
3. No question has a negative answer.
4. Some problems may have more than one correct answer. In such cases, grid only one answer.

5. **Mixed numbers** such as $3\frac{1}{2}$ must be be gridded as 3.5 or 7/2. If $\boxed{3\,1\,/\,2}$ is entered into the grid, it will be interpreted as $\frac{31}{2}$, not $3\frac{1}{2}$.)

6. **Decimal answers:** If you obtain a decimal answer with more digits than the grid can accommodate, it may be either rounded or truncated, but it must fill the entire grid.

Answer: $\frac{7}{13}$

Write answer in boxes → ← Fraction line

Grid in result

Answer: 2.5

← Decimal Point

Acceptable ways to grid $\frac{2}{3}$ are:

Answer: 210 – either position is correct

NOTE: You may start your answers in any column, space permitting. Columns you don't need to use should be left blank.

31

A tree with an initial height of 1 meter grows at an average rate of 1.2 meters per year. At that rate, how many years will it take for the tree to reach a height of 19 meters?

32

A partially filled gas tank contains 2 gallons of gasoline. If a fuel pump can pump at 0.5 gallons per second and the maximum capacity of the tank is 14 gallons, after how much time (in seconds) will the tank be full?

33

The graph of the function $g(x) = 2x^2 - 6x + c$ contains the point $(2, 5)$ in the standard xy-coordinate plane. What is the value of c?

CONTINUE

4 **4**

34

Andy and Jen plan to save a combined $420 each month, and Jen will contribute $80 more than Andy each month. How much (in dollars) will Andy have contributed after six months?

35

$$x^2 + y^2 - 6x - 8y = -16$$

The equation above defines a circle in the xy-coordinate plane. What is the length of the circle's radius?

36

Lawnmowers Sold

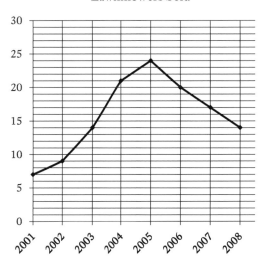

The line graph above shows the number of lawnmowers sold at a local hardware store between the years 2001 and 2008. According to the graph, the number of lawnmowers sold in 2001 is what fraction of the number sold in 2004?

CONTINUE

37

$$h(x) = \frac{1}{(x+3)^2 + (x+3) - 42}$$

For what value of $x > 0$ is the function $h(x)$ above undefined?

38

Anthony deposited $1,200 into a bank account that pays interest at an annual rate of 1.5 percent. Anthony's friend Shaun found an account that earns 3 percent interest compounded annually and made an initial deposit of $1,000 into this account at the same time Anthony made his. After ten years if neither Anthony nor Shaun deposit or withdraw any additional money into their accounts, how much more money will Anthony have in his account than Shaun will have in his? (Round your answer to the nearest dollar and disregard the $ sign when gridding your response.)

STOP

If you finish before time is called, you may check your work on this section only.
Do not turn to any other section.

Practice Test Answer Keys

Question Types

Reading Question Types

WIC   **Words in Context:** These questions ask about the meaning or use of specific words or phrases as they are used in the passage.

COE   **Command of Evidence:** These questions are usually in two parts, with the first being a challenging reading comprehension question and the second question providing line numbers to choose from for the best evidence for the correct answer. When these questions are paired, **both** questions are coded as **COE** in the answer keys.

IG   **Informational Graphic:** These questions are based on what the test calls "supplemental materials," such as graphs, tables or maps.

RC   **Reading Comprehension:** These questions make up the remainder of the test questions, asking about such things as tone, main ideas, or inferences.

Writing Question Types

SEC   **Standard English Conventions:** These questions are based on rules for grammar and correct usage, covering topics such as punctuations, pronoun reference, sentence structure and more.

EOI   **Expression of Ideas:** These questions are based on the context of the passage, so there are no rules to learn to answer them. They often ask students to do certain compositional tasks, including ordering of sentences or paragraphs, transitioning between ideas, adding or deleting text, and much more.

Math Question Types

HOA   **Heart of Algebra:** These questions involve the kind of basic algebraic translation, equation solving, and linear expression found in a first-year Algebra class.

PAM   **Passport to Advanced Math:** These questions involve the kind of algebraic form changes and higher level functions found both in a first-year and a second-year Algebra class.

PSD   **Problem Solving and Data Analysis:** These questions include manipulating data from graphs and tables, as well as data representation topics such as percent, probability, and statistics.

ATM   **Additional Topics in Math:** These questions include geometry and trigonometry topics, plus a few lesser-taught topics such as complex numbers.

How to Score your SAT Practice Test

Math

1. Count the number of correct answers on Sections 3 and 4 and add them up to find your raw score.

2. Use the Raw Score Conversion Table on the following page to convert your raw score to a scaled score on the 200–800 point scale.

Evidence-Based Reading and Writing

1. First count the number of correct answers on Section 1 (the Reading Test). That is your Reading raw score. Use the Raw Score Conversion Table to convert your Reading raw score to a scaled score.

2. Next, count the number of correct answers on Section 2 (the Writing and Language Test). That is your Writing and Language raw score. Use the Raw Score Conversion Table to convert your Writing and Language raw score to a scaled score.

3. Add your Reading scaled score to your Writing and Language scaled score, and multiple the sum by 10. This is your Evidence-Based Reading and Writing Test score.

Example

> Tarika took SAT Practice Test 1 and answered 35 of the 52 questions correctly on the SAT Reading Test and 24 of the 44 questions correctly on the SAT Writing and Language Test. Using the Raw Score Conversion Table for Test 1, she calculates that she received an SAT Reading Test score of 29 and an SAT Writing and Language Test score of 26. She adds 29 to 26 (giving a total of 55) and then multiplies 55 by 10 to determine her SAT Evidence-Based Reading and Writing Section score of 550.

Total Score out of 1600

Add your Evidence-Based Reading and Writing Section score to your Math Section score. The result is your total score on the SAT Practice Test on a scale of 400–1600.

Answer Explanations Icons

 Indicates that a test-taking strategy can be applied

 Warns of a common error to avoid

 Alerts to the possibility of using an alternative method

Test 1: Answer Key

Reading Test

Q	A	TYPE	Q	A	TYPE	Q	A	TYPE	Q	A	TYPE	Q	A	TYPE
1.	C	RC	11.	A	COE	21.	B	RC	31.	B	COE	42.	A	COE
2.	D	WIC	12.	B	COE	22.	D	RC	32.	B	COE	43.	C	COE
3.	A	RC	13.	C	RC	23.	D	WIC	33.	A	RC	44.	D	RC
4.	A	COE	14.	D	RC	24.	C	COE	34.	C	RC	45.	C	RC
5.	D	COE	15.	A	COE	25.	B	COE	35.	D	COE	46.	C	WIC
6.	C	RC	16.	B	COE	26.	C	COE	36.	B	COE	47.	D	COE
7.	A	WIC	17.	C	WIC	27.	B	COE	37.	C	WIC	48.	D	COE
8.	B	COE	18.	C	WIC	28.	D	WIC	38.	A	WIC	49.	B	RC
9.	D	COE	19.	C	RC	29.	A	RC	39.	C	RC	50.	C	RC
10.	A	RC	20.	B	IG	30.	D	RC	40.	A	COE	51.	B	RC
									41.	C	COE	52.	B	IG

Writing and Language Test

Q	A	TYPE	Q	A	TYPE	Q	A	TYPE	Q	A	TYPE
1.	A	EOI	12.	C	SEC	23.	B	EOI	34.	D	EOI
2.	B	EOI	13.	B	EOI	24.	B	EOI	35.	C	EOI
3.	D	EOI	14.	B	EOI	25.	C	EOI	36.	D	EOI
4.	B	EOI	15.	D	SEC	26.	C	SEC	37.	C	SEC
5.	B	SEC	16.	D	SEC	27.	A	SEC	38.	B	EOI
6.	D	SEC	17.	B	EOI	28.	D	SEC	39.	B	EOI
7.	A	SEC	18.	C	SEC	29.	B	EOI	40.	D	EOI
8.	A	EOI	19.	C	EOI	30.	B	SEC	41.	B	SEC
9.	C	SEC	20.	A	EOI	31.	D	EOI	42.	B	EOI
10.	B	SEC	21.	D	SEC	32.	A	EOI	43.	A	SEC
11.	A	EOI	22.	D	EOI	33.	A	SEC	44.	D	EOI

Math Test – No Calculator

Q	A	TYPE	Q	A	TYPE	Q	A	TYPE
1.	C	HOA	11.	A	ATM	16.	3 or 6	HOA
2.	A	HOA	12.	C	PAM	17.	6	PAM
3.	C	PAM	13.	A	HOA	18.	4/5 or 0.8	ATM
4.	B	HOA	14.	D	PAM	19.	3/8 or 0.375	HOA
5.	B	PAM	15.	D	PAM	20.	8	ATM
6.	C	HOA						
7.	B	PAM						
8.	B	PAM						
9.	C	HOA						
10.	A	HOA						

Math Test – Calculator

Q	A	TYPE	Q	A	TYPE	Q	A	TYPE	Q	A	TYPE
1.	B	HOA	11.	D	HOA	21.	B	PSD	31.	11	HOA
2.	C	ATM	12.	A	PSD	22.	B	PSD	32.	2	PAM
3.	B	HOA	13.	D	PSD	23.	C	PSD	33.	$5 \le x \le 6.25$ or $5 \le x \le 25/4$	HOA
4.	A	PSD	14.	C	PAM	24.	D	ATM	34.	5	PSD
5.	C	PSD	15.	C	HOA	25.	C	PAM	35.	7	HOA
6.	D	PSD	16.	A	PSD	26.	B	PAM	36.	90	PSD
7.	B	PAM	17.	C	PSD	27.	B	HOA	37.	64	PAM
8.	C	PSD	18.	A	PSD	28.	C	PSD	38.	3/2 or 1.5	ATM
9.	D	HOA	19.	B	PAM	29.	C	PSD			
10.	A	PAM	20.	B	HOA	30.	C	PAM			

Test 1: Raw Score Conversion Table

Raw Score	Reading Test	Writing and Language Test	Mathematics Test
0	10	10	200
1	10	10	200
2	10	10	210
3	11	11	230
4	12	12	240
5	13	13	260
6	14	14	270
7	14	15	280
8	15	16	300
9	16	16	310
10	17	17	320
11	17	18	330
12	18	18	350
13	18	19	360
14	19	20	370
15	19	20	380
16	20	21	390
17	20	21	410
18	21	22	420
19	21	23	430
20	21	23	440
21	22	24	450
22	23	24	460
23	23	25	470
24	24	26	480
25	24	26	490
26	25	27	500
27	25	27	510
28	26	28	520
29	26	29	520
30	27	29	530
31	27	30	540
32	28	30	540
33	28	31	550
34	29	32	560
35	30	32	560
36	30	33	570
37	31	34	580
38	31	34	580
39	32	35	590
40	32	36	600
41	33	37	600
42	34	39	610
43	34	39	620
44	35	40	630
45	36		640
46	37		650
47	38		660
48	38		670
49	39		680
50	39		690
51	40		700
52	40		710

Raw Score	Reading Test	Writing and Language Test	Mathematics Test
53			730
54			740
55			760
56			770
57			790
58			800

Test 2: Answer Key

Reading Test

Q	A	TYPE	Q	A	TYPE	Q	A	TYPE	Q	A	TYPE	Q	A	TYPE
1.	D	COE	11.	C	RC	21.	B	RC	32.	A	COE	43.	C	COE
2.	C	COE	12.	D	RC	22.	C	WIC	33.	B	COE	44.	C	COE
3.	C	RC	13.	A	RC	23.	A	COE	34.	C	RC	45.	A	RC
4.	D	RC	14.	A	COE	24.	C	COE	35.	C	RC	46.	D	WIC
5.	B	RC	15.	B	COE	25.	B	RC	36.	C	WIC	47.	D	RC
6.	C	WIC	16.	C	COE	26.	D	RC	37.	A	RC	48.	B	RC
7.	A	RC	17.	C	COE	27.	C	RC	38.	A	WIC	49.	C	COE
8.	C	WIC	18.	A	WIC	28.	D	COE	39.	B	RC	50.	B	COE
9.	D	COE	19.	D	WIC	29.	D	COE	40.	B	RC	51.	B	RC
10.	B	COE	20.	C	IG	30.	B	WIC	41.	A	COE	52.	B	WIC
						31.	D	IG	42.	B	COE			

Writing and Language Test

Q	A	TYPE	Q	A	TYPE	Q	A	TYPE	Q	A	TYPE
1.	B	SEC	12.	A	SEC	23.	C	SEC	34.	B	EOI
2.	B	SEC	13.	C	SEC	24.	C	EOI	35.	A	EOI
3.	A	SEC	14.	D	EOI	25.	B	EOI	36.	C	SEC
4.	A	EOI	15.	C	EOI	26.	C	EOI	37.	D	EOI
5.	D	EOI	16.	B	EOI	27.	A	SEC	38.	B	SEC
6.	C	SEC	17.	C	EOI	28.	B	SEC	39.	C	EOI
7.	B	EOI	18.	B	SEC	29.	C	SEC	40.	C	SEC
8.	B	SEC	19.	A	SEC	30.	D	EOI	41.	A	SEC
9.	A	EOI	20.	B	EOI	31.	A	SEC	42.	D	EOI
10.	A	EOI	21.	C	SEC	32.	A	EOI	43.	A	SEC
11.	C	SEC	22.	D	EOI	33.	D	EOI	44.	B	EOI

Math Test – No Calculator

Q	A	TYPE	Q	A	TYPE	Q	A	TYPE
1.	B	HOA	11.	A	HOA	16.	1 or 3	PAM
2.	D	ATM	12.	A	PAM	17.	8	HOA
3.	D	PAM	13.	B	PAM	18.	1.25 or 5/4	HOA
4.	C	HOA	14.	A	PAM	19.	140	HOA
5.	D	PAM	15.	D	HOA	20.	3/5 or .6	ATM
6.	B	HOA						
7.	C	PAM						
8.	C	HOA						
9.	C	PAM						
10.	D	ATM						

Math Test – Calculator

Q	A	TYPE	Q	A	TYPE	Q	A	TYPE	Q	A	TYPE
1.	B	PSD	11.	B	PSD	21.	A	HOA	31.	2.5 or 5/2	PSD
2.	D	HOA	12.	D	HOA	22.	B	ATM	32.	200	HOA
3.	C	HOA	13.	C	PAM	23.	C	PAM	33.	5	PAM
4.	A	PSD	14.	D	PSD	24.	B	PAM	34.	6.48	PSD
5.	A	HOA	15.	A	PSD	25.	C	HOA	35.	15	ATM
6.	C	PSD	16.	B	PSD	26.	C	PSD	36.	650	PSD
7.	C	PAM	17.	B	PSD	27.	C	PSD	37.	8	PAM
8.	B	HOA	18.	D	PAM	28.	A	PSD	38.	1024	PAM
9.	B	PAM	19.	C	PSD	29.	A	ATM			
10.	D	PSD	20.	A	HOA	30.	C	HOA			

Test 2: Raw Score Conversion Table

Raw Score	Reading Test	Writing and Language Test	Mathematics Test
0	10	10	200
1	10	10	200
2	10	10	210
3	11	11	230
4	12	12	240
5	13	13	260
6	13	13	270
7	14	14	280
8	15	15	300
9	16	16	310
10	16	16	320
11	17	17	330
12	18	18	350
13	18	18	360
14	18	19	370
15	19	19	380
16	19	20	390
17	19	21	400
18	20	21	420
19	20	22	430
20	21	22	440
21	22	23	450
22	22	23	460
23	23	24	470
24	23	24	480
25	24	25	490
26	24	26	500
27	25	26	510
28	25	27	510
29	26	28	520
30	26	28	530
31	27	29	530
32	27	29	540
33	28	30	550
34	28	31	560
35	29	32	560
36	30	32	570
37	30	33	580
38	30	34	580
39	31	35	590
40	31	35	600
41	32	37	610
42	33	38	610
43	33	39	620
44	34	40	630
45	34		640
46	35		650
47	36		660
48	37		670
49	38		680
50	38		690
51	39		700
52	40		710
53			720
54			740
55			760
56			770
57			790
58			800

Test 3: Answer Key

Reading Test

Q	A	TYPE	Q	A	TYPE	Q	A	TYPE	Q	A	TYPE	Q	A	TYPE
1.	B	RC	11.	D	RC	21.	D	RC	32.	C	RC	43.	D	RC
2.	D	RC	12.	C	RC	22.	B	RC	33.	A	WIC	44.	D	RC
3.	C	COE	13.	A	RC	23.	D	WIC	34.	B	COE	45.	C	RC
4.	B	COE	14.	C	WIC	24.	A	RC	35.	B	COE	46.	B	COE
5.	B	WIC	15.	C	COE	25.	C	WIC	36.	A	RC	47.	D	COE
6.	D	WIC	16.	B	COE	26.	C	COE	37.	B	WIC	48.	B	WIC
7.	A	COE	17.	B	WIC	27.	D	COE	38.	C	RC	49.	C	WIC
8.	B	COE	18.	D	IG	28.	D	RC	39.	D	COE	50.	D	COE
9.	D	RC	19.	B	IG	29.	B	RC	40.	C	COE	51.	D	COE
10.	C	RC	20.	D	IG	30.	A	COE	41.	C	RC	52.	C	IG
						31.	B	COE	42.	D	RC			

Writing and Language Test

Q	A	TYPE	Q	A	TYPE	Q	A	TYPE	Q	A	TYPE
1.	C	SEC	12.	C	EOI	23.	D	SEC	34.	D	SEC
2.	D	SEC	13.	B	EOI	24.	C	EOI	35.	A	EOI
3.	D	EOI	14.	A	EOI	25.	A	EOI	36.	D	SEC
4.	D	EOI	15.	A	SEC	26.	D	SEC	37.	C	SEC
5.	C	EOI	16.	C	EOI	27.	A	EOI	38.	A	EOI
6.	C	SEC	17.	C	SEC	28.	C	SEC	39.	D	SEC
7.	A	EOI	18.	A	SEC	29.	A	EOI	40.	D	EOI
8.	B	EOI	19.	B	EOI	30.	D	SEC	41.	C	SEC
9.	D	SEC	20.	A	SEC	31.	B	EOI	42.	C	EOI
10.	B	SEC	21.	A	SEC	32.	D	EOI	43.	B	EOI
11.	A	EOI	22.	D	EOI	33.	C	EOI	44.	B	EOI

Math Test – No Calculator

Q	A	TYPE	Q	A	TYPE	Q	A	TYPE
1.	B	HOA	11.	C	HOA	16.	0	HOA
2.	D	HOA	12.	B	ATM	17.	105	ATM
3.	D	PAM	13.	D	PAM	18.	2.5 or 5/2	ATM
4.	B	HOA	14.	B	PAM	19.	9	PAM
5.	C	PAM	15.	A	PAM	20.	7	PAM
6.	A	HOA						
7.	B	PAM						
8.	C	HOA						
9.	B	PAM						
10.	A	HOA						

Math Test – Calculator

Q	A	TYPE	Q	A	TYPE	Q	A	TYPE	Q	A	TYPE
1.	A	HOA	11.	D	PSD	21.	D	HOA	31.	$2 \le x \le 3$	HOA
2.	A	PAM	12.	A	HOA	22.	C	PAM	32.	183	HOA
3.	D	PSD	13.	D	PAM	23.	C	HOA	33.	2	PSD
4.	A	PSD	14.	B	HOA	24.	B	PAM	34.	120	ATM
5.	C	HOA	15.	C	HOA	25.	C	PSD	35.	60	PSD
6.	B	PSD	16.	C	PSD	26.	D	PSD	36.	110, 111, 112, 113, 114, or 115	ATM
7.	A	PAM	17.	A	PSD	27.	D	ATM	37.	.999	PAM
8.	C	PSD	18.	D	HOA	28.	B	PAM	38.	73.8	PAM
9.	C	PSD	19.	C	PSD	29.	A	PAM			
10.	C	PSD	20.	A	PSD	30.	B	PAM			

Test 3: Raw Score Conversion Table

Raw Score	Reading Test	Writing and Language Test	Mathematics Test
0	10	10	200
1	10	10	200
2	10	10	210
3	11	11	220
4	12	12	230
5	13	13	250
6	13	13	270
7	14	14	280
8	15	15	300
9	16	16	310
10	16	16	320
11	17	17	340
12	18	18	350
13	18	19	360
14	18	19	370
15	19	19	380
16	19	20	390
17	20	20	400
18	20	21	410
19	21	22	420
20	21	22	430
21	22	23	440
22	23	23	450
23	23	24	460
24	24	24	470
25	24	25	480
26	25	26	490
27	25	26	500
28	25	27	500
29	26	28	510
30	26	28	520
31	27	29	520
32	27	29	530
33	28	30	540
34	28	31	540
35	29	31	550
36	29	32	560
37	30	33	570
38	30	33	580
39	31	34	580
40	31	35	590
41	31	36	600
42	32	38	610
43	32	39	610
44	33	40	620
45	34		630
46	34		640
47	35		650
48	36		660
49	37		670
50	38		680
51	39		690
52	40		700

Raw Score	Reading Test	Writing and Language Test	Mathematics Test
53			710
54			730
55			750
56			770
57			790
58			800

Test 4: Answer Key

Reading Test

Q	A	TYPE	Q	A	TYPE	Q	A	TYPE	Q	A	TYPE	Q	A	TYPE
1.	B	RC	11.	B	RC	21.	B	RC	31.	D	COE	42.	B	RC
2.	D	COE	12.	B	WIC	22.	C	WIC	32.	C	COE	43.	A	WIC
3.	C	COE	13.	B	COE	23.	C	RC	33.	A	RC	44.	D	RC
4.	C	RC	14.	C	COE	24.	A	WIC	34.	B	RC	45.	B	WIC
5.	B	RC	15.	D	RC	25.	D	COE	35.	C	WIC	46.	D	COE
6.	D	COE	16.	C	WIC	26.	D	COE	36.	A	RC	47.	A	RC
7.	C	COE	17.	A	COE	27.	A	RC	37.	B	RC	48.	C	COE
8.	A	WIC	18.	C	COE	28.	B	RC	38.	C	WIC	49.	A	COE
9.	B	WIC	19.	C	IG	29.	B	COE	39.	D	COE	50.	C	WIC
10.	A	RC	20.	A	IG	30.	C	COE	40.	D	COE	51.	B	RC
									41.	C	IG	52.	D	RC

Writing and Language Test

Q	A	TYPE	Q	A	TYPE	Q	A	TYPE	Q	A	TYPE
1.	A	SEC	12.	D	EOI	23.	D	EOI	34.	B	SEC
2.	C	SEC	13.	A	EOI	24.	C	EOI	35.	A	SEC
3.	B	EOI	14.	D	SEC	25.	D	SEC	36.	C	EOI
4.	C	SEC	15.	B	SEC	26.	D	EOI	37.	B	EOI
5.	A	EOI	16.	A	SEC	27.	C	SEC	38.	A	EOI
6.	B	SEC	17.	C	EOI	28.	C	SEC	39.	C	SEC
7.	A	EOI	18.	C	EOI	29.	B	EOI	40.	D	EOI
8.	D	EOI	19.	D	SEC	30.	A	EOI	41.	B	EOI
9.	C	SEC	20.	B	SEC	31.	B	SEC	42.	A	SEC
10.	B	EOI	21.	B	EOI	32.	D	SEC	43.	C	EOI
11.	B	EOI	22.	C	EOI	33.	A	EOI	44.	D	SEC

Math Test – No Calculator

Q	A	TYPE	Q	A	TYPE	Q	A	TYPE
1.	D	HOA	11.	C	ATM	16.	2	PAM
2.	B	PAM	12.	C	HOA	17.	0	HOA
3.	B	HOA	13.	A	PAM	18.	0.8 or 4/5	ATM
4.	B	HOA	14.	A	PAM	19.	28	HOA
5.	B	HOA	15.	C	PAM	20.	144	PAM
6.	A	HOA						
7.	A	PAM						
8.	C	ATM						
9.	B	HOA						
10.	C	PAM						

Math Test – Calculator

Q	A	TYPE	Q	A	TYPE	Q	A	TYPE	Q	A	TYPE
1.	A	HOA	11.	B	PSD	21.	B	PSD	31.	15	HOA
2.	C	PSD	12.	C	PSD	22.	C	PSD	32.	24	HOA
3.	C	HOA	13.	C	PAM	23.	B	PSD	33.	9	PAM
4.	A	HOA	14.	A	PSD	24.	B	PAM	34.	1020	HOA
5.	A	HOA	15.	D	ATM	25.	B	PAM	35.	3	ATM
6.	D	PSD	16.	D	PSD	26.	C	ATM	36.	1/3 or .333	PSD
7.	D	PSD	17.	D	HOA	27.	B	HOA	37.	3	PAM
8.	C	PAM	18.	B	PSD	28.	C	PSD	38.	49	PAM
9.	B	PSD	19.	B	HOA	29.	B	PAM			
10.	A	PAM	20.	C	PSD	30.	C	PSD			

Test 4: Raw Score Conversion Table

Raw Score	Reading Test	Writing and Language Test	Mathematics Test
0	10	10	200
1	10	10	200
2	10	10	220
3	11	11	230
4	12	12	240
5	12	13	260
6	13	13	270
7	14	14	280
8	15	15	300
9	15	16	310
10	16	16	320
11	17	17	340
12	17	18	350
13	18	18	360
14	18	19	370
15	19	19	380
16	19	20	400
17	19	20	410
18	20	21	420
19	20	21	420
20	21	22	440
21	21	23	450
22	22	23	460
23	22	24	470
24	23	24	480
25	24	25	490
26	24	26	500
27	25	26	510
28	25	27	520
29	26	27	520
30	26	28	530
31	27	29	540
32	27	29	540
33	28	30	550
34	28	31	560
35	29	31	560
36	29	32	570
37	30	33	580
38	30	33	590
39	31	34	590
40	31	35	600
41	32	36	610
42	33	38	620
43	33	39	620
44	34	40	630
45	34		640
46	35		650
47	36		660
48	37		670
49	37		680
50	38		690
51	39		700
52	40		710
53			730

Raw Score	Reading Test	Writing and Language Test	Mathematics Test
54			740
55			760
56			770
57			790
58			800

Answer Explanations for Test 1

Reading Test

Passage 1

The first passage of the SAT reading test is always a literary passage, and so the key elements to look for are different than they would be in an informational or argumentative passage. For this passage, it is essential to identify the central characters and understand their relationships to each other. Another important aspect is tone: understanding the tone of not only the narrator but also the various characters will make the passage as a whole much more clear. In this passage, Henry Tilney is a bit pedantic, and he enjoys teasing both his sister Eleanor and friend Catherine Moreland. He tends to speak with an ironic tone. Eleanor teases her brother back and also uses irony regularly in her speech. Catherine is not quite as quick as the Tilneys. She speaks earnestly in all her words and often doesn't seem to understand exactly what Henry and Eleanor mean when they speak. Perhaps you can sympathize! Two tips for this passage and others like it:

1. Read the introduction! It is the clearest indication of both the full names of the characters and their relationships to each other—the narrator uses the name Catherine, while the other characters always call her "Miss Moreland." The fact that they are one and the same is easy to miss if you don't read the introduction!

2. Mark each character's initials in the margins to indicate who is speaking when. The speeches often proceed without any tags to indicate who is speaking, and the questions ask about specific characters' words, so doing so will help keep things straight and lead to correct answers.

1 **C** **RC** You need to understand Henry's character as a whole to get this one correct. Choice (A) is not supported by lines 3–4 at all—he may not like the book, but that's not what he says here.

Choices (B) and (D) are there to tempt you to see Henry's words as sincere—only choice (C), which indicates that Henry is choosing to pretend not to understand and that he is teasing Catherine, fits with the character and the lines referenced.

2 **D** **WIC** This is a words-in-context (WIC) question that is based on an idiomatic expression rather than the dictionary definition of the words, so don't just think about what the words mean.

Re-read the sentence starting in line 8 and replace the phrase with your own words to fit the context. Eleanor says that her brother finds fault with her way of speaking all the time and that he is now "treating Catherine the same way." Looking at the answer choices, only (B) and (D) are close to this, but (B) is incorrect because the treatment is in no way romantic!

3 **A** RC It is important to consider this reference as a continuation of the same teasing speech the last question referred to. (B) might be tempting, because her knowledge of these men does show that she is well-read, but she is not mentioning them for the purpose of showing off—she is teasing her brother for being pedantic in response to Catherine's use of the word "nicest."

4 **A** COE This is the first of a pair of Command of Evidence (COE) questions. The test often sneaks these on the bottom of one page so that you won't notice that it is only one part of a two-part question!

Don't try to answer it without first going to the line references provided in question 5. After reviewing those lines, we can readily choose (A), as explained below. Choice (B) is particularly tempting without making reference to the specific lines—we know that Henry is mocking Catherine, and there is no reason to believe that he doesn't disapprove of what he speaks of. Choices (C) and (D) are easier to rule out—they both suggest he is being sincere in his use of the word "nice."

5 **D** COE You want to read these lines before choosing your answer to question 4: the correct answer here is easy to pick out if you work carefully. Further, once you have this one correct, the previous question is delivered to you on a silver platter with a nice bottle of wine. Choices (A) and (B) feature Eleanor and Catherine, respectively, so we are unlikely to understand Henry's intention from their words. Choice (C) is immediately after the lines referenced in question 4, but it provides no clue as to his purpose in using the word "nice" in the preceding lines. Choice (D) gives us a direct statement of his complaint: "But now every commendation [mention of praise] on every subject is comprised in that one word [nice!]." Thus, we can choose (D) and go back and pick (A) for question 4, because it references the overuse of the word "nice."

6 **C** RC This question requires you to make an inference about the reading preferences of Catherine based on the passage as a whole. Luckily, she has talked about little else but her reading preferences throughout the passage! We know that she enjoys the gothic novel *The Mysteries of Udolpho* (lines 1–2), and she tells us she doesn't like other kinds of reading much, other than poems and plays, and that she particularly doesn't like history (lines 34–37). Based upon this, the word "novel" in choice (C) makes this answer a good bet.

Another way to answer this question is to use the process of elimination and cross out the wrong answers. Choice (A) is the easiest answer to dispose of, since it is clearly a book about history, but (B) or (D) might be tempting, given that one mentions plays and the other mentions journeys, but you have to make sure that the ENTIRE answer is correct, not just part of it. Both of these answers present texts of historical analysis—of the accuracy of speeches and of the impact of an explorer. This kind of "serious history" is just what she does not enjoy!

7 **A** WIC   This (WIC) question simply requires that we return to the text to get its meaning.

Choice (B) tempting if you don't go back to the passage—"a newly developed technology" sounds like a great definition for an invention until you read how the word is used in the passage. When we re-read the lines, we can see that "invention" must mean something like "made up": only choice (A) gives us an answer that fits with this meaning. "Fabricated" means made up—don't rule the answer choice out if you don't know this word!

If you don't know the word "fabricated," you can eliminate all the other choices and still get to the right answer. We know that choice (B) is irrelevant to the passage, and choice (C) is relevant to the topic but does not make sense in either line 45 or 48. Choice (D) is somewhat tempting for a careful reader who realizes that invention is used to mean something that is not true, but the inference required is too large: we cannot assume that the authors are intending to deceive anyone based on what the passage states.

8 **B** COE   This is the first of another COE pair, and answering the second question first makes this otherwise very difficult question very easy. Once you see that the answer to question 9 is (D), you know that she calls the speeches "embellishments" written by the authors themselves and that she likes them. An almost perfect match for choice B!

9 **D** COE   This is a perfect example of how to use the strategy of answering the second question of a COE pair first. You want to find which section tells Ms. Tilney's view of the speeches in history books, and only choice (D) actually does this at all.

Choice (A) seems to answer the question, but it is Catherine Moreland's view of speeches in history books, and so is irrelevant! Choice (B) is Ms. Tilney's statement, but she is merely reflecting Catherine's view back to her, not speaking her own view at all.

Choice (C) is tricky: it is Ms. Tilney speaking, but she speaks about the supposed *facts* recorded in history books, not the speeches. Beware! This answer corresponds perfectly to choice (D) in question 8, so you have to be certain to read carefully to determine which lines actually answer the exact question asked.

10 **A** RC   Unless you are quite erudite, reading the footnote is essential to answer this question. In it, you learn that the gentlemen mentioned in the question are historical figures whose deeds are recorded in history books by contemporary historians, such as those mentioned in lines 61–62. Knowing that this comparison is the general purpose allows us see that (A) and (D) seem like possible answers.

Choosing between these two answers can be done in two ways: (1) if you understand her point, Ms. Tilney is expressing a preference for the "inventions" of contemporary historians, which makes choice (A) the best choice; (2) if you closely examine the two answers, choice (D) suggests that the speakers of the past are compared to "later rhetoricians," persuasive speakers, but she is comparing past speakers to historians, not other speakers. Remember that often just one word can make a tricky answer choice incorrect!

Passage 2

This passage is a social science passage, and it is part of what the test makers refer to as the "great global conversation," which is comprised of contemporary or classic readings on significant social or political topics. In this passage, Mary Fisher addresses the then-emerging issue of the AIDS crisis. This passage is neatly organized into relatively short paragraphs, and it is clear in its rhetorical purpose throughout. Fisher wants to inform her audience about the realities of AIDS and call for sympathy and support for those who suffer from the disease, and all of the passage is clearly directed toward these aims. The passage includes a pair of graphs—this is worth noticing upon initial reading, but don't bother studying or trying to perfectly understand the graphs before you start the questions. When questions ask directly about the graphs, use them to answer those questions, but don't worry about them as you complete the rest of the passage and questions.

11 A COE This is the first of a pair of COE questions. The context of the passage suggests that the author might support the actions described in each of these answer choices, but only one is stated in the passage directly—choice (A).

To understand why the lines in the next question support this answer choice, you must understand the third paragraph in detail. It begins by suggesting that HIV patients are often stereotyped and goes on to explain why this stereotyping is unfair and misguided. This is an instance where using the line numbers in the second COE is very helpful!

12 B COE Choice (A) describes the dangers of AIDS but does not include specific suggestions about how to respond. That comes later. Choice (C) describes the effect membership in the Republican Party has had on the author, but does not relate directly to the primary discussion in the passage. Choice (D), similar to choice (A), describes the fears associated with AIDS along with how people perceive those fears. Choice (B) explains that AIDS patients are worthy of compassion and support. This is in stark contrast to the stereotypes that are often negatively applied to such people, as described in this paragraph.

13 C RC In this context, "though" is used to mean "despite the fact that." The author begins sentences with "though" to show how she is affected by AIDS despite the fact that she is not a member of the populations most directly and strongly impacted by the disease at that time in America. In this way, she is showing how she is similar to people within those groups and how she is an example of how faulty the stereotypes about AIDS victims are.

14 D RC Notice that the author states in this sentence that "people with HIV have *not* entered some alien state of being." The author here is arguing that AIDS patients are not fundamentally different from other people. Choice (D) is correct, as the author is contradicting the mistaken assumptions of others about AIDS patients, but the word "belie" may not be familiar to you, which could make it hard to choose this answer.

Even if you do not know this word, you can still get this correct if you know what you are looking for, which is that "AIDS patients are not fundamentally different from other people." If we know that this is the correct idea based on the passage, we can use this information to rule out all the other answers. Choices (A) and (C) are clearly opposite to the intended idea of the passage, and choice (B) treats the description as if the "alien state" were about physical characteristics, which we know it is not.

15 A COE This is another COE question that can be answered most effectively by using the answer choices in the following question to find the answer in the passage. Carry on to question 16!

16 B COE Here, choice (B) provides the best evidence, although noticing this requires looking at the context of the lines and not only the lines themselves. Without reading the start of the paragraph in which lines 36–40 appear, it would be difficult to notice that the "them" in these lines refers to President and Mrs. Bush. The other answer choices discuss only the responses to President Bush's response to the AIDS crisis, rather than the way in which he himself responded.

17 C WIC Always consider the full context of a word for any WIC question. All four choices arguably work grammatically and choice (D) is particularly tempting in the context of the individual sentence by itself, but only choice (C) fits the context in the paragraph as a whole. This part of the passage is discussing the hypocrisy of ignoring the AIDS epidemic. The first sentence of the paragraph—all the way back in line 46—is the most direct indication of the best meaning of "integrity" in line 50, so remember to look at the context fully to choose the best meaning!

18 C WIC Choice (B) is a very tempting answer, especially if you read the introduction to the passage. It is arguable that the author is referring to her own party as "we," but she is not using "you" to refer to those "who don't wish to show compassion." Choice (A) is incorrect because some people in the category of "you" (those without fear) are included in "we" as well, regardless of exactly how "we" must be defined here. Choice (D) may be tempting because the author has AIDS. However, she is speaking primarily to an audience that does not and is advocating action by those who do not. Rather, "you" refers to people who do not fear that AIDS may impact them or people they care about. Choice (C) best defines "we" and "you" in this context.

19 C RC Answer this question for yourself based on the passage rather than going directly to the answer choices. The quotation describes the reactions of the public during the Holocaust and is referenced to relate that reaction to the public response to the AIDS crisis. Choice (A) refers to the devastation caused rather than the public response, so is easy to rule out if you have answered the question for yourself before reading the answer choices. The quote is not primarily religious in nature nor does it primarily relate to a theological issue, which rules out choice (B).

 Choice (D) is tempting, because it suggests that the historical precedent is applicable to the current discussion, but it is incorrect because the quote does not provide the proper response but a dangerously ignorant response. Choice (C) alone shows that the analogy between the two is based on that response—one which suggests that a widespread problem is "not my concern."

20 B IG This informational graphic (IG) question can be tricky, as the two graphs look quite similar at first glance. If you look closely, however, you will notice that the scale of each graph is quite different. The numbers on the Adult Cases graph are much higher than those on the Pediatric Cases graph. Choice (B) is therefore correct because there were many more adult cases than pediatric cases. The graphs do not give the necessary information to know if either of choices (A) or (D) is true. Choice (C) is false because the two graphs are very similar in appearance, which tells us that the rates of change in both data sets have been similar over time.

Passage 3

This passage is one of two science passages on the test. Because science passages tend to be loaded with terms and names, be sure to circle all terms and names as you read them in the passage. This habit will keep you focused as you read and is often useful for finding key information to answer questions. In this case, the article presents information on a specific topic rather than a specific study or researcher, so you need to keep names like Fetz, Nicolelis, Donoghue, and Chen straight so that when you are asked about specific people's work or ideas, you can find them quickly. It is also, as always, important to identify the main idea of the passage: here, the article discusses research and developments in brain–machine interfaces and considers their applications and possibilities.

 21 B RC Use the main idea of the passage to answer these first two general questions! This passage focuses on the advancements discovered through research into a treatment option for some forms of paralysis, which makes (B) the best choice.

22 D RC The trick to this question is finding an answer choice that correctly characterizes the author's main point as optimistic, but not too optimistic. The passage does not claim that the brain-machine interface technologies being discussed are a cure for paralysis, but rather that they have promising and interesting applications, as in choice (D).

23 **D** WIC Like many WIC questions, this one includes the most common meaning of the word as an incorrect answer, "transport" (B).

 This is a great question to answer for yourself based on the passage instead of going straight to the answer choices. This sentence is about how technology is being advanced through the insights gained by the research discussed in the passage, so a good write-in for this question would be something like "bring forward," "advance," or the correct answer, "stimulate" (D).

24 **C** COE This is a COE question, so make sure to use the answer choices in the following question to help figure out which answer is best for this question. Choice (C) is correct and matches the correct line numbers in the following question.

25 **B** COE Notice that only choice (B) actually features a quote from Fetz! Lines 56–59 discuss the brain-machine interface research of Fetz and his team, but nothing about the development of related technology. Lines 15–18 and Lines 89–92 might seem tempting, but the previous question begins with "[a]ccording to Fetz." Lines 15–18 are by Nicolelis, and 89–92 are quotes by Chen, not Fetz. Choice (B) is correct because lines 31–35 give Fetz's description of how the development of brain-machine interface research is operating in parallel with the development of related technology.

26 **C** COE This is another COE question that should be answered by using the line numbers in the second question of the pair. Choice (C) here is best because it is explained as an advantage of using electrodes implanted deep within the brain as described in the passage.

27 **B** COE Choice (B), lines 50–52, describes a way in which electrodes implanted deep within the brain are superior to other types of electrode sensors. The lines in choices (A) and (C) explain a result of a study involving the use of brain electrodes but not an advantage of the use of that kind of electrode over others. The lines in choice (D) make no direct mention of brain embedded electrodes.

28 **D** WIC This is another WIC question, but one that uses a (probably) familiar word in a very unusual way. The sentence involves a feeling only within the mind, rather than one brought about as a result of physical presence, so choice (D), "imagined," most closely matches the odd use of "phantom" in this sentence.

29 **A** RC This is another great question to illustrate the importance of writing in your own answer! If you don't do so, choice (D) will probably be tempting, because it presents a fairly accurate claim about the reference, but does not give the *reason* that Nicolelis made the reference. In the passage, "they like grapes" is mentioned shortly after Nicolelis tells us that the monkeys can reliably steer wheelchairs to get grapes. The reason that it matters to us that the monkeys like grapes is that the grapes provide a motivation for them to learn to use the wheelchairs well. That way they can get the grapes that they like!

30 D RC

Hopefully you circled the names in this passage so it was easy to look up "Fetz" and "Chen" in the passage when trying to figure out what their attitudes were. Fetz has a few positive and optimistic comments about the advancing technology, such as those mentioned in lines 31–35 and 59–61. Chen, on the other hand, focuses on the current limitations and how we still have a long way to go before this technology will be as helpful as possible as in lines 83–85.

Choice (D) alone shows the proper relationship, contrasting the "tentative" Chen with the "optimistic" Fetz.

Passage 4

This is a paired passage, and it is a fairly difficult one because of how old it is and because of the level of rhetorical sophistication of each speaker. The topic of these passages is history, as each of the pair presents an excerpt from the famous Lincoln-Douglas debates. Often, it is best to read the first passage and then answer the questions about it only (31–34, in this case) and then read the second passage and answer the questions about it (35–38) and finally to do the ones about the two together. This prevents the perspective and information in the second passage from "intruding" into your answers on the first, and vice versa. However, it is also essential to understand how the two relate to each other. As you read the second passage, you want to ask yourself what it has in common with the first passage and how it is different from it. In this case, the two share a common topic—slavery in the United States—but come to opposite conclusions about what should be done about it, based primarily on differing views of the United States as a whole and the relationship between the collective and the individual states that make it up.

31 B COE

Notice that this is the first of a paired COE set. Skip 31 for a moment, and move on to question 32. After you have decided that answer choice (B) for question 32 is correct because author refers to the founding fathers as "great men" in lines 9–15, come back to this question. Let's try to match up "great men" to one of our answer choices. If you know all of these words, you can readily choose (B)—"paragons," meaning "exceptional people"—as the best answer.

Some of these answer choices include pretty hard vocabulary words, so you may not know all of them. You can still use the process of elimination to find the right answer. Choice (C) may be the easiest to cross off because "conservatives" is fairly familiar and does not have the same meaning as "great men." Choice (D), "heroes," doesn't seem to quite capture the author's attitude toward the founding fathers correctly—he doesn't remark upon their courage or other heroic traits. We've thus got it narrowed down to two choices, so we've got a 50-50 chance if we are unfamiliar with the remaining words. If you recognize the root word "chronos," meaning time, in choice (A), you can probably eliminate "anachronisms," which means something or someone out of its proper time, such as a dinosaur in 1920s New York or a stopwatch on the wrist of the Odysseus.

32 B COE

Remember that for this question you are looking for the line numbers where you can find the answer to question 31: how does the author view the founding fathers? In line 11, the author places Washington and other founding fathers along side "the great men of that day." Therefore (B), the answer choice containing line 11, is correct.

33 A RC If you read the passage carefully, you know that the author speaks primarily about his belief that the country can and should continue to exist divided into slave and free states. How does he make this argument? The author insists that "people necessarily required different laws and regulations in different localities" (lines 19–20) and that "[o]ne of the reserved rights of the States, was the right to regulate the relations between Master and Servant." In other words, each state is different and should be allowed to make its own laws regarding slavery. Therefore, answer choice (A) is correct.

34 C RC The author describes the contrasting geographical features of New Hampshire and South Carolina to emphasize that each state is different and therefore needs different laws. If you followed the author's argument as you read, you can quickly choose (C) as the correct answer. Although choice (B) also indicates that the author is emphasizing differences between the states, he does not argue that these differences are irreconcilable. In fact, he claims that the various states can continue to coexist despite their differences.

35 D COE This is the first question about Passage 2, and that is where you need to look for the answers to this and the next three questions.

Notice that question 35 is the first of a pair of COE questions, which means that you should answer question 36 first and then come back to this question afterward. According to the correct answer for question 36, the author says that the institution of slavery has always created discord and division. Therefore (D), the answer choice that describes slavery as a source of conflict, is the correct answer to 35.

36 B COE Choosing the correct answer to this question may be a little trickier than other Command of Evidence questions you have encountered. Answer choices (B), (C), and (D) all direct you to lines in the passage that describe characteristics of slavery recognized by the author. In the line numbers from choice (B) we learn that the author views slavery as an institution that has always been "an element of division."

In the lines from choice (C)—probably the most tricky answer to eliminate—the author expresses that slavery is an institution that has existed in some states for 80 years, but in the context of conceding that the states are different in this regard, which is not his point about slavery, but his opponent's. In the lines from choice (D), the author expresses the founding fathers' view that slavery is an institution that they restricted by ending the slave-trade and curtailing its spread to new Territories. Each of these choices might seem as though it contains an answer to the question, but only (B) gives the author's own view about the institution of slavery.

37 **C** WIC Be careful! The word "constitution" is used in both Passage 1 and Passage 2. However, in each passage the word is used differently. Remember: words may change their meaning depending on the context in which they appear. No matter how tempted you may be to answer a WIC question without referring back to the passage, *always* look back at the line number you are directed to in the question.

 If you don't look back, you might choose (A), "governing document," because "Constitution" is used in line 16 and line 30 to refer to a particular governing document. In line 66, however, "constitution" has the connotation of "composition," and so (C) is the correct choice.

38 **A** WIC Again, to answer this WIC question look back at the passage. In this case, we are directed to line 82. If you are unfamiliar with the word "abrogation," don't worry!

 Simply substitute a word of your own that makes sense in the context of the sentence and then try to match that word with an answer choice. From the sentence in which "abrogation" appears, we learn that the founding fathers cut off the source of slavery by the "abrogation" of the slave trade. What is another word that makes sense here? Maybe "elimination" or simply "cutting off" which is used in line 81. Now it's easy to realize that the answer is (A), "abolition."

39 **C** RC This is the first question that refers to the authors by name and it's important to know who said what!

 Before you read the passages, did you read the introduction? This is where you'll find which author wrote which passage (Hint: Douglas wrote Passage 1, and Lincoln wrote Passage 2). Throughout the passage, Douglas argues that the founders of the country supported the right of states to make their own laws governing slavery. Lincoln does not agree with him, as stated in (B). Rather, Lincoln argues at the end of Passage 2 that the founding fathers created national laws to keep slavery from spreading. The answer choice which best states these positions is (C).

40 **A** COE Another COE pair! Are you getting the hang of these?

Let's hold off on this question for a moment and answer 41 first. After finding in the line numbers from question 41 where in the passages the authors agree, it's not hard to answer this question. According to our answer from 41, both authors agree that the country is made up of unique states. If you compare this to the answer choices, you will see that (A) is the correct answer.

41 **C** COE The authors of these passages don't seem to have many beliefs in common, but for this question we are looking for where they do agree. Re-read the lines you are directed to in the answer choices, and compare what is stated in the first passage to what is being said in the second passage. Answer choice (C) is correct because it directs you to places in the passages where both authors talk about the physical differences as well as the differences in local institutions that exist in different parts of the country.

Passage 5

Another science passage, this one is a bit more rhetorically complex than the previous science passage, but it is still filled with names and terms, so circling these as you encounter them is a good strategy. It is, however, less of a mere overview of a topic and more of a purposeful argument, using evidence to support a claim. That claim is that a curious pattern of migration can be accounted for by the continents having drifted apart through time. Understanding how the evidence and argument work together in this passage will help you to answer many of the questions.

42 **A** COE

This is the first of another COE pair. Go ahead and answer question 43 first and then come back to this one when you have decided what lines best represent the author's description of the turtles' journey. You will have found that the answer to 43 is (C) because it best matches one of the answers listed for this question. All you have to do now is indicate which answer that is—choice (A), "a curious phenomenon."

43 **C** COE
Don't be fooled by the line numbers in answer choice (C), the correct answer. Just because the lines direct you to a question rather than a statement doesn't mean that you aren't provided with an understanding of the author's position. The author uses a rhetorical question in lines 40–42 to emphasize that the 2,000 mile migration of the green turtle is an unusual and surprising behavior (this matches nicely with choice (A), the correct answer to question 42). Indeed, the fact that a question is the best evidence supports the idea of its being curious, as it has aroused the author's curiosity enough to ask the question! Choice (A) is not about the turtles' migration at all, and choices (B) and (D) reveal details about the turtles' journey, but not the author's perspective about it.

44 **D** RC

For this question, let's read through all the answer choices and eliminate those that don't describe the structure of the passage. Choice (A) is incorrect because the passage is not a narrative, and the author discusses the turtles' migration habits over millions (not hundreds) of years. Choice (B) is incorrect as well. Although the passage explains the theory of plate tectonics, this theory is neither revolutionary nor the main focus of the passage. Choice (C) also incorrectly identifies the structure of the passage as an "interpretation of turtles' motives." The words "interpretation" and "motives" are inappropriate references for the nature of the passage as a whole and the way the turtles are described in the passage, respectively. The author only briefly mentions that green turtles migrate to breed on sandy beaches, but this can hardly be labeled as a "motive," a term which is restricted to human reasoning for actions. We have eliminated three answer choices and only (D), the correct answer, remains.

45 **C** RC
This is an analogy question, which many students find quite difficult because it requires you to go beyond what is directly in the passage. In order to get it correct, you have to understand the point being made in the lines referenced: the idea the author conveys in these lines is that researchers should pay attention to geological history in order to understand some aspects of modern biology. Choice (C) is correct because it describes an approach to studying genetic characteristics of a (human) animal without paying attention to the geology of the past, a direct violation of what Gould advocates in lines 6–10.

46 C WIC   This is a WIC question that gives a (likely) familiar word which has shades of meaning that can make the term more or less positive. "Astounding" suggests that one is stunned, which can mean alarming or even horrifying in extreme cases, but these words are both too negative to suit this sentence.

   Choice (B) makes good sense of the sentence as a whole, but "astonishing" does not mean "good," so this is not an acceptable synonym.

47 D COE   This is the first of a pair of COE questions, but it is one of the pairs that you may find easier to approach by answering the two questions together rather than by simply answering the second one first. See below for the reason that solving the second question in isolation from the first might be difficult. To easily eliminate the incorrect answers to this question, refer back to lines 25–59. If you had originally read through the chosen sections particularly closely, you should now be able to cross out (A) and (B) from question 48 fairly quickly and then cross out answers that don't relate to choices (C) or (D). (A), (B), and (C) are all either irrelevant or inaccurate based on the passage, so the best answer is choice (D) for question 47, which restates what the author says in choice (D) of question 48.

48 D COE   If you take on the line numbers first in this pair, you should be able to fairly readily eliminate choice (A), as it is clearly just a single reference to one aspect of history that is not developed or central to the passage as a whole. Since we know that the passage as whole—and these paragraphs in particular—is primarily about the turles' migration, we can also eliminate (B) fairly readily, because it discusses the turtles' breeding and feeding habits without direct reference to their migration.

Choices (C) and (D) might both seem possible, as they are both about the migration, which is the main point of these paragraphs. There are two ways to make the right choice between them. Since choice (D) gives the claim about the migration and choice (C) merely asserts that the migration is completed successfully, you may be confident enough to choose (D) and then match it up with (D) in 47. However, if you cannot choose between them, go back to the first question and think about which answers might relate to which lines. In question 47, we can eliminate (A), (B), and (C) as not clearly related to either choice (C) or (D). Choice (D) in 47 is a perfect fit for lines 48–52.

49 B RC   This is a tough question because it only gives line numbers and doesn't ask a specific question at all.

Thus, you want to revisit lines 48–73 quickly to remind yourself of the purpose of these lines and then read through the answer choices to eliminate answers that don't fit with what you find in the passage. We can quickly rule out choices (C) and (D) because although the passage explains that coral reefs prevent the erosion of islands, it does not say whether either Ascension or Iceland are surrounded by reefs. (A) is also incorrect. The passage indicates that Africa and South America, not North America, were at one time contiguous, and it gives no indication that the continents will reconnect. (B) is the correct answer. We can infer from the author's description of island formation along ridges that new islands may continue to be formed in this manner along the Mid-Atlantic Ridge.

50 C RC   This is a very tough question, because Carr's theory is fairly complex and it is explained only very briefly in lines 48–82, requiring the reader to pick up pieces of his explanation along the way.

Choice (A) is tempting, but it contains two key inaccuracies. First, it claims that the island itself has moved, which is not what the theory suggests. Second, it indicates that the turtles have always swum to the *same* island, but Carr refers to the island they initially swam to as "proto-Ascension" in line 76, which is the clearest indication that the island is *not* the same. Choice (B) is incorrect because it situates the change in an evolving ability in the turtles, whereas the theory is based on change in the geology of their migration, not their swimming skills. Choice (D) is *very* similar to choice (C), but it claims that the Mid-Atlantic Ridge destroyed the turtles' migratory island, whereas the passage claims that sea waves eventually eroded the islands away. Choice (C) accurately represents the theory as explained in the passage, and thus is correct.

51 B RC   In lines 79–82, the author compares the gradual lengthening of the turtles' migration to the process of a jogger who runs a little farther every day until finally covering many miles in a single run. Illustrating a concept by making a comparison to an example in this fashion is called an analogy, which makes choice (B) correct.

If you are not familiar with all the vocabulary in the answer choices—especially if you are not sure what an analogy is—you can still get this question correct by using process of elimination. You can eliminate (A) because no elements or ideas are repeated and (D) because the extreme length of the turtles' journey is a fact rather than an exaggeration. Choice (C) is probably an unfamiliar word for most students, so you may have to take your best guess and between (C) and (B), which at least gives you a 50-50 chance. If you recognize the "meta" root—Greek for "change," as in metamorphosis and metaphor—and the "nym" root—from the Greek word for "name," as in synonym and antonym—you might be able to guess that metonymy means "a change of name." As a literary term, "metonymy" refers to the use of a closely associated term in the place of another term, as when we speak of the executive branch of the US government in the phrase "the White House released a statement today." The White House is literally a house, so it doesn't do anything at all! And now, you know what metonymy is, and that's a lot of knowledge for a wrong answer.

52 **B** IG   This question is one of the few IG questions that requires you to use your ability to interpret visual information. Take a look at the maps that accompany the passage. What do they show? Could they support the explanations in the passage?

 You want to answer this core question for yourself first, so that you can eliminate the two wrong answers—the "Yes" or "No" pairs—immediately. The maps seem to show the positions of the continents millions of years ago and their positions as we know them today, which supports the author's claim that the turtles' journey has lengthened over time because continents drifted apart, and so (B) is the correct choice.

You may notice that answer choice (C) also provides a correct interpretation of the maps—nowhere is the turtle breeding ground labeled. However, this does not mean that the map does not provide other information to support the author's claim as choice (B) makes clear, which is why the essential first step on IG questions is to figure the answer out for yourself before you even read the answer choices. Often, wrong answer choices provide accurate information about the figures, but this information does not answer the question that was asked.

Writing and Language Test

1 A EOI Because the entire paragraph follows a chronological progression, the information about the time these events took place is important to add. If you are uncertain about whether to add the phrase, notice that none of the other three answers are true about the phrase!

2 B EOI Again, the chronological arrangement of the paragraph is the key to answering this question. Because the date 661 is earlier than any other date in the passage, we want to move it to beginning of the whole passage.

3 D EOI Since all the other options include redundant material, the best answer is (D).

Always notice when one answer is shorter than the others: it is often the correct answer, and a good clue to look for redundancy or wordiness in the other options.

4 B EOI This passage is obsessed with dates, and choice (B) has got 'em! The question asked for specific chronological information, and (B) is the most specific.

Don't be fooled by choice (D)—a century is a long time, but it is not as specific as exact years.

5 B SEC This is a parallelism question, so we need all the items in the list to be the same grammatical structure. Choice (B) provides one gerund, overseeing, and then lists four objects, all nouns.

Remember that lists cannot mix verb forms and nouns!

6 D SEC Since what comes before the comma and what comes after it in this sentence are both independent clauses, we need to fix the comma splice in the original sentence. While there are many ways to punctuate two independent clauses in a sentence, choice (D) provides one—a semi-colon can always replace a comma to correct a comma splice.

7 A SEC This subject-verb agreement question requires us to find the subject for the underlined verbs—when you go back in the sentence, you should find that "Ayatollah" is the subject, which is singular, so we need both verbs to be singular forms, as they are in (A).

Two quick tips:

- Notice that "authorities" is the closest noun to these verbs, but it is NOT the subject. Since it is part of a nonessential and is the object of a prepositional phrase, it CANNOT be the subject of the sentence.

- Notice that choice (B) and (C) both "mix and match" verb forms, giving one singular and one plural form. Since a subject cannot be simultaneously singular and plural, you can rule both of these out, even if you cannot tell whether "Ayatollah" or "authorities" is the subject of the sentence.

8 A EOI This is a standard but tricky question type on the new SAT, one which makes you choose the best transition word. The choice here is not at all grammatical—all options are grammatically correct—nor is it based on how it "sounds." Rather, you must choose based on the context of passage as a whole.

This question is particularly tricky. "Finally" is tempting, since this is the last paragraph of the passage. However, none of the transition words indicated provide an appropriate introduction to the paragraph. Consider:

"However" indicates contrast, and this last paragraph is summarizing the passage, not offering something different. "Therefore" indicates causality, but the previous paragraph has not given the reasons for the deviation mentioned but merely given the ways in which Iran has deviated from the rest of the Middle East. Although "Finally" is tempting, it doesn't make sense in the passage. The whole passage thus far has been arranged chronologically, but this last paragraph is a summary of the whole, and this sentence actually goes back to the beginning of the passage, rather than being the "final" event discussed.

Always remember to read well past the underlined section on a "transition" question, because you need to understand what follows the underlined portion to know how to move from the previous part of the passage to the new section.

9 C SEC This is a misplaced modifier question, which is rarely tested on the new SAT, but is easy to get correct if you recognize it. Because the sentence starts with a participle—an "-ing" or past tense verb form used as an adjective—the subject of the sentence MUST be the person or thing doing the action of the participle. Thus, the subject of the sentence must be the ulema themselves, not their power. Choice (D) also seems to make "ulema" the subject, but introduces the faulty form "ulemas's."

Remember that 's and s' are used at the end of nouns to show POSSESSION, not to make them plural.

10 B SEC This is an idiom question, which many students find tricky. Technically, an idiom is not based on any rule—the term comes from a Latin term meaning "only like itself," so we cannot memorize or study any rule to know what is correct about these "one of a kind" questions.

The best method to determine the right answer for an idiom is to read through all the options and choose the one that sounds best and expresses the intended meaning of the sentence. "Unique of" and "unique towards" are simply faulty forms, but "unique to" is wrong because of context. Iran's history cannot be "unique to" others—the history discussed is "unique to" Iran. Thus, "unique to" is acceptable idiomatically, but it does not make sense in this sentence.

11 A EOI This is a sentence-combining question that asks which choice is most effective; thus, all the choices are grammatically correct. The best choice for these types of questions is the one that shows the relationship between the ideas of the two sentences and does not repeat information needlessly. Choice (A) is the most concise expression, and it includes all the essential information contained in the two sentences.

12 C SEC This is another idiom question. The phrase "not only" in answer choice (C) correctly parallels with the phrase later in this sentence, "but also."

You will almost never see one of these two phrases without the other in a correctly arranged sentence.

13 B EOI This is a transition question that asks you to decide which word best fits the meaning of the sentence as it related to the rest of the passage, rather than which fits best grammatically or sounds the best.

This sentence provides information that shows a strong contrast with that of the previous two sentences. "However" works well to show this transition. A second way to find the correct answer here is to consider the other answer choices: "Therefore," "thus," and "because" all are used to show a causal relation (i.e. one thing causing another), and so don't work here. Also, because all three mean basically the same thing, none of them can be correct.

14 B EOI This passage is all about how college professors have become increasingly rare, so this sentence fits nicely to start this paragraph. Notice also that the explanations given in the other three answer choices are all false.

15 D SEC Answer choices (A), (B), and (C) are all pronouns that must refer to either community colleges or liberal arts colleges, but the sentence doesn't make sense with either of these options as the antecedent. Choice (D) makes clear who the subject of the sentence is by providing a new subject, "these instructors."

16 D SEC This is a pronoun-antecedent number-agreement question. The antecedent of the pronoun is "these instructors" for the previous sentence, and so we need a plural pronoun here. Only choice (D) uses the plural and correctly agrees "they" (plural) with "teachers" (plural).

17 B EOI Often when a question asks for which word works best in context, going by what sounds best is a good starting point to narrow down the choices. "Thing" is too informal. "Event" refers to something happening only at a specific time, whereas the occurrence described is ongoing. "Activity" refers to a specific action, whereas "phenomenon" describes a general circumstance like the lack of continuity and depth described here.

18 C SEC Use a comma along with a coordinating conjunction (remember the acronym FANBOYS) to join together two independent clauses, much like you would use a period or a semi-colon. Both parts of this sentence are independent clauses because they could each be a separate full sentence. Choices (B) and (D) don't work because, even though a period or semi-colon could work here, they both add a subordinating conjunction, making the second clause subordinate.

19 C EOI

This question is tricky because it requires you to pay close attention to the wording of the graph. Notice that the graph doesn't show the percent of tenured faculty, but rather the percent of tenure *track* faculty. Choice (A) is not correct because it mixes up tenured with tenure track. (B) and (D) are arguably true statements, but aren't shown through the information in the graph.

20 A EOI

At this part of the passage, the material is transitioning from an explanation of the problem into an analysis of its cause. The rhetorical question presented in choice (A) does a great job of introducing this new part of the passage. The other answer choices are all grammatically correct and true statements, but leave us without a transition statement to get from the discussion of the current problem to that of the issues causing it.

21 D SEC

This question requires you to think about subject–verb agreement and verb tense. When trying to figure out if a verb should be singular or plural, try to find the simple subject of the sentence—who or what is doing the verb.

Be careful: many students will try to figure out subject-verb agreement by what sounds best with the noun closest to the verb, but this often leads to an incorrect answer. The word "adjuncts" is closest to the verb, which "sounds" correct with the verb "are."

However, words in prepositional phrases are NEVER the subject of the sentence, so you can cross out the entire phrase when you are trying to find the subject of the sentence. Once you do so, you will be left with "use" as the only noun that could be the subject of the verb. Since "use" is singular, we need to choose a singular verb, which eliminates choices (A) and (C). Then, to check the tense, look at other verbs in the sentence that aren't in the underlined section. If the other verbs are in past, present, or future tense, stick with that same tense unless there's a specific reason to change. In this sentence, "receive" is present tense, suggesting that we should stick with present tense and choose "is." Also, think about when the setting is in the passage. Here in this passage, we're talking about the present day in general, so we want to keep the verb tense present to keep that clear!

22 D EOI

The tricky part of this question is recognizing the difference between percent and number. The graph shows the percentage of tenure track professors decreasing and the percentage of non-tenure track professors going up, but it doesn't tell us anything about the changing number of either.

23 B EOI

This question is easier to answer after reading the next couple of sentences in the passage for context. Choice (B) best introduces the topic by describing Stalin as he relates to the subject of the passage—Soviet control of music in Russia.

24 B EOI

This is a redundancy question. All four of the choices are grammatically correct and essentially identical in meaning. Choice (B), however, is the most concise and avoids any unnecessary extra wordiness.

25 **C** EOI   Choices (B) and (D) do not refer to specific members of Shostakovich's family, so those are out. Between choices (A) and (C), (C) is a better answer because it describes the experiences of the specific family members individually, rather than broadly and grouped together, as in choice (A).

26 **C** SEC   "Nor" must be paired with "neither" in this instance, but "neither" is incorrect because it would create a double-negative. Choice (C) is better than (D) because "either" is unnecessary in this context, and because it is in the wrong place in the sentence in choice (D). "To" starts an infinitive phrase. If we put "either" between "to" and the verb form "comply," we create a parallel structure error, because we cannot possibly put "or" between "to" and "represent."

27 **A** SEC   This is a long sentence with a complex structure. When looking at the punctuation rules for this part of the sentence, note that you don't use commas to separate a short prepositional statement from the rest of a sentence. Further, the prepositional statement "on a basic level" could not be a full sentence, so it doesn't work to separate it from the rest of the sentence using a comma with a FANBOYS word, as in choice (C), or a period as in choice (D).

28 **D** SEC   This question is about the correct form of the verb. First, we need to use the past tense, because the sentence begins narrating past events with this verb, as shown by the use of the verb "understood" as the narration continues in the following sentence. The second aspect in choosing the right answer to this question is recognizing the verb: "lie" can mean both to speak something untrue—as in to lie about what happened—and to be placed or situated, as in to lie about the house.

In this case, we need the second meaning, which is conjugated differently than the first. "Lied" is the past tense of the first version, but the past tense of the second is "lay," which is why (D) is the correct answer. Another difficulty about this question is that many students confuse the forms of the words lie and lay. The verb "to lay" requires an object, where the verb "to lie" does not. Here, the verb is immediately followed by two prepositional statements and has no direct object itself. Therefore, we must use the verb "to lie" in this case. However, the past tense of "to lie" is "lay," so this is a difficult question if you have not memorized these irregular forms!

29 **B** EOI   This sentence, while true and correctly following the first sentence of the paragraph, adds unnecessary detail to the passage that detracts from the main point of the paragraph.

The reasons given in choices (A), (C), and (D) for saying yes or no are all incorrect as well.

30 **B** SEC   This is a prepositional idiom question. Just as you would walk "in" a hallway and not "on" a hallway and sit "in" a car and not "among" a car, so too would nouns adhere "to" themes, rather than "with," "among," or "of" them.

31 **D** EOI   This sentence is complicated and detailed, with more music jargon than any of the other sentences in the passage for no apparent reason, so it has to go.

If your first reaction was to feel that the sentence should be added, read the "Yes" explanations carefully: neither of them is true!

32 **A** EOI   Choice (A) is most consistent with the information in the rest of the passage.

The difficult language of choice (C) makes it a tough choice to rule out for many students, as they assume that answers with harder words are "better." "Visceral" refers to the quality of being felt deeply in the body, rather than only through reason. "Polemical" means relating to controversial or critical use of language, like sarcasm, a hostile or bitter comment, or a caustic or cutting phrase. These words do not do as good a job as "moving and satirical" do to reflect how Shostakovich's music is described through the rest of the passage, and they introduce a style that doesn't fit with the more common language used throughout the passage.

33 **A** SEC   Choices (C) and (D) have incorrect subject–verb agreement because they do not correctly pair "listeners" with "are" or "listener" with "is." Choice (B) is overly broad because it refers to "every listener," rather than listeners generally, and because "is being" suggests that all listeners are being, at this very moment, taken aback by the horrors mentioned.

34 **D** EOI   This sentence disrupts the flow of the paragraph: the topic of the paragraph—and the entire passage—is the controversy regarding these specific genes.

35 **C** SEC   This is a pronoun question. Here, each of the answers choices except (C) either uses a vague pronoun, making it unclear which noun that pronoun is replacing, or uses the wrong pronoun.

"Myriad" is a singular non-person entity, so "it" is the correct pronoun to use. Similarly, the Hospital at the University of Pennsylvania is also a singular non-person entity that must be referred to as "it." Answer choices (A) and (D) use the plural "their" and "they" to refer to these singular nouns. Choice (B) uses an ambiguous pronoun—it is ambiguous exactly which of the two nouns "its" refers to. Further, the tense is incorrect in choice (B): we need to use the past tense, as all the other answer choices do.

36 **D** EOI   The graph shows that BRCA1 Positive people are at a much greater risk (almost eight times the risk) of contracting breast cancer than the general population. Choices (A) and (C) incorrectly present this information.

Be careful: choice (B) presents correct information but in a way that does not support the point of the paragraph—that the BRCA1 gene is useful in testing for cancer risk factors.

37 C SEC This is a sentence structure question.

 To evaluate the structure of a sentence, one trick is to remove any prepositional phrases, appositives, and subordinate clauses, then see if the core subject/verb part of the sentence still makes sense. In choice (A), after removing those things, we are left with "The case ruling," which is not a complete sentence. In choice (B), after removing the extra parts, there is no main verb for "case" at all, and choice (D) is actually a comma-splice: the run-on is created by turning the subordinate clause into an independent clause and using only a comma to combine them.

38 B EOI "However" is the best transition in this context because it means "regardless of that," referring to the information in the previous sentence. The other transition words do not show the correct relationship between the previous paragraph and the new information in this paragraph.

39 B EOI Choices (C) and (D) explain only why one party would dislike the ruling, but not both.

 Choice (A) is concise and so is an attractive choice, but it is not as good an answer as choice (B), because choice (A) does not give any information to explain why both parties were not pleased with the Court's finding. Choice (B) explains in just enough detail for the reader to understand why both Myriad and the plaintiffs disliked the ruling.

40 D SEC "Except" means "not including" as in, "I like every *Star Wars* movie except for the first three." "Accept," on the other hand, means to recognize, agree, or receive, as in "I am willing to accept that I may never get to go to Mars." Here, the parties asked the Court to decide the case, so "accept" is the correct term. Both choices (C) and (D) have the same meaning and are grammatically correct, but choice (D) is more succinct and so is the better choice.

41 B SEC The noun being replaced by a pronoun in the underlined section here is "the Supreme Court," which is a single non-person. Therefore, "it" is the correct pronoun.

42 B EOI Choice (C) takes a stance on the issue that eliminates the neutral tone the writer uses in the context of the rest of the passage. Choice (D) is quite concise, but overly so, as it doesn't explain what cDNA is, and that term is likely to be unfamiliar to most readers. Between choices (A) and (B), (B) is worded more clearly—choice (A) interrupts the flow of the sentence by putting a clause and an appositive phrase between the subject and verb, and also creates ambiguity with the use of "it."

43 A SEC A colon should be used to connect an independent clause with a quote, as in choice (A).

44 **D** EOI It can be difficult to notice without careful inspection, but paragraph 5 takes place chronologically after paragraph 6.

 Here's how to know what to do with ordering these paragraphs: paragraph 5 explains the significance of the "landmark precedent," which was set through the decision of the Supreme Court, which is explained in the paragraph currently marked 6. Thus, the paragraph describing the court decision must precede the one explaining the consequences and importance of that decision.

Math Test – No Calculator

Multiple-Choice Questions

 1 **C** HOA   Plug in 2 for x in both binomials on the left side of the equation:

$$(2-1)(2+3) = k+2$$
$$(1)(5) = k+2$$
$$5 = k+2$$
$$3 = k$$

⚠️ You may be tempted to FOIL (double distribute) the binomials because sometimes that kind of form change is useful, but since the value of x is known, it is best to just plug 2 into the equation as written. FOILing will only lead to extra work, which may cause unforced errors.

2 **A** HOA   The surest way to solve this is to backsolve the choices.

You can begin by plugging the choices into the first equation since it is simpler. Quickly, you will notice that only choice (A) works in the equation $a-b=12$ since $19-7=12$. You can verify that choice (A) is correct by also plugging it into the second equation to see that $2(19)-5(7)=3$.

💡 Alternatively, you can use the elimination method by first multiplying the top equation by 2 to arrive at $2a-2b=24$. Then, subtracting the bottom equation gets you $3b=21$ or $b=7$. Choice (A) is the only choice where b is 7. Though this algebraic method is valid, it has a higher chance of yielding errors than backsolving the choices.

 3 **C** PAM   Though plugging in numbers is an option for this problem, it is significantly more tedious on this problem than on most others, especially without the use of a calculator. The algebra here requires that you recall that squaring simply means multiplying something by itself, so calculate $(3a^2+6b^2)(3a^2+6b^2)$ by FOILing:

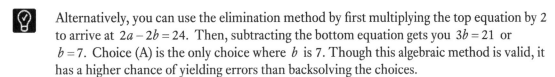
$$9a^4 + 18a^2b^2 + 18a^2b^2 + 36b^4 = 9a^4 + 36a^2b^2 + 36b^4$$

⚠️ Beware: powers cannot be distributed over addition. The common error here is to solely square both terms in the binomial. Luckily, that result does not yield one of the choices.

💡 When you get an answer that isn't one of the choices, as could happen for this question if you mistakenly distribute the power, the test is telling you that you've made a mistake. Consider it a gift, and either look for a calculation error or think about a different method.

4   **B** HOA   In most SAT formula interpretation problems there are two kinds of numbers: numbers, like the 35 in this question, that are constant values unattached to any variable; and numbers, like the 8 in this question, that act as coefficients to variables. These coefficients are rates of increase or decrease because they change linearly as the variable changes. Since the 8 in this question is a coefficient for both the variable representing hours and the variable representing number of guests, it means the restaurant charges $8 per hour per guest. Choice (A) is irrelevant because the formula has no mechanism for a maximum (like a $\leq$ symbol), choice (C) is an example of a constant because flat rates cannot increase or decrease, and choice (D) indicates a decrease which could only happen if there were a negative sign in the formula.

5   **B** PAM   Plug in 4 for a and solve for x:

$$\frac{\sqrt{x^2-9}}{4}=1$$
$$\sqrt{x^2-9}=4$$
$$x^2-9=16$$
$$x^2=25$$
$$x=\pm 5$$

Since $x<0$, x must $=-5$. Therefore $x-5=-10$.

6   **C** HOA   Like in question 4, you have a formula here with both a constant number and a coefficient number. The coefficient 24.45 is the rate per session so that $24.45x$ changes as x changes, increasing by 24.45 every time x increases by 1.

7   **B** PAM   If $h(2)=20$, then:

$$3(2)^3 - a(2) = 20$$
$$3(8) - 2a = 20$$
$$24 - 2a = 20$$
$$-2a = -4$$
$$a = 2$$

So $h(x)=3x^3-2x$, and $h(-1)=3(-1)^3-2(-1)=-3-(-2)=-1$.

8 B PAM You can begin this problem by multiplying both sides by a^4 yielding $a^{2x^3} = (a^{12})(a^4)$.

It is important to remember your exponent rules here. When you multiply terms with the same base, the exponents are added, so you get $a^{2x^3} = a^{16}$. Since you have the same base on both sides, you can now just conclude that $2x^3 = 16$ or $x^3 = 8$. This means that x must equal 2, and since you are asked for 2^x, you get 2^2 or 4.

Alternatively, you can make the left side of the original equation equal a^{2x^3-4} by using a different exponent rule. The remaining algebra would be similar from there.

9 C HOA Set the prices for plan A and plan B equal to each other and solve for m:

$$3.85 + 0.45m = 7.65 + 0.25m$$
$$0.45m = 3.80 + 0.25m$$
$$0.20m = 3.80$$
$$m = 19$$

Alternatively, you can backsolve the choices into each formula. Without a calculator, the difficulty of the backsolving calculations may prove prohibitive, but remember that you can backsolve at any stage of the above solution. So, for example, it may be easier to plug the choices in to $0.20m = 3.80$ than it is to complete the algebra.

10 A HOA A better case can be made for backsolving in this problem than in the previous one, since choices (A) and (D) are very easy to multiply by even the most complicated decimals. Still, the algebra may prove just as simple:

$$3.85 + 0.45m = 8.35$$
$$0.45m = 4.50$$
$$m = 10$$

11 A ATM When an expression is divided by a complex number, you should multiply the top and bottom of the fraction by the conjugate (change the middle sign) of the bottom. This is, in effect, multiplying by 1, like when you want to get a common or rational denominator, so you are changing only the form and not the value. The benefit is that the bottom will no longer be a complex number because i will be eliminated:

$$\frac{(4+2i)}{(2-i)} \cdot \frac{(2+i)}{(2+i)} = \frac{8+4i+4i+2i^2}{4+2i-2i-i^2} = \frac{8+8i+2(-1)}{4-(-1)} = \frac{6+8i}{5}$$

If you recognize that you will need to multiply by the conjugate on both the top and the bottom and that the choices all have different tops and different bottoms, then you can save time by just doing half the work.

12 **C PAM** The difficulty level of isolating variables in formulas can vary wildly.

⚠️ This problem is made to look more complicated than it is because the formula itself has so many operations. However, since you are only asked to solve for P, you need only divide both sides by everything else on the right side of the equation, namely $\left(1+\dfrac{r}{n}\right)^{nt}$. This leaves P alone on the right and $\dfrac{A}{\left(1+\dfrac{r}{n}\right)^{nt}}$ on the left.

13 **A HOA** Try to first find the slope-intercept form of each line. Line q has a slope of -2 and a y-intercept of 8, so the equation for line q is $y=-2x+8$. Line p has a slope that can be found by plugging the two points into $\text{slope}=\dfrac{\text{rise}}{\text{run}}=\dfrac{y_2-y_1}{x_2-x_1}$, so its slope is $\dfrac{5-7}{0-2}=\dfrac{-2}{-2}=1$. Line p has a y-intercept of 5, so its equation is $y=1x+5$. Set the equations equal to each other, $-2x+8=1x+5$, and solve to get $x=1$. This means that $a=1$ because a is the x-value at the point of intersection. Plug 1 in for x in the second equation to get $b=1(1)+5$, so $b=6$. The question asks for $a-b$, so $1-6=-5$.

14 **D PAM** In order to subtract these two fractions, you will need to get each one over the common denominator $(x+2)(x-3)$. That means multiplying each fraction on top and bottom by the denominator of the other:

$$\frac{1}{(x+2)}\bullet\frac{(x-3)}{(x-3)}-\frac{1}{(x-3)}\bullet\frac{(x+2)}{(x+2)}$$
$$=\frac{x-3}{x^2-x-6}-\frac{x+2}{x^2-x-6}$$
$$=\frac{-5}{x^2-x-6}$$

◈ An alternative method is to plug in a number for x in both the original expression and the answer choices to see which choice matches. That involves many calculations, so is not ideal as a primary method in this example.

💡 However, you could, if time permits, consider using that method as a check of the algebra above so that you are only plugging in to the answer you believe to be correct. For example, if you let $x=2$, then the expression in the question becomes $\dfrac{1}{4}-\dfrac{1}{-1}=\dfrac{5}{4}$ and answer choice (D) becomes $\dfrac{-5}{2^2-2-6}=\dfrac{-5}{-4}=\dfrac{5}{4}$.

15 D PAM If you FOIL the left side of the first equation you arrive at $6x^2 + 3bx + 2ax + ab$.

Since this equals $6x^2 + cx + 6$, you can conclude that $3bx + 2ax = cx$, or $3b + 2a = c$, and that $ab = 6$. Some of this is misdirection, a common hallmark of tougher SAT problems.

You need only recognize that $3b + 2a$ is half of the $4a + 6b$ from the second equation, so therefore c must be half of 12, or 6.

Student-Produced Response Questions

16 HOA 3 or 6

The number of multiple-choice questions has to be less than 8 because 8×8 is already more than the 60 total points. If you consider all possibilities between 1 and 7 multiple-choice questions, you can calculate the remaining points available for True/False questions and determine if the resulting number is a multiple of 3. For example, 2 multiple-choice questions will equal 16 points, leaving behind 44 points for True/False questions, but 44 is not a multiple of 3, so there cannot be 2 multiple-choice questions. On the other hand, 3 multiple-choice questions (24 points) leave 36 points available, and 6 multiple-choice questions (48 points) leave 12 points available. Both 36 and 12 are multiples of 3, so both 3 and 6 multiple-choice questions are valid options. Of course you only have to discover one of them to answer this correctly.

When it is clear from the wording of a "grid-in" problem that multiple answers will be accepted, trial and error is often a useful method.

17 PAM 6

First add 12 to both sides to arrive at $2b^2 = 72$. Divide by 2 to find $b^2 = 36$, so $b = \pm 6$. The question specified that $b > 0$ (and negatives cannot be gridded anyway), so b must be 6.

18   ATM $\dfrac{4}{5}$ or .8

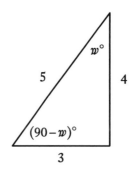

$w°$

5

4

$(90-w)°$

3

Draw a right triangle and label one of the acute angles as having a measure of $w°$. Because the tangent ratio is equal to $\dfrac{\text{opposite}}{\text{adjacent}}$ (SOH-CAH-TOA), you can label the leg opposite your marked angle as 3 and the other, adjacent, leg as 4. By the Pythagorean Theorem the hypotenuse has to be 5 because $\sqrt{3^2 + 4^2} = 5$.

It also helps to remember that 3-4-5 is a Pythagorean Triple. The acute angle that isn't $w°$ must have a measure of $(90-w)°$ because the two acute angles in a right triangle must be complementary. Therefore $\sin(90-w)°$ equals the side opposite the $(90-w)°$ angle, now 4, divided by the hypotenuse 5, so $\dfrac{4}{5}$.

19   HOA $\dfrac{3}{8}$ or .375

For a system of two equations to have infinitely many solutions, one of the equations must be a multiple of the other so that if you divide it through by a constant you will get the other equation exactly. Since 64 is 4 times 16, the second equation must be 4 times the first equation, and thus $3 = 4a$ and $2 = 4b$. From these equations you can arrive at $a = \dfrac{3}{4}$ and $b = \dfrac{1}{2}$, so $ab = \dfrac{3}{8}$.

20   ATM   8

Since the circumference of a circle is equal to $2\pi \times \text{radius}$, a full turn of $360°$ can be said to be equivalent to 2π radians. The simplest way to look at this problem is to recognize that since the x and y coordinates of point P are equivalent, the segment connecting point P to the origin must cut halfway through the third quadrant. Thus the angle θ must be $\dfrac{5}{8}$ of a full turn. $\dfrac{5}{8}$ of 2π is equal to $\dfrac{10\pi}{8}$, so $a = 8$.

Math Test – Calculator

Multiple-Choice Questions

1 **B** HOA   To find the total lemonade sales, add the small cup sales to the large cup sales. The small cup sales will equal the number of small cups, s, times the price per small cup, \$2.25, which will give $2.25s$. Add this to the large cups sales, $3.50l$, and you get $2.25s + 3.50l$.

2 **C** ATM   Since the figure has two pairs of parallel lines, each of the four intersections has congruent angles at each respective corner. Angle 1, in the northeast corner of its intersection, is congruent to the angles in the northeast corners of each intersection, including the intersection where angle 2 resides. This means that angle 1 and angle 2 are supplementary (add to 180°), and angle 2 must measure 50°.

3 **B** HOA   This word problem translates to:

$$3a + 17 = 50 - 6$$
$$3a + 17 = 44$$
$$3a = 27$$
$$a = 9$$

 You may think the problem is done here, but you must remember to keep your eye on your target, which in this case is $9a$. The final answer is $9(9) = 81$. If you remain aware of this ultimate goal throughout the problem, you can skip the final step above and simply multiply $3a$ by 3 to achieve the same result.

4 **A** PSD   When two variables are inversely proportional, they multiply to make a constant product, which in this problem is the mass of the gas.

$$\text{Density} \times \text{Volume} = \text{Mass}$$
$$(0.50)(4) = 2$$

When you change the values for density and volume, they should continue to yield a product of 2:

$$\text{Density} \times 10 = 2$$
$$\text{Density} = \frac{2}{10} = 0.20$$

5 **C** PSD   First you must find the new volume after a 30 percent decrease:

$$\text{New Volume} = \text{Old Volume}(1 \pm \text{Percent Change})$$
$$4(1-0.3) = 4(0.7) = 2.8$$

Again, you will use the inverse proportion relationship and the constant mass of 2 in order to find the density after the volume change:

$$\text{Density} \times 2.8 = 2$$
$$\text{Density} = \frac{2}{2.8} = 0.71$$

6 **D** PSD   In order to convert units, you must understand how to make conversion ratios. For example, when the question tells you that 10 liters = 1 dekaliter, you can place these values in a fraction, and because the two values are equivalent, the fraction will always equal 1, regardless of which unit is placed in the top or bottom:

$$\left(\frac{1 \text{ dekaliter}}{10 \text{ liters}} = 1 \ \text{ OR } \ \frac{10 \text{ liters}}{1 \text{ dekaliter}} = 1 \right)$$

Since this question asks you to convert 6 dekaliters into milliliters, you are merely changing the form (units) of the value by multiplying it by conversion ratios that equal one:

$$6 \text{ dekaliters} \times \frac{10 \text{ liters}}{1 \text{ dekaliter}} \times \frac{1000 \text{ milliliters}}{1 \text{ liter}} = 60,000 \text{ milliliters}$$

How do you know how to place your conversion ratios? Notice how the initial unit of dekaliters is canceled out by the dekaliters in the denominator of the first fraction, and the unit of liters is canceled out by the unit of liters in the denominator of the second fraction, thus leaving milliliters as the only uncanceled unit. Making sure that all the undesired units cancel out is a great way to ensure you've done your steps correctly!

7 **B** PAM You are asked to find an equation that is equivalent to $y = 2x^2 - 8x - 20$ and which displays the vertex of the parabola. If you recall that the axis of symmetry for any parabola of the form $y = ax^2 + bx + c$ is the line $x = \dfrac{-b}{2a}$, you can work out that the x-coordinate of the vertex is $\dfrac{-(-8)}{2(2)} = 2$. Plugging 2 into the function yields a y-coordinate of -28, which is only seen in choice (B).

◇ You can also backsolve the answer choices to see which can be simplified to the initial equation. Answer choice (B) is the only one to simplify correctly:

$$y = 2(x-2)^2 - 28$$
$$y = 2(x^2 - 4x + 4) - 28$$
$$y = 2x^2 - 8x + 8 - 28$$
$$y = 2x^2 - 8x - 20$$

◇ Alternatively, you could put $y = 2x^2 - 8x - 20$ into your graphing calculator and use that to calculate the vertex $(2, -28)$, which can only be seen in choice (B). You can find this either by expanding your window and visually estimating the vertex or by using $\boxed{\text{CALC}}$, i.e. $\boxed{\text{2ND}} \to \boxed{\text{TRACE}}$, and selecting the `minimum` feature.

8 **C** PSD The total number of apartment buildings is supposed to equal 15,000. If you add up the populations for the four cities from the graph, you will find that they sum to 15 units on the vertical axis. This means that each unit must equal 1,000 since 15 times 1,000 will give you your desired total of 15,000.

9 **D** HOA The easiest way to find the answer is to write an equation for how many calories are in one bag: if there are a chips that have 10 calories, $10a$ represents the total calories from the 10 calorie chips, $12b$ the calories from the 12 calorie chips, and $14c$ the calories from the 14 calorie chips. Since the total number of calories must equal 700, you get the equation $700 = 10a + 12b + 14c$, which can only be found in choice (D).

◇ Backsolving allows you to examine several possibilities and learn from them. Since the question stipulates that a bag must contain *exactly* 700 calories worth of chips, only a choice that includes an equal sign with a 700 is valid. This eliminates choices (B) and (C). A brief examination of choice (A) shows an incorrect relationship between the variables and calorie numbers, so only (D) can be correct.

10 **A** PAM   In order to isolate t, perform the following steps:

$$d = 171.3 + 55t$$
$$d - 171.3 = 55t$$
$$\frac{d - 171.3}{55} = t$$

Remember to check by plugging in numbers: if you plug an ordered pair into the original equation, the same values should also work in the new equation. For example, (1, 226.3) works in both the original and the new equations for (t, d), so you know you have found your answer.

11 **D** PAM   To find the unknown time, plug the distance of 400 for d into the initial equation:

$$400 = 171.3 + 55t$$
$$228.7 = 55t$$
$$4.16 = t$$

Alternatively, you can backsolve by plugging each of the choices in for t and assessing which one gives you a d equal, or closest, to 400.

12 **A** PSD   Like in question 6, you must use conversion ratios to change units, except that this question has some added difficulty. If you want your answer to be in the amount of days it would take for a single printer to run these books, you can use:

$$10,000 \text{ books} \times \frac{300 \text{ sheets}}{1 \text{ book}} \times \frac{1 \text{ minute}}{50 \text{ sheets}} \times \frac{1 \text{ hour}}{60 \text{ minutes}} \times \frac{1 \text{ day}}{10 \text{ hours}} = 100 \text{ days}$$

Note that you will be expected to know one conversion ratio (1 hour = 60 minutes) that is not supplied.

This question requires careful examination of all the data in the table. You should notice that the number of days the printers run per week and the number of employees running the printers are irrelevant. However, if there are 50 printers running, you must divide your total time by the number of printers to arrive at a final answer of 2 days.

13 **D** PSD   First find the C-axis, which is the vertical axis, labeled as Cost. Since the line represents the cost of one pizza according to the number of toppings, and the number of toppings at the C-intercept is zero, then you know the C-intercept represents the price of one pizza without any toppings.

14 **C** PAM You are being asked to determine the equation of a line in $y = mx + b$ form. Right off the bat, you should be able to see the value for b, the y-intercept, is 7, which means that choices (A) and (B) are out. Looking at choices (C) and (D), you now must examine the line more closely to determine if it has a slope of 0.5 or 1. Using points such as $(0, 7)$ and $(2, 8)$, you should be able to employ the slope formula to arrive at option (C).

$$\frac{\text{rise}}{\text{run}} = \frac{y_2 - y_1}{x_2 - x_1} = \frac{8 - 7}{2 - 0} = \frac{1}{2} = 0.5$$

You can also use your graphing calculator to graph each choice in the $\boxed{Y=}$ menu. Then use either the $\boxed{\text{GRAPH}}$ function or $\boxed{\text{TABLE}}$ function to compare each choice to the graph or, respectively, two associated points from the table.

15 **C** HOA Since you want a formula that expresses when the pool is full or overflowing, you must find the answer choice in which the sum of the initial water volume (3,250 gallons) and the volume added by the hose, 25 gallons per minutes over x minutes ($25x$), is greater than or equal to 9,500 gallons.

16 **A** PSD You can find the percentage of the total group represented by each choice very easily on a calculator by dividing the number in each respective group by 152, the total number of people surveyed. For example, choice (A), males who prefer Macs, consists of 48 individuals, which constitutes a portion that is $\frac{48}{152} = .3158$ of the total. This translates, by simply moving the decimal point two places to the right, to about 32 percent.

You can tackle this problem through approximation as well: 32 percent is just a little bit less than one third, or 33.3 percent. If you approximate one third of 152 by dividing 150 by 3 in your head, then you get 50. When you examine each of the choices carefully, Males who prefer Macs is the closest to 50.

17 **C** PSD You are given the speed of orbit in billions of km per hour. To find the speed as kilometers per hour, complete the following steps, noting that 4.9 billion should be written as 4,900,000,000 and that there are both 365 days in the average year and 24 hours in a day:

$$\frac{4,900,000,000 \text{ km}}{12 \text{ years}} \times \frac{1 \text{ year}}{365 \text{ days}} \times \frac{1 \text{ day}}{24 \text{ hours}} = 46,613 \text{ km/hour}$$

18 **A** PSD The median number of 45 would be found by arranging the numbers of flowers on each bush in order from smallest to largest and then selecting the middle number. The average of 34 would be found by adding up all the numbers of flowers and then dividing by the number of bushes. However, here you are not given any of the numbers in the set so you have to examine the impact each of the answer choices would have on either the median or average:

- Choice (B) is suspect because, depending on the numbers in a set, a mode can have little to no effect on the median or average. For example, if all but one number in a set only appeared once, then a number that appeared twice would be the mode, but a number appearing twice would not explain how the average number of flowers could be so much smaller than the median.

- Choice (C) seems like a reasonable idea, except that since a median and an average are both ways of describing the middle of a set of numbers, you would expect many numbers between 34 and 45. This does not, though, explain why there is such a large difference between them.

- Choice (D) says that there is little variance in the numbers of flowers, which means that the numbers don't deviate much from the average. If this were true, then there would not be such a large gap between the median and average.

- Choice (A) is correct because if some bushes had very few flowers (for example, if a small but significant number of bushes had zero flowers), then the median would be relatively unaffected while the average would be driven down. Imagine you have a list of the integers from 0 to 50. The average and the median would each be 25. If you then changed the lowest twenty numbers to all be 0, that would lower the average dramatically while leaving the median unchanged.

19 **B** PAM Since you are looking for the maximum of the function $f(x)$, you should look for the highest point on the graph, which has a height of 5. The question asks for the input value that yields the height of 5, which in this case is -2.

⚠️ Note that 5, the greatest y-value, is a choice, but you were asked explicitly for the value of x at the maximum.

20 B HOA You can solve this complicated system of equations by starting with either choice (B) or (C) and then backsolving.

If you start with choice (C), 2,149 weekend customers would result in 1,973 weekday customers in order for the total customers to add up to 4,122. If you multiply the number of weekend customers by the weekend price and add that to the number of weekday customers multiplied by the weekday price you get $2{,}149(15) + 1{,}973(11) = 53{,}938$. This is only slightly larger than the desired total sales of 53,234. This means we need fewer of the higher-value weekend customers, which points to choice (B). Repeating the above steps shows choice (B) to be correct: $1{,}973(15) + 2{,}149(11) = 53{,}234$.

It is instructive to examine the algebraic method of solving a system of equations problem like this, even though it requires more steps in this particular case,

let x = weekday parkers; let y = weekend parkers

$11x + 15y = 53{,}234$ and $x + y = 4{,}122$

$11(4{,}122 - y) + 15y = 53{,}234$

$45{,}342 - 11y + 15y = 53{,}234$

$4y = 7{,}892$

$y = 1{,}973$

21 B PSD There were 400 students surveyed, so to find the median value, you'd want to arrange the numbers of hours each student spent on homework from least to greatest and find out the number of hours the 200th and 201st students spent on homework. Luckily, the table has already placed the students in order, so you merely need to start at either the top or the bottom of the table, and add the number of students for each row until you find the row that contains the 200th and 201st students. The first 30 students (20 underclassmen and 10 upperclassmen) spent one hour on homework, and 120 more spent two hours. Since you have now accounted for 150 of the 400 students and there are 170 total students who spent three hours on homework, the 200th and 201st would surely reside there.

22 B PSD Based on the table, you might expect 10 underclassmen and 10 upperclassmen to have spent five hours on homework. However, the table represents the findings when 200 underclassmen and 200 upperclassmen are surveyed. This means it is likely that 5 percent of students, 10 out of 200, study for five hours whether they're underclassmen or upperclassmen, and since there are actually 80 more underclassmen than upperclassmen in total, there should be about four more underclassmen (5 percent of 80) who study for five hours.

23 C PSD When you are changing the value of something by a percentage, you can use the following formula: New Value = Old Value$(1 \pm$ percent change as decimal$)$. Multiple percent changes can be arranged in a single step. In this case:

New Population (p) = Original$(1 - 0.3)(1 + 0.47)$

$p = \text{Original}(0.7)(1.47)$

$\text{Original} = \dfrac{p}{(0.7)(1.47)}$

24 **D** ATM For this question, it is important to remember the equation for a circle is $(x-h)^2 + (y-k)^2 = r^2$, where (h, k) represents the center point, and r represents the radius. Your goal should be to change the given equation to this form, which can be accomplished by "completing the square" for the expression $y^2 - 10y$. The x^2 term is already a completed perfect square. When the coefficient of the squared term is 1, as it is here, you can complete a perfect square trinomial by halving the second term, -10 in this case, squaring that half, and then adding your result to the expression. So by adding the square of -5 we will create a set of terms that will be equivalent to the square of a binomial in y. Don't forget that you must add on both sides of the equal sign:

$$x^2 + y^2 - 10y + (-5)^2 = 9 + (-5)^2$$
$$x^2 + y^2 - 10y + 25 = 9 + 25$$
$$x^2 + (y-5)^2 = 34$$

In this form it is clear that $r^2 = 34$, so $r = \sqrt{34}$. Had you been asked for the center, you could also use this form to recognize that it would be $(0, 5)$.

25 **C** PAM Isolating a variable in a formula requires all the same algebraic skills that you've learned to solve for a value in an equation. Essentially, you need to undo what has been done to the variable you are looking for, while remembering that whatever is done to one side of an equal sign must be done to the other. The first move here in isolating m is to divide both sides by 2π to arrive at $\dfrac{T}{2\pi} = \sqrt{\dfrac{m}{k}}$. Then square both sides to find $\dfrac{T^2}{4\pi^2} = \dfrac{m}{k}$.

Lastly, multiply both sides by k to isolate m: $\dfrac{T^2 k}{4\pi^2} = m$.

 This problem can also be done by plugging in numbers for the variables. Since the calculations for each choice can get tedious, this problem is a good candidate for employing the plugging-in-numbers strategy as your check. If you are able to complete the primary method above, but are unsure if you've done all of the exponent work properly, consider choosing $m = 8$ and $k = 2$. This will ensure that you get a nice number, 4, under the square root in the original equation, and it will compute to a T value of 4π. Then plug 4π and 2, respectively, in for T and k in choice (C) and see that it gets you $m = 8$. If you'd made an error and didn't get choice (C), this maneuver would discover that error and allow you to continue the work of plugging in numbers as your new primary method.

26 **B** PAM Here plugging in numbers should be your primary method, especially since there is no extra work to be done with the choices. Consider masses $m_1 = 25$ for object 1 and $m_2 = 1$ for object 2 to satisfy the conditions mentioned. Then work out T for each object:

$$T_1 = 2\pi\sqrt{\frac{25}{k}} = 2\pi(5)\sqrt{\frac{1}{k}} = 10\pi\sqrt{\frac{1}{k}} \text{ and } T_2 = 2\pi\sqrt{\frac{1}{k}}.$$

So the period for object 2 is $\frac{1}{5}$ that of object 1.

27 **B** HOA First examine the lines $y = \frac{1}{3}x + 2$ and $y = \frac{1}{2}x + 4$ on your graphing calculator, looking for the point of intersection. If you are in a standard window, you may want to expand the left side a little by changing the Xmin to −20 under the WINDOW menu. You'll see that these two lines clearly cross in the third quadrant, actually at the point $(-12, -2)$. Though points on the line $y = \frac{1}{2}x + 4$ are not valid for the graph of $y > \frac{1}{2}x + 4$, the points just above that line are. Also, points both on and just below the line $y = \frac{1}{3}x + 2$ are valid for the graph of $y \le \frac{1}{3}x + 2$, so it is clear that there are points in that third quadrant that satisfy the system of inequalities.

Most calculators allow you to graph shaded inequalities by toggling with the ENTER button through the line/shade options to the left of the Y in the Y= menu. However, this often results in hard-to-read graphs if your calculator does not feature multiple colors, so it is sufficient to simply examine the lines in the manner recommended above.

28 C PSD If Clara's score is 5 percent higher than the class average, then it can be represented by 1.05a, where a stands for the class average. Thus, by solving for a when this is set equal to 85, you arrive at $\frac{85}{1.05} = 80.95 \approx 81$. Notice that the question asks for an answer that expresses your answer rounded to the nearest whole number, so the approximate value of 81 is sufficient.

We often think of scores on tests as percentages because many tests are calculated that way. For example, if you score 19 out of 20 on a vocabulary test, your teacher may write 95 on your test because you answered 95 percent of questions correctly. This example, though, does not stipulate that scores were percentages, yet it is easy to be fooled into thinking that if Clara scored 5 percent higher than the average, she must have scored 5 *points* higher than the average. For this reason, many students will incorrectly choose choice (B), 80. Remember, questions toward the end of a math section (this one is, after all, the third-to-last multiple-choice question in section 4) will likely involve a little more work or critical thought than simply subtracting 5. Treat each question with a level of respect commensurate with its position in a section or sub-section.

29 C PSD This question is based on the statistical conclusion that a representative sample can be used to approximate a total. Since Emily chose one shelf from each of her nine bookshelves, you can average the numbers in the table to reasonably estimate an average shelf among the 108 shelves that she has. That average, 94.22, can then be multiplied by 108 to approximate the total number of books in her collection at 10,176. Though there are flaws in this method if you are looking for a certain level of exactitude, the fact that no choice other than (C) comes close to 10,176 allows for a lot of latitude.

30 C PAM The Remainder Theorem states that if r is the remainder when a polynomial $p(t)$ is divided by $(t-a)$, then $p(a)=r$. This is what choice (C) says. If you have not taken a higher-level Algebra or Pre-calculus class, you may not have seen the Remainder Theorem, but your knowledge of factors of quadratic functions should help you navigate such questions.

A polynomial function $p(t)$ has a linear factor, $(t-a)$, if $p(a)=0$. You see this often in math classes when the polynomial function is quadratic. For example, $(t-5)$ is a factor of $t^2 -8t +15$ because that polynomial can be written as $(t-5)(t-3)$, and if you were to plug 5 into the polynomial, you would get a result of 0. This is true for all levels of polynomials, so choice (B), which claims that $(t-3)$ is a factor of $h(t)$, is invalid since $h(3) \neq 0$. You also have no basis to conclude one way or the other whether $(t+3)$ is a factor of $h(t)$, so choice (A) is out.

Student-Produced Response Questions

31 HOA **11**

Since 15 inches is an initial value and 2.5 inches per week is a rate, you can set the expression $15 + 2.5w$, where w represents weeks, equal to 42.5. Then isolate w:

$$15 + 2.5w = 42.5$$
$$2.5w = 27.5$$
$$w = 11$$

When time allows, you should make it a point to check your algebra by plugging your answer back in to the original equation.

Backsolving known choices is not an option on grid-in questions, but guess and check is. For example, if you could not figure out the equation that models this situation, you can start guessing possible answers that are easy to compute, like 10. After 10 weeks at 2.5 inches per week, the plant would have grown 25 inches beyond its initial height of 15 inches, giving you 40 total inches. It is not a far leap to realize that one more week will get you to 42.5 inches.

32 PAM **2**

A point should be thought of as (x, y) or $(x, f(x))$, so if $(3,8)$ is a point on the graph of $f(x) = x^3 - bx^2 - x + 2$, then:

$$8 = (3)^3 - b(3)^2 - (3) + 2$$
$$8 = 27 - 9b - 3 + 2$$
$$8 = 26 - 9b$$
$$-18 = -9b$$
$$2 = b$$

You can now check your answer by simply putting $x^3 - 2x^2 - x + 2$ into the $\boxed{Y=}$ feature on your calculator and seeing whether $(3,8)$ shows up on $\boxed{\text{TABLE}}$ ($\boxed{\text{2ND}} \rightarrow \boxed{\text{GRAPH}}$).

33 HOA $5 \leq x \leq 6.25$ or $5 \leq x \leq \dfrac{25}{4}$

If Joe reads at his slowest rate of 32 pages per hour over the entire 200 pages, it will take him $\dfrac{200}{32}$, or 6.25, hours. On the opposite end of the spectrum, if Joe reads at his fastest rate of 40 pages per hour over the entire 200 pages, it will take him $\dfrac{200}{40}$, or 5, hours. Any answer between, and including, these two numbers are possible lengths of time, in hours, that Joe might need to complete those pages.

34 PSD **5**

To find the average number of books read, you need to calculate the total number of books read and then divide by the number of students. The easiest way to calculate a total when you have data in a bar graph (or frequency table) is to add the products of each pairing of books read and students. For example, since five students read three books each, there were a total of 15 books read by those five students. This calculation yields:
$3(0)+1(1)+2(2)+5(3)+2(4)+7(7)+1(8)+4(10)=125$.

Notice that five, six, and nine books read are not included because no students read those numbers of books. The number of students, essentially the sum of the heights of each bar, is $3+1+2+5+2+7+1+4=25$. Lastly, you find the average by dividing 125 by 25, arriving at 5. It should be reassuring that the calculation resulted in a whole number, especially since the question did not mention rounding your answer.

35 HOA **7**

Since each day consists of 24 hours, d days has $24d$ hours. If d days and 6 hours totals 174 hours, you can use the equation $24d+6=174$ to answer this question. The solution, $d=7$, gives you the amount of full days that Herman was away. Like question 31, guess and check is another valid option here.

36 PSD **90**

You can use the previously-mentioned percent change formula here,

New Value = Old Value$(1 \pm$ percent change as decimal$)$:
$150(1-.40)=150(.60)=90$

37   PAM   **64**

The algebra required for this problem is:

$$(2x+3)^2 - (4x-7) =$$
$$(2x+3)(2x+3) - (4x-7) =$$
$$4x^2 + 6x + 6x + 9 - 4x + 7 =$$
$$4x^2 + 8x + 16$$

From this, you can conclude that $a = 4$ and $c = 16$, so $ac = (4)(16) = 64$.

 There are at least two common algebraic errors to beware of in this problem. First, realize that squaring a binomial like $(2x+3)$ requires four separate multiplications, not, as is often thought, just a squaring of $2x$ and 3 individually. Also, remember to distribute the negative sign through the second binomial. It is easy to miss that and end up with a -7 instead of a $+7$ at the end of the third line above. That would give you a c value of 2 and an answer of 8. Since this is a grid-in question, there are no choices to act as a safety net, so these possible missteps can be deleterious.

 Since there are many possible pitfalls to the algebra, a good checking mechanism is valuable in a problem like this. One option is to put both your final trinomial, $4x^2 + 8x + 16$, and the original left side of the equation, $(2x+3)^2 - (4x-7)$, into the $\boxed{Y=}$ feature of your graphing calculator and make sure that either the graph or table of both are the same as one another.

38   ATM   **1.5 or $\dfrac{3}{2}$**

The formula for the volume of a cone, supplied in the introduction to each math section, is $V = \dfrac{1}{3}\pi r^2 h$, where r is the base radius of the cone and h is its height.

If the volume of Darin's cone is 810π in^3 and its height is 30 inches, then you can solve $810\pi = \dfrac{1}{3}\pi r^2 (30)$ to determine the radius of the cone in inches:

$$810\pi = \frac{1}{3}\pi r^2 (30)$$
$$810\pi = 10\pi r^2$$
$$81 = r^2$$
$$9 = r$$

Since the diameter is twice the radius, the diameter must be 18 inches long.

But be careful: you were asked for the diameter in <u>feet</u>. 18 inches equals 1.5 feet. Two words were underlined in the question, "diameter" and "feet," so take note, because it is easy to forget that you are looking for a diameter when the formula you are using references the radius, and it is easy to forget that the answer should be in feet when the dimensions you are given are in inches.

Words that are underlined, italicized, or in all capitals should be circled as well because you are likely to overlook these kinds of emphasis markers when you are in the midst of a complicated set of algebraic maneuvers.

Answer Explanations for Test 2

Reading Test

Passage 1

The first passage on every SAT reading section is always a literary passage, which takes a slightly different approach from the more informative and rhetorically oriented passages on the rest of the test. This passage is excerpted from Oscar Wilde's comical ghost story "The Canterville Ghost," and it is essential to read the introduction in order to minimize the disorientation caused by the start of the passage, which begins when the conflict between the family and the ghost has already begun. As you read, it is important to mark the names of characters as they are introduced in order to keep them straight, as the questions ask about different specific characters' ideas and actions. Finally, it is important to get a sense of the tone of the passage as a whole: the family's response to their haunting is patently absurd, and the narrator reports it with a dry wit.

 D COE

 We jump into this passage with a COE question immediately, and it is a tough one for almost any reader to get without using the strategy of answering the questions as a pair. Many readers may read the question and not realize that there was a gift given at all, so you really want to read those line number choices first! Thus, make sure you answer question 2 before you answer question.

C COE   You want to read through these options to see which tells us why the gift was given. Choice (A) tells us that the Minister was upset that his present was not accepted, which tells us that he gave a gift, but nothing about *why* he gave it. Choices (B) and (D) make no reference to the gift at all and are thus easily ruled out. Choice (C) references the gift he gave—the Rising Sun Lubricator—and that he gave it in the hope that it would silence his chains, which points directly to choice (D) in the previous question.

C RC   This question can be answered in terms of the tone of the narrator throughout the passage as a whole, but the specific reference given is a particularly clear indication of the kind of voice the narrator uses. When we read the lines referenced, we see that the narrator refers to the Minister's reproach of his children's hurling pillows at the ghost as "impolite" as a "just remark" and then apologizes for having to report that the twins "burst into shouts of laughter" at their father's reproof.

You should write in your own term for this, perhaps something like "mocking" or "ironic," and then match it up with Choice (C).

If you cannot come up with your own term for the narrator's tone, you can also use process of elimination. Choice (A) is then wrong because the narrator is not in the story, which would require a first-person narration from one of the characters in the story itself. Choice (B) is incorrect because he is not "inept," or unskillful, as an observer. Choice (D) may be difficult to rule out because the words are difficult, and the word "apologist" may be tempting due to the narrator's apparent apology, but the narrator is not being sincere, and so this answer does not fit.

4 D RC This question, too, is based on the narrator's style throughout the passage, but the specific reference explains that little Virginia "for some unexplained reason" was upset at the sight of a fresh blood-stain every morning. Since any rational person—particularly a small child—would be quite understandably distressed about a blood stain, the term to write in for the tone here is "ironic." This leads to choice (D).

Another way to get this question is to consider that questions 3 and 4 need to "fit" with each other and the passage as a whole, and "subtly ironic" is an appropriate tone for a "wry commentator," while none of the others are good fits with that idea.

5 B RC Question 5 is a good example of a question with misleading line numbers: the reference in line 50 is where the key terms are, but the entire paragraph leading up to this sentence is needed to understand how the term is used. The ghost has knocked over a suit of armor and hurt himself, and the Minister is pointing a revolver at him. The instruction that the narrator describes as "Californian etiquette" is to hold up his hands, so this is an ironic use of the term "etiquette." Thus, choices (A), (C), and (D), all of which suggest that the term is meant more or less in earnest, are incorrect, leaving only choice (B).

Another way to get this question is to write in your own idea for the purpose, which would be something like "make fun of the Minister." This makes (B) and (C) seem possible, as both "satirical" and "derisive" fit with making fun, but (C) suggests that he is mocked for being polite, and the minister is not being polite!

6 C WIC This is a great example of a WIC question that requires you to go back and re-read the sentence to get correct. No one's first idea of what the word "covered" means is "aimed at," unless you have just read the word in the context of its use in line 48. In the sentence, he "covered" the ghost with his revolver, which refers to the idiomatic use of covered that suggests having a weapon pointed at someone. Seeing this makes choice (C) an easy pick.

7 A RC To answer this question, go back and re-read not only the sentence referenced in the question but also the ones before and after it. Once you do this, you can see that the references are there to suggest the powerful effect that the ghost's hauntings have had on people in the past, which is a perfect fit for choice (A). The other choices are tempting only if you do not return to the passage and read it for yourself.

8 C WIC This is a very difficult WIC question: it gives a common word used in a way that is archaic and almost certainly unfamiliar to most students. If you know this now obsolete use, you can quickly pick choice (C).

However, even if you are not familiar with the word's use in this sentence, you can use the context and eliminate answers that don't make sense. The ghost hears footsteps approaching, and so he "hesitates in his fell purpose." If we read each of the answers in, we can see that (A) and (D) do not make sense, because they imply that his purpose is already lost. Choice (B) is not impossible, but it doesn't make nearly as much sense as the correct answer, which suggests that he hesitates in his "evil" purpose.

 9 D COE This is the first part of a COE pair, so you should always use the COE paired question strategy: try to answer the second question first and then come back to this one.

10 B COE Use the paired question strategy and start by using a process of elimination to get this question correct and then go back to get 9. Choices (A), (C) and (D) tell us what the ghost does and what evidence he leaves behind of his actions, but none provide any specific response of the family. Only choice (B) tells us that they were "amused" by the blood-stain and made bets on what color it would be. This matches well with choice (D) in #9, because amusement is a very odd response to a ghost.

Passage 2

This passage is a social science passage that discusses issues of economics, agriculture, public health, and the environment. There is a lot of information here, and so the strategy of circling names, dates, terms and figures is a necessity, both to help keep everything straight as you read and to access needed information to answer questions later. You also want to write down the main purpose of the passage—to show a problem in Uganda and what one entrepreneur is doing to help address that problem. There is also a table with the passage, but remember that you don't really need to pay attention to it until you get to a question about it.

11 C RC This is a great example of a question with deceptive line numbers. Although it asks about lines 5–12, the clearest articulation of the purpose of these lines comes in lines 18–19, which shows that the story illustrates the kinds of problems Moses wanted to solve with his company, which matches choice (C) perfectly.

 You can also get this one correct by thinking about the introductory anecdote in terms of the purpose of the passage as a whole. This story illustrates the kinds of problems that Moses' company tries to address, which nearly corresponds to choice (C).

12 D RC This is a tone question, and we recommend the following strategy for such questions: use a 5-point system to "score" the tone of the passage, and then find the answer choice that matches your "rating." If the author's tone is very critical and negative, it would be a 1, whereas a passage that is merely informative ranks a 3, and a passage that is very positive—like this one—gets a 5. You can use the even numbers for slightly less strong tones. Once we know that the tone here is a 5, it is easy to choose (D), easily the most positive description of the tone.

13 **A** RC Answering this question correctly requires a basic understanding of the structure of the passage. If you understand that the first part introduced the problem and the rest of the passage discusses a partial solution to the problem, it is easy to choose (A).

If you are stuck on a question like this, you can use the specific language in each answer choice to "match up" with what you find in the passage at the indicated point. Choice (B) suggests that these lines introduce the problem: not only has the problem already been introduced, but these lines also do not articulate any problem at all. Choice (C) is incorrect, because both social and environmental impacts have already been brought up prior to these lines. Choice (D) is entirely inaccurate—these lines are not about restoring forests, they are about using farm waste. Choice (A), however, is directly supported by the language of the transition, which indicates a change from a past time to what is being done to address a problem four years later.

14 **A** COE This is an ideal example to illustrate why it is much better to go directly to the line number references in the second of a COE question pair. The entire passage is filled with the problems of burning wood, so we want to let the test lead us to the correct places to look for the answer to this question.

15 **B** COE Once we know by carefully reading the previous question that we are looking for lines that show a specific problem caused by burning wood, we can read through these line references and find which provides such a problem.

Choice (A) is a very tempting answer, as it starts talking about problems caused by wood-burning, but it only addresses the fact that these problems are widespread—it does not actually give any specific problems. Choices (C) and (D) are easier to eliminate, as both only talk about ways in which Moses and his group are trying to improve things. Choice (B) tells us about the toll on health that wood burning takes, which makes it the correct answer for this question and also clearly points to choice (A) in the previous question.

16 **C** COE This COE question requires close reading of the lines for the next question—in one form or another, all of these answers come up in the course of the passage, so just go on to the next question and find the lines that answer this exact question about the unsold char left over from Moses' kilns.

Once you choose (C) for question 17, you may still struggle between choices (B) and (C) if you do not understand how percentages are used in the passage. Choice (B) suggests that the farmers double their yield; however, the passage says that they increase harvests by more than 50%. To double yields, they would have to increase by 100%.

17 **C** COE Once you know what you are looking for—the usefulness of unsold leftover char—this question is quite easy to solve by process of elimination. Choice (A) discusses benefits to families, choice (B) discusses the profits from sold char, and choice (D) gives a quote about how individual employees have benefited from the program. Only choice (C) discusses the unsold leftover char at all, and so is, of course, the correct answer.

A WIC   This WIC question asks about a common word with a few meanings, so you must read the sentence again to determine how "value" is used in this sentence. First, you should notice that it is a verb, not a noun, and then replace it with your own word. In context, one word you could use instead of "value" is "appreciate," which is an exact match with choice (A).

   Choice (B) "enjoy" would make the sentence mean roughly the same thing and it is almost certainly true that people enjoy the opportunity Moses's company offers. However, the best strategy for these questions is not simply to read each choice into the sentence and pick the one that sounds best, but to replace the word with your own term first and then match it. Only resort to putting each of the answers in place of the selected word if you are stuck between two based on your own replacement word or if none of the words are a good fit with your word.

19 D WIC   Like #18, this is a WIC question on a common word with several uses. In this sentence, "credit" refers to a financial transaction based on a loan given to be repaid later, which is a perfect match with choice (D).

20 C IG   This is a fairly straightforward IG question. Proceed by eliminating answers that are untrue or unsupported. Choice (A) is made up of two parts, and inaccuracy in either part is enough to rule it out. The first part is a claim that the author has exaggerated the severity of deforestation, but, even if the second part were true, it would not make this initial claim accurate. Choice (B) is clearly inaccurate based on the table. Choice (D) is impossible to determine based on the table.

Passage 3

This is a science passage that not only presents a lot of information but also has a clear argumentative purpose. In order to handle the first aspect well, you want to be sure to circle all of the names, terms, dates, and numbers given in the passage. In order to understand the rhetorical aspects of the passage, you should do two things: First, you should pay attention to the way the passage develops, underlining key words like "easy to overstate" in line 52 and "the problem arises" in line 65. Second, you should write a good summary—something like "Though genetics has produced advancements in the field of medicine, our understanding of DNA is imperfect and other factors in understanding health must still be attended to." Again, note that there is a table, and be prepared to attend to it when you come to a question that addresses it.

21 B RC   This question is an ideal example of a question to write in your own answer for before looking at the answer choices. When you go back to the first paragraph, you will find that it is full of facts about what has happened recently in genetics. Thus, you want to write down "background info," and then choose (B), which is a perfect match.

  Choices (C) and (D) are somewhat tempting if you do not figure this out for yourself at first, as they all are at least partially accurate, so be sure to trust your own reading ability (*and the answer you wrote down*), and not the answer choices on the test.

22 C WIC   This is a WIC question: follow the strategy of going back to the passage, considering what the term means in context, and writing down your own answer before you look at the answer choices. While "cloud" can mean darken, the literal meaning of darken makes no sense in this context, so choice (B) is not a good answer.

  In context, both choices (A) and (D) make good sense of the sentence as a whole with these words swapped in for "cloud." However, "cloud" simply does *not* mean either limit or hamper, and so they are both incorrect.

23 A COE   This is a paired COE question, so you want to go on and do the next question first. Onward to #24!

24 C COE To get this question correct, you want to read the previous question and look through these lines to see which one provides a specific benefit of genetic research. Choice (C) gives one—the possibility of identifying and being proactive about certain diseases—and this matches choice (A) in #23 perfectly.

25 B RC This question requires you to understand the larger structure of the passage as a whole, as the paragraph referenced is the one in which the author shifts from the advances offered by genetic research to the dangers and limitations of such research. If you write this in as your own answer to the question, you will easily recognize Choice (B) is a perfect fit for the idea.

26 D RC   Always write in your own answers for all questions about tone. In this case, if you re-read the paragraph in which this idea is mentioned, you will find that the author disagrees with the notion that "DNA is destiny" and warns against accepting the view. Thus, a word like "warning" would be a good answer, and "cautionary" is the best fit.

  We can also get this correct by thinking about the main idea of the passage as a whole and eliminating answers that don't fit. Choice (B) is too positive about the idea, and choices (A) and (C) are too negative, as the author is neither disinterested nor cynical.

27 C RC   This is another question to use the strategy of writing in your own answer based on the passage before going to the answer choices. The passage uses quotation marks to indicate that the term is a misnomer, as the sentence says it was "previously thought" of in this way but is not seen as "vital." Choice (C) exactly matches this idea.

  Choice (A) might seem like a close fit for the idea, but the author of the passage never "mocks" anything in the passage. Remember to read closely and make sure that every word of the answer fits properly with the passage as a whole.

28 D COE This question is very close to the main idea of the passage as a whole, and so you may be able to answer it based on a strong understanding of the passage, which makes clear that choice (D) is correct.

 However, the strategy of treating COE questions as a pair makes this question even easier. Thus, you can also just go on to question 29…

29 D COE After reading the previous question, you can read through these four choices and see which offers the author's response to the overemphasis upon genetic factors in dealing with diseases, and Choice (D) offers the clearest answer to the question. These lines also clearly match choice (D) on question 28. Choice (A) is too early in the passage, when the author is still just reporting advances. Choice (B) merely indicates that there is an overemphasis, not a response to it. Choice (C) indicates one of the limitations of genetic research, not a way of limiting the dependence upon it.

30 B WIC
 In this WIC question, choices (B) and (D) both give more common alternative meanings of "stock," so be sure to go back to the passage to understand its use in line 88. When we re-read the full sentence, we find a familiar word in an odd context, in this case the idiomatic phrase "putting too much stock into," which means depending upon too much or having too much faith in. When we consider the context of this idiom, it is easy to choose (B), which fits well with the word "faith."

31 D IG This an IG question, but it is a particularly difficult one, because it requires you to work with both the passage and the table. In order to get it correct, you need to read through the answers and carefully eliminate any that are incorrect. So let's do that, in order:

 Choice (A) is tempting, because the table divides up cases between the general population and those with BRCA mutations, but there are two problems: first, the table never gives a total for us to determine percentages from, and second, the passage never suggests that these mutations are solely responsible for causing breast cancer in those who have them.

Choice (B) is probably easier to rule out, because the table gives only percents, no numbers of cases at all.

 Choice (C) is also tempting but is incorrect because we do not have the "average" age for any population, only the median, and we don't have a way to calculate the median between the various groups listed in the table.

Choice (D) is correct—the passage tells us in line 85 that only 10% of patients diagnosed with breast cancer have BRCA mutations, and so 90% of cases are from the general population, which has only an 11% risk of breast cancer.

Passage 4

This is a paired history passage that falls into the "great global conversation" category that the SAT is using on each test. These readings are OLD and HARD. Be sure to read the introductions to each passage on the test: they convey essential information, such as the date and author. In this case, many test takers should notice the dates 1790 and 1791 and skip this passage for the time being. For a test taker who is not going for a top score and is not a very strong reader, simply gridding in answers for each question and moving to the next passage saves time and energy and will likely allow the last passage to be finished in its entirety. For a test taker who is going for a top score, skipping this passage will allow you to come back to it and do it last, when you can take all the time you have left and not worry about still needing to finish the (much easier) last passage. This passage is drawn from the opposed political writings of Thomas Paine and Edmund Burke. Both passages are highly rhetorical, using imagery and metaphor to express complex political and historical ideas, further increasing the difficulty of these passages for most readers. Burke writes a lament of the loss of the traditional order that took place in the French Revolution, focusing on Marie Antoinette to illustrate his point. Paine responds directly to Burke in this excerpt, calling attention to the abuses of the system that Burke praises.

32 **A** COE

This is the first of a COE pair—remember always to check through all the questions and mark these pairs before you start, because those sneaky test makers will put the first of a pair at the bottom of a page so that you will try it without using the second question. Don't do it! Go on to #33, and you will find this question fairly easy, despite the difficulty of the language in the selection.

33 **B** COE

Once you have read question 32, read through these options to see which gives the author's initial assessment of Marie Antoinette. Choice (A) does not give any assessment, it merely affirms the author's having seen her at a particular time and place. Choice (C) refers to a later time, as he claims that he could not dream of her later troubles upon first seeing her. Choice (D) is back to that initial moment of seeing her, but he references the response he expected from others, not his own assessment of her. Choice (B) is the author's rapturously poetic description of Antoinette, which admires her beauty in claiming that she "decorated" the world around her and her charm in saying that she "cheered" that world as well. Her physical beauty is also suggested in comparing her to a glittering star, and her personality is indicated as "full of life, splendor and joy." This is the correct answer and clearly points to choice (A) in #32.

34 **C** RC
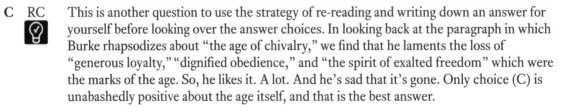
This question asks you to analyze the author's use of the rhetorical scheme of repetition at the opening of clauses (that's anaphora, for those of you who love Greek words). For this type of question, you always want to re-read the referenced sentences and then answer the question in your own words. Here, you might write something like "to show his surprise." This neatly matches choice (C).

35 **C** RC
This is another question to use the strategy of re-reading and writing down an answer for yourself before looking over the answer choices. In looking back at the paragraph in which Burke rhapsodizes about "the age of chivalry," we find that he laments the loss of "generous loyalty," "dignified obedience," and "the spirit of exalted freedom" which were the marks of the age. So, he likes it. A lot. And he's sad that it's gone. Only choice (C) is unabashedly positive about the age itself, and that is the best answer.

36 C WIC This WIC question asks about a word that may be familiar to some, but it is used in a very specific way by the author, so we want to go back to the passage and put our own word into the sentence before looking at the answers.

In the sentence, we find that Burke claims that, in the age of chivalry, "vice" was less evil, because it had no "grossness." Based on what he has said about the age prior to this sentence, its emphasis upon order, gentility, and honor, we can assume that he means that vice was not vulgar in that previous age, which leads us to choice (C).

If you have a hard time with the context on your own, you can try reading the four answer choices into the sentence and see which might be said to make vice seem less evil. Choice (A) should seem very unlikely, as well-washed sinners should hardly be less evil, and choice (B) cannot sensibly be possessed by vice, as it cannot be disgusted in reaction to itself. Choice (D) is likely tougher to rule out, especially if you don't know what "largess" is, so you may have to take a guess between (B) and (D). If you do know what largess is— generosity—this answer is way off, as losing generosity would only make something worse.

37 A RC This question is somewhat atypical, in that it is most readily answered by simply working carefully through the answer choices. A sharp reader may read answer choice (A) and immediately recollect that this analogy is used repeatedly in the passage (the whole of the first paragraph and the last sentence of the selection in particular).

However, if that answer doesn't immediately strike you as correct, you can eliminate the others by simply checking if they are true.

Choice (B) is perhaps the most tempting, as lines 56–59 are certainly a fairly personal attack; however, in order to be prevalent, we should expect to find more than a single instance. Choice (C) is simply inaccurate: if you try to find parallel logical claims or uses of evidence, you will not find them! Choice (D) misunderstands the theatrical references— they are all accusations of Burke, not his own attempt to be theatrical.

38 A WIC This is a WIC question that is just a hard word. If you know the term—perhaps from studying Poe's "Purloined Letter" in an English class—you can readily choose (A), as it is the only meaning of the word.

If you don't know the word, you can still get this question by process of elimination. Reading the choices into the sentence, you will find that choices (A) and (C) are sensible substitutions in the sentence as a whole because both make a negative meaning and could be done by a hand. From there, you can choose one and have a 50/50 chance, or, if you have time to come back to this question at the end and can give it more time, you can choose (A) because being "stolen" from oneself would be more likely to cause "degeneration" than simply being "hidden," which isn't negative enough.

39 B RC This is a main idea question in disguise.

 It can be solved by understanding Paine's specific metaphor at this point, but it can also be solved by recognizing how this fits into the overall point that Paine makes, that Burke is more interested in externals of the old system that he sees as glorious than the real suffering of human beings. Only choice (B) gets at this idea. If you understand his metaphor, that a bird's plumage—the visible feathers—are the external aspects of the old system that Burke laments losing, while the bird's death refers to the suffering the system caused, you can readily choose (B) as well, which reflects this idea exactly.

 40 B RC If you wrote down a quick sentence comparing these two passages before you started the questions, it should show that these two are directly opposed, with Burke on the royalist/aristocratic side of the French Revolution and Paine on the common people's side. This makes (B) the obvious choice.

 Another way to solve this question is to use process of elimination. Because the two do not agree, you can eliminate (C) and (D) immediately. If you waver between (A) and (B), re-read the introductory information: since the passages are from 1790 and 1791, respectively, they cannot be from "very different times."

 41 A COE This is the first of a COE pair. You know the drill: go on to the next question, and don't waste time here! This is probably the hardest question in this set, as it asks you to understand a difficult part of the first passage and then connect it to the second passage. Let the test do the work by reading through those choices, and then you will easily be able to choose (A).

 42 B COE Once you read over question 41, read these excerpts and ask yourself: does Paine talk about the experience of the lower classes (those "in servitude") in these lines? Lines 39–42 criticize Burke's writing style, but does not address any issue of the Revolution itself. Lines 51–52 again criticize Burke's writing as "unkind to nature," but does not address specifics. Lines 59–60 speak of Burke's "hero," which is an aristocrat, not one of those "in servitude." Thus, only choice (B), which discusses the "wretched lives" of those imprisoned in the Bastille, addresses the question, and it is the correct answer. It also clearly points to choice (A) in #41.

Passage 5

This is a science passage that references two books to discuss a biological concept, "flexibility in behavior response." The passage's structure is easy to recognize and you should mark its parts as you read: it opens with wasps as a counter example, then identifies the advantage humans have over such wasps, and then articulates three "complex and interrelated sources" for this biological advantage, each neatly discussed in its own numbered paragraph. Circling terms and names is a very helpful strategy here, as there are a few of both, and the questions ask about specifics in many cases.

43 C COE This question might not be too difficult to answer if you read the whole passage and understood the rhetorical function of this introduction, but you can still use the answer choices to the second part of this COE pair. Choice (C) reflects the structure of the passage—the author uses an example to illustrate a biological concept and then illustrates how humans and certain other species can transcend that tendency.

44 C COE Lines 25–27 clearly articulate the relevance of the wasps in the initial example to the passage as a whole, so this is the correct answer. Choice (A) is within the paragraph, but it draws the central conclusion of this paragraph rather than indicating its significance in terms of the passage as a whole. Choice (B) reinforces the idea of determinism that is central to the first paragraph, but still does not situate it within the context of the passage as a whole. Choice (D) is too late in the passage, as it doesn't discuss the wasp example at all.

45 A RC Answer this question by using process of elimination. All of the information to answer the question is contained in the first paragraph, so doing so won't take long. When you check the first choice, you will see that each egg is in its own partition, which makes this NOT a part of the cycle.

Be sure to underline the word NOT in the question. If you go through all the answer choices and mark those you are not sure about, confirm that you have chosen the one that is FALSE when you bubble in your answer choice.

46 D WIC This is a WIC question with a fairly difficult word and a few difficult choices.

If you know that steadfast means constant, you can readily pick (D), assuming that you also know that assiduously means the same thing. If your knowledge of these somewhat difficult words is not certain, you can still get this question by reading through the answers and using process of elimination. Choice (A) doesn't make sense—although steadfast can suggest bravery, the wasps are certainly not brave. Choice (B) is a harder word, but you can break it into pieces to get an idea of its meaning. The root word "vocal" means something related to the voice, and "un" means not, and "equi" means equal. So the whole must mean something like "not equally voiced," which is a poor fit here. (By the way, "unequivocal" actually means completely clear, not in any way ambiguous.) Choice (C) may be tempting, because digging to its own death certainly is unfortunate, but the word is a poor match with our original word, which seems to be made up of the words "steady" and "fast," neither of which suggests "unfortunate." Thus, you are left with choice (D), and you can choose it even though you may not have any idea what "assiduously" means.

47 D RC   This is a question that demands re-reading, and it is a great example of why the strategy of writing down an answer for yourself before reading the answer choices is so important. The direct discussion of these two books is in the second paragraph, so you will want to re-read lines 25–40 and then write down what you find to be the relationship between the two. First, you will see that the author mentions a "common theme" between the two books in lines 26–27. Then, you will see that one of Bonner's aspects of "culture" is "freedom from… 'single response behaviors'" in lines 33–34. Then, Gould goes on to discuss Wilson's use of "freedom from genetic programming of specific behaviors" (lines 36–37)—the same concept Gould just mentioned in Bonner—as central to human potential. Thus, we could write something like the following: "Bonner's concept of culture includes the aspect that Wilson's book is all about." That is a perfect match for choice (D).

  While (A) and (B) are fairly easy to reject, choice (C) may be tempting. It includes many of the correct concepts, but does not put them into the proper relationship, as neither says that flexibility determines brain size.

  This is a fairly difficult question. On questions you are not sure of, always mark the question on the packet and return to it after you complete all the questions for the passage. Often, later questions will help you understand earlier ones better, and you may even re-read a part of the passage on a later question that makes the answer quite clear. In this case, answering question 48, which also refers to both writers, will almost certainly make this question easier.

48 B RC If you already answered 47 correctly, this question should be very easy, as it is based on the same paragraph in the passage but asks an easier question.

  If you weren't sure about 47, you can use process of elimination to answer this question. Choice (A) says that these are "exclusively" human traits, meaning that they can never be found in any other creature, and the passage directly contradicts this idea, even in the title of Bonner's book. Choice (C) is not supported by the passage—larger brains are an aspect of flexibility, but there is no suggestion that it directly determines either culture or flexibility. Choice (D) is directly contradicted by the passage—the main idea of the passage is an exploration of the biological benefits of culture and flexibility. Thus, choice (B) is correct.

49 C COE This is a difficult COE question because it makes you think analogically, which many test takers find challenging.

  In order to give yourself the best chance, go on to the next question and read through the line number options to see which gives the best answer to how a larger brain is beneficial, and then it will be much easier to choose which of these options is most analogous to the specific reference given in the passage. Once we know that a larger brain is better because its size allows for more circuitry, we can see that this corresponds best with a larger puppet having more strings to allow for greater movement.

50 B COE Use process of elimination here. Choice (A) claims that humans have a proportionally larger brain but doesn't give a specific benefit of our sizable grey matter.

 Choice (C) is probably the most tempting wrong answer. It doesn't give a specific benefit to a larger brain; it simply gives an impressive fact about the amount of information the brain holds. Choice (D) is an easier answer to rule out, because it asserts what allowed our brains to become large, not a benefit of that size. Choice (B) is the correct answer, but it is hard because of the specific language used, which doesn't appear to correspond directly to the language of the question. The "material substrate" is the size of the brain itself, and so these lines suggest that the advantage of larger brains is the greater growth in circuitry that comes along with the larger brain.

51 B RC Use process of elimination on any question that asks "which of the following." In order to eliminate answers here, you want to read each and then check the fourth paragraph of the passage, the one in which Gould discusses neotony. We can find support for each of the answers (A), (C), and (D), but choice (B) is not supported by the passage, which says that human brains are slowed by neotony. The passage says in lines 62-63 that the process of maturation is slowed down, not that the brain itself is slower.

If you are running out of time as you get to the end of the test, you can also get this question correct by reading through the choices with the basic idea that neotony=good, and then choose (B), which is negative.

52 B WIC This is a WIC question, and it is best to solve it using our strategy of writing in your own word in place of the word the question asks about. The sentence reads "A bat has committed its forelimbs to flight..." Gould is saying that a bat must use its forelimbs for flight, so a good fill in might be "devoted," which makes (B) an obvious choice.

Writing and Language Test

1 B SEC In this question, only the punctuation changes, so you want to recognize that this question tests punctuation. It is probably easiest to start with the semi-colon, because all semi-colons must have a complete sentence both before and after. The part before the semi-colon is not a complete sentence, so we can eliminate (A); however, since we do need a comma, we can also eliminate choice (C). The second punctuation mark determines the right answer between (B) and (D), and the "comma FANBOYS" in (B) is a correct way to combine independent clauses, while (D)'s "semicolon FANBOYS" is, for the purposes of the SAT, always wrong.

2 B SEC This is a tricky parallelism question. The original version is incorrect because one cannot compile volunteers. Choice (C) is incorrect because it lacks a coordinating conjunction.

This is a tricky choice to rule out because it looks okay on its own, but if you read through the sentence, you will "hear" the lacking conjunction and realize that it cannot be correct. Choice (D) is incorrect both because it puts an extra comma after "records" and because it commits a parallelism fault by adding the gerund phrase "supervising volunteers" in a list of objective nouns.

3 A SEC This is another sentence structure punctuation question. The easiest way to get this is to conduct an independent clause inspection on both sides of the semi-colon—each part could be its own sentence, so it is correct as it is!

4 A EOI For all add/delete questions, first decide about adding or deleting it based on the larger context of the passage. Since this detail is irrelevant, it has to go, meaning that (C) and (D) are wrong. Choice (A) directly articulates this exact reason for deleting the underlined portion, so it is correct.

5 D EOI For ordering questions on the SAT, it is essential to read the entire passage rather than skipping from one question to the next. If you were reading the entire passage, you probably noticed not only that sentence 2 was out of place when you read it but also that it needed to be moved down. This leaves us with only choices (C) and (D).

Choice (C) is not easy to eliminate: if you assume that the tasks listed at the close of sentence 3 are exhausting and repetitive, then the beginning of sentence 2 might seem to fit there. However, those tasks were listed as specifically assigned to the writer, not to "everyone in the office," so the second half does not fit. Further, if sentence 2 is put before sentence 4, that sentence seems to be merely redundant. Thus, choice (D) is the only answer that puts the entire paragraph into a logical and coherent order.

6 C SEC This is a subject–verb agreement and verb tense question. The correct answer is (C), which gives the present tense singular form.

⚠️ Don't be fooled by the fact that the start of the sentence is in past tense—it refers to a specific past action, while the rest of the sentence and the following one use present tense to discuss canvassing in general. Further, the test gives no simple past option, so don't pick past perfect or present perfect (choices (B) and (D), respectively) in an effort to try to put this in the past.

7 B EOI Answer the basic question for yourself first: does this fit here, and is it relevant? The answer is yes, so we can eliminate choice (C) and (D) immediately. Once we do so, it is not hard to determine that choice (A) does not provide a sound rationale for the addition, while choice (B) does.

◆ If you are not sure whether this should be added, you can also use process of elimination. We have already rejected (A) as unsuitable, and (C) and (D) are also easy to eliminate. Choice (C) suggests that the information is already implicit in the passage, and this is simply untrue. Choice (D) provides a reason that doesn't make sense—if this clause doesn't add enough detail, how does not adding it solve that problem?

8 B SEC This is a misplaced modifier question. According to the original version of the sentence, the voters were canvassing, but the sentence is talking about the writer canvassing, so that is incorrect. Choices (B) and (D) correct this problem, but choice (D) introduces a new problem, because there is no subject for the verb "got." Thus, choice (B) is correct.

9 A EOI Remember to underline the key words in the question: you want to pick the answer with the most vivid depiction of the week's experience. Only choice (A) gives specific details about what activities the writer did during this week, and so that is the correct answer.

10 A EOI This is a transition word question, so you need to understand the sentence before the underlined word as well as the one that follows it. In this case, the sentence before discusses the low success rate of the calls made, while the sentence after emphasizes that the work was worth doing anyway. Thus, we want a word that suggests contrast, and only "Nonetheless" does so.

11 C SEC This is another verb tense question. Because the end of the passage is discussing the way the author felt in the past about something further in the past, we need to use past perfect tense, which places events further in the relative past than other events, here.

◆ If you don't know your tenses that well, don't despair. You can also get this correct by simply reading through the full sentence with each choice in place. You will find that choices (A), (B), and (D) all make it sound like it is happening at the moment, which doesn't make sense in context.

12 A SEC This question tests the use of the coordinating conjunction "and." When "and" is used to join two independent clauses (an independent clause is a group of words that could function as an independent sentence), then the SAT requires the use of a comma before the "and." Choice (A) is the only answer choice that uses a comma before "and."

13 C SEC This is a tricky question because nothing sounds wrong in the part of the sentence that has been underlined. However, the sentence as a whole has a comma splice problem. A comma splice occurs when two independent clauses are joined by just a comma and no coordinating conjunction. In this sentence, the comma is not underlined, and so there is no error in the comma. So we have to change the underlined part to make it work with the rest of the sentence. Answer choices (A) and (D) create independent clauses after the comma, so they are both incorrect. Answer choice (B) "of whom" is incorrect because "whom" can only be used to refer to a person, not a benefit. Thus the correct answer is (C).

14 D EOI This is a vocabulary in context question. Answer choices (A), (B), and (C) are incorrect, because you can't have large "numbers" of power, large "totals" of power, or large "aggregates" of power. The correct answer is "quantities," because it is the only answer choice that is idiomatically correct when used with the adjective large and applied to nuclear power.

15 C EOI This is a sentence combining question, often one of the most difficult question types on the writing test.

Use process of elimination to make your choice. Read each choice carefully and remember that you want to choose the answer that most concisely and clearly shows the correct relationship between the ideas. Choices (B) and (D) both contain some repetition, and choice (A) is incorrect because it emphasizes the energy produced rather than the danger of the waste.

16 B EOI For all yes/yes/no/no questions, start by answering the question for yourself. Is this a good addition here? Yes, because it explains the disaster referenced in the preceding sentence. Once you know this, you can cross off (C) and (D), and then choose (B) after reading over the two remaining options, because it fits best with your own answer.

17 C EOI This is a transition word question.
In order to get this question, read the sentence before the underlined word and the sentence that follows it, and then determine the relationship for yourself. In this case, the previous sentence gave a death toll of 4,000, but the following sentence suggests a much higher number. Therefore, we want to choose a word which will emphasize this disparity, which is choice (C).

18 B SEC This is a subject–verb agreement question.
To answer such questions, always find the subject of the underlined verb and make sure that the verb fits with it. The subject here is "book," which is singular, and we say that a "book reveals" rather than a "book reveal." Thus, answer (B) is correct.

19 A SEC This is a punctuation question with many punctuation marks in the underlined portion. However, only the first and last punctuation marks are changed in any of the answers, so those are the only ones you need to consider. In the original version of the sentence, a pair of dashes sets apart an interrupting element—a list of types of energy sources—from the rest of the sentence, which is a correct use of dashes, so you want to choose "NO CHANGE."

20 B EOI Like question 14, this question asks you to choose the best word based on the context of the sentence.

Just read each choice in the sentence and choose the one that is most natural sounding. Although each word is nearly synonymous, when you read each in the full sentence, you will find that only "supplying" makes sense to convey the idea of meeting the energy needs of the world, so the best answer is choice (B).

21 C SEC This question combines two elements of usage: affect vs. effect and a prepositional idiom. Take these two on one at a time. Most people find the second element easier, especially if they are not sure about the difference between affect/effect. To most readers, "of" simply sounds like the correct idiom, and it is. Unfortunately, there is no rule to memorize for idiom questions, because idioms are elements of correct usage in any language that are not dictated by any clear logic or rule, but simply are deemed correct due to accepted use. Once you have ruled out choice (B) and (D), you need to know the difference between "affect," which is usually a verb, and "effect," which is usually a noun. (The relationship is actually more complex than this, but, for the purposes of the test, this distinction should be all you need.) In this case, we want "effect" because the word is preceded by "the," which is a signifier of a noun.

If this rule seems confusing, try to replace the "effects" with "consequences" and "affects" with "alters." In this case, you would say "… be mindful of the consequences of our actions" not "… be mindful of the alters of our actions."

22 D EOI This is an informational graphic question, so you want to read through the choices and check each against the graph. Choice (A) is incorrect because petroleum is less than double either coal or natural gas, not double the two combined. Choice (B) is incorrect because the two amounts are equal. Choice (C) is incorrect because it says 1 "million," while the graph is in quadrillions. Choice (D) is correct, which can be determined fairly quickly by seeing that the three largest sources alone are more than 80 quadrillion Btu, so the 8 indicated for nuclear power is necessarily less than 10%.

23 C SEC This is another misplaced modifier question, and it is a tricky one, because the original version seems to make sense. However, since the introductory phrase suggests standing in Shakespeare's shadow, not that of his plays, only another person, not that person's work, can stand in Shakespeare's shadow. Only choice (C) makes Marlowe the subject of the sentence, and he is the one who is so cursed as to stand in the shadow of the bard of Avon.

24 **C** **EOI** Underline the key words in the question, "<u>Marlowe was an influence,</u>" and this question becomes quite easy. Choices (A) and (B) merely suggest that both playwrights wrote histories, without any reference to influence, while choice (D) suggests the influence is in the other direction. Only choice (C) suggests that Marlowe influenced Shakespeare, and so that is the right answer.

25 **B** **EOI** Holy irrelevant (and annoyingly pedantic) information, Batman! You should know before reading the answer choices that this has got to go, and thus only even look at choices (A) and (B). Since (A) is not true, the right answer is (B).

26 **C** **EOI** Each of these choices is grammatically correct, and so you must choose the option that is the most concise and relevant. Choice (A) has repetition of ideas in claiming that the plays are "unstructured," made of "loosely connected" actions, and lack "dramatic unity." That's three ways to say roughly the same thing, which is a trifle excessive. Further, the phrase "seem to exist merely" is needlessly wordy. Choice (B) also offers three similar descriptors and adds and awkward phrase tacked on to the end. Choice (D) sends us off-topic, bringing up later plays that are irrelevant to the paragraph. Choice (C) reduces the total number of words and limits repetition of ideas without losing any essential meaning, and so is the best answer.

27 **A** **SEC** This question requires you to decide whether to use singular or plural nouns and pronouns and also to decide about the correct form of the verb. Rather than worrying about both at once, divide and conquer. First, check out the verb form. We want past tense—both "made" and all other verb forms in the sentence are also past—and only choice (A) has it. Thus, the singular/plural question is an irrelevant distraction.

28 **B** **SEC** Another grammar-based question that tests two concepts at once, this also requires addressing one error at a time.

Start with the decision between who and whom, and use "he" and "him" in the clause to check which is correct. If "he" is correct, choose "who," and if "<u>him</u>" is correct, choose "who<u>m</u>." Since we would say "he was a weak…" not "hi<u>m</u> was a weak…" you want to rule out (A) and (C). The comma tests whether the information in the "who" clause is essential—if it is, you don't put a comma before who, but if it is non-essential, you must put a comma before who.

There are two ways to make this decision. The first is logical—you can ask yourself, is this information needed to know who is being talked about, or is it just extra fun facts about him? Since this is just extra info, we want to put a comma there. The second is grammatical—if I read the sentence with this clause dropped out, does it sound like a complete sentence? Since the answer to this is yes, the information is non-essential, and we need a comma. Either way, the answer is (B).

29 C SEC This is a third "two-fer" grammar question, testing punctuation and parallelism. However, since the punctuation is easier to differentiate, start by using the differences in punctuation to rule out wrong answers.

Choice (A) puts a colon before the list of things to be combined, and many students have memorized that a colon can be used to introduce a list. However, that use of a colon demands that a grammatically complete independent clause precede the colon, and that is not the case here, so (A) is incorrect. Choice (B) puts a comma before a prepositional phrase, setting it apart from the rest of the sentence. There is no reason to put a comma there, so this answer is wrong.

Remember to ask, "Why would I NEED a comma here?" not "Could I conceive of a world in which someone might put a comma here?" or—even more dangerous—"Do I hear a 'pause' here?" Choice (D) is almost identical to choice (B), except that it adds a word and changes the comma to a dash. Since we didn't need a comma, we certainly don't need a dash either. Choice (C) is the right answer because it doesn't add unnecessary punctuation and it is displays proper parallelism. Notice that, again, you don't actually need to deal with the parallelism issue, because punctuation alone leads you to the right answer.

30 D EOI This is a word choice question, in which you must choose the best word for the context. Logically, one cannot be shrouded, drowned, or inundated by a corrupting influence: all of these are suggestive of metaphorical meanings that the text does not support. Thus, choice (D), overcome, is the best answer in this context.

31 A SEC This is a difficult question, because it is based on making a logical comparison. The introductory phrase creates a comparison with Edward, who is a character in the play discussed in the passage. Only choice (A) makes a comparison between two characters—Edward and one in a morality play—while all the others compare Edward to a type of play, which is not logical.

32 A EOI If you have been reading the whole passage, this question should be fairly simple. When you get to sentence 6, there is nothing jarring or out of place, so it is correct where it is.

Many students will miss this question, because they are sure that any ordering question must require moving the selected element. There is no reason that this must be so: if there is nothing wrong with where it is, it's probably in the right place.

If you are not confident enough to choose (A) without trying out the others, you can put the sentence in each of the other spots and find good reason to reject each: putting it before sentence 1 would be very confusing: there is not yet any context to make this claim, because the author hasn't told us anything about the play yet. Putting the sentence after 3 or 4 would interrupt the ongoing discussion of Marlowe's play in sentences 1–5 with a sentence that brings up Shakespeare, so (C) and (D) are also not good choices.

33 **D** EOI Notice that there is no grammatical difference between the verbs, which means that this is not a verb agreement question. Once you realize that fact, you should recognize that this is a redundancy question and pick choice (D), which avoids repeating information already implicit earlier in the sentence.

34 **B** EOI This question combines redundancy and style. Choice (A) is wrong because it is needlessly wordy and redundant in using more and more unneeded words, while choices (C) and (D) both are stylistically inappropriate. Choice (C) is both horrifyingly opinionated and a bit superciliously pedantic in its choice of expression, while choice (D) sounds like a stupid slang way to say stuff.

35 **A** EOI Underline the key words of the question—"specific support" and "main idea"—and then choose the one that meets those specifications. The main idea of this paragraph is that the use of GM crops is on the rise, and only choice (A) gives specific, statistical data to support that idea.

36 **C** SEC This is a punctuation question based on sentence structure. Because the sentence is a dependent clause followed by an independent clause, we need only a comma, and choice (C) provides it.

Some students just try to memorize patterns, and so assume that (D), with its "comma FANBOYS" use, must be correct. Remember to figure out the structure of the whole sentence first, and then make your choice, rather than trying to just look at the answer choices in isolation.

37 **D** EOI This is a transition word question that tests the best way to introduce the new idea of this paragraph relative to the previous paragraph. In this case, the relationship is basically a continuation of the previous paragraph's topic with a specific example, but none of the choices that provide a transition word show this relationship. Thus, you want choice (D), which starts the paragraph without any specific transition word.

38 **B** SEC This is a fairly basic pronoun question. "They" is incorrect because there is no plural antecedent, so we need to choose "He," which refers to the single researcher, Seralini.

39 **C** EOI Remember that sentence combining questions are not about connecting the ideas in a grammatically correct way but about most concisely and clearly expressing the relationship between the ideas of the sentences. Choice (C) is the only choice that does so.

40 **C** SEC This is a tricky question, because it looks like a transition word question, but it isn't.

First, underline the word "LEAST" in the question, so that you make sure that you are approaching the question correctly, and then double check your underlined word before gridding your answer in, just to make sure that you chose the least acceptable answer. Choice (C) is unacceptable because starting the sentence with "Though" makes this sentence a fragment.

41 A SEC This question tests both subject–verb agreement and verb tense. Attack one problem at a time: first, find the subject, which is "size," and then cross off (B) and (D), both of which use "were." "Size were" does not work, and it doesn't sound correct, either.

Don't just look at the noun closest to the verb to determine subject–verb agreement. Remember that any word in a prepositional phrase can never be the subject of a sentence, so you can ignore all the words from "of 200" to "of 10." Now you have to decide on the tense. To determine the correct tense, you must look at the other verbs in the sentence. This sentence says that scientists "pointed out"—past tense—this problem, so you need to make this verb past tense as well, which means that choice (A) is correct.

Don't be distracted by the present tense verb later in the sentence. Although "recommends" is in present tense, it switches to present tense to indicate that the recommendation is still true, whereas the details of this specific experiment are completed in the past, so you need to use past tense for verbs regarding the experiment.

42 D EOI This ordering question is fairly easy to get if you pay close attention to the key words in the sentence to add. Because it discusses concerns about the experiment, it must be after sentence 4, which is the first sentence that suggests that there were concerns about it. With choices (C) and (D) remaining, we can confidently choose (D), because the sentence starts by bringing up "Another concern," and so has to be added after the first concern was explained, which takes place in sentence 5.

43 A SEC This is an apostrophe question, and the easiest way to get it is to recognize that there is nothing wrong with the original version and choose (A) right away. The sentence calls for singular possession—there is only one Seralini in the passage and it is his experiment, which makes "Seralini's" correct.

However, if you are not so sure, you can use process of elimination to see why each of the other choices does not work. (B) and (C) both use plural possessives, but there is only one Seralini involved in the experiment and only one team, so these do not make sense. Choice (D) is incorrect because the word "teams" needs to be possessive in order to be correct.

44 B EOI Underline the key words in the question: the answer to the question the essay asks is both "uncertain" and "essential to determine." Choices (A) and (C) fail to emphasize the importance of finding the answer, while choice (D) suggests that the answer is clearly that GM foods are unsafe. Thus, choice (B) is correct.

Math Test – No Calculator

Multiple-Choice Questions

1 B HOA The expression for total expenses includes two costs that vary from flight to flight, t and g, which express the time flown and fuel consumption, respectively, of a given flight. Neither of those values would be impacted by a rise in fuel costs. The letter C represents a fixed cost related to servicing and storing a plane, which is also not affected by fuel price changes. Only X, a rate which is described to be in dollars per gallon, could be a fuel price. The other rates involved, namely t and g, make no mention of a monetary unit like dollars.

2 D ATM Although this question identifies i as the imaginary base number equivalent to $\sqrt{-1}$, you can treat the i like a variable here. You can distribute the 3 and combine like terms, so that $3(4-3i)+2i=12-9i+2i=12-7i$. It's true that when i is squared it calculates to –1, but that doesn't happen in this problem.

In each math section of the SAT, the multiple-choice questions graduate from easy ones to medium ones to hard ones. Though difficulty is somewhat subjective, you can take for granted that a question numbered 2 will be simpler than most. The Imaginary Number System is not a basic concept and is often not taught until the later years of high school, so any question about imaginaries that comes this early in a section should involve only simple calculations on i.

3 D PAM The rule for fractional exponents is $x^{\frac{a}{b}} = \sqrt[b]{x^a}$ or $\left(\sqrt[b]{x}\right)^a$. Therefore, $x^{\frac{3}{4}} = \sqrt[4]{x^3}$.

The fractional exponent rule is easily confused with the negative exponent rule because negative exponents give you fractions. Many of the exponent rules feel unnatural or counterintuitive, so take the extra second when applying them on SAT problems.

If you start with the basic premise that anything taken to the power of 1 does not change, then it is easy to see how whole numbers taken to powers greater than 1 increase where those taken to powers less than 1 decrease. Roots, like square roots and cube roots, also tend to make numbers smaller. Armed with these concepts, if you don't know how to apply the exponent rule stated above you can tackle this problem by first recognizing that $x^{\frac{3}{4}}$ should be smaller than x (assuming x is a whole number) but not significantly so. Choice (A) provides two operations that each make x smaller, so you can rationalize that it would decrease the value of x too much. The same can be said for choice (C). Choice (B) has an increasing step that seems to override its decreasing step since the exponent 4 is greater than the root 3. Since plugging in numbers is difficult in a problem like this, particularly since you don't have the use of your calculator, this kind of size estimation can come in handy in a pinch.

4 C HOA To find the total dollar amount paid by the group, add the entree sales to the soda sales. The entree sales will equal the number of entrees, d, times the price per entree, \$5.25, which will give $5.25d$. Add this to the soda sales, $1.50p$, and you get $5.25d + 1.5p$.

5 D PAM Factoring the trinomial is the most direct way to arrive at the answer, but you don't have to factor blindly. The choices make clear that the answer will be the square of a binomial, so you know that the two factors must be identical. Since the first and last terms of the trinomial are each perfect squares, you can simply look to their square roots to fill the binomials:

$$4x^4 + 20x^2 y + 25y^2$$
$$= (2x^2 + 5y)(2x^2 + 5y)$$
$$= (2x^2 + 5y)^2$$

Though plugging in numbers is an option here, the numbers might get too large to do so comfortably without a calculator. Backsolving the choices, however, is a decent alternative. Just remember that squaring a binomial requires FOILing (double distributing).

6 **B** HOA   There are multiple ways to attack a system of equations. The most obvious method in this question, though not the quickest, is the elimination method (also known as linear combinations), where you multiply one or both equations by a number in order to induce the elimination of one of the two variables by adding or subtracting the equations. An example of that process follows:

$$
\begin{array}{ll}
4(3a - 4b = -14) & \Rightarrow \quad 12a - 16b = -56 \\
-3(4a - 3b = -7) & \Rightarrow \quad \underline{+\ -12a + 9b = 21} \\
& \qquad\qquad\quad -7b = -35 \\
& \qquad\qquad\qquad b = 5
\end{array}
$$

$$
\begin{array}{l}
3a - 4b = -14 \\
3a - 4(5) = -14 \\
3a = 6 \\
a = 2 \\
a - b = 2 - 5 = -3
\end{array}
$$

If it occurs to you that a method will call for as many steps as the one shown above, expect that there might be a shortcut. If you find that shortcut, you save time and limit the opportunities to make an error. In systems questions like this one, look for calculations on the equations that get you where you want to go. Notice that this question does not ask you to solve explicitly for a or for b. You need only solve for $a - b$, so it is fair to say that the longer solution above carried some extra steps. If you simply add the two original equations first, you will arrive at a multiple of the expression you're looking for, leaving you one step away from the finish line:

$$
\begin{array}{r}
3a - 4b = -14 \\
\underline{+\ 4a - 3b = -7} \\
7a - 7b = -21 \\
7(a - b) = -21 \\
a - b = -3
\end{array}
$$

7 **C** PAM   For a quadratic function $f(x) = k(x - a)(x - b)$, where a and b are real numbers, the function will equal to 0 whenever $x = a$ or $x = b$. The graph in this question has $f(x) = 0$ at $x = -1$ and $x = 3$ since those are the values where the graph crosses through the x-axis. Therefore, $(x - (-1))$ and $(x - 3)$ must be factors of $f(x)$. $(x - 3)$ is a choice, so that is the correct answer.

8 **C** HOA   Plugging in numbers is an excellent option in this question because the numbers given are small enough to allow for reasonable calculations without a calculator. When an equation is involved, the numbers you choose must make the equation true. For example, if you let $p = 8$ and $q = 6$, the proportion is valid. Using those same numbers in the expression gives:

$$
\frac{12q}{p} = \frac{12(6)}{8} = \frac{72}{8} = 9
$$

It is not prohibitive to do this problem algebraically, but that will involve substitution. First, cross multiply the equation to arrive at $4q = 3p$. Since the expression requires $12q$, just multiply this equation by 3 on both sides to arrive at $12q = 9p$, and substitute for the $12q$ in the expression to get

$$
\frac{12q}{p} = \frac{9p}{p} = 9.
$$

9   **C**   **PAM**   A quick examination of the choices can reveal the correct answer in short order. Since squaring any real number produces a non-negative result, there are no y-values for choices (A) and (B) that can ever be less than -4. Similarly, the absolute value of any real number will always produce a non-negative result, so any y-value from choice (D) will be greater than or equal to a non-negative and thus cannot be less than -4 either. Choice (C), on the other hand, will always have a positive sum within the parentheses because you are adding a positive with a squared number, and this positive sum is then negated by the negative sign on the outside. Therefore, (C) has the only chance of being the correct answer. You can check by plugging in a number for x in choice (C). For example, if $x = 2$ then $y < -8$. This check does not verify that y will always be less than -4, but it does provide a strong enough confirmation.

Questions involving a comparison of equations or inequalities can often be made clearer by sketching graphs. The graph of choice (A) is an up-facing parabola, drawn with a dotted line, with a vertex at $(4, 0)$ and shaded down. Since all of the points on this parabola have non-negative y-values, there will surely be points in the shaded area that are greater than -4. Choice (B) has a similar graph, only the parabola is drawn with a solid line and the vertex is at $(-4, 0)$. Choice (C) graphs as a down-facing parabola (dotted line), with a vertex at $(0, -4)$ and shaded down. This will clearly only encompass y-values less than -4. To make sure, you can also sketch choice (D), a V-shaped graph with a vertex at $(4, 0)$ and shaded up.

10   **D**   **ATM**   First mark the diagram to show that angles c and d have equal measures since they are vertical angles. Now, since these angles are equal and the sum of the measures of b and c equals the sum of the measures of f and d, you can conclude that the measures of angles b and f must be equal as well. This verifies statement (I). Once you know that two pairs of equal angles exist in two triangles, then the third pair must also be equal since the sum of the angles of any triangle must always total $180°$. This verifies statement (III) since angles a and e are those two remaining angles. There is no basis to state that (II) is correct, so (D) is the correct choice.

Be careful of figures that are labeled "not drawn to scale." This diagram makes it look as though the segments that are farthest from each other are parallel. If this were true, then angles e and b would have to be equal because they have an alternate interior relationship. Since you cannot assume they are parallel, you cannot make that case.

This problem is also a good candidate for plugging in numbers. If, for example you set $\angle b = 60°$ and $\angle c = 50°$, you can find all of the other angles using rules of triangles, vertical angles and the given equivalent sums. This shows statements (I) and (III) to be correct and statement (II) to be incorrect.

11 **A** **HOA** With a single point and the slope of a line you can always find the equation of the line. You can use either point-slope form or slope-intercept form. In slope-intercept form, plug 3 and −5 in for x and y, respectively as follows:

$$y = mx + b \Rightarrow -5 = \frac{4}{3}(3) + b$$
$$-5 = 4 + b$$
$$b = -9$$

Since the equation of the line would be $y = \frac{4}{3}x - 9$, it is clear to see that $(0, -9)$ would be a point on that line, because that is the y-intercept.

You can also use the slope formula, $\text{slope} = \frac{\text{rise}}{\text{run}} = \frac{y_2 - y_1}{x_2 - x_1}$, for this problem and plug in each of the choices (backsolving) along with $(3, -5)$ to see which works out to a slope of $\frac{4}{3}$.

12 **A** **PAM** This problem can be done quickly if you know some simple but obscure formulas. No matter what type of solutions a quadratic equation of the form $ax^2 + bx + c = 0$ has—rational, irrational or imaginary—you can find the sum of the solutions by calculating $\frac{-b}{a}$ and the product of the solutions using $\frac{c}{a}$. Here you only need the sum, so

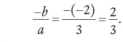

$$\frac{-b}{a} = \frac{-(-2)}{3} = \frac{2}{3}.$$

If you don't use the sum and product formulas, you can still find the solutions to any quadratic equation using the quadratic formula (this quadratic is not factorable) and then add them together:

$$x = \frac{-b \pm \sqrt{b^2 - 4ac}}{2a} = \frac{2 \pm \sqrt{4 - (-48)}}{6} \Rightarrow x = \frac{2 + \sqrt{52}}{6} \text{ or } x = \frac{2 - \sqrt{52}}{6}$$

The sum of those solutions works out to

$$\frac{2 + \sqrt{52} + 2 - \sqrt{52}}{6} = \frac{4}{6} = \frac{2}{3}.$$

13 B PAM First multiply both sides of the equation by $nx - 5$ to eliminate the denominators:

$$(nx - 5) \cdot \frac{16x^2 + 28x - 19}{nx - 5} = (-4x - 2)(nx - 5) - \frac{29}{nx - 5} \cdot (nx - 5)$$

$$16x^2 + 28x - 19 = -4nx^2 + 20x - 2nx + 10 - 29$$

$$16x^2 + 28x = -4nx^2 + 20x - 2nx$$

Since the coefficients of x^2 on either side are 16 and $-4n$, you can solve $16 = -4n$ for n and get $n = -4$. This is easily verified by showing that the $28x$ on the left side of the equation can be arrived at by plugging in $n = -4$ on the right to get $20x - 2(-4)x = 28x$.

  You can plug in numbers on this problem as well. Though it is often wise to avoid plugging in 1 for a variable on questions where the variable is in the choices, this question has no such restriction and is hard to work out with larger numbers and no calculator assistance. If you plug 1 in for x, you will see the following:

$$\frac{16 + 28 - 19}{n - 5} = -6 - \frac{29}{n - 5}$$

$$\frac{25}{n - 5} + \frac{29}{n - 5} = -6$$

$$\frac{54}{n - 5} = -6$$

$$54 = -6n + 30$$

$$24 = -6n$$

$$-4 = n$$

14 A PAM If two exponential expressions in an equation can be rewritten in the same base (without having to use logarithms), the solution to such an exponential equation becomes much simpler. Since 25 can be written as 5^2, and since the powers on the left side can just be multiplied, you can change this equation to $5^{3ab} = 5^2$. Therefore, $3ab = 2$, which means $36ab = 12(2) = 24$.

  Plugging in numbers can work here, but you should be very selective and chose a number for one of the variables that will make it easy to solve for the other variable. For example, letting $a = \frac{1}{3}$ makes it fairly clear that b will have to equal 2. Then working out $36ab$ just entails substituting: $36\left(\frac{1}{3}\right)(2) = 24$.

15 **D** HOA Whether the $-\dfrac{3}{7}$ is distributed or not, it is a coefficient of the variable A, so it can be thought of as a rate of decrease of $\dfrac{3}{7}$ Jagons for every increase of one Ambloo. Since statement (II) says this exactly, it must be correct. Statement (I) is stipulating a decrease of one Ambloo, which will, as stated, have the opposite affect of increasing the number of Jagons by $\dfrac{3}{7}$, so statement (I) is also correct. Since a decrease of one Ambloo will increase the number of Jagons by $\dfrac{3}{7}$, a decrease of $\dfrac{7}{3}$ Ambloos will increase the number of Jagons by $\left(\dfrac{7}{3}\right)\left(\dfrac{3}{7}\right)$, so the increase in Jagons will be one, as statement (III) contends. All three statements are correct.

Student-Produced Response Questions

16   PAM   **1 or 3**

This problem tests your ability to distribute, recognize a quadratic, and factor. First, simplify by dividing both sides by x to give the following:

$$x^2(x^2-10)=-9$$

Then, distribute the x^2 through the parentheses on the left side, and bring the -9 over to the left side of the equation:

$$x^4-10x^2+9=0$$

From here, you need to factor and then recognize that the resulting binomials are both in 'difference of perfect squares' form which can then be further factored to give four possible solutions.

$$x^4-10x^2+9=0$$
$$(x^2-9)(x^2-1)=0$$
$$(x+3)(x-3)(x+1)(x-1)=0$$
$$x=-3,\ x=3,\ x=-1,\ \text{or}\ x=1$$

Since the problem specifies that x must be greater than zero, only the positive solutions are correct.

17   HOA   **8**

Given a system of linear equations, you can either use substitution or linear combination. It's worth noting that in this system, the first two equations can align nicely to cancel out two variables and let you solve for x.

 Substitution can work for this problem, but it will take much longer and many more steps, given that there are three variables. It's generally a good idea to check for nice cancellations in the linear combination method first.

Add the first two equations:

$$w + x - y = 4$$
$$+ (x - w + y = 6)$$
$$2x = 10$$
$$x = 5$$

Then substitute 5 for x in the third equation to arrive at $w = 7$. Finally, substitute 5 for x and 7 for w into either of the first two equations to solve for y and you will get 8.

 Because the most efficient way to solve this question involves finding both x and w before you arrive at y, there is a danger of stopping too early, especially since there are no answer choices. Make sure you either underline the "ask" of each question before beginning your work to help remind you what you are looking for or reread each question after the work is complete before moving on to the next.

18   HOA $\dfrac{5}{4}$ or **1.25**

Use common denominators to combine the fractions on each side of the equation, and then simplify both sides.

$$\frac{11}{15}x - \frac{8}{15}x = \frac{2}{12} + \frac{1}{12}$$
$$\frac{3}{15}x = \frac{3}{12}$$
$$\frac{1}{5}x = \frac{1}{4}$$

Then, simply multiply both sides by 5 to solve for x, leaving you with $x = \dfrac{5}{4}$ or 1.25.

19 HOA **140**

The key to this problem is correctly writing your equations based on the statements given. The statement "each football jersey costs $40 more than each hockey jersey" can be written algebraically as $F = H + 40$.

The statement "2 hockey jerseys and 4 football jerseys cost $1,000" can be written as $2H + 4F = 1000$.

With two equations and two variables, either linear combination or substitution will work to solve for H. In this instance, substitution is far easier since you can directly substitute $H + 40$ for F in the second equation. Solving for H yields:

$$2H + 4(H + 40) = 1000$$
$$2H + 4H + 160 = 1000$$
$$6H = 840$$
$$H = 140$$

20 ATM $\dfrac{3}{5}$ or **.6**

Since the triangles are similar, $\angle L \cong \angle NOP$, so $\cos \angle L = \cos \angle NOP$. The cosine ratio is $\dfrac{\text{adjacent}}{\text{hypotenuse}}$, so you will need to find the hypotenuse, ON, of $\triangle NOP$. Using the Pythagorean Theorem, you get $ON = \sqrt{a^2 + b^2} = \sqrt{6^2 + 8^2} = 10$. Thus,

$\cos \angle L = \cos \angle NOP = \dfrac{6}{10} = \dfrac{3}{5}$.

First, make sure to label the segment lengths given. To find the $\cos \angle L$, you'll need the adjacent side LM, which is given, and the hypotenuse LN. The triangles are similar, so, after finding $ON = 10$ using the Pythagorean Theorem as above, you can set up a proportion to find LN.

Sometimes it is helpful to redraw and label the two triangles separately, which can make it easier to see the relationships between sides and set up the correct proportions.

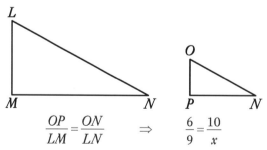

$$\frac{OP}{LM} = \frac{ON}{LN} \quad \Rightarrow \quad \frac{6}{9} = \frac{10}{x}$$

Cross multiply and solve for x to get $LN = 15$. Now you have both the adjacent side and the hypotenuse for the larger triangle, so $\cos \angle L = \dfrac{\text{adjacent}}{\text{hypotenuse}} = \dfrac{LM}{LN} = \dfrac{9}{15} = \dfrac{3}{5}$.

Math Test – Calculator

Multiple-Choice Questions

1   **B**   PSD   Three of the most important points on this graph are the three turning points, also known as relative extrema (or maxima and minima). The first of these, at around 4 minutes, is a relative maximum. It shows Brian changing direction from moving away from his home to moving toward his home. The third turning point, at around 16 minutes, does the same. But the second turning point, a minimum at around 9 minutes, shows a change from moving toward his home to moving away again, and that is what you are looking for.

2   **D**   HOA   Use the equation $p = mv$ to find the object's mass based on the known momentum and velocity:

$$4 = m(12)$$

$$\frac{1}{3} = m$$

Then use this mass to determine the momentum when the velocity is 27 m/s:

$$p = \left(\frac{1}{3}\right)(27) = 9$$

3   **C**   HOA   The ratio "two out of every 45 people" can be put into the proportion $\frac{2}{45} = \frac{x}{675}$, where the top numbers represent how many people receive the prize out of the numbers of people represented by each bottom number. This equation can then be cross-multiplied to get

$45x = 1350$ or $x = 30$.

◆   Since this section allows the calculator, you can easily backsolve this problem. First divide $2 / 45$ to get $0.0\overline{4}$. Then divide each of the choices by 675. Only $30 / 675$ gives you the same decimal. This is a great example of how alternative methods for doing or checking problems are enhanced when you have the use of your calculator.

4   **A**   PSD   Probabilities can be thought of as the ratio $\frac{\text{desired outcomes}}{\text{total outcomes}}$.

In this case, the desired outcomes include club members who like both sugar and cream in their coffee (4) and those who like neither sugar nor cream (1). Since there is no overlap between these two groups you can simply add the 4 and the 1 to get 5 desired outcomes out of the 27 total outcomes.

5   **A**   HOA   The given velocity of 13 m/s can be plugged into the equation for v_f, giving you the equation $13 = 6 + 2t$. Solving for t yields 3.5 seconds.

Though backsolving is a fine way to do this problem, it doesn't simplify the work in any way. Still, after getting 3.5, you can plug it back into the equation for t. This should result in a v_f value of 13. Such checking is quick and guarantees that you won't miss a problem because of an unseen calculation error.

6 C PSD Since there is no overlap between club and premium members, you can add the two percentages to find that approximately 20% of shoppers are either one or the other, and thus 20% of the 730 purchases could reasonably have been made by club or premium members. When you have the use of your calculator, the simplest way to arrive at 20% of 730 is to multiply $(0.20)(730)$ to get 146.

7 C PAM Since this problem involves the subtraction of polynomials, the most dangerous step is in the distribution of the subtraction sign to each of the terms in the second polynomial. Take the time to write out each step.

$$R - S = (5x^2 - 13x + 2) - (-2x^2 + 2x + 7)$$
$$= 5x^2 - 13x + 2 + 2x^2 - 2x - 7$$
$$= 7x^2 - 15x - 5$$

This problem can be done by plugging in numbers, but that might not be ideal because of the amount of steps involved. Still, you can plug in numbers to check your answer. Using 2 for x yields

$$(5(2)^2 - 13(2) + 2) - (-2(2)^2 + 2(2) + 7) = (-4) - (3) = -7.$$

It is best to rely on the calculator to do this work, as long as you plug the 2 into its own set of parentheses every time to avoid PEMDAS errors. Then, if you are checking choice (C), just plug 2 in to get $7(2)^2 - 15(2) - 5 = -7$ to see that your answer is correct.

8 B HOA When a formula is modeled by a linear equation like this, the coefficient, $-3,046,$ is the rate at which y changes every time x increases by 1. Since the question is only asking you for the significance of 3,046, you must indicate that the rate is a decrease in value to account for the negative sign. Also, (B) is the only choice that describes a rate.

9 B PAM A composition of functions like this requires that you apply the inside function first and then plug the result into the outside function. Since $C(53) = 44,$ you must plug 44 into the R function. $R(44) = 31,$ so $R(C(53)) = 31.$

10　D　PSD　Though you could use unit conversion methods like dimensional analysis to work this problem out, the given information states a formula that will cut down on steps, $C = \dfrac{mg}{f}$. For the Kia Soul Hybrid, $f = 105$, so $C = \dfrac{(305)(\$2.50)}{105} \approx \$7.26$.

Though you should always do the busywork to be certain, a quick examination of the choices and a little common sense can lead you in the right direction too. Choices (A), (B), and (C) all indicate costs that are from less than 2 gallons of gas, and even though the Kia Soul Hybrid has the best fuel economy of all the cars listed, it is still unreasonable to expect a 300-plus mile long trip to use under 2 gallons of gas or cost under $5.00. This kind of numerical estimation and common-sense evaluation can be more useful on the non-calculator section or on a problem where you are running out of time, but they shouldn't be dismissed as at least valuable ways to double check your work on any problem.

11　B　PSD　This question mentions gas price fluctuations to remind you that you cannot assume a certain price per gallon, like, for example, the $2.50 per gallon from #10. Still, since you are asked to calculate the cost for a Ford Mustang making the same drive with the same gas price as the Ford Fusion, it really doesn't matter whether you know the gas price or the length of Route 48. Just plug the cost for the Fusion, along with its fuel economy number, into the formula: $12.97 = \dfrac{mg}{47}$, so $mg = 609.59$. Then use that value for mg in the formula for the cost of driving the Mustang: $C = \dfrac{mg}{f} = \dfrac{609.59}{26} \approx 23.45$.

12　D　HOA　A close examination of this equation reveals that whatever comes out of the absolute value signs must add with 1 to make 0. The only number that adds with 1 to make 0 is −1. Since absolute value signs make everything non-negative, no value will work.

You can also backsolve the answer choices. On a TI-84 calculator, press the MATH button, hit the right arrow to get to the "number" tab, and then press ENTER . You should now see absolute value signs that you can use to reconstruct the left side of the equation, using the values from the answer choices substituted in for x. You should find that none of the numbers work, and therefore only option (D) remains.

If you ever forget how to get to a particular function, like absolute value, on the calculator, remember that there is an alphabetized catalog of all the calculator's functions that can be accessed by hitting 2ND + 0 (CATALOG) .

13 C PAM If you feel the least bit shaky about your algebraic fraction skills, then this problem is best approached by plugging in numbers. Since there is more going on in the left side, you should assign easy numbers to d_i and d_o such as $d_i = 2$ and $d_o = 3$. The equation $\frac{1}{d_o} + \frac{1}{d_i} = \frac{1}{f}$ becomes $\frac{1}{3} + \frac{1}{2} = \frac{1}{f}$, and using your calculator you can find $0.8\overline{3} = \frac{5}{6} = \frac{1}{f}$ which yields $f = 1.2$. From there, plug your values of $d_o = 3$ and $1.2 = f$ into the answer choices until you get our answer of $d_i = 2$. This happens with choice (C) because

$$\frac{f\,d_o}{d_o - f} = \frac{1.2(3)}{3 - 1.2} = \frac{3.6}{1.8} = 2.$$

◈ The most dynamic algebraic way to do this problem is to multiply the entire equation through by the least common denominator of all three fractions, $d_o d_i f$. That will give you $d_i f + d_o f = d_o d_i$. To solve for d_i bring the terms that have d_i in them to one side and factor d_i out so it can be isolated:

$$d_o f = d_o d_i - d_i f$$
$$d_o f = d_i (d_o - f)$$
$$\frac{d_o f}{d_o - f} = d_i$$

14 D PSD Though you can backsolve this problem by determining the percentage that the number represented by each choice comes out to when taken out of the 300 total students, it is even simpler to just take 26% of 300 by typing (.26)(300) on your calculator. That will result in the number 78, which is the number of males who prefer peanut butter and jelly.

15 A PSD At a rate of 280 eggs per year, m months yields the following unit conversion:

$$\frac{m \text{ months}}{1} \times \frac{1 \text{ year}}{12 \text{ months}} \times \frac{280 \text{ eggs}}{1 \text{ year}} \times \frac{1 \text{ dozen}}{12 \text{ eggs}} = \frac{280m}{(12)(12)}$$

◈ Performing unit conversions on rates can be tricky for some test takers, so you may want to try plugging in a number for m to tease out n. For example, say the number of months, m, is 1. You can find the number of dozens of eggs, n, the chicken lays in that 1 month, by calculating

$$\frac{280}{12} = 23.\overline{3}, \text{ and } \frac{23.\overline{3}}{12} \approx 1.94 \text{ dozen.}$$

This means that you are looking for a number close to two when you plug $m = 1$ into the choices. Only choice (A) comes close.

16   **B**   PSD

When you encounter a large table like this on the SAT, make sure to take the time to carefully examine all table headings and descriptions. Otherwise, it can be very easy to get confused by mismatched units. For example, there are numbers in the millions and hundreds of thousands in the table and numbers in the hundreds of millions offered in the answer choices. The values in the table are actually in thousands of dollars, so you can add three zeros to the end of each one. The question is asking how much the values for Education (second column) changed on average from Fiscal Year 13 to Fiscal Year 16. The easiest way to do this is to find out how much the total change was and then divide that value by the three years over which the change occurred:

$$\frac{\$7,718,943,000 - \$6,933,564,000}{3} \approx \$261,793,000$$

This number is closest to choice (B).

17   **B**   PSD

This problem asks for the answer choice that is closest to the following ratio:

$$\frac{\text{Human Services FY15}}{\text{Human Services FY14}} = \frac{3,956,955}{3,696,711} \approx 1.07$$

Note that it's okay both to drop the last three zeros for the data points (as long as you do it for both numbers in the ratio) and to round the answer, since you are just looking for the choice that comes closest. From there, work out the ratio of each of the answer choices to see which ratio is closest to 1.07.

Choice (B) yields $\frac{211,233}{197,421} \approx 1.07$.

18   **D**   PAM

To understand this question, it's important to know that $f(x)$ represents the y-values for the curved graph and $g(x)$ represents the y-values for the line graph. So the question is essentially asking you to find how many x-values yield the result that the sum of these y-values equals twice the y-value for the curve. Another way of putting that is to say that $f(x) = g(x)$.

You can also reach this conclusion by doing a little algebra, subtracting $f(x)$ from both sides of the given equation:

$$\begin{aligned} f(x) + g(x) &= 2f(x) \\ -f(x) \qquad\quad &\;\; -f(x) \\ \hline g(x) &= f(x) \end{aligned}$$

These y-values will be equal when the graphs intersect. There are three such points.

19   **C**   PSD

Probability questions often require you to find a desired outcome and place it in a ratio over total possible outcomes for a given circumstance. In this question, you should only consider shoppers who spent under a $100 (the middle column of the table), and you are asked for the probability that one of these shoppers made their purchases at the mall. So your ratio should look like this:

$$\frac{\text{People who shopped at the mall and spent under \$100}}{\text{All people who spent under \$100}} = \frac{36}{19 + 36} = \frac{36}{55}$$

Make sure to use only the 36 mall shoppers who spent under $100 and not include the 39 shoppers who spent over $100.

20 A HOA Since the question is asking about Jasmine's profit, be careful to examine the correct equation, $J(n) = 4n - 30$. Remember that the constant term -30 represents her initial profit before she sells any orange juice, and the coefficient 4 reflects the rate at which the profit increases for each cup of orange juice sold. The question asks for the number that describes how Jasmine's profit changes with number of cups sold, so 4 is correct.

21 A HOA There are many ways to approach this problem, but the quickest way may be to graph the functions for Perry's and Jasmine's profits in your graphing calculator to see where each has a higher profit. In the $\boxed{Y=}$ window, enter $4x - 30$ into $Y_1 =$ and $(5/2)x - 12$ into $Y_2 =$, hit the $\boxed{\text{WINDOW}}$ button to adjust your Xmax to 32 and your Ymax to a number large enough to see where the lines cross, and then hit $\boxed{\text{GRAPH}}$. You can hit the $\boxed{\text{TRACE}}$ button to move your cursor along the graphs. Read the coordinates along the bottom of the screen to determine which function starts with a higher value, and an approximation of where they cross. You should notice that $Y_2 = (5/2)X - 12$ (Perry) initially has a higher profit, but after $x = 12$, $Y_1 = 4X - 30$ (Jasmine) has a higher profit. Though it is not necessary for this problem, you can use the "calculate" feature to find the exact value of the graphs' intersection.

 This problem can be approached algebraically as well. If you set Perry's and Jasmine's functions equal to each other, you can solve for the number of cups they would each have to sell for their profit to be the same:

$$\frac{5}{2}n - 12 = 4n - 30$$

$$-12 = \frac{3}{2}n - 30$$

$$18 = \frac{3}{2}n$$

$$12 = n$$

Since their profits are equal when each sell 12 cups, you can limit your choices to (A) and (B). Then recognize that early on, for example when neither has sold any cups so Perry's profit equals -12 and Jasmine's profit equals -30, Perry has greater profits than Jasmine. Therefore (A) is the only correct choice.

22 B ATM In order to be an endpoint of the diameter of a circle, a point must be on that circle, and thus make the equation work out, so you can backsolve this problem by plugging the points into each choice. The point $(-2, 6)$ works in choice (B) because $((-2) - 2)^2 + (6 - 3)^2 = (-4)^2 + (3)^2 = 16 + 9 = 25$, but you must be careful because $(-2, 6)$ also works in choice (D) since $((-2) - 6)^2 + 6^2 = 64 + 36 = 100$. However, if you try $(6, 0)$ in both of these choices, you'll see that it only works in choice (B).

While this problem may have been good for backsolving, other circle problems may not be. Make sure you remember the equation for a circle is $(x-h)^2 + (y-k)^2 = r^2$ where (h, k) is the center point of the circle and r represents its radius. You can determine the length of the diameter by using the distance formula with the two given points:

$$d^2 = (x_2 - x_1)^2 + (y_2 - y_1)^2$$
$$d^2 = (6-(-2))^2 + (0-6)^2$$
$$d^2 = 100$$
$$d = 10$$

If 10 is the diameter, then the radius is 5, and only choice (B) has the correct value for $r^2 = 25$. Alternatively, you could have focused on finding the center of the circle, which will be at the midpoint of the diameter, but since there are two choices with the same center point you would still have to figure out the radius to distinguish between them.

23 C PAM To understand this question, it's important to know that $g(0)$ represents the y-value when $x = 0$. By looking at the graph, you can see that this y-value is 3. In other words, $g(0) = 3$.

The question is asking for options that have a y-value of 3, which include option I as shown, option II since $g(3) = 3$, and option III since $g\left(\dfrac{11}{2}\right) = g(5.5) = 3$.

B PAM You can put this function into the graphing calculator alongside the function $y = 2$ (since David's friend will catch the stone at a height of 2 meters) and then ask the calculator to find the intersection between the resulting line and parabola. There will, of course, be one intersection when $x = 0$ — this is when David originally throws the stone. The other occurs at 2.857, which rounds to 2.9.

On a TI-84 calculator you can use $\boxed{\text{2ND}}$ + $\overset{\text{CALC}}{\boxed{\text{TRACE}}}$ → `intersect` to find this.

 If you try to backsolve this problem, it may look as though none of the answers work. When the correct answer, 2.857, is rounded to the nearest tenth, you most certainly get 2.9, but if you were to plug in 2.9 for t, the resulting value of h will be 1.391. That is still closer to 2 than any of the other choices, but it makes it look as if you've done something wrong.

 This problem can also be solved using algebra. You can plug in 2 for h and solve for t as follows:

$$2 = -4.9t^2 + 14t + 2$$
$$0 = -4.9t^2 + 14t$$
$$0 = -t(4.9t - 14)$$

Then isolate the binomial to find the solution that doesn't represent David's initial throw at $t = 0$:

$$4.9t - 14 = 0$$
$$4.9t = 14$$
$$t = \frac{14}{4.9} \approx 2.9$$

 C HOA A good way to understand a subtraction sign inside of an absolute value is to translate it as follows: $|a - b| < 4$ means the distance between a and b on a number line is less than 4. Another way to express the exact same idea is $-4 < a - b < 4$.

For this question, you need an expression that shows the difference in hours between Jane's predicted time x and her actual time y as being less than 0.25 hours (15 minutes converted into hours). Choices (A) and (B) do not work because they essentially say that the difference between x and y is equal to and less than 15 <u>hours</u>, respectively. Choice (D) tries to describe the difference between x and y as being less than 2.75 hours, which means the discrepancy between her prediction and the actual amount of time it takes her to finish her homework could be large, like two and a half hours. Only choice (C) properly limits the difference to something less than 0.25 hours.

 C PSD This experiment's design suffers from a selection bias. Participants in a study should not know whether they are part of a control or experimental group. Allowing them to decide whether they receive the generic or name-brand medicine might influence how effective they perceive the medication to be and skew the results of the study.

27   **C**   **PSD**   In order to solve this problem in an accurate and time-efficient manner, it is very important to be organized with your calculations. Using the table to arrange the information is highly recommended. You can represent the *Space Battles* regular tickets with the variable x, which means the 3D tickets sold for that movie should be $2x$. Similarly, you can call the *Servitors* 3D tickets sold y and its regular tickets sold $1.25y$ (25% more than a value equals 1.25 times it). In each cell, multiply the amount of tickets sold by the price per ticket:

	Regular Sales (\$)	3D Sales (\$)	Total Sales (\$)
Space Battles	$(10)(x)$	$(14)(2x)$	3040
Servitors	$(10)(1.25y)$	$(14)(y)$	1272

For each movie you can add Regular Sales to 3D Sales to get Total Sales, so

$$10x + 14(2x) = 3040 \qquad\qquad 10(1.25y) + 14y = 1272$$
$$38x = 3040 \qquad\qquad\qquad 26.5y = 1272$$
$$x = 80 \qquad\qquad\qquad\qquad y = 48$$

Now plug these variables back into the third column of the table to determine the 3D sales for both movies: $14(2(80)) + 14(48) = 2912$. So the percent of 3D movie sales is

$$\frac{\text{3D Sales}}{\text{Total Sales}} = \frac{2912}{3040 + 1272} \approx .6753 \approx 68\%.$$

28   **A**   **PSD**   You can backsolve this problem, but the algebraic way is also handy. Since you are looking for how the number of miles *changed* from one day to the next, you can use the percent change formula, $\text{New} = \text{Old}(1 \pm \%\text{change})$. Plug in the percent as a decimal and 428 miles as your *New* value:

$$428 = \text{Old}(1 + .35)$$
$$\text{Old} = \frac{428}{1.35} \approx 317$$

29   **A**   **ATM**   One way to think about this problem is to envision the volume of the ring as the volume of a wide, flat cylinder with a smaller cylinder cut out of the middle of it. The larger cylinder would have a diameter of 24mm (obtained from the figure: 20mm + 2mm + 2mm). This would make its radius 12mm, so you can calculate its volume:

$$V = \pi r^2 h = \pi (12)^2 (6) = 864\pi.$$

The smaller cylinder is the empty region in the middle of the ring that has a diameter of 20mm, a radius of 10mm, and a volume of $V = \pi(10)^2(6) = 600\pi$.

So the volume of the hollowed out cylinder comes out to $864\pi - 600\pi = 264\pi \approx 830\text{mm}^3$. Since you are looking for the choice that comes *closest* to the volume of gold used to make the ring, there is no need to worry about the curved edges. All other choices are significantly larger than choice (A), and technically the curved edges would make the volume of gold a little smaller.

30 **C** HOA Perhaps the quickest way to attack this problem is to use your graphing calculator.

Backsolve each of the choices by plugging them in for the slope, m, in $y = mx$ using the

$\boxed{Y=}$ feature. Then go to the table by hitting $\boxed{2ND}$ + $\overset{\text{TABLE}}{\boxed{\text{GRAPH}}}$ and check so see if the y-value

when $x = 27$ is the same as the x-value when $y = 48$. Choice (C) yields the points

$(27, 36)$ and $(36, 48)$.

You can also plug the points $(27, k)$ and $(k, 48)$ into the equation $y = mx$ to get the equations $k = 27m$ and $48 = km$. If you now substitute by plugging $27m$ in for k in the second equation, you get the following:

$$48 = (27m)(m) = 27m^2$$
$$m^2 = \frac{48}{27} = \frac{16}{9}$$
$$m = \sqrt{\frac{16}{9}} = \frac{4}{3}$$

Student-Produced Response Questions

31 PSD 2.5 or $\dfrac{5}{2}$

Since the question asks about the median, it's a good idea to re-write the data set in order. Because there is an even number of numbers in the set, the median is the average of the two middle numbers:

$$35, 36, 36, \mathbf{37}, \mathbf{40}, 44, 46, 83$$

$$\text{median} = \frac{37 + 40}{2} = 38.5.$$

The mode is the number which appears most often in a data set, which in this case is 36. Therefore the difference between the median and mode is $38.5 - 36 = 2.5$.

32   HOA   **200**

This problem requires careful reading to avoid getting mixed up by the given information. The easiest way to get to the answer is to recognize that since the player lost 3 points for every chip remaining and had 50 chips left, the player must have lost a total of 150 points to arrive at the final score. Since the player ended with 50 points, he must have started with 200.

 You can also create an equation based on the information given about the game, showing that the player started with a certain amount of points (P), the player lost 3 points for every chip he had at the end of the game (c), and that the player ended up with 50 points:

$$P - 3c = 50$$

Substituting 50 for c, since we're told the player had 50 chips remaining, gives an equation that can be solved for P.

$$P - 3(50) = 50$$
$$P - 150 = 50$$
$$P = 200$$

33   PAM   **5**

First distribute and combine like terms, and then organize the terms in the form $ax^2 + bx + c$ as shown:

$$-x(2x + 1) + x(7 + x) =$$
$$-2x^2 - x + 7x + x^2 =$$
$$-x^2 + 6x$$

Then, since a is the coefficient on the x^2 term and b is the coefficient on the x term, you know that $a = -1$ and $b = 6$, so $a + b = 5$.

34   PSD   **6.48**

Understanding how the data is represented in the histogram is key to solving this problem. The x-axis represents numbers of hours of sleep, and the y-axis represents how many students got a certain number of hours of sleep. So, the first bar shows that 2 students got 4 hours of sleep, the second bar shows that 3 students got 5 hours of sleep, and so on. To find the average (arithmetic mean) number of hours slept, you'll want to add up the total number of hours slept and divide by the total number of students. You can write out each data point to do this, but it is simpler to multiply each number of students by the corresponding number of hours:

$$\text{Average} = \frac{\text{Sum}}{\text{Number of Students}} = \frac{2(4) + 3(5) + 8(6) + 6(7) + 5(8) + 1(9)}{2 + 3 + 8 + 6 + 5 + 1} = \frac{162}{25} = 6.48$$

35   ATM   **15**

It's important to understand in this problem that the original square patio is only being extended in one direction, so what is referred to as the width of the new rectangular patio will be the original side length of the square. The new length is "5 feet shorter than 5 times the width," which can be written $L = 5w - 5$. Drawing a picture for this problem is immensely helpful:

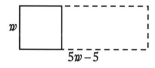

Since you're given that the area of the rectangular patio will be 1050 ft^2, and the area of a rectangle is simply its length times its width, you can create the equation $w(5w - 5) = 1050$. This is a quadratic equation, $5w^2 - 5w - 1050 = 0$, which you can solve in multiple ways (factoring, graphing, the quadratic formula). Since you are allowed the calculator on this section, it is most efficient to graph $y = 5x^2 - 5x - 1050$ and find the x-intercepts either by analyzing the table or using $\boxed{\text{2ND}}$ + $\boxed{\text{TRACE}}^{\text{CALC}}$ $\rightarrow$ zero. You'll see that both -14 and 15 are correct algebraic answers, and since you can't have a negative distance, the width must be 15. The width of the rectangle is also the side length of the original square patio, and therefore 15 is the answer.

 If you don't recognize the opportunity to use the graphing element of the calculator to solve the quadratic equation above, one algebraic option is to factor:

$$5w^2 - 5w - 1050 = 0$$
$$5(w^2 - w - 210) = 0$$
$$5(w - 15)(w + 14) = 0$$
$$w = 15 \text{ or } \cancel{w = -14}$$

36 PSD **650**

You are given that the average price per guitar needs to be $500. Ignacio has already sold 14 guitars and has 6 more to sell for a total of 20 guitars. The total amount of money brought in from all guitars sold will be $11(425) + 3(475) + 6(x)$, where x represents the average price of the 6 remaining guitars to be sold. The formula for average yields:

$$\text{Average Price} = \frac{\text{Sum of Prices}}{\text{Number of Guitars}} = \frac{11(425) + 3(475) + 6x}{20} = 500$$

$$6100 + 6x = 10,000$$

$$6x = 3900$$

$$x = 650$$

37 PAM **8**

Since the units don't match up, first convert the 2 million calculations per second into a number of calculations per minute:

$$\frac{2 \times 10^6 \text{ calculations}}{1 \text{ second}} \times \frac{60 \text{ seconds}}{1 \text{ minute}} = 1.2 \times 10^8 \text{ calculations per minute}$$

Then, dividing the desired rate of calculations, 1.92 billion per minute, by the current rate tells you that the rate must increase $\frac{1.92 \times 10^9}{1.2 \times 10^8} = 16$ times over. Since you know that the technology doubles every two years, it will take 4 years to increase to 4 times as fast, 6 years to increase to 8 times as fast, and 8 years to increase to 16 times as fast.

38 PAM **1024**

Referring to the given information that the supercomputer doubles its computing power every two years, you know that in 20 years it will have doubled ten times. This is the same as 2^{10} or 1024, which will be the multiple by which the computing power has increased.

Since you are looking for a relative increase in computing power over 20 years, you can also assign an initial computing value of, for example, 1 calculation per second, and then multiply that number by 2 ten times, an easy enough task with your calculator. This will yield 1024, and since you started at 1 calculation per second, you can say that the supercomputer is now 1024 times as powerful.

Answer Explanations for Test 3

Reading Test

Passage 1

You are told in the introduction that this Literary Fiction passage was written in 1854, so prepare for some difficult vocabulary and an old-fashioned writing style. Because this is fiction, there are several things to pay attention to that are not relevant to the other informational and argumentative passages in this section. It is important to understand the feelings and motivations of the main character, what is happening in the story, and the relationship between characters.

This particular passage has two parts: the first part is a character description emphasizing the seriousness of Mr. Thomas Gradgrind, who we later learn is a schoolteacher, and the second part depicts his lesson to his students, showing his literal-minded character in action. As you read, you should develop a sense of Gradgrind's personality and how that is reflected in his interaction with his students in the classroom. As with many older passages as well as fictional passages, rather than writing a summary of the passage as a whole, it may be easier to write in the margins of each paragraph or section what the main point of that part of the text is—doing so will assure your understanding of the passage as you read and also prove useful in answering the questions.

1 B RC   This question directs you to the first paragraph and asks what its function is.

Before you look at the answers, look back briefly to remind yourself what the narrator says in lines 1–15. As you've hopefully already noted, this is part of the narrator's description of Gradgrind's character, giving a description of him that reflects the seriousness of his approach to life. The correct answer is thus (B). Gradgrind is introduced as a very serious person guided by strong beliefs.

If your impression of the first paragraph was too general, you may need to use a process of elimination to rule out the wrong answers. You can eliminate (A) because while the paragraph indicates Gradgrind's passionately held beliefs, it doesn't discuss his activities or personal interests. Choice (C) is incorrect because the narrator does not compare Gradgrind to his students. Instead, Gradgrind is compared to some "non-existent persons" with the same last name, but these people are imaginary, not his actual relatives, and this makes choice (D) an incorrect answer.

2 D RC   Do NOT fall into the trap of using the answer choices to try to answer this question. For many students, a question like this, which asks about a metaphor used in the passage, seems to be a difficult "interpretive" question, which might make it seem that multiple answers are possible.

Instead of looking at the answers, re-read the sentence referred to in line 21, and you will see that the author explains the metaphor directly, stating that Gradgrind sees his students as little pitchers that he can fill "full of facts." This should make very clear that choice (D) is correct.

3 C COE

Questions 3 and 4 are a set of paired evidence-based questions. After reading question 3, but not its answer choices, look at question 4 and then come back to question 3.

In choosing (B) as the correct choice for Question 4, you've determined that lines 24–30 tell you how Gradgrind views his task as an educator. Apparently, he is like a "cannon loaded to the muzzle with facts" and sees in his students "imaginations that were to be stormed away." This matches nicely with (C), which is the correct answer to this question.

Although the language in lines 24–30 might seem to suggest that Gradgrind helps his students mature ("clean out of the regions of childhood…"), he does this through impersonally conveying information—no indication is given that he personally mentors his students (in fact, everything about his character and approach as outlined in the passage indicates he would NOT do so), which is why choice (D) is incorrect.

4 B COE

You need to find the place in the passage where you learn how Gradgrind views his job as a teacher. Of all the lines you are directed to look back at, only lines 24–30 express how Gradgrind's outlook affects how he interacts with his students. Choice (B) is correct.

5 B WIC

The sentence containing the word in question describes Gradgrind as "a kind of cannon." "Discharge" completes this cannon metaphor.

Take a look at line 27 and try to determine a good synonym for "discharge" in the context of a cannon. When referring to a gun or cannon, discharge means "sending out a bullet or cannonball." A synonym to write in might be "firing" or "shot." This matches the correct answer choice (B).

If you don't know what discharge means in this context, just realizing that this sentence is comparing Gradgrind to a cannon is helpful: the only answer choice that seems to have anything to do with a cannon is choice (B).

6 D WIC

Another word in context! This is a tricky one—it's an archaic word, which means it is no longer in common use, so you'll have to use context clues to understand what it means.

Try to think of a word that works in place of "behoof." In context, you could replace the phrase "for the general behoof of," with "for the general benefit of," so "benefit" would be a good choice, and look!—that matches (D), the correct answer.

If you are unable to put a word in for behoof in the sentence, you can simply read the answer choice into the sentence and see which makes the most sense. Choice (A) and (C) are easy to eliminate: (A) is incorrect and rather silly. Clearly, the students aren't about to put horseshoes on a horse (and certainly aren't going to wear horseshoes themselves!). Choice (C) doesn't work, because he is not mocking all of the students (though he certainly is being unkind to girl number twenty!), so general mockery is inaccurate. Choice (B) is tougher to eliminate, but also doesn't quite make sense. He is not taking away anyone's difficulties in what he is saying here, so this doesn't make sense. However, he does see himself as benefiting the others by humiliating Sissy for her ignorance and allowing the others to show their knowledge, making (D) correct.

7 A COE For this COE question pair, take a look at Question 8 first and then come back to Question 7. Lines 67–71 tell us that Bitzer is, like Sissy, being lit by the window. Thus, it is proximity to Sissy that makes Gradgrind choose Bitzer, so choice (A) is correct.

8 B COE The implied question in Question 7 is "Why does Gradgrind call on Bitzer?" Thus, you need to find the line numbers that tell you the answer.

Choice (A) is the trickiest to eliminate, because it is actually the part in which Gradgrind chooses Bitzer, but it does NOT give any indication WHY he did so. However, in lines 67–71—choice (B)—the narrator suggests that perhaps Gradgrind calls on Bitzer because he is sitting in the same ray of sunlight that is shining on Sissy, so choice (B) is correct. Choice (C) is simply a description of Bitzer, without reference to Gradgrind, and choice (D) is merely Bitzer's definition of a horse, neither of which tell us anything about why he was chosen.

9 D RC Write in your own answer for this question, probably something like "detailed and factual." Once you have done so, it is clear that choice (D) is correct.

Do NOT go directly to the answer choices, many of which may seem tempting in offering a sophisticated "interpretation" of the description! Both choices (B) and (C) might seem like "cleverer" answers than (D), but (D) is perfectly accurate, and the text offers no clear support for the other answers.

10 C RC All the answer choices to this question have two parts: an adjective and a reason that would justify the answer. If you can determine that either part of the answer is incorrect, you can eliminate that answer choice entirely.

Start by writing down your own word to describe the tone, such as "pleased," or, if you understand the character a bit better, "pompous." Once you have written down this word, you can eliminate answer choices based on the initial word. Choice (A) is incorrect because the practical, straightforward Mr. Gradgind would be unlikely to speak ironically; in his mind, Sissy did not know what a horse is and needed to be told. Choice (B) is incorrect because Gradgrind would be unlikely to express any type of humor. Also, Gradgrind approves of Bitzer's very detailed definition. Choice (D) is also incorrect: remember, Gradgrind is eager to fill his "little pitchers" with facts, and he enjoys every opportunity to do so. Choice (C) is correct, since "gloating" is a good fit for "pleased" or "pompous." Gradgrind proudly announces that Sissy now fully understands his definition of a horse, and in his mind, Bitzer's recitation of a very factual answer proves that he has succeeded in his duty.

Passage 2

This passage is the text of a presidential speech. Remember: a lot of thought goes into both *what* the president should say and also *how* he should say it. As you read a speech, it is important that you determine its purpose. Here, Reagan attempts to convince Congress to support the bipartisan measure for economic reform. It is also essential that you understand the structure of the speech—The first paragraph explains the context of the occasion (the country is facing many economic challenges) and the general topic of the speech (the task of restoring the economy). The second paragraph expresses the urgency of fixing the economic problems by addressing their cause—"government is too big, and it spends too much." In the next four paragraphs, Reagan attempts to convince the audience that a solution is possible, explains the best solution, and points out problems with an alternative plan. The final paragraph sums up the speech by restating the problem, the possibility of resolving the problem, the solution he supports, and the urgency of the situation. A good summary might read something like, "Reasons congress should support the bipartisan economic plan."

11 **D** RC If you wrote down the main point for this passage, you have already answered this question! Choice (D) clearly corresponds to the main point of the passage, so that is the correct answer.

12 **C** RC Write in your answer to this question, which should be something like "provide background for the need for the proposed plan." This clearly corresponds to choice (C), which is the correct answer.

 At first glance, choice (A) might also seem to be a tempting answer, because it is close to the main point. However, make sure to examine this paragraph in the context of the entire speech. Reagan is certainly describing a troubling state of the economy, but he doesn't view it as irreparable, meaning impossible to fix, or he would not be proposing measures to fix it!

13 **A** RC Here we want the answer choice that corresponds to a statement that Reagan would *not* make.

 Remember, when answering a question that calls for a negative answer using a word like "not" or "except," underline and circle that negative word. This helps you focus and remember not to accidentally pick an answer choice that gives a true statement. Look back at lines 13–27. This is the second paragraph, in which Reagan says that Congress must act quickly because "[o]ur government is too big, and it spends too much." This directly conflicts with the course of action suggested in choice (A). The other choices all provide statements that reflect Reagan's views as expressed in line 13–27.

14 C WIC   Even if you know what the word "candor" means, you should go back to line 37 and re-read the sentence to understand its meaning in context. If you don't know what "candor" means, notice that it is a part of a list used to describe the spirit of communication Reagan has used, so it should be positive, and it should fit well with the positive tone of "openness, and mutual respect." Choices (A) and (D) are both too negative, and choice (B) "careful reverence," doesn't fit with openness and respect nearly as well as choice (C), "impartial honesty," which matches the dictionary definition of "candor," which means "frankness, honesty."

Choice (A) may distract you. It contains the word "sincere," as well as "obfuscation," which may make it a difficult option to reject if you do not what that word means. Since obfuscation means that something is hidden or disguised—the opposite of openness—it is a poor choice. Don't choose an answer with difficult vocabulary that you don't know if another choice effectively answers the question with only familiar words!

15 C COE   This is the first question of a COE pair. Check out Question 16 first and then come back.

Once you've identified that lines 66–70 contain the answer to this question, you can answer this question. In those lines, Reagan states that the committee measure projects too much spending, which matches answer choice (C).

16 B COE   Question 15 asks you to identify a specific reason that Reagan says Congress should reject the House Budget Committee's measure. If you've taken note of the structure of his argument, you have noticed that the sixth paragraph is where he lays out the problems with the House's measure. Answer choices (B), (C), and (D) all direct you to lines in this paragraph, but only in the lines in choice (B) does Reagan state a *specific* problem he sees in the measure—that it involves spending $141 billion more than does the bipartisan bill.

17 B WIC   If you aren't familiar with this expression, can you picture what would happen if you were literally to "cut through the fog?" You would go from being able to see only the fog, to seeing what it has covered or hidden. Reagan is using this idea metaphorically here. He is urging the audience to look through or clear away distractions so they can see the reality of the problem clearly. This is a good match for choice (B).

18　**D**　IG　NOTE: This is the first of three questions on the graph that accompanies this passage. In order to answer this question, you will need to understand the information the graph gives you, so you should take a moment to familiarize yourself with the graph as you answer this question. The title of the graph indicates that it displays the inflation rates in America from 1975 to 1985. Note that the given rates are based on data from January 1 of each year. The bottom axis shows the year, and the side axis shows the inflation rate. The inflation rate for each year is indicated on the graphed line.

Since the answer choices make reference to evidence in both the passage and the graph, start with those based on the graph, which will be easier to check quickly. So, does evidence from the passage or the graph support the idea that inflation rates began falling before the proposals in the passage were implemented? If you look back at the blurb before the passage, you will see that Reagan gave his speech in April of 1981. Therefore, you want to look at the year 1981 on the graph—the easiest way to check it is to actually draw a line straight up from 1981. Doing so will make clear that on January 1, 1981, the inflation rate was 11.8, lower than the previous year's rate of 13.9. Therefore the correct answer is choice (D).

19　**B**　IG　Looking back at lines 1–3, you can determine that the election the question refers to occurred in November 1980. The graph shows that in January 1980 the inflation rate was 13.9 percent. This is more that twice the rate it was in 1977 when the inflation rate was 5.2 percent, so choice (B) is correct.

Don't get distracted by choices (C) and (D): the graph simply doesn't provide enough information to draw any conclusions about overall economic growth or mortgage interest rates.

20　**D**　IG　This question asks what the trend of the graph is between 1977 and 1983. This is the period in which the inflation rate rises to its highest point on the graph and then falls again. Only answer choice (D) correctly describes a period where the inflation rate both rises and falls dramatically. Stability implies no or little change, which is clearly inaccurate, while expansion and recession both imply economic situations that move in only one direction (though a graph of inflation only is insufficient evidence to show either in any case!).

Passage 3

Questions 21–31 are based on a pair of passages rather than a single passage. Begin by reading the background information printed above Passage 1, which reveals that these passages are from 1844 and 1859, so prepare for some sophisticated rhetoric and antiquated diction.

 Recall that the strategy for paired passages is to read Passage 1, answer the questions on Passage 1, then go back and read Passage 2, and answer the questions on Passage 2. Finally, answer the questions that ask about the relationship between both passages. These two passages describe the authors' thoughts on the similarities and differences between different categories of animals and how these traits can be accounted for. The author of Passage 1 theorizes that the species of animals could be ordered according to variations of their traits, although not necessarily in a neat, linear fashion. He suggests that these variations are designed to suit their needs, but he offers no clear conception of how these variations came to be. The author of Passage 2 agrees with the author of Passage 1 on the key point that it is reasonable to conclude that species descended from similar species. However, he is unsatisfied with this explanation because it does not include an acceptable description of that process.

21 **D** RC The line numbers in this question are distracting: although lines 13–15 contain the list, they do not give any indication of the author's intention in their arrangement. Do not simply read the list referenced and determine if the answer choice seems to fit the list in your own opinion, as the question asked about the author's design, not the list itself.

Instead, read back to lines 7–10, in which the author states that "there are general appearances of a scale beginning with the simple and advancing to the complicated." This makes clear that the author is arranging them in this order as choice (D) indicates.

Choice (B), although seemingly also true on first glance, is incorrect because it does not follow from the author's stated ideas as choice (D) does.

22 **B** RC Reread lines 1–6, and summarize for yourself what the author is saying. The author says that the different life forms of the animal kingdom cannot be strung along one line, but they require a more complicated arrangement, sometimes double lines and sometimes a circle or many circles.

Thus, you should write down something like "shows complexity" before reading over the answer choices. This idea matches nicely with choice (B).

23 **D** WIC For this words in context question, re-read the sentence with the word "impress." What is a good replacement for "impress" in context? It would make sense to say "tending to *mark* its own features on that which succeeds." *Imprint* is the only answer choice that fits with "mark," so that's the correct answer.

24 **A** RC Reread lines 21–27, focusing on the indicated key words. The author explains that, although every animal is distinctive, each seems to be modeled on a basic design. Any differences are alterations to suit the animal to its particular conditions. The words "fundamental plan" and "designed" suggest that animal forms are in some way the result of a conscious process, so jot down something like "purpose or design." This idea is stated in choice (A).

25 C WIC   In the first sentence of Passage 2, the author proposes that each species seems to be variously descended other species. What word could you substitute for "mutual affinities" that would make sense in this context and support the authors focus on what makes species resemble each other? "Common attributes" would be a good write in for this question. Although answer choices (A) and (C) use the word "shared" which support the idea that organic beings are alike, the author is discussing shared attributes, not abstract things like values, so choice (C) is correct.

26 C COE   This questions introduces a COE pair. Answer questions 27 first and then come back.

Be careful to check ahead for these problems. When the first half of a COE pair appears at the end of a page, as this one does, it can be easy to miss the second half until after you have answered the first half. Once you have identified lines 79–88 as answering this question, all you need to do is determine which answer choice summarizes the process described in those lines. Choice (C) does this best.

27 D COE   You are looking for the line numbers where the author explains what accounts for the specific variations between living things. He talks about these "means of modification" in lines 79–88, choice (D), where he describes a process of natural selection. Choice (A) merely suggests that existing species may be variations of previous species, and choice (B) and (C) both offer examples of explanations the author rejects.

28 D RC   Write down your own answer for this question before looking at the answer choices. Preposterous means absurd or ridiculous, and repetition is a rhetorical device that is often used for emphasis. Thus, repetition of *preposterous* in these lines emphasizes that the explanation that external conditions alone cause variation is absurd. Just jotting down the words "emphasize" and "absurd" should be enough to make clear choice (D) is the best answer.

29 B RC   This is the first question that asks you to consider the relationship between the two passages. Make sure you consider the similarities and differences between the two authors' perspectives as you answer. This question asks how the second passage responds to the first. Read the passage summaries above. Do the two come to the same conclusion? The author of Passage 2 agrees with the observation of the author of Passage 1 that animals seem to descend from similar animals, but he provides a description of the process by which variations of animal types come to exist, which makes choice (B) the best answer.

Choice (D) might seem a tempting choice. It also suggests agreement ("concurring") and disagreement ("quibbling"), but the specifics of the agreement and disagreement are inaccurate. The author of passage 1's final conclusion is that species modify themselves to meet external conditions, and that is exactly what the author of passage 2 disagrees with. Further, it is the logic of the claim itself, not its structure, that the author of passages questions.

30 **A** COE   This questions introduces a COE pair.

    However, before you go to question 31, you need to make sure you understand this question. It refers to lines 27–35, in which the author of Passage 1 describes the sequence of each species as advancing from previous types, showing similarities to the previous form as well as impacting the forms that follow. Now you can go to question 31 and find which line numbers match up with the response of the author of Passage 2 to this observation. Armed with the knowledge provided in lines 72–76, you can see that choice (A) provides a good description of the author of Passage 2's response to this view.

31 **B** COE   Remember that the author of Passage 2 (Darwin) is critical of the author of Passage 1 (Chambers) because Chambers does not provide an explanation for the process by which species descend from other species. Darwin expresses this in choice (B), lines 72–76. Choice (A) merely repeats Chambers' own view, while choices (C) and (D) are from the part of the passage when Darwin moves on to present his own ideas.

Passage 4

This passage is a courtroom statement given by civil rights leader Nelson Mandela in South Africa in 1964. From the context, you can expect argumentative writing. Indeed, Mandela addresses the issue of white supremacy in his country, describes the consequences of social, legal, and political inequality, and explains a solution. A good summary of the main point might be something like "South Africans need equal rights to undo the legal and social effects of racism."

 C RC This question asks you to determine the main point of the author, and if you followed our strategy of writing down the main point before starting the questions, you will be able to tell that the correct answer is clearly choice (C).

 If you do not determine the main point for yourself first, many of the wrong answers to this question seem tempting. Choice (A), although related to a portion of the author's argument, is an overstatement of the ideas presented. The ideas stated in choice (B), that whites in South Africa are racist towards Africans, and (D), that policies need to be put in place, are both partially correct, but neither reflects the main point of the passage as a whole. However, all three wrong answers here might seem possible if you haven't already identified the main point before looking at the choices, so be sure to use that strategy!

 A WIC Look back at line 5 and write down a word that might be a good substitute for menial. "Unskilled" or "low-status" would be good choices, and these match up well with the correct answer, "lowly." Choice (B), "manual," might be tempting; after all, the next sentence discusses jobs that require carrying or cleaning. However, the main idea of the paragraph as a whole suggests that Mandela is characterizing these tasks not merely as physical labor, but as something whites look at as beneath them, as too "lowly" for them to do.

 B COE This is the first question of a COE pair. Once you have underlined the key words in the question—probably "reflects" and "whites view Africans"—move on to 35, and then come back when you have answered that question.

You have found that lines 5–9 contain the answer to this question. What do they say? As stated in choice (B), these lines demonstrate that whites see Africans as servants who will perform menial tasks for them.

 B COE Question 34 asks how the author suggests whites view Africans. Answer choice (B) directs you to the lines where he describes how whites expect Africans to perform menial tasks.

 Choice (A) may be tempting, but note that lines 1–5 only states that "White supremacy implies black inferiority," not that this is how whites actually view Africans. That whites do view Africans as inferior is stated in other portions of the passage, but not within these specific lines.

 Further, if you did initially select choice (A), you could determine when evaluating number 34 that no choice matches up with these lines. Choice (D) in number 34 is much too large an inference to make based on lines 1–5, even if inferiority were an accurate expression of the author's claims about the way white South Africans view native Africans.

36 A RC This question asks you to consider the function of the third paragraph, so be sure to look back and remind yourself what the author says in lines 31–48. This is the paragraph where the author explains several negative social consequences of poverty and the breakdown of family life. In the previous paragraph, he has claimed that poverty and the breakdown of family life are themselves the consequence of discriminatory pass laws. Choice (A) expresses the relationship between these paragraphs.

⚠ Don't be distracted by choice (B). Although the third paragraph examines the societal costs of a law, the author did not previously explain a list of its benefits and only expresses a critical view of the policy.

37 B WIC This word-in-context question asks for a substitute for a very common word—"meet."

⚠ Be careful! This does not mean the question is easier—often common words can have unusual contextual meanings, and the test-makers are probably testing one here. Although "meet" most often means "encounter" or "join" those words won't work here.

💡 Instead of thinking about what "meet" usually means, re-read the sentence and write down your own replacement word—maybe "fulfill," "satisfy," or "answer"? This should lead you away from the more common definitions presented in choices (A), (C), and (D) toward the correct answer (B).

38 C RC This question asks about why the author is using repetitive sentence structure in the fourth 💡 paragraph, so go back to lines 49–73 and look for repeated elements. In the fourth paragraph, the author lists the grievances of Africans by first stating what they want to be allowed to do in the future and then what they don't want, which is to be limited to what they are allowed to do now. For example: "Africans want to perform work which they are capable of doing, and not work which the Government declares them to be capable of." The repetition of "want to" and "not" throughout the paragraph highlights the difference between desire and current reality, as stated in answer choice (C).

39 D COE Notice that this is the first question of another COE pair, so you want to read the question carefully and underline the key words, such as "white South Africans resist granting equal rights to Africans." Underlining the key words helps you be certain that you are looking for exactly the right thing in the lines referenced in the next question. After finding that lines 75–78 provide the answer to this question, you can choose (D) as the best expression of the author's ideas about why equal rights are resisted by white South Africans. In lines 75–78, the author expresses that whites are concerned about the potential political majority that Africans would represent if they were granted the right to vote. This is best summarized in answer choice (D).

40 C COE You are looking for the answer to question 39: what is the main reason whites resist granting equal rights to Africans? You can find the answer near the end of the passage. In lines 75–78, the author expresses his view that whites fear democracy—giving Africans equal voting rights—because the majority of voters would be African. Choice (C) is therefore correct.

Choice (D) may be tempting because lines 81–85 mention that "enfranchisement of all will result in racial domination," but explains that this is "not true," and instead provides the author's own view of what the effects of enfranchisement would be, whereas the text in 75–78 discusses this fear itself and does so more specifically than in lines 81–85.

41 C RC Recall that repetition is a rhetorical device often used for emphasis. In repeating the word ideal, the author is stressing his belief that a different system—a democratic system—is possible. In lines 86–91, the author says this system would bring freedom, harmony and opportunity—a better reality than the present system he criticizes throughout this passage. The author's purpose in repeating the word is best expressed by choice (C). Although choice (A) also says the purpose of the repetition is to highlight an aspect of the author's ideal, the author isn't saying his dream is impractical. Rather, he hopes "to live for and to achieve" his ideal.

42 D RC Before looking over the answer choices, write down your own answer. Based on the passage as a whole, the author believes that pass laws are very harmful, and he has nothing good to say about them. Choices (A) and (B) can be quickly eliminated because they are both too positive though answer choice (A) contains some difficult vocabulary. "Salutary" means beneficial, and "deleterious" means harmful. Choice (A) is thus incorrect because the author's view of pass laws are that they are harmful both to individuals and to families. Choice (B) is incorrect because the author doesn't say anything positive about the purpose or "design" of the law, only its harmful consequences. Choices (C) and (D) are both negative, so you will have to read them closely to choose the best answer. Choice (C) is incorrect because the author doesn't characterize the arrests he discusses as "illegal"—the pass laws in place actually make them specifically legal—although he does blame the law for the breakdown of family life. Choice (D) correctly identifies the author's attitude toward pass laws. In addition to expressing the author's view that these laws are responsible for the breakdown of family life, this answer choice also identifies the issue of harassing police encounters that the author discusses in lines 21–27.

Passage 5

This contemporary science passage outlines some of the historical developments in our understanding of the brain and brain injuries, particularly stroke, and advancements in the treatment of stroke injuries. The passage concludes with a projection for future developments for treatment. A graph accompanies the passage. Read the passage and answer the first 9 questions. When you come to question 52, which asks about the graph, go back to analyze what information the graph presents.

43 **D** RC
This question asks about the primary intention of the passage—use the summary you should have already written of the main point of the passage, and you will have an easy time answering this question. Your summary of the main point should indicate that the author summarizes the history of developments in understanding strokes, which is reflected in choice (D).

44 **D** RC
For a tone question, always quickly jot down your own word to describe the tone of the passage before looking at the answer choices. You might write down a word like "informational," which makes it easy to choose (D).

Some students have a hard time coming up with words to describe the tone an author uses. If that's you, just try to rate the tone from very positive (5) to very negative (1), with 3 for a neutral tone. You might rate this passage a 3 or 4, meaning it is fairly neutral or slightly positive. You can eliminate choices (A) and (B) for being too strong, (A) in a negative way and (B) in that the passage is not strongly persuasive, and thus is not rhetorical. Choice (C) may be harder to eliminate, especially if you are uncertain what "measured" means as a tone (which would actually be too negative in this case), but "inquisitive" doesn't fit the passage at all. Remember that for an answer to be correct, the entire answer must be correct, so don't get distracted by words like "pedantic" or "measured," which you may not be sure about as words for an author's tone, but use the parts you know to eliminate answer choices.

45 **C** RC
Re-read the relevant part of the passage and find the answer for yourself. Hippocrates and Willis are discussed in paragraph 2. Hippocrates described seizures and observed that paralysis on one half of the body was related to injury on the other half of the brain. Immediately after these facts are presented, Willis's work is explained. Willis studied arteries in the brain and discovered the dye injected into a carotid artery on one side of the brain would be expelled on the other side. In this way, Willis expanded on Hippocrates earlier discovery, as in choice (C).

46 **B** COE
This is a paired COE question. Answer question 47 first and then come back to this one.

Now that you have correctly identified the correct line numbers where the answers to this question can be found, what do those lines say? Lines 39–44 explain that disease in the carotid artery causes symptoms that can be warning signs for future strokes, which corresponds best with choice (B).

47 D COE You are looking for where the author discusses the importance of the carotid artery to an understanding of strokes. In lines 39–44, the author explains the discovery that carotid artery disease could cause attacks which could warn of future strokes, so choice (D) is correct.

Although the line numbers in answer choices (A) and (B) also direct you to points in the passage where carotid arteries are mentioned, these lines lack a discussion of a connection between the carotid arteries and strokes.

48 B WIC This WIC question asks for the definition of "minute." Make sure you go back to line 78 and write in your own word for "minute" as it used in the sentence.

If you don't do this, you might think they are asking for a substitution for the word that means "the equivalent of 60 seconds" and choose (C). If you look back however, you will see that you need to find an adjective that describes a pellet small enough to deliver treatment to a tissue in someone's body, and so choice (B) is correct.

49 C WIC Take a look back at line 90 and see if you can think of a good substitute for "dramatic" here. Perhaps "substantial" or "sizable" or choice (C), "impressive"?

Although choice (D), "drastic," might be a good replacement in some contexts, here we want a word with a positive connotation, and the connotation of "drastic" is negative.

50 D COE This is the first of a COE pair.

Before you move on to the next question, be sure to take the time to carefully mark the key words in the question to be sure you understand exactly what the questions asks.

At first glance, you might think that the question merely asks what someone can do that helps prevent stroke, but the question specifically asks what might "minimize the damage from a stroke," not what might prevent one from happening in the first place.

Once you have found that only choice (D) provides an answer to question 51, it is easy to choose (D) for this question, as it clearly reflects what lines 64–68 indicate about the importance of early diagnosis and treatment.

51 D COE Once you have carefully marked the preceding question so you know just what you are looking for on this question, you can read through each set of lines to see whether it provides any evidence about what might minimize the damage an individual suffers from a stroke. Choice (A) discusses how to identify diseased carotid arteries, which might be a sign of future strokes, but does not directly discuss strokes at all. Choices (B) and (C) both discuss different actions that might lead to or prevent strokes, but neither one talks about minimizing damage caused by a stroke. Thus, choice (D), which discusses the new-found importance of rapid diagnosis and immediate treatment, is the correct answer, as it leads into the passage's discussion of how stroke may become a temporary and treatable illness.

52 **C** IG   This question is based on the accompanying graph. Before tackling this question, take a look at the graph to see what it says. The horizontal axis of this graph marks every tenth year from 1950 to 2010. The vertical axis indicates the number of deaths per 100,000 people. The bold black line on the graph indicates the number of actual deaths. The solid, straight black line indicates the number of deaths if the rate hadn't declined. The dashed black line indicates the expected death rate if the rising rate had continued.

The question asks how many deaths per 100,000 people would have been expected in 2010 had the death rate continued to climb. To find this answer, go to the graph. Make sure you are looking at the correct line—you want to be reading the dashed line. In 2010, it appears that a little under 600 deaths per 100,000 people were expected. This corresponds best with answer choice (C), 590.

Writing and Language Test

1 C SEC This question is testing the correct use of commas with subordinate clauses or phrases. The main clause of this sentence is "Immunization has been a tremendous boon for world health." The phrase "the process of inoculation and vaccination through the artificial introduction of infectious material" is a non-essential element of the sentence (specifically an appositive phrase). Non-essential elements of a sentence should be separated from the rest of the sentence with commas or dashes, one before the phrase and one after the phrase. This rule is followed in answer choice (C). Choices (A) and (B) are incorrect because they introduce one of the needed commas but not the other. Choice (D) is incorrect because a colon should only be used after a clause that could be a full and complete sentence by itself.

If you can remove a phrase from a sentence and the sentence still makes sense, then put a comma on either side of the phrase. It is considered "non-essential."

2 D SEC This question is testing the correct use of pronouns. Anytime you use a pronoun, make sure it has a clear antecedent—the noun that the pronoun is replacing. In this sentence, the pronoun "it" is ambiguous. Even though we can tell "it" probably refers to immunization, grammatically it could also refer to world health. Choice (A) is therefore incorrect because the pronoun is ambiguous. By contrast, choice (D) has no ambiguity and is therefore the right answer—the reader is clear that it is immunization that is under attack. Choice (C) is incorrect because of the ambiguity of "its" and because "its" lacks an apostrophe which would be needed to form the contraction "it's (meaning "it has"). Choice (B) uses a plural pronoun when there is no plural noun in the previous sentence for the word "that" to refer to.

3 D EOI This is a redundancy question. The SAT has a strong preference for concise language, so avoid repeating information, especially in the same sentence. Choice (D) is the most concise choice. The other choices each include redundant information. We don't need to say "it is important" and "we must" in the same sentence.

Always notice when one answer is shorter than the others: it is often the correct answer and is a clue to look for redundancy and wordiness in the other options.

4 D EOI In this question, you need to decide whether to include one of the phrases provided after the word polio. Choices (A), (B), and (C) each provide correct additional information in a grammatically correct way. However, the extra information given in each of these choices is unnecessary and does not advance the discussion in the passage. Additionally, the information is more or less the same in each of choices (A), (B), and (C), so if any of them were the right answer, all of them would have to be the correct answer.

Once again, notice that one answer is much shorter than the others. This is a clue that you should be looking for redundancy or to see if the additional information is necessary.

5 C EOI This question is testing transitions. Choice (C) provides the clearest transition phrase, illustrating that the information that follows happens as a reaction to the events in the preceding sentence. Choice (B) is incorrect because it provides redundant information. The sentence already ends with "in 1952," so we don't need to say the year at the beginning of the sentence. Choice (D) is incorrect because "however" is used to show a contrast, but the events discussed in this and the previous sentence are closely connected. Choice (A) is not as good an answer as choice (C) because it is less specific and overemphasizes the causal nature of the connection. "Therefore" is used to show a specific "A" leads to "B" type connection where the second statement is true as a result of the first one. For example, I like all flavors of ice cream; therefore, I like vanilla ice cream.

Always read a sentence before and a few sentences past the underlined portion of a "transition" sentence so that you are clear on what kind of transition needs to be made. For example, are you looking for a contrast, an example, further clarification, causality, etc.

6 C SEC By looking at the answer choices, it is clear that this question is testing a vocabulary word and the use of commas. We use a comma when we are connecting two independent clauses with a coordinating conjunction (for, and, nor, but, or, yet, so). We also use a comma when separating three or more items in a list (e.g. A, B, and C). The underlined portion in this sentence contains a list but the list only consists of two things, so it does not require a comma. This eliminates choices (B) and (D). Choice (A) is incorrect because it incorrectly uses "affective" instead of "effective." "Effective" means successful. "Affective" means relating to feelings and attitudes. Therefore, choice (C) is correct.

7 A EOI This question is asking for the best choice of word. Choice (A) best matches the tone of the passage. Choices (B) and (C) and (D) are less formal and somewhat awkward when used here.

8 B EOI This is a Writer's Intention, or goal question. Remember that you should underline the goal anytime a question gives you a specific goal to try to meet. Here, the goal is to show "a link between low rates of vaccination and higher rates of infection." You are not just looking for the sentence that sounds best or fits best in the context of the overall paragraph. You must meet the goal you underlined. Choice (B) is the only one that links low vaccination rates with higher infection rates. The other choices do not specifically show the relationship between the two—they tell us that nations with low vaccination rates are experiencing polio, but do not go as far as choice (B) in connecting the low vaccination rates with the high rates of polio infection.

9 D SEC This question is testing your knowledge of "it's" and "its." Make sure you know the difference!! "It's" is the contraction of "it" + "is." "Its" (with no apostrophe) is the possessive of "it" and means belonging to it. "Its' " is not a word and will never be in the correct answer choice. This sentence is referring to the use of it, which is possessive, rather than "it is use," and so the correct answer must be either choice (C) or (D). Choice (C), however, uses the incorrect form of the verb 'to be' (has/having) and makes the sentence into one big dependent clause, which makes the sentence incomplete. Choice (D) uses the correct form of "its" and avoids introducing any errors in the verb.

10 B SEC   This question is testing the correct use of a restrictive clause—a clause that isn't necessary to form a grammatically complete sentence but is necessary for the reader to understand the relevant context of the sentence. The first portion of the sentence (before the underlined portion) is an independent clause—it could be a full and complete sentence ending after the word "article." The remaining portion of the sentence is part of a restrictive clause. Restrictive clauses often begin with the word "that," which makes choice (B) correct. Both choices (A) and (C) are clearly incorrect when you read them to yourself, as they are missing a "that" or "which" and choice (D) is incorrect because it uses the wrong verb tense.

11 A EOI   This question asks you to use information from the graph and the passage, but you only need a little information from the passage here. The passage tells us that the polio vaccine was introduced in 1955. The graph tells us that since 1955 the number of cases of polio infection primarily decreased (with some fluctuations at first) until they reached 0 around 1964. The number then stays at 0 for the rest of the time shown on the graph. Thus, choice (A) fits the information in both the passage and the graph. Choice (B) is wrong because it incorrectly states that the number of reported polio infections only decreased after 1955, and yet there was an uptick in the late 1950s. Choice (C) incorrectly states that polio infections in the US sometimes rose to levels close to 1955 after the introduction of the vaccine. Choice (D) incorrectly attributes only a small portion of the decrease to vaccination, which we know to be incorrect based on the information in the passage about the success of the polio vaccine.

12 C EOI   This is a goal question. Always remember to underline the goal in the question to help you choose the correct answer. In this case, you must pick the answer choice that "specifies some of the artistic techniques that were banned." Choices (A), (B), and (D) all specify that techniques were banned, but only choice (C) actually provides specific examples of what some of those techniques were.

13 B EOI   This is a sentence combining question. You must choose the best way to combine the two sentences provided. Choice (B) is the shortest of the choices, and it does not introduce an error, any redundancy or a vague pronoun.

Have a strong preference towards the shorter choices in sentence combining problems. As a general rule for this kind of question, the shortest answer choice is usually correct unless there is something specifically wrong with it.

14 A EOI   Choice (A), (B), and (C) all have the same meaning but choice (A) presents the most concise option. The context is sufficient that choice (A) is not vague—we know "there" refers to the library because there is only one location mentioned in the sentence before the underlined portion. Choices (B) and (C) provide redundant information by mentioning the library again. By now you should have realized that the SAT hates redundancy! Choice (D) would only make sense if we were coming back to a discussion after going on a tangent to discuss something else in between, which didn't happen here.

15 A SEC By looking at the answer choices, you can see that this question is testing punctuation—specifically placement of commas or semi-colons. Remember that a comma is generally used with "and" only when separating two independent clauses (sentence units that could be full standalone sentences) and when separating items in a list of three or more. In this sentence, there is only one independent clause so no comma is needed before the "and." Thus, choice (A) is the correct one. Choice (B) incorrectly places a comma before the "and." Choice (C) incorrectly uses a semi-colon before the "and," which is incorrect because semi-colons are only used to separate two independent clauses. Choice (D) incorrectly separates a verb and the object of that verb with a comma.

It can be tempting to place a comma before an "and" in a sentence with multiple verbs. However, we only put a comma before an "and" if the "and" is joining two independent clauses, so make sure that there is a subject and a verb on either side of the "and" before placing a comma there.

16 C EOI The author should not make the addition here because this sentence distracts from the main point of the paragraph. The focus of this paragraph, as with the previous and the following paragraphs, is on the narrator's artistic development. The author's experience in the United States is a relatively minor portion of the overall passage and additional details about movies and food are unrelated to the main topic of artistic growth.

Remember that for additions, you are not deciding whether a sentence is grammatically correct. You are deciding if the new sentence adds a *necessary* detail to the paragraph. If it seems to go off topic, then choose No.

17 C SEC By looking at the answer choices, you can see that this question is testing punctuation. This question is perhaps best answered using a process of elimination. Choice (A) is incorrect because a colon may only be used immediately following a portion of a sentence that could be a complete stand-alone sentence. The portion here before the colon could not be a full sentence because of the word "titled" immediately prior to the colon. Choices (B) and (D) are incorrect because a comma should not be placed between the verb "titled" and the object of that verb "Words and Scenes…" Placing a comma between the verb and its object is grammatically similar to writing "I like, ice-cream," or "I watch, movies," both of which would be similarly incorrect due to the unnecessary commas.

18 A SEC This is a subject-verb agreement question. To choose the correct verb form for a subject, read the sentence with the subject and the verb next to each other. Here, that would mean reading the sentence without the extra detail phrase surrounded by two commas ("including...prohibited"). At that point, it becomes much easier to "hear" that choice (A) is correct. The subject of the sentence is artwork. "The artwork" is singular, as it refers to the art as one combined group. Choice (B) is therefore incorrect, as "were" is used for plural nouns, or singular nouns in hypothetical cases, which also doesn't apply here. Choices (C) and (D) both lack a "to be" verb (like "was"), and therefore incorrectly attribute the artwork as actively doing the verb, as if the artwork is displaying, rather than being displayed.

Subject-verb agreement questions are tricky when the subject and verb are separated by a subordinate clause or phrase. Always cross these phrases out so that you see the subject next to the verb.

19 B EOI Here, the underlined portion should mean "a group." Choice (B), "an enclave," refers to a group or place different from the character of the surrounding people or locations, which best fits the meaning here.

20 A SEC This question tests the use of parallelism in a sentence. The sentence contains a list of three things, each beginning with an article (a, an, the). The sentence reads: "[M]y distance...created within me" and then a list of three things—first "**a** nostalgia for my childhood home," and second "**an** urge to see the rolling hills of the Chinese countryside." The third item in the list must therefore also start with an article to parallel the first two, which choice (A) does.

21 A SEC This sentence contains a list of people whom the narrator met. Each group in the list should be separated with a comma. Choice (A) does this correctly. Choice (B) uses a dash, which cannot be correctly used to replace a comma in a list. Choices (C) and (D) both incorrectly introduce apostrophes to words that should not be made possessive, and they introduce other errors in structuring the list.

22 D EOI This passage is presented in chronological order. Paragraph 4 discusses the narrator's return to China, which is further described in paragraph 6, and referenced at the end of paragraph 5 as something the author would like to do. Paragraph four should therefore be placed between paragraphs 5 and 6, as in choice (D).

23 D SEC This is a parallel structure question. That means you need to make sure the different parts of the sentence (in this case items in a list) are all in the same format. The format here should be "verb" followed by "noun." You can see the format in most of the list: "Craft [verb] a theme [noun], develop [verb] rules [noun], supervise [verb] artists [noun]..." Only choice (D) follows the format for the whole list by using the verb "manage" followed by the noun "supply chain." Choices (A), (B), and (C) each incorrectly omit a verb or noun from one of the items in the list.

24 C EOI This is a Writer's Intent question in which we are tasked with picking the choice that best meets a specific goal. Remember to underline the goal. Here, the goal is to match the writer's tone and uphold the main idea of the paragraph. The main idea of this paragraph is that the design challenges described by the author are difficult, although not insurmountable. The tone of the passage is fairly serious—the author does not rely on colloquial or slangy terms. Choice (B) is overly informal. Choices (A) and (D) both overemphasize the difficulty of the task by suggesting that it is nearly or completely impossible, rather than only challenging.

25 A EOI This is a vocabulary question. "Ensure" means to make certain. "Insure" means to protect against loss, especially through arranging repayment for such a loss (like with car insurance). "Unsure" means hesitant or undecided. Here, "make certain" is closest in meaning, and thus choice (A) is the correct response. Choice (D) is incorrect because it changes the meaning of the sentence in an undesirable way. With choice (A), the sentence means that playtesting is a means through which the author can **make sure** the ideas will make sense to others. Without the underlined portion, the sentence would mean that playtesting helps with making the ideas make sense to others. This changes the emphasis from one of guaranteeing the ideas make sense to one of helping make it more likely that the ideas make sense. Based on the emphasis in precision in the passage, the meaning provided through choice (A) best fits the overall context.

26 D SEC The sentence containing the underlined portion consists of two independent clauses: "[M]ost of this work goes into the game" and "some of it gets saved for publicity materials." One way of joining two independent clauses together is to use a comma and a coordinating conjunction (for, and, nor, but, or, yet, so). Choice (D) does this and is the correct answer. Choices (A) and (C) incorrectly combine a semi colon with a coordinating conjunction ("but"). Choices (B) and (C) incorrectly use the plural "themselves" instead of the singular "itself" to refer to "the game," a singular noun.

Remember—a semi-colon is never used before a coordinating conjunction.

27 A EOI This is a Writer's Intent question, which means you should underline and focus on the specific goal the question is asking you to achieve. In this case, the goal is pick the choice that "most logically follows" the last sentence. The previous sentence described the option of publishing through a professional publisher as being the least financially rewarding, meaning that it doesn't pay much money. The correct response, choice (A), correctly relates information on this topic by providing the explanation for why this is true. Choices (B), (C), and (D) all discuss topics relevant to the passage, but none that logically explain the concept discussed in the previous sentence.

28 C SEC This is a subject-verb agreement question. The subject of the sentence, "possibility," is a singular noun acting in the present tense and so should be matched with "is," as in choice (C).

When determining subject-verb agreement, ignore clauses beginning with "which" separated by two commas. This sort of phrase or clause contains grammatically unnecessary information that could be deleted without making the sentence incomplete. Generally, when answering this kind of question, locate the specific subject that is doing the verb and place it immediately next to the verb so that you can hear if they agree.

29 A EOI For yes/yes/no/no questions, start by answering the question yourself. Is this a good addition here? Yes, because the sentence helps explain the meaning of "crowd funding websites," a term with which the reader might not be familiar. Choices (B), (C), and (D) are all incorrect because they each provide an incorrect rationale for stating yes or no.

30 D SEC "Not only" must usually be accompanied with "but also," as in "not only one thing but also another." Because "not only" appears in the non-underlined portion of the text, "but also" should follow. Choice (B) is incorrect because it introduces an unneeded comma. Choices (A) and (C) are incorrect because they each fail to complete the "not only ... but also" idiom.

31 B EOI The sentence we are adding contains the term "this difficulty" without any explanation of which difficulty it is referring to. Therefore, it should be placed immediately after the sentence that mentions the difficulty in question, which is sentence 1. The author claims it is difficult to make large profits by selling board games, and the additional sentence gives the reason for the difficulty.

32 D EOI This is a transition question. You must decide if one of the transitions provided best introduces the paragraph or if no transition is needed. In this case, were a transition word or phrase to be used, it would need to introduce the idea that the concept being immediately described is new and somewhat different from the previous discussion, like "Additionally." Instead, choices (A), (B), and (C) all use concluding words, so choice (D) must be correct.

Note also that because choices (A), (B), and (C) all have the same meaning, if one of them were correct, the other two would have to be correct as well. The SAT won't give you multiple correct answers to a question.

When given the choice between three options that start a sentence or paragraph with a transition word or phrase and one that starts the sentence or paragraph with no transition, the last option (no transition) is nearly always the correct answer on the SAT.

33 C EOI This is a tone question. The passage maintains a fairly serious and straightforward tone and avoids much use of colloquial or slangy terms. Choice (C) is the best option here because it maintains this tone. Choices (A), (B), and (D) all use metaphoric or symbolic language in a way that fails to match the style of the rest of the passage.

34 **D** SEC   This question tests two grammar concepts: the use of commas and colons.

Nonessential elements contained in the middle of a sentence should be separated from the rest of that sentence using either two commas or two dashes. In this sentence, the nonessential element is "perhaps surprisingly." (We could remove this phrase from the sentence and it would still make sense.) A comma is used at the start of this element, so a second comma must be used to complete it. Although a dash and a comma can be used together in the same sentence, they cannot be paired together to surround a nonessential element. Choice (D) is the only choice to correctly complete this comma pair. The colon used in choice (D) is correct because it is used to connect something that can be a full and complete standalone sentence with a list or quote, in this case a list of one thing, the British Medical Journal. A list of one item still counts as a list for using a colon.

35 **A** EOI   The heart of this question is "what is the main idea of this passage?" This type of question can be difficult to answer without first reading the rest of the passage, so it is fine to initially skip it, then come back after working through the rest of this passage. This passage details the contributions to medicine by the author Charles Dickens. Despite all providing arguably correct statements of fact, only choice (A) presents this main idea.

36 **D** SEC   This question is testing the use of apostrophes. When a singular noun ends in an "s," make it possessive by adding either an apostrophe after the "s" or an apostrophe and an additional "s" at the end of the word. For example, to make the name "Chris" possessive, we could use Chris' or Chris's. In this sentence, the singular "Dickens," should be possessive because it owns or controls a "keen eye." It is the keen eye of Dickens. Choice (D) is the only choice that correctly uses an apostrophe to make the name "Dickens" possessive.

37 **C** SEC   This question is testing the rules for using commas between adjectives in a list.

Adjectives should be separated with commas only when they are non-cumulative. You can test this by trying to rearrange the order of the adjectives and seeing if the new order makes sense, or by seeing if you could put the word "and" between the adjectives. If either of these works, it means the adjectives are noncumulative and therefore should be separated with commas. In this case, it wouldn't make sense to insert an "and," as in "modern and medical" or to rearrange the order, as in "medical modern approach," so these adjectives are cumulative and should not be separated with commas.

38 **A** EOI   This question is asking you to choose the best word based on the context of the sentence. The sentence is describing an influence behind Sydney Burwell's research and the word "inspired" expresses that meaning. Choices (B) and (C) provide words that do not fit the meaning of the sentence. Choice (D) does not fit the tone of the passage, nor does it make sense in the context of research happening many decades after the inspiring event.

39 D SEC Use "who" and "whom" to refer to people and "that" and "which" to refer to things. Here, "an obese boy" is being referred to. Choices (A) and (C) are therefore incorrect.

To decide between "who" and "whom," determine if the word itself is the subject or object of the sentence. The subject will be doing a verb in the sentence. If the word is a subject, use "who" because only subjects do verbs. If not, use "whom," the object form of the pronoun because objects receive verbs. Here, the underlined portion is doing the to be verb, "is," and so we should use "who."

Another way to decide between who and whom is to make the sentence starting with the word "who" or "whom" into a question and then to see what type of pronoun you would use to answer the question. Pick "who" if you used a subject like "I," "she," "they," or "us," or "whom" if you used an object like "me," "her," "them," or "us." In this sentence, the question you would ask would be "Who/whom is consistently either sleeping or extremely drowsy?" The answer would be "**He** is sleeping or drowsy." "He" is a subject like "who," so we should use "who."

40 D EOI Sentence 3 uses the possessive pronoun "their" twice. This sentence, therefore, should be placed in the paragraph in a location that will clarify the antecedent of these pronouns – who "they" are. Sentence 1 contains only a singular noun, Dickens, and so cannot be correct. Sentence 4 does contain two nouns, Joe and Dickens, but it's clear that they are not the people being referred to in sentence 3. Sentences 2 and 6 both contain the antecedents of "their," the researchers, but only sentence 6 references these researchers coming to conclusions, which is what Sentence 3 refers to.

41 C SEC This is both a subject verb agreement and a verb tense question. Tackle it one piece at a time. The subject of the verb "to lead" in this sentence is "this portrayal," a singular noun. The verb should therefore be in singular form, which eliminates choices (A) and (B). Choice (D) (and choice (B) too) is in the past tense which is incorrect as the rest of the sentence up to this point has been in present tense. Choice (C) is singular and in the present tense.

42 C EOI This is a sentence combination question.

Remember that you want to choose the answer that most concisely and clearly shows the relationship between the ideas. Choice (C) does this. Although choices (A), (B) and (D) show the correct relationship, they all contain some level of redundancy and wordiness, repeating the word "London" for example.

43 B EOI Remember for a yes/yes/no/no question, answer the question for yourself. Should the sentence be deleted? Yes. The focus of this paragraph is on how Dickens' writing led to increased interest in certain fields of medical study. While the underlined sentence is arguably true, it does little to support the focus of this paragraph and is out of place among the other sentences in the paragraph.

44 **B** EOI The goal in this question is to choose an example that demonstrates the main idea of the passage as a whole using a "vivid example." The main idea of this passage is that Charles Dickens' writing is celebrated as providing meaningful assistance to the field of medicine. Only choice (B) describes Dickens' contribution to medicine and uses Barley the gout sufferer as a vivid example.

Math Test – No Calculator

Multiple-Choice Questions

1 **B** HOA To find x, subtract 12 from both sides to get $3x = 9$. Dividing by 3 gives you $x = 3$. You are not done yet because the question asks for $2x + 8$. Plugging in results in $2(3) + 8 = 6 + 8 = 14$.

⚠ Since choice (D) is 3, the value you determined x was equal to, this problem is a little dangerous. You've got to be careful to re-read the *ask* (i.e. the thing you are ultimately asked for) before you move on to the next question. In so doing, you will realize that this question is looking for an expression of x and not for x itself.

2 **D** HOA Since the absolute value of a number is never negative, you can eliminate choice (C). You can also eliminate choices (A) and (B) because the absolute value of a number plus a positive integer will always be positive. To confirm choice (D), you can set the expression equal to −1 and confirm that it is true for some value a.

$$|a - 2| - 2 = -1$$
$$|a - 2| = 1$$
$$a = 3 \text{ or } a = 1$$

3 **D** PAM Since $f(6) = -6$, you can write $-6 = \frac{c}{3}(6) + 2$. Solving for c:

$$-6 = 2c + 2$$
$$-8 = 2c$$
$$c = -4$$

Therefore, $f(x) = -\frac{4}{3}x + 2$. Plug in $x = -9$. $f(-9) = -\frac{4}{3}(-9) + 2 = 12 + 2 = 14$

⚠ Notice that −4 is a choice, but you are not asked for the value of c. Just like in question 1, make sure that you always answer the *ask*.

4 **B** HOA This is a direct translation problem where you simply convert the words into an algebraic equation. 9,600 workers joined between 1960 and 1985, and this is three times the number n that joined between 1986 and 2010. So 9,600 = 3n. Do not be intimidated by all the numbers in the question. Four of them are dates whose only purpose is to indicate the two different time periods, so they have no bearing on the equation.

5 C PAM FOILing (using double distribution) is the most direct way to arrive at the answer. You can either FOIL right away or first distribute the 2 into the first binomial as follows:

$$2(3x-1)(-x+4) \ = \ (6x-2)(-x+4) \ = \ -6x^2+24x+2x-8 \ = \ -6x^2+26x-\text{\textsterling}$$

You can check choice (C) by picking a number for x and substituting it into the original equation and into answer choice (C). You should get the same result for both. Though you can do the entire question by plugging a number for x into the original expression and <u>all four</u> choices, without a calculator that can be unpleasant and invite errors. In this case, plugging in a number is better as simply your checking method.

6 A HOA A system of linear equations with no solutions means the lines expressed by the graphs of those equations are parallel and the coefficients of x and y in one equation are multiples of the respective coefficients in the other equation. Taking the coefficients of y, -3 can be multiplied by $\frac{5}{3}$ to get -5. So a must be $\frac{5}{3}$ times 2, which yields $\frac{10}{3}$. This is, perhaps, more easily seen when using a proportion:

$$\frac{2}{a}=\frac{-3}{-5}$$
$$-10=-3a$$
$$\frac{10}{3}=a$$

A more time-consuming approach would be to manipulate each equation into slope-intercept form ($y=mx+b$). Since parallel lines have the same slope, you would set the slopes equal and solve for a.

7 B PAM The average rate of change in the number of visitors over a period of time is equal to the change in the number of visitors divided by the change in time.

$$\frac{320-20}{18-6}=\frac{300}{12}=25$$

8 C HOA Although this is a system of equations problem, you cannot back solve because the question asks for $x+y$ rather than just x or just y. One way to find $x+y$ is to use the elimination method to solve the system of equations for x and y separately, and then add those values.

Always explore possible ways to simplify equations or expressions. You can solve this problem more quickly if you recognize that the equation $6x-4y=14$ is divisible by 2, so that $3x-2y=7$. Now subtract $2x-3y=3$ from this new equation, and you will be left with $x+y=4$.

$$\begin{array}{r} 3x-\ 2y\ =7 \\ \underline{-(2x-3y)=3} \\ x+\quad y\ =4 \end{array}$$

9 **B** PAM The graph of $y=(x+7)^2$ is a parabola with a vertex at $(0,-7)$. The line $y=16$ is horizontal. The parabola and line intersect at two points with y-values of 16, so set y equal to 16 and solve. Since you have the equation $(x+7)^2=16$, you can take the positive and negative square root to solve for x.

$$x+7=4 \qquad x+7=-4$$
$$x=-3 \qquad x=-11$$

Point M is $(-3,16)$ and point N is $(-11,16)$. The distance between them is the difference in x-values, $|-3-(-11)|=8$.

10 **A** HOA If $A=80°$, $80n=360$, so $n=4.5$. Since the exterior angle is greater than $80°$, $n<4.5$. Therefore, the greatest number of sides, which must be a whole number, is 4.

This is an easy enough problem to back solve. Choice (C), for example, yields $A=60°$ and choice (B) yields $A=72°$, whereas choice (A) yields $A=90°$, so that is the only choice where $A>80°$.

11 **C** HOA The total paid before tax can be represented by $d+d+d-6=3d-6$. To find the price after tax, you can find 110% of $3d-6$ (100% is the original cost and you add the 10% tax to that). The easiest way to find percent of a number is to convert the percent to a decimal and multiply: $1.10(3d-6)=3.3d-6.6$. Dividing by 3 gives you $1.1d-2.2$.

Since there is a variable, d, in both the question and the answer choices, this is an opportunity to plug in numbers if you are more comfortable with them. Pick a number for d and write it down. If you pick $d=10$, then two gifts each cost $10 and the third gift costs $4. The total is $24 before tax. To find the price after tax, you can find 110% of $24. Convert the percent to a decimal and multiply: $1.10(24)=26.40$. This is the total cost, but the question asks for the amount paid by each gift giver. There are three people, so divide 26.40 by 3. Each person paid $8.80. Notice that all of the answer choices include the variable d, so you must plug $d=10$ into each answer choice to see which one gives you 8.80. Choice (C) would show $1.1(10)-2.2=11-2.20=8.80$.

12 **B** ATM The wording of this question may be intimidating, but all it requires you to do is to simplify the complex fraction $\dfrac{6-5i}{2+i}$ into the form $a+bi$. First, multiply both numerator and denominator by the complex conjugate of the denominator, $2-i$. You will need to FOIL and remember that since $i=\sqrt{-1}$, $i^2=-1$.

$$\frac{6-5i}{2+i}\cdot\frac{2-i}{2-i} = \frac{12-6i-10i+5i^2}{4-2i+2i-i^2} = \frac{12-16i-5}{4-(-1)} = \frac{7-16i}{5}$$

This is equivalent to $\dfrac{7}{5}-\dfrac{16}{5}i$, so $b=-\dfrac{16}{5}$.

13 D PAM   The equation of the quadratic function is written in factored form, so you can easily see that the x-intercepts of the parabola are at $x=-3$ and $x=5$. Since a parabola is symmetric about a line through its vertex, the x-value of the vertex must be halfway between -3 and 5. Therefore, $m=1$. To find n, plug in 1 for x in the equation.

$$y = a(1+3)(1-5)$$
$$y = a(4)(-4)$$
$$y = -16a$$

Since n is the y-coordinate of the vertex, $n=-16a$.

14 B PAM   This is a case of exponential growth where the population is increasing annually by a percentage of its current amount. The formula $A = P(1+r)^t$ represents exponential growth where P represents the principal (initial) amount, r the annual rate of change (as a decimal), and t the number of years that have passed. In this problem, A is written as $P(t)$, the principal is 43,560 and the rate is 0.155. The equation for population is $P(t) = 43,560(1+0.155)^t$, which is equivalent to $P(t) = 43,560(1.155)^t$.

Choice (D) is easily mistaken for the right answer since it only lacks the 1 that must be added to the rate. A quick examination of choice (D), however, reveals that, over time, the population will decrease not increase.

15 A PAM   To simplify the rational expression $\dfrac{8x+2}{3x-1}$, you can use polynomial long division. It looks

intimidating, but the process is identical to long division of whole numbers. First,

determine how many times the divisor, $3x-1$, goes into the dividend, $8x+2$ by asking

yourself how many times does $3x$ go into $8x$. It goes in twice, so multiply the divisor

$3x-1$ by 2 and subtract it from $8x+2$.

$$
\begin{array}{r}
2 \\
3x-1 \overline{)8x+2} \\
-(6x-2) \\
\hline
2x+4
\end{array}
$$

The result, $2x+4$, is the remainder. Since remainders can be written as fractions

(remainder over divisor), the answer is $2+\dfrac{2x+4}{3x-1}$.

◆   Another approach is to plug in a number for x in $\dfrac{8x+2}{3x-1}$. If you let $x=1$, for example,

then $\dfrac{8(1)+2}{3(1)-1}=\dfrac{10}{2}=5$. Plug $x=1$ into each answer choice to see which one equals 5.

Choice (A) works because $2+\dfrac{2(1)+4}{3(1)-1}=2+\dfrac{6}{2}=2+3=5$.

◆   This can also be a back solving problem. It requires getting common denominators in order
to add or subtract in the choices, but that can still be less tedious or easier to execute than
the previously discussed methods.

Student-Produced Response Questions

16   HOA   0

There are multiple ways to solve a system of equations, but the elimination method is the
quickest here.

$$
\begin{array}{lll}
2a+4b=12 & \rightarrow & 2a+4b=12 \\
2(5a-2b=30) & \rightarrow & 10a-4b=60 \\
& & \overline{12a=72} \\
& & a=6
\end{array}
\qquad
\begin{array}{l}
2a+4b=12 \\
2(6)+4b=12 \\
12+4b=12 \\
4b=0 \\
b=0
\end{array}
$$

17   ATM   **105**

In an isosceles triangle, the two angles opposite the two congruent sides are also congruent. The triangle on the left has a right angle, so the other two angles, which can both be called a, each measure $45°$. Since $b = \frac{2}{3}a$, $b = \frac{2}{3}(45) = 30$. The other two angles in the triangle on the right must measure $75°$ since they are congruent and $\frac{180-30}{2} = 75$. Angle c is supplementary to the $75°$ angle, so $m\angle c = 105°$.

18   ATM   **2.5 or 5/2**

Since D is the midpoint of $\overline{AB}$ and $AB = 8$, $AD = DB = 4$. E is the midpoint of $\overline{AD}$, so $AE = ED = 2$. It is also useful to note that $\triangle ABC$ is a 3-4-5 right triangle. Since the legs measure 6 and 8, the hypotenuse $\overline{AC}$ measures 10 (you could also find this using the Pythagorean Theorem). DE is $\frac{1}{4}$ of AB, so FG is $\frac{1}{4}$ of AC. $\frac{1}{4}$ of $10 = \frac{5}{2}$.

19   PAM   **9**

Substitute $w = 12\sqrt{2}$ into $\frac{1}{4}w = \sqrt{2x}$ and solve for x:

$$\frac{1}{4}(12\sqrt{2}) = \sqrt{2x}$$
$$3\sqrt{2} = \sqrt{2x}$$
$$3\sqrt{2} = \sqrt{2} \cdot \sqrt{x}$$
$$3 = \sqrt{x}$$
$$9 = x$$

20 PAM **7**

To find a real number solution for x, you can factor the polynomial since it is both factorable (by grouping) and set equal to zero. Rewrite the equation by factoring out the GCF (greatest common factor) of the first two terms and the GCF of the last two terms. Notice that you'll have $x-7$ in both products. Factor out $x-7$ and solve:

$$x^3 - 7x^2 + 3x - 21 = 0$$
$$x^2(x-7) + 3(x-7) = 0$$
$$(x-7)(x^2+3) = 0$$
$$x-7 = 0 \quad x^2 + 3 = 0$$
$$x = 7$$

Since $x^2 + 3$ can never equal zero if x is a real number, 7 is the only solution.

Any solution to an equation is checkable by plugging your answer back in. Since there is no safety net of choices in this problem, take the time, if you have it, to plug 7 in. At first that will seem daunting because it looks like you need to work out 7^3 without a calculator. Notice, though, that the first two terms, 7^3 and $7(7^2)$, really mean the same thing, so they subtract to zero:

$$7^3 - 7(7^2) + 3(7) - 21 \;=\; 0 + 21 - 21 \;=\; 0.$$

Math Test – Calculator

Multiple-Choice Questions

1 A HOA To write an equation representing this situation, think about how much money Flannery starts with and how much she needs at the end of the day. She begins with $300 and then makes $45 an hour, represented by $45n$. However, she must pay a fee of $150 before leaving work. This can be expressed by $300 + 45n - 150$. This must equal her goal of $420. By subtracting 300 from each side, you get choice (A).

$$300 + 45n - 150 = 420$$
$$45n - 150 = 120$$

 Be careful: if you start with $300 + 45n - 150 = 420$ and combine like terms, you get $45n + 150 = 420$, which is not one of the choices. When your answer doesn't obviously match one of the choices, first check to see if one of them is just a different form of your expression or equation.

2 A PAM To determine the function f, you only need to find the slope of f since the four answer choices all have different slopes. In the table, each time a increases by three, $f(a)$ increases by one. Slope is $\dfrac{\text{rise}}{\text{run}}$ or $\dfrac{\text{change in } y}{\text{change in } x}$ and since a is the x-value and $f(a)$ is the y-value, the slope is $\dfrac{f(a_2) - f(a_1)}{a_2 - a_1} = \dfrac{1}{3}$. This will be true no matter what pair of coordinate pairs you choose. The only linear equation with a slope of is $f(a) = \dfrac{1}{3}a - 3$, choice (A).

3 D PSD Answer this question by the process of elimination. Choices (A) and (B) are incorrect because the tweets both increased and decreased after December 17th. Choice (C) is incorrect because the maximum number of tweets occurred around December 25th, not December 31st. That leaves choice (D). Be mindful of the word "generally." It is true that tweets generally increased until December 25th and then generally decreased, even though you could find brief periods where this doesn't hold.

4 **A** PSD   One way to get an answer is by backsolving. Since the answer choices are in ascending order, start with one of the middle choices. If you pick Choice (B), divide 550 by 600 to determine if it is equal to 87.5%. Since $\frac{550}{600} = 0.91\overline{6}$ or $91.\overline{6}\%$, 550 is too large. Therefore, the correct answer is (A).

You can double check that $\frac{525}{600} = 0.875 = 87.5\%$.

You can also easily take 87.5% of 600 by multiplying $(0.875)(600)$ on your calculator. It will give you 525. The only danger here is that the 24 mentioned in the question is extraneous, so make sure to avoid the temptation to use it in your busywork.

5 **C** HOA   This is a two-part question. First, find z by translating the statement "when 4 times some integer z is subtracted from 12, the result is 32" to the algebraic equation $12 - 4z = 32$ and solving it.

$$12 - 4z = 32$$
$$-4z = 20$$
$$z = -5$$

Now, multiply z by 3 and add 7 to get $3(-5) + 7 = -15 + 7 = -8$.

Notice that –5 is a choice, even though the question does not ask for z. Before moving on to the next problem, always re-check the *ask* from the problem you've just completed to be sure you've answered it.

6 **B** PSD   Since the total population is 1.25 million people and the populations for each country range from 1.5 to 3.4, the units for the vertical axis cannot be millions, Choice (C), or hundreds of millions, Choice (D). Choice (A) is incorrect because thousands is too small. In thousands, 2.2 would represent 2,200. The sum of 2200, 3100, 1500, 3400, and 2300 is 12,500, which is not 1.25 million (1,250,000). Therefore, the correct answer is (B), hundreds of thousands.

7 **A** PAM   The best approach is to draw the graph of the function $g(x)$ as a line that passes through quadrants I, II, and III. The function $g(x) - 2$ is a line parallel to $g(x)$ but shifted down 2 units. Draw $g(x) - 2$ so it passes through quadrants I, III, and IV. Using your sketch, you can see that $g(x)$ must have a positive slope and a y-intercept between (0, 2) and the origin. If the y-intercept of $g(x)$ were any higher on the y-axis, $g(x) - 2$ would not pass through quadrant IV. If it were any lower than the origin, $g(x)$ would miss quadrant II.

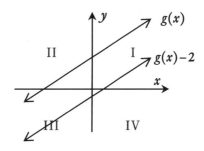

355

8   C   PSD   Since 75 seconds is equivalent to 1.25 minutes ($75 \div 60 = 1.25$), Laura reads 2 pages in 1.25 minutes. To find how many pages she reads in an hour (60 minutes), you can set up a proportion with the ratio $\dfrac{\text{pages}}{\text{minutes}}$, and solve it by cross-multiplying:

$$\frac{2}{1.25} = \frac{x}{60}$$
$$1.25x = 120$$
$$x = 96$$

◈   You can also use conversion ratios to change units all in one step:

$$1 \text{ hour} \times \frac{60 \text{ minutes}}{1 \text{ hour}} \times \frac{60 \text{ seconds}}{1 \text{ minute}} \times \frac{2 \text{ pages}}{75 \text{ seconds}} = 96 \text{ pages.}$$

9   C   PSD   Participants who smoked between 6 and 25 cigarettes per day fall under the smoking status of "Moderate (6–15)" and "Heavy (16–25)." The probability that one of these participants was "Underweight" can be determined by:

$$\frac{\text{Number of Underweight, Moderate and Heavy smokers}}{\text{Number of total Moderate and Heavy Smokers}} = \frac{35 + 47}{575 + 1046} = \frac{82}{1621} = 0.051.$$

10   C   PSD   The key is to determine the scale on both the x and y-axes of the graph. Each vertical line represents an increase of 2 cm on the x-axis (Height) and each horizontal line represents and increase of 2 cm on the y-axis (Reach). There are four boxers with a reach of at least 184 cm, and the shortest has a height that is half-a-box to the left of 180cm, so 179 cm.

11   D   PSD   Calculate the ratio of height to reach for boxers A, B, C, and D. Boxer D has the smallest ratio: $\dfrac{191}{198} = 0.965$.

12   A   HOA   You can backsolve by plugging each answer choice into the inequality. Remember, you want the one that is NOT a solution, meaning the choice that does not make the inequality true. If you start with choice (A) and plug in 3 for x, the inequality becomes $4(3) - 3 \geq 2(3) + 7$ or $9 \geq 13$. Since this is a false statement, (A) is the correct answer.

💡   Though you could solve this inequality algebraically, you'd still want to check your answer, so why not, as we did above, just cut right to the chase and start with the checking?

13 D PAM   Every time the age of the sample increases by 5730 years, the number of Carbon-14 atoms decreases by half. Since the number of C-14 atoms decreases by a different amount each time (e.g. the difference between 3.2×10^{12} and 1.6×10^{12} is 1.6×10^{12}, but the difference between 1.6×10^{12} and 8.0×10^{11} is 8.0×10^{11}), the relationship is not linear. That eliminates choices (A) and (B). It cannot be choice (C), exponential growth, because the number of C-14 atoms is decreasing, not increasing. That leaves choice (D), exponential decay.

Be careful when determining the relative size of numbers written in scientific notation. 8×10^{11} is *smaller* than 1.6×10^{12} because the exponent is smaller.

14 B HOA   The *C*-intercept is the total monthly cost of using the gym zero times. This represents the base cost of a gym membership each month since you would pay that amount for a month even if you never use the gym.

15 C HOA   All four equations are in slope-intercept form where m is the slope and b is the *y*-intercept (or in this case the *C*-intercept). Since the *y*-intercept is approximately 35, you can eliminate choices (A) and (D) as those equations have *y*-intercepts of 0. To determine the slope of the line, take two points on the line and calculate $\frac{\text{rise}}{\text{run}}$ or $\frac{y_2 - y_1}{x_2 - x_1}$. It appears that the line passes close to (0, 35) and (2, 40). The slope of a line that goes through those points is $\frac{40 - 35}{2 - 0} = \frac{5}{2} = 2.5$. This is much closer to 2, the slope of choice (C), than to $\frac{1}{2}$, the slope of choice (B), so Choice (C) is the best equation.

16 C PSD   The range, the spread between the largest and smallest values, will change the most once the outlier 25 is removed from the set. With 25 included, the range is $25 - 5 = 20$, and without 25 included, the range is $15 - 5 = 10$. The median is unaffected by the removal of 25, remaining at 7. The mean is only slightly changed, decreasing from 9.17 to 8.23.

Generally, the mean and median should not change drastically with the addition or removal of one number in a large enough set. An exception to this would be the addition or removal of an extreme outlier. For example, if the number 5,000 were added to the set in this problem, the mean would be greatly altered. Of course, if there were a 5,000-story apartment building on Elm Street, the change in the mean number of stories would be the least interesting fact about that street.

17 A PSD Since the team practices 6 days a week and the players drink 200 gallons of water per practice, they consume 1200 gallons per week. The filter pours water at a rate of 9 gallons per minute, which is equivalent to 540 gallons per hour. To find the number of hours spent filling water containers, divide 1200 gallons by 540 gallons per hour: $\frac{1200}{540} = \frac{20}{9}$ hours.

You can also use conversion ratios:

$$\frac{200 \text{ gallons}}{1 \text{ day}} \times \frac{6 \text{ days}}{1 \text{ week}} \times \frac{1 \text{ min}}{9 \text{ gallons}} \times \frac{1 \text{ hour}}{60 \text{ minutes}} = \frac{20}{9} \frac{\text{hours}}{\text{week}}.$$

18 D HOA Solving for p yields $14p \geq 12$ or $p \geq \frac{6}{7}$. Plugging $\frac{6}{7}$ for p into $11 - 7p$ will give you the maximum possible value since plugging in anything larger will create a smaller final difference: $11 - 7\left(\frac{6}{7}\right) = 11 - 6 = 5$.

A trick here is to recognize that $11 - 7p$ is equivalent to $14p - 22$ divided by -2. Thus, divide both sides of the inequality by -2. Remember to flip the inequality sign whenever you multiply or divide by a negative number!

$$\frac{14p - 22}{-2} \geq \frac{10}{-2}$$
$$11 - 7p \leq 5$$

Since $11 - 7p$ is less than or equal to 5, the maximum possible value is 5.

19 C PSD The probability that someone who had dinner at the food court did not eat Chinese food can be represented by $\dfrac{\text{Pizza for Dinner + Burgers for Dinner}}{\text{Total Dinners}} = \dfrac{52 + 53}{150} = \dfrac{105}{150}$.

Notice that you only need the information from the "Dinner" row. Don't be confused by the extra information in the table.

20 A PSD Use the equation $c(x) = (T + G)x + I + R$ and the table to write equations for the total cost of renting a truck from company A and from company C.

Company A: $c(x) = (0.60 + 0.10)x + 35 + 20 = 0.70x + 55$

Company C: $c(x) = (0.75 + 0.15)x + 0 + 50 = 0.90x + 50$

To find the range of miles when the cost for company A will be greater than or equal to the cost for company C, set up an inequality and solve for x.

$$0.70x + 55 \geq 0.90x + 50$$
$$5 \geq 0.20x$$
$$25 \geq x \quad \text{a.k.a.} \quad x \leq 25$$

21   **D**   HOA   The slope of the line in any linear function of x is the coefficient of x, which, in this case, is $T + G$. Both the truck rental T and the gas expenses G are in dollars per mile. Choice (D) is the only answer that makes sense because it is the cost of <u>per mile</u> expenses.

22   **C**   PAM   The key phrase in this question is "exponential rate." To grow at an exponential rate means to increase by a certain percentage of oneself. You can eliminate Choice (A) because the annual rate of change was constant, $10. Similarly, you can eliminate Choices (B) and (D) because they have constant growth rates, $110.10 and $100, respectively. You are left with Choice (C). Here the balance grew by a greater amount each year (10.50, 11.03, 11.57), which is a sign of exponential growth. You could do calculations to show a consistent exponential growth in choice (C), but they are unnecessary once you eliminate the other choices.

23   **C**   HOA   If $h - k = 0$, then $h = k$. You can sketch a line where the x-intercept (h) and the y-intercept (k) are equal. The slope of the line must be negative.

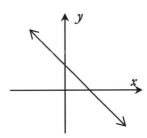

◆   Calculate the slope of the line to be $\dfrac{k-0}{0-h} = \dfrac{k}{-h}$. Since $h = k$, substitute to get a slope of $\dfrac{h}{-h} = -1$.

24 **B** PAM First simplify $f(b) - g(b)$, distributing the negative sign to every term of $g(b)$.

$$f(b) - g(b) = (4b^2 - 3b + 5) - (20b^3 - 15b^2 + 25b)$$
$$= 4b^2 - 3b + 5 - 20b^3 + 15b^2 - 25b$$
$$= -20b^3 + 19b^2 - 28b + 5$$

Unfortunately, $\dfrac{-20b^3 + 19b^2 - 28b + 5}{5b - 1}$ doesn't look pretty. In this form, it doesn't appear to be equivalent to any of the answer choices. The next step is to divide using polynomial long division.

$$5b - 1 \overline{)\,-20b^3 + 19b^2 - 28b + 5} \quad \text{(quotient } -4b^2 + 3b - 5\text{)}$$
$$\underline{-(-20b^3 + 4b^2)}$$
$$15b^2 - 28b$$
$$\underline{-(15b^2 - 3b)}$$
$$-25b + 5$$
$$\underline{-(-25b + 5)}$$
$$0$$

Now, just notice that $-4b^2 + 3b - 5$ is simply $-f(b)$.

When a problem looks terribly difficult, like this one, always consider what a change of form might do. Here, $g(b)$ can be factored to $5b(4b^2 - 3b + 5)$, which means $g(b) = 5b \cdot f(b)$. So $\dfrac{f(b) - g(b)}{5b - 1} = \dfrac{f(b) - 5b \cdot f(b)}{5b - 1} = \dfrac{f(b)(1 - 5b)}{5b - 1} = -1 \cdot f(b)$.

Plugging in a number for b can also make the question easier. If you use, for example, $b = 2$, then $\dfrac{f(2) - g(2)}{5(2) - 1} = \dfrac{15 - 150}{9} = -15$. Choice (B) also yields –15 when $b = 2$.

25 **C** PSD A good strategy is to plug in numbers for the initial radius and height of the tank. If you let $r = 1$ and $h = 1$, then the initial volume is $V = \pi r^2 h = \pi (1)^2 (1) = \pi$. If the aquarium increases the volume by 50%, the new volume will be 1.50π. An 18% increase of the radius will make the new radius 1.18. To determine the new height, solve the following equation:

$$1.50\pi = \pi (1.18)^2 h$$
$$h = \frac{1.50\pi}{(1.18)^2 \pi} = \frac{1.50}{1.3924} = 1.077$$

Since the new height is 1.077, it is a 7.7% increase from the initial height of 1.

When the choices have variables in them, it is wise to avoid using special numbers, like 0 or 1, when plugging in. However, since this problem has four numeric choices, there is a clear benefit to using a simple number like 1 for both the original radius and the original height.

26 D PSD   An important distinction to make is that the data points represent the *actual* dependency ratio for Japan for each year since 1995. The line of best fit represents an estimate of the dependency ratio for each year. Choice (A) is incorrect because there is no actual data for the dependency ratio in 1995. The line of best fit indicates that the dependency ratio was likely 0.416, but you have no way of knowing if that is the actual ratio. Choice (B) is incorrect because it has the numerator and denominator of the dependency ratio reversed. The corrected statement would say, "In 2005, the number of people whose ages were below 15 or above 65 was 51 percent of the number of people of working age in Japan." Choice (C) is incorrect because the actual dependency ratio for Japan does not increase by 0.103 each year; the estimated dependency ratio (as predicted by the line of best fit) increases by 0.103 each year. Since the data points don't form a true line, there is no standard increase. Choice (D) is correct because the data point at 7 years (2002) has a dependency ratio of 0.48. Therefore, in 2002, Japan had 48 people that were not of working age for every set of 100 working-age people.

27 D ATM   First, find the slope of using the slope formula $\dfrac{y_2 - y_1}{x_2 - x_1}$.

$$\text{Slope of } \overline{AB} = \frac{1-3}{5-1} = \frac{-2}{4} = -\frac{1}{2}.$$

The slope of a line perpendicular to $\overline{AB}$ is the negative reciprocal of $-\dfrac{1}{2}$ which is 2. You can eliminate choices (A) and (B) since they both have a slope of $\dfrac{1}{2}$. Since the perpendicular line intersects $\overline{AB}$ at its midpoint, find the midpoint by taking the average of the x-values and y-values of the endpoints A and B.

$$\text{Midpoint of } \overline{AB} = \left(\frac{1+5}{2}, \frac{3+1}{2}\right) = (3, 2)$$

The midpoint must be on the line you are looking for, so you can plug $(3, 2)$ into the equations $y = 2x - 1$ and $y = 2x - 4$ to see if it is on either the line from choice (C) or the line from choice (D). Since $2 = 2(3) - 4$, choice (D) has the correct equation of the perpendicular line.

28 B PAM   This is an example of exponential growth where the population of mosquitos increases by a percentage of itself. The formula $A(t) = P(1 + r)^t$ exhibits exponential growth where P represents the principal (initial) amount, r the rate of change (as a decimal), and t the number of times the rate is compounded. In this problem, the principal is 200 and the rate is 0.50. Since the population increases by 50% every two weeks, it is compounded once every fourteen days. This is represented by $\dfrac{d}{14}$. For example, if $d = 14$, the rate is compounded once because $\dfrac{14}{14} = 1$; if $d = 21$, the rate is compounded 1.5 times because $\dfrac{21}{14} = 1.5$. The equation is therefore $A(t) = 200(1 + 0.5)^{\frac{d}{14}}$ or $200(1.5)^{\frac{d}{14}}$.

29 **A** PAM   If $f(x)+5=0$ has exactly one real solution, then the graph of $f(x)+5$ has only one x-intercept. Add 5 to each answer choice (because you want $f(x)+5$) and graph each new function on your calculator. The graph of $y=x^2+10x+25$ has one x-intercept, so choice (A) is correct. When taking section 4 of the SAT with a graphing calculator, never forget that sometimes the best way to analyze a function is to just let the calculator show you what it looks like.

30 **B** PAM   A good strategy is to plug in numbers for A and B. Since B is two less than A, let's pick $A=4$ and $B=2$. Then substitute those values for A and B into the two equations.

$$R=16(2)^4=16(16)=256$$
$$P=4(2)^2-5=4(4)-5=16-5=11$$

Now, plug $R=256$ and $P=11$ into the answer choices to see which equation is true. Only (B) is correct.

Choice (A): $11 \neq \dfrac{256}{16}+5$

Choice (B): $11 = \dfrac{256}{16}-5$

Choice (C): $11 \neq \dfrac{256}{4}$

Choice (D): $11 \neq 4(256)-5$

Since $B=A-2$, you can rewrite the second equation as $P=4(2)^{A-2}-5$ or $4\left(\dfrac{2^A}{2^2}\right)-5=2^A-5$. Since the first equation yields $\dfrac{R}{16}=2^A$, you can rewrite $P=2^A-5$ as $P=\dfrac{R}{16}-5$.

Student-Produced Response Questions

31   HOA $2 \leq x \leq 3$

If Allie types 30 words per minutes, she could type 5400 words in 180 minutes

$\left(\dfrac{5400}{30} = 180\right)$. If Allie types 45 words per minutes, she could type 5400 words in 120

minutes $\left(\dfrac{5400}{45} = 120\right)$. Since there are 60 minutes in an hour, 120 minutes is equivalent to

2 hours and 180 minutes is 3 hours. Therefore, it will take Allie anywhere between 2 and 3

hours, inclusive. You can therefore give any number in this range, such as 2, 2.5, 2.99, or 3.

32 HOA **183**

This is a classic systems of equations problem. Let G be the number of sunglasses Genie sold and S be the number of sunglasses Sarah sold. Since they sold a total of 299 sunglasses, $G + S = 299$. Genie sold 67 fewer sunglasses than Sarah, so $G = S - 67$. You could solve this system of equations several ways, but it is already set up for the substitution method since the second equation has G isolated.

$$G + S = 299$$
$$G = S - 67$$

Substitute the second equation into the first and solve for S.

$$G + S = 299$$
$$S - 67 + S = 299$$
$$2S - 67 = 299$$
$$2S = 366$$
$$S = 183$$

33 PSD **2**

Since 1 acre = 1 chain × 1 furlong, 1 acre = 66 ft × 660 ft = 43,560 square feet. The plot of land has an area of 87,120 square feet, so to find the number of acres, divide 87,120 by 43,560 and the result is 2 acres.

34 ATM **120**

An arc is a portion of the circumference of a circle, and the ratio of arc length to circumference is equal to the ratio of its central angle to $360°$.

$$\frac{\text{arc length}}{\text{circumference}} = \frac{\text{central angle}}{360}$$

Since the circumference of a circle is equal to $2\pi r$, the circumference of this circle is $2\pi(12)$ or 24π. You can set up the following proportion and solve for x, the central angle

$$\frac{8\pi}{24\pi} = \frac{x}{360}$$

$$\frac{1}{3} = \frac{x}{360}$$

$$x = 120$$

35 PSD **60**

If 60% of the total acceptances are male and there are 240 male acceptances, then $240 = 0.60x$ where x is the number of total acceptances.

$$x = \frac{240}{0.60} = 400$$

Thus, there must be 400 total acceptances. Since there are currently 340 (240 boys and 100 girls), the college should accept 60 more girls.

36 ATM **110, 111, 112, 113, 114, or 115**

A sector is a portion of the area of a circle, and the ratio of sector area to circle area is equal to the ratio of central angle to $360°$.

$$\frac{\text{sector area}}{\text{area of circle}} = \frac{\text{central angle}}{360°}$$

The diameter of the circle is 10, so the radius is 5. Since the area of a circle is πr^2, the area of this circle is $\pi(5)^2 = 25\pi \approx 78.54$. The area of the sector is between 24 and 25, so you can pick any value between 24 and 25, inclusive, to set up the proportion. For example, pick 24.5:

$$\frac{24.5}{78.54} = \frac{x}{360}$$

$$78.54x = 8820$$

$$x = 112.3$$

Rounding to the nearest degree, this would be 112. Picking a different value for the sector area (between 24 and 25) would yield a different central angle. The possibilities are 110, 111, 112, 113, 114, or 115.

37 PAM **.999**

Since the rate at which a man loses height is a percentage of his current height, this is an example of exponential decay. The formula $A(t) = P(1-r)^t$ models exponential decay where P represents the principal (initial) amount, r the rate of change (as a decimal), and t the number of times the rate is compounded. In this problem, you are given the equation $H = 76v^t$. Notice the similarity to the decay model: v can be represented by $1-r$. The rate 0.1% can be written as a decimal so $r = .001$. Thus, $v = 1 - r = 1 - .001 = .999$.

38   PAM   **73.8**

Use the given equation $H = 76v^t$ and $v = .999$ from question 37 to solve for Mr. Celio's height when he is 70.

 Be careful because t is the number of years in the future after age 40. Therefore, t should be 30, not 70.

$$H = 76(0.999)^{30} = 73.8$$

Answer Explanations for Test 4

Reading Test

Passage 1

The first passage on every SAT reading section is a literary passage, which usually requires a somewhat different approach from that used for the more information heavy passages on the rest of the test. This passage describes a series of events taking place over a short period of time. As you read, mark names and places and write a short summary of the action every 15 lines or so. The story starts by showing Jimmy, a child from Rum Alley, in a fight with several other children from Devil's Row until he is rescued by an older boy. Notice that the author does little to take sides in describing the action, and that it is not until near the end of the passage that we learn how the conflict began.

 B RC Write in your own answer for this open-ended question: most of the text of the passage is devoted to describing the violent action as it takes place, which is what you would want to write down before going to the answer choices. He describes the action in a mostly neutral way, almost like a reporter, so that we aren't left feeling like one side or the other represents good or evil. This makes (B) clearly the best answer!

 If you are not sure what to write down, you can use a process of elimination to get to the correct answer, but this is risky, because each answer is at least partly accurate. Choice (A) is incorrect because it suggests that the intent of the author is to pass judgment on the guilty although the passage doesn't "clearly" assign guilt at all. Further, he does not overtly mock (C) the people in the fight, though they may be ignorant and brutal, nor does the author make any call to action in response to the events described, though he may suggest justice is lacking in the actions portrayed (D).

 D COE Solve COE questions as a pair: go on to the answer choices in 3 to see which explains why the incident began. Once you have recognized that 76–81 provides the correct answer to this question, you simply have to find the answer choice that best matches what it says. Jimmy's words in 80–81 are in the vernacular of the street boys in the passage, so this may actually be harder than you might think! Jimmie was going to beat up ("lick") a Devil's Row boy ("dat Riley kid"), but then the others ganged up on him ("dey all pitched on me"). With this loose translation of Jimmie's words, choice (D) is clearly correct.

3 **C** **COE**

As you read through the choices for the best answer to the reason the incident started according to Jimmie, there are two key "tricks" to get to the correct answer. First, the passage is not completely chronological, as choice (A), the earliest reference (lines 1–4) to the fight, does not necessarily explain why it started. Second, the question asked why the fight started "according to Jimmie"; thus, we can eliminate answers that do not present Jimmie's perspective. If we have paid attention to the fact that the question asks for Jimmie's view, we can streamline the process as only (B) and (D) present Jimmie's view, and, of these, (D) is clearly the only one that gives any reference to why the fight started.

If you did not focus on the question's reference to Jimmie's perspective, you can still get to the correct answer, as choices (A) and (B) present actions in the middle of the fight, and choice (D) talks about "causes of retreat" rather than causes of the fight in the first place.

4 **C** **RC**

Before going to the answer choices, write down your own idea about how Jimmie is described. This paragraph describes Jimmie's appearance. He is bruised and bloodied and his clothes are torn. Notice the contrast between the description of Jimmie's hurt appearance and the description in the last sentence of the paragraph, in which we are told that he looks like "a tiny, insane demon." Thus, you might write something like "beaten but still fighting." Choice (C) fits best with this, as he is pitiable for being beaten and fierce as he still fights on.

Alternatively, since the paragraph gives no insight into his motivations, you can eliminate choices (A) (noble), (B) (foolish and ignorant), and (D) (arrogant), all of which require insight into the mind of the character.

5 **B** **RC**

This is an especially difficult question because it requires us to infer why the author included a specific description that doesn't seem to be important to the plot.

To answer inference questions like this one, it is essential to answer the question for yourself before looking at the answer choices. The lines referenced describe people watching what happens, but do not show them caring enough to do anything about it. Thus, writing down "shows apathy in outsiders" will help you get to the correct answer, which is (B).

If you were unable to write in an answer or are not sure which fits best, remember to use elimination by taking out answers that involve too specific or too large an inference. Choice (A) suggests that the other people referenced somehow have contributed directly to the conflict, which is much too large an inferential leap. Choices (C) and (D) are inaccurate, as people appear curious enough to watch the fight and no one is described as doing purposeful labor.

6 **D** **COE**

This is the first of a pair of evidence-based questions, so read this question carefully, and move on to the lines in the next question. As explained in the explanation for question 7, after reviewing the lines, we should choose (D), because the Devil's Row boys ran away from the older, larger boy who joined the scuffle.

7 C COE The boys from Devil's Row don't retreat from the conflict until near the end of the passage, making choices (A) and (B) easy to eliminate. On the other hand, choice (D) is too late in the passage: it describes the boys from Rum Alley leaving, which is after the Devil's Row boys retreat. Choice (C) describes the older boy, Pete, coming to the scene and hitting one of the boys, who then runs away, followed by the rest of the Devil's Row children. This does tell us why the Devil's Row children retreated—they were faced with an older and larger boy to fight.

8 A WIC It is especially important to write-in your own answer for question like this before you read through the answer choices. A good write in for this would be something like "fighter" or "defender." In both sets of lines, "champion" is used to describe Jimmie, who we are told little about in the story except that he is from Rum Alley and fights with children from Devil's Row, despite being outnumbered. Choice (A) is closest to this meaning.

9 B WIC This is another great question to do a write-in answer before looking at the answer choices. In context, the word must refer to the people who are, as described, turning slowly towards their home street: the Rum Alley children who came forward in line 82 to exchange stories.

Although contingent often means "depending upon" (A), it does not in this context.

This is a good example of why it is important to view these types of questions in their exact context, rather than focusing on what the word in the question usually means, as the SAT often tests a secondary or tertiary meaning of a word or phrase.

10 A RC This question is a great example of why it is often important to read the context before or after specific sets of lines being asked about in a question. Lines 88–89 explain exactly what is happening in lines 89–93, that the boys are telling to each other "distorted versions" of the fight. The lines this question is asking about describe some of those distortions (A). The author indicates neither the size nor scale of the fighting in these lines, nor how it turned out (B).

Choices (C) and (D) may be tempting, but both require logical leaps that we should not make. The passage does not indicate that the boys exaggerating the story created actual misunderstandings (C), nor that it is generally true that people distort previous events when retelling them (D).

Passage 2

This passage describes historical events but mostly uses modern language. Its difficulty comes from the presentation of a potentially unfamiliar subject using some scientific terminology that can be challenging to follow. Circling names and potentially unfamiliar terms as you read the passage can provide a loose outline to use when skimming for answers in the text. The passage includes a graph at the end, but don't worry about understanding it in detail initially. You should read the entire text portion of the passage before working through the questions, but you don't need to analyze the graph until it comes up in a question. Remember to write down a short main idea for the passage after reading it: a good main idea for this passage would be something like "Modern relevance of founders' views of climate change theories."

 11 B RC Use the main idea that you wrote down to narrow down the choices for this question. Choice (B) is the best fit as it suggests the possible relevance of older views of climate change today.

 Although the passage does state that the founders believed in a type of global warming, choice (A) is incorrect because that belief is not presented as a reason why people today should take action on climate change. Choice (C) is incorrect because the passage does not present climate change views as consistent from the past up to today. The passage describes several past people's interest in climate change, but not their attempts to advocate in favor of changes to prevent climate change. Even more so, the passage suggests that it is a more modern occurrence. Choice (D) is outside of the scope of the passage; the passage does nothing to suggest that man-made climate change is unlikely to be possible today.

12 B WIC If you know the meaning of "ambivalent," having a mix of positive and negative feelings or ideas, choosing (B) is relatively easy.

 However, if the word is unfamiliar, you can use the strategy of putting in your own word based on the context. There are two context clues that help us learn the meaning of this word. First, the sentence before the one containing "ambivalence" tells us that the US has had a lot of climate change skepticism recently. The second clue is later in the sentence in lines 5–9, where the passage tells us that the founders were "far from" the modern American response in that the founders were vocal supporters of climate change theories. Therefore, you might write in "+/–" to indicate that ambivalent must mean both positive and negative, which makes "uncertainty" (B) the correct response.

 13 B COE For paired-evidence questions like this one, remember to read through the lines in the second question before reading through the answer choices in the first. Once you have found that in choice (C) the passage describes in lines 43–46 that colonists believed man-made climate change could be brought about through colonization, it is easy to choose (B).

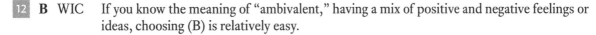

14 C COE   After reading through question 13 but before reading through its answer choices, you should read through the lines in the answer choices here. Choice (A) refers to neither founders nor climate change, and choice (B) tell us that disagreeing with the ideas put forth in choice (A) was patriotic, but these views are not about man-made climate change. In lines 43–46 (C), however, the passage explains that the colonists argued in support of man-made climate change in response to negative climate beliefs about North America coming from England. Choice (D) discusses a specific founder, but does not suggest that he believed in man-made climate change.

15 D RC   This question is an excellent example of one that can be answered much more easily by those who circled character names while reading the passage. Doing so makes it easier to quickly skim the text to find where these two people are mentioned—paragraph 3. These two are described as believing that the climate of the new world was inferior to that of Europe. This belief provided motivation to the founders to take an interest in the study of man-made climate change; it was a way for the founders to show that the efforts of colonials were improving the condition of the new world. Choice (D) is therefore correct.

16 C WIC   Write down your own word to take the place of "eager" in the sentence. A good phrase to write would be "interested in": don't worry if the part of speech doesn't match! The context clue for this word appears in the sentence right after the one containing the word. We are told that Jefferson worked hard to dispute the idea that American animals were inferior to European animals. This shows that he was especially interested in refuting such claims. Being interested in doing something does not fit with restless (A) or nervous (B) or prepared (D). Choice (C), keen, is correct because it refers to Jefferson's eagerness or enthusiasm, which is the secondary meaning of "keen."

17 A COE   Make sure to read through the lines in question 18 to help answer this question rather than answering this one first. Lines 97–100, choice (C) below, explain that people today can use the example of the mistakes made by the founders regarding man-made climate change to help avoid making similar mistakes, which fits perfectly with choice (A) here.

18 C COE   Using the lines in the answer choices on this question helps answer question 17, especially because question 17 is fairly open ended. The lines in choice (A) compare the founders' views with the modern American response, but do not suggest how we should apply the founders' beliefs to modern climate concerns. The lines in choice (B) contain little information and do not make mention of modern concerns. The lines in choice (D) reference "degeneracy theorists," who were not directly discussing climate change. The lines in choice (C) describe specifically that modern climate advocates can avoid making the same mistakes as those made by the founders described in the passage, making choice (C) correct.

19 C IG This question asks us about the graph. The best time to read through the graph in detail is right after reading this question but before reading through the answer choices. The graph shows the annual mean temperature and five year average temperature in the US from 1880 to 2015. The annual mean goes up and down over and over as does the five-year average, but both seem to be increasing overall. Choice (C) correctly summarizes this information.

You can also use a process of elimination by checking each choice against the graph. Choice (A) is inaccurate both because the temperature increases and decreases from year to year and because the graph does not cover the time before 1880. Choice (B) is inaccurate because the temperature has fluctuated by more than plus or minus 1 degree. Choice (D) is incorrect because the fluctuations during Jefferson's time (the 1700s and early 1800s) are not shown on the graph.

20 A IG The variation in average temperatures from year to year is shown to be much greater than the variation in the five year average temperature, making choice (A) the correct response. The fact that a difference was measured enough to be shown on the graph indicates that choice (B) is incorrect. Choice (C) is incorrect because the overall trend is an increase rather than a decrease. Choice (D) is incorrect because the change in average temperature from year to year is nearly always greater than 0.1 degrees.

Passage 3

This science passage describes the discovery of a scientifically valuable fossil and subsequent creation of a publication that included stereoscopic images. Some of the terminology and French names in this passage can be difficult to follow, so it is especially important to underline main ideas and circle relevant terms and names in the passage as you read. Some students find that taking short notes on each paragraph, written beside the passage, helps make it easier follow along. Before you move on to the questions, remember to write down the main point of the passage as a comprehension check, perhaps something like "stereoscopic fossil images allowed wider study."

21 B RC The La Chapelle fossil is central to the entire passage, so this is a difficult question because of how open-ended it is. However, the best place to start searching the passage for the answer to this question is in the first paragraph, in which the fossil is introduced. The answer is in lines 9–11: "…excavations of the skeleton revealed that it was more complete than anything else in the fossil record," which indicates that (B) is correct.

If you do not feel confident about where to find the answer to this question, skip it initially, and come back to it at the end and eliminate answers based on what you know is untrue based on the passage and the other questions. None of the other choices are supported by the passage, but it can be very time-consuming to start by trying to look for support for the inferences in each answer choice.

22 C WIC Write in your own word for this before looking at the answer choices, especially since this term is derived from Latin and a specialized term for archaeology. Here, the meaning of "in situ" is provided immediately before the term is used: "undisturbed archaeological context." "Undisturbed context" would be an excellent write-in and leads us to choice (C).

23 C RC The second paragraph of the passage describes the Bouyssonie brothers sending the remains to Boule, and Boule's subsequent actions. Boule studied the fossil in detail then produced a publication. The passage does not describe Boule's work as if it was unexpected or contrary to what the Bouyssonie brothers had planned, so we can reasonably infer that the brothers intended that Boule would look into the fossil in this way, which makes Choice (C) correct.

24 A WIC Eminent is being used to describe Marcellin Boule, who we are told is a director at a prestigious museum. From the context, we can tell that eminent is a positive adjective that describes someone who does important scientific research. "Top in field" could be a good write-in for this question, but if you have trouble coming up with a specific word or phrase, a couple of up arrows to indicate the word being very positive would be a great start. Of the choices, "distinguished" is the closest in meaning and is correct.

Don't choose an answer just because it may be unfamiliar: choice (C), "grandiose," is a tempting choice if you aren't completely sure what it means because it sounds like "grand," which is very positive. "Grandiose" means impressive in size, appearance, or style, and usually refers to something unnecessarily or pretentiously grand.

25 **D** **COE**   As with all COE questions, go ahead to the next question's answer choices before choosing the best answer here.

     However, be sure that you understand the question before reading over the answer choices for the next question—this question asks about the way that the focus shifts in the passage as a whole, which is a movement from the artifact to a discussion of the stereoscopic plates used to present it in a book. Once you have identified that lines 36–42 show this transition, it is easy to choose (D) for this question!

26 **D** **COE**   The question above asks about the movement of the passage from before the second paragraph to what comes after the second paragraph. Thus, you need to think about the movement of the passage as a whole as you read over the options. The first paragraph discusses the discovery of the fossil, and the third paragraph and the rest of the passage describe the book's use of stereoscopic images. Choice (A) introduces the topic of the second paragraph, Boule, but does not relate to the larger movement of the passage as a whole. Choice (B) discusses the book itself and its significance, but does not discuss the key aspect of the stereoscope that the rest of the passage focuses on. Choice (C) discusses what Boule wrote in the book, but does not quite get to the use of stereoscopic imagery. Only choice (D) gets us from Boule's book about the fossil to its use of stereoscopic plates, which then are the focus of the remainder of the passage.

27 **A** **RC**   Kaleidoscopes are briefly mentioned in the third paragraph (top of the second column). In the sentence immediately following the sentence in the passage that mentions kaleidoscopes, the passage describes stereoscopes as having a "particular trick": "to give a two-dimensional image an illusion of depth." This trick being "particular" suggests that it is a way in which stereoscopes are different from other optical toys listed in the previous sentence, like kaleidoscopes. Choice (A) is therefore correct.

     Don't be fooled by answer choices that present material verbatim from the passage—the whole answer must be correct to be the best answer. Choice (C) mentions the kaleidoscope being an "optical toy," which is language lifted directly from the passage, but the passage suggests that stereoscopes are another "optical toy," so this is not a difference.

28 **B** **RC**   Go back to the passage so that you can answer this for yourself. The author creates an analogy between stereoscopic prints and modern data sharing to help the reader understand the importance and effect of those prints being provided in the book, as indicated in choice (B). Choice (A) is incorrect because this connection does not help one visualize the stereoscopic prints, only understand their importance and connection to modern science. Choice (C) is incorrect because this sentence does not explain *how* the stereoscopic prints were produced. Choice (D) is incorrect because the emphasis here is on the similarities between providing stereoscopic images and modern data sharing, not the differences.

29   B   COE   Remember to complete paired evidence questions by using the line numbers in the second question to figure out which choice is correct for the first question. We can eliminate Choices (A) and (C) based on the information contained in the line numbers in the following question. Choice (B) is correct because the stereo cards, we are told, are valuable for getting a better understanding of the fossils they depict. Choice (D) is incorrect because, although the stereo cards are described as valuable, the passage does not state that this was the first instance of stereoscopic images used in a scientific publication.

30   C   COE   Use these line numbers after reading through the previous question to help answer that one. Choice (A) discusses the stereoscopic device in general, not the specific plates used in the book. Choice (B) talks about need for "proxies," but doesn't mention stereoscopic images at all. Choice (C), however, provides the most specifically detailed information about the scientific value of the specific stereo cards included in the *L'Homme* publication, and is therefore correct.

   Choice (D) may seem difficult to eliminate if you are not careful to identify exactly what the question asks, since it mentions Boule's use of stereograms in the book, but it references the long-term effect, not the immediate response of Boule's contemporaries.

Passage 4

Expect the SAT Reading Test to contain at least one passage that is over one hundred years old. Most students find that older passages are usually more difficult and take longer to get through. To manage your time best, plan to skip older passages initially and save them for last. This particular passage is a persuasive speech given to support women's right to vote. Focus on the individual arguments made in each paragraph—take short notes beside each paragraph to see how the argument fits together.

31 **D** COE   For paired evidence questions, make sure to read through the line numbers in the second question before reading through the answer choices in the first question. The author constructs her argument through several means, so this question could be answered in several varying correct ways. However, only one answer choice given actually answers the question correctly. If you were able to see that lines 29–33 were correct for question 32, you can quickly see that choice (D) matches them, as the author provides an argument for why preventing women from voting constitutes a violation of the constitution.

If you were unable to rule out all the wrong answers on question 32, you can still get this pair correct by recognizing that none of the answer choices match either choice (B) or (D) for question 32, as both essentially suggest the same thing—that women are actually people!

32 **C** COE   Use the information contained in the line numbers from this question to answer the previous question, rather than answering them separately one after another. Re-read the indicated lines and ask yourself whether these lines indicate how her argument is constructed. Choice (A) does not do so, because it is entirely a quote, and thus does not show her argument. Choice (B) is harder to rule out, because in these lines she makes an argument that "we" means all the people, women and men. However, it doesn't directly reference the issue of a woman's right to vote—it only presents a piece of evidence that leads to her primary argument. Choice (C) shows the specific way in which the author constructed her argument for women's right to vote, and it matches with the specific correct answer to the previous question. Choice (D) asks a rhetorical question, but does not tie directly to the question of women's right to vote.

33 **A** RC   Make sure to write in a short answer to this question before you look at the answer choices. The author is giving a persuasive speech in which she uses strong rhetoric to convince her audience. Choice (A), "forceful," is correct, because it focuses on assertiveness and powerful use of language. Choice (B), "pedantic," means overly precise and finicky. Choice (C), "irate," means angry and can be a difficult answer choice to cross out, especially if you did not write in your own answer before looking at the choices. Although we may be able to infer that the speaker is upset at the situation she describes, her use of language focuses on reasoned arguments, not unreasoning anger, as suggested by "irate." Choice (D), "despondent," means down, discouraged, or despairing, and does not fit the energetic and dynamic language and arguments provided in the passage.

34 **B** RC   As with many questions that contain specific line numbers, the answer to this question is contained not within the lines given, but rather in the following paragraph, so be sure to read the broader context to answer the question correctly. In paragraph 3, the author makes reference to specific language used in the preamble to the Constitution to advance her argument, which makes choice (B) correct.

35 **C** WIC Go back to the sentence and write in your own replacement word. In the paragraph containing line 33, the speaker makes the argument that prohibiting women from voting is unconstitutional. When the speaker states that disfranchisement is "a violation of the supreme law of the land," this is what she is referring to—the Constitution. She speaks to the top most elevated source of law. A good write-in for this question would be something like "top" or "most important." Choice (C), "highest," is therefore correct. Although choices (A) and (B) can work in meaning for "supreme" in some instances, neither works in this context, as the speaker is arguing that disenfranchisement violates the chief source of law, not that the Constitution is flawless or above questioning.

36 **A** RC Lines 33–38 make two specific arguments about disenfranchisement—that it is unconstitutional and that it is undemocratic. Either or both would make a good write-in for this question before reading through the answer choices. Continue reading the sentence immediately following lines 33–38 to see a continuation of the discussion of why the lack of women's right to vote is undemocratic. Choice (A) is correct. Choice (B) is overly strong through its use of the word "forever." Choice (C), although a probable consequence of a lack of women's suffrage, is not discussed at all in lines 33–38.

Choice (D) is tempting, but it is overly specific, in that although lacking the vote does deprive women of "the blessing of liberty," it does not necessarily deprive non-white males from that blessing.

37 **B** RC This paragraph can be difficult to read because of its sentence structure. Nearly the entire paragraph is one long complex sentence with lots of clauses. The sentence essentially states that denying women the vote is "the most hateful aristocracy ever" and that other common types of inequality are relatively less objectionable because this inequality enters "every home of the nation." Choice (B) is correct because this paragraph indicates that the "oligarchy of sex" is the most widespread of the oligarchies described.

38 **C** WIC The most relevant portion of the sentence containing the word in question reads "no State has a right to make any law, or to enforce any old law, that shall abridge [meaning decrease or restrict] their privileges [things that people are allowed to restrict] or immunities." Immunities therefore must refer to something other than privileges that the State lacks a right to do. In context, this suggests that restricting or decreasing someone's immunities would be negative. Think also about the word itself: "immunities." To be "immune" is to be resistant to or protected from something. Vaccines like the flu shot are also called immunizations. Here, "resistances" or "protections," would both be excellent write-in words, and "protections" is the correct answer, choice (C).

Choice (D), "inoculations" does mean the same thing as immunizations in the context of vaccines, but generally not in other contexts.

39 **D** COE Using the line numbers in the following question, we can see the author explain that discrimination against women is unconstitutional "precisely as is every one against Negroes." Choice (D) is therefore correct.

40 D COE   Make sure to read through the given lines after reading through the previous question, but work on both questions together as a pair. Choice (D), lines 60–63, is correct because in these lines the author directly makes the argument that discrimination against women and blacks is prohibited by the constitution in the same way.

41 C IG   Be careful not to get confused by this graph's *x*-axis (at the bottom of the graph). You should read the notes listed next to a graph when answering a question about that graph to make sure you understand how the data is being represented. The graph shows that the percent of the over-21-year-old population that voted increased from 25% to about 37% at the start of women's suffrage, then, over the next 10 years, fluctuated between around that level and 48% at the most. The primary inference we can draw is that voter turnout increased noticeably following women's suffrage and maintained that increase for at least the following 10 years. Choice (C) is therefore correct. Choice (A) may or may not be a true statement, but the graph does not suggest whether it is or isn't true—the graph doesn't include information on the outcomes of specific elections or the participation of specific individuals. Choices (B) and (D) under and overestimate respectively the impact of women's suffrage on voter participation.

Passage 5

This set of paired passages is the second science question set on the reading section. Remember to focus on circling proper nouns and underlining words and phrases that seem important or especially confusing. Read through Passage 1, then answer questions 42–45 before reading Passage 2, as these questions only deal with Passage 1. Then read Passage 2 and answer the remaining questions. Splitting up the passages in this way makes managing the timing a little easier and decreases how much material you have to keep in mind when answering some of the questions. The first passage describes a portion of the life cycle of some insects and explains the natural interrelations of insects in human terms. The second passage critiques the personification of natural phenomena, especially in the description of insects. Note that Passage 1 uses this type of language numerous times.

 B RC Re-read these lines and their context and write your own answer down before going to the answer choices. In this image, the author intends to suggest that prey and predator perfectly fulfill their roles. If you wrote something like this down first, it is very easy to pick Choice (B).

 If you found the passage difficult to understand, you can also use a process of elimination to rule out incorrect answers. Always be on the lookout for specific words that make an answer choice incorrect. Choice (A) is incorrect because, although well suited for their individual roles, the passage does not tell us that insects are "comfortable" in their particular roles. Indeed, it seems a stretch to believe that prey insects are "comfortable" with being eaten. Choice (C) is incorrect because the relationship, although well established and simple, does not benefit the prey, at least as far as we know from the information in the passage, meaning that the relationship is not mutually beneficial. Choice (D) is incorrect because we are not given information about the predator and prey making sounds to each other.

 A WIC This paragraph describes the relationship between a larva being eaten by a parasite and the parasite itself. In lines 2–7, for example, the passage states "the Anthrax [fly]…must…be made incapable of opening his victim's body…harmonious relation between the eater and the eaten." Choice (A) correctly describes this relationship – the "victuals," "foster mother," and "vessel" all refer to the thing being eaten by the Anthrax fly.

 D RC Re-read these lines and identify the purpose of these references for yourself. The author uses "founder" and "melting pot" when describing insect behavior to make the behavior seem more human in order to make it easier to understand. Choice (D) correctly captures this intention.

45 B WIC "This restriction" as it is used in lines 14–15 refers to the restriction described in the previous two sentences—that "the Anthrax [fly]…must, for his own protection, be made incapable of opening his victim's body." This restriction is described therefore as a necessary limitation on the fly's behavior, making choice (B) correct.

If you are unable to come up with your own word for this question, you can carefully eliminate the wrong answers instead. Choice (A) is incorrect because this limitation is inherent to the fly's being and not a result of a conscious choice of will. Choice (D) is similarly incorrect because there is no choice being made. Choice (C) is incorrect because the restriction is described in such a way as to help us understand why it would need to be that way, rather than something surprising or unexpected.

46 D COE Before you can answer this question, you must understand the claim referred to in the question. Re-read these lines and you will see that the claim described in this question is that there is a tension between knowing that insects should be described using scientific terms, rather than human terms that fall into traditional human stories of good and bad, "pain and destruction," etc. The best example of this in the answer choices is choice (D), lines 29–33, as these lines describe an old human story as an analogy to a fly parasitically digesting a larva. The other sets of lines describe natural phenomena using more scientific terms.

47 A RC Write in your own answer for this question after re-reading the first paragraph. The first paragraph of Passage 2 discusses a complaint that natural history is so often described in human terms and that this is an inappropriate mode of discussion within the field of science. This is the problem described that many scientists have in their writing, making choice (A) correct.

If you are not sure what the point of the first paragraph was, you can attempt to match up the language of the answer choices with the paragraph and eliminate answers that don't match. There is no common misconception mentioned, so (B) doesn't work; there is no contrast established between data and explanation, so (C) won't do; he isn't arguing against objectivity, so (D) is no good.

48 C COE Lines 33–35 include a description of insect behavior using human story in the way Passage 2 criticizes. Using the line number ranges in the following question, we can see that the author of Passage 2 states in lines 50–51, "wasps should not be described in human terms," and then goes on to mention some specific human themes that are often inappropriately used to describe insect behavior. Choice (C) is correct because the author of Passage 2, as illustrated by these lines, likely would deny that human themes and stories should be drawn from and used to describe insects.

49 A COE Choice (A) is correct because these lines most specifically provide the author's complaint about the type of language and comparisons made in lines 33–35 in Passage 1.

50   **C**   WIC   The author of Passage 2 describes insect behavior as being instinct based—a sort of programmed mode of acting unrelated to the kind of conscious thought and decision making undertaken by humans. The author also describes, as we have seen questions about already, the issue of scientific phenomena, especially insect behaviors, being described using human terms and stories. Choice (C) correctly summarizes this contrast as between "scientific fact" (the instinct based behavior) and "human interpretation" (the stories).

51   **B**   RC   The two passages relate to each other in that the first passage discusses a specific type of insect behavior using language that personifies the insects and applies their behaviors to human stories, and the second passage criticizes discussing insects in that way. Choice (B) best summarizes this connection.

       Choice (A) might seem tempting because Passage 2 criticizes Passage 1. Choice (A) is incorrect because the way Passage 1 describes its findings is separate from its research methodology. Research methodology is how one collects data, not how one describes it.

52   **D**   RC   Re-read these lines and write in your own answer for what the author intends in these descriptions. Lines 69–82 contain a mix of insect behaviors described in scientific terms and in human terms. These are used to contrast the inappropriate ways in which insect behaviors have been described, as in choice (D). Choice (A) is incorrect because the type of language being criticized is used in the lines as examples. Choice (B) is incorrect and unrelated to the discussion—the implication that relations in the natural world are efficient is made in Passage 1, but Passage 2 does not disagree. Choice (C) is incorrect, although it be difficult choice to eliminate. Choice (C) is incorrect because the methods described are being thoughtfully critiqued, rather than mocked. The difference is in the tone and use of language.

Writing and Language Test

1 **A** SEC — The object of the verb "was" in this sentence must be who "the best known figure" is referring to, Bob Dylan. It is not correct to make his name possessive here because his name is an object and does not possess anything. Were we to make "Dylan" possessive, the sentence would mean that "the best known figure" was Dylan's songs, rather than Dylan himself. Choice (D) is incorrect because it introduces a comma splice error. Because we could read the portion of the sentence before and after the comma in choice (D) each as separate full complete sentences, the punctuation used would have to be a period, semi-colon, etc., rather than only a comma. Choice (A) correctly relates "Dylan" with "the best known figure" and avoids introducing any errors.

⚠ Choice (C) is incorrect because "who's" is an abbreviation of "who is," just as "they're" is an abbreviation of "they are" and "he's" is an abbreviation of "he is". Remember that when pronouns take apostrophes, they don't signify possession: rather, they signify contraction of the pronoun and the verb "to be."

2 **C** SEC — When evaluating whether to surround a portion of a sentence with two commas or two dashes, determine whether the information contained in the clause or phrase to be surrounded is essential to make the sentence full and complete. In this sentence "Masters of War" and "Blowin' in the Wind" are essential to understanding the sentence because those are the specific songs that railed against war profiteers, etc. Because the names of the songs are essential to the sentence, they should not be surrounded with commas or dashes, which makes choice (C) correct.

⚠ Choice (D) is incorrect because the commas surrounding the names of the songs suggest that all of Dylan's songs railed against war profiteers. As the rest of the sentence makes clear, other songs had different messages.

3 **B** EOI
💡 — This question is asking us to revise the underlined portion to provide additional description to better connect with the main idea of the paragraph. Therefore, you should read through the rest of the paragraph, answering questions 4–6 along the way, before answering this question. The main idea of the paragraph is that Dylan surprised the audience at the Newport Folk Festival by playing rock music, rather than his traditional folk music. Choice (B) is the only choice that mentions that this festival is a traditional folk music festival. This is the correct response because it helps clarify why it was surprising that Dylan did not play the music that was expected, because the festival was intended for the type of music he had previously played.

4 **C** SEC — As indicated by the use of "did," the past tense of "do," this sentence is in the past tense. Choice (C) is correct because "led" is the past tense of "to lead." Choice (A) is incorrect because it uses the plural form of the verb, "lead," which would be appropriate to use for a plural subject acting in the present, neither of which is the case here. Choice (B) is in the present tense, which conflicts with the past tense "did" earlier in the sentence. Choice (D) is incorrect because it is in the present perfect, which also conflicts with the past tense "did" earlier in the sentence. The past perfect is denoted with "had" instead of "has."

381

5 A EOI Use process of elimination. Choice (A) is correct because it uses appropriate vocabulary to match that of the rest of the passage and it's the simplest choice. Choices (B) and (C) both use overly formal language, which also does not quite capture the correct meaning in this case. Choice (D) is overly informal due to its use of the colloquial "folks."

6 B SEC Use process of elimination. Choice (A) is incorrect because a comma is ordinarily only used along with "and" when separating items in a list of three or more things and when separating independent clauses in the same place that you could use a period or semi-colon. Choice (C) is incorrect because it lacks a comma that would be needed to connect the participle phrase "playing new songs without political themes" with the rest of the sentence. Choice (D) is incorrect because, by introducing a new subject into the clause following the comma, it creates a comma splice error. A comma alone (without a coordinating conjunction – FANBOYS) cannot be used in place of a period to separate two things that could each be separate standalone sentences.

7 A EOI On all "yes/yes/no/no" questions, always try to figure out your own answer before looking at the answer choices. Think: Is the information provided in the underlined part relevant to the main idea of the preceding paragraph? The main idea of this sentence and the paragraph as a whole is that, when performing at the Newport Folks Festival, Dylan unexpectedly played new music of a different type than what he usually played. The underlined portion should be deleted because the information it presents is off topic and distracts from this main idea.

8 D EOI For transition word questions, always read the sentence or two before the underlined part and understand what's happening there.

Here, the sentence beginning with the underlined portion is describing a conclusion of the previous sentence. "Thus" means the same thing as "hence," "therefore," and "as a result," and is thus appropriate here. "Universally," as in choice (A), is overly strong; the second sentence of the paragraph clearly states that the response "was mixed, with both boos and cheers audible ...." "Furthermore," as in choice (B), means the same as "in addition," and would be appropriate if the last sentence of the paragraph was presenting additional information on the same topic rather than summing it up. "Conversely," as in choice (C), is used when showing a contrast—something different from what was previously described.

9 C SEC There is little context by which we can determine that the sentence must read "reaction was" or "reactions were"; however, the negative view the Newport audience had towards the performance is described using the singular "response" in paragraph 3, suggesting that the singular "reaction" is more appropriate than the plural "reactions" here. Both are correct in terms of subject-verb agreement. Choices (A) and (B) are incorrect because both include a comma splice error in which a comma is used in place of a period or semi-colon to connect two independent clauses together. To use a comma in this way, it must be accompanied by a coordinating conjunction (FANBOYS) like "but," as in choice (C).

10 B EOI On all main idea questions, write down a quick main idea before you look at the answer choices. The main idea of this passage is that Bob Dylan did not only play one type of music (folk) even though many of his fans would have preferred that he did, and choice (D) is the only one that is consistent with the main idea.

 This is a very difficult type of question, and you can also use process of elimination here. Choices (C) and (D) all provide entirely new information. Choice (A) is overly general and does not relate to the main idea of this essay.

11 B EOI Because this sentence begins with "Dylan claims he didn't necessarily mean to offend…," it should be placed immediately after a discussion of Dylan's offensive conduct. The conduct Dylan undertook that bothered so many of his fans was playing rock music instead of folk music in the Newport Folk Festival, as described in paragraph 2. The best location for this new sentence therefore is at the end of the discussion of Dylan's playing the music, at the end of paragraph, 2 as in choice (B).

12 D EOI Use process of elimination. "Unexpected," "unforeseen," and "inexplicable" all have similar meanings, which make all of them unlikely to be the correct answer. Further, none of them make sense when used to describe the known effects of a practice as shown through studies. Choice (D) is therefore correct.

Whenever "Delete the underlined portion is an option," always consider it carefully. If the underlined portion can be deleted to create a simpler sentence and it conforms to the meaning intended by the author, it is probably the right answer.

13 A EOI Always pick the simplest answer! The SAT has a strong preference in the Writing section for concise, efficient language. For questions that, without providing a more specific goal, ask how best to combine two sentences, prefer the shortest answer choice that makes sense and avoids introducing an error, especially a vague pronoun. Choice (A) is correct because it is short and simple, and it combines the sentences without introducing redundancy, which each of the other choices contain.

14 D SEC The "colleagues" in this sentence conducted the testing but are not possessing it and so should not be made possessive through use of an apostrophe, as in choices (A) and (B). Choice (C) is incorrect because it uses the present tense "tests" when the sentence should be in the past tense as indicated by the word "conducted" earlier in the sentence. Choice (D) correctly avoids an apostrophe error and uses the correct tense, "tested."

15 B SEC This question tests pronoun agreement as well as subject-verb agreement. The results mentioned in this sentence refer to those of "Jacobs and his team," as in the previous sentence, and should therefore be the plural "their results" rather than the singular "its results." Choices (A) and (C) are incorrect for that reason. Choice (D) is incorrect because it combines the plural "results" with the singular "has" and creates a subject-verb agreement error. "Have" would be the correct word to use in choice (D), as in "results have served."

16 **A** SEC Use process of elimination. In choice (B), the semi-colon is incorrect because you don't have a full independent clause after the semi-colon. In choice (C), you need the adverb "particularly," not the adjective "particular," and in choice (D), there are two errors: the colon is incorrectly used and "in particular" is the correct idiom, not "in particularly."

17 **C** EOI As always, for "yes/yes/no/no" questions, always answer the question before you look at the answer choices. Do you think the passage needs the underlined portion? The answer should be yes, because the underlined portion offers helpful specific guidance about the amount and type of exercise.

You could also use process of elimination here. Choices (A) and (B) are incorrect because the reasons they provide for deleting the underlined portion are not true. The underlined portion does not contradict an emphasis on exercise; it merely suggests that even small amounts of exercise provide benefits. This information is not implied earlier in the sentence, as stated in choice (B). Choice (D) is incorrect because the underlined portion does not define "aerobic exercise."

18 **C** EOI Always pick the simplest answer! Choices (A), (B), and (D) all redundantly reuse the word "symptoms." Reusing that term has the effect of making the sentence read "…[A]erobic exercise…can reduce **symptoms** for those who suffer from…**symptoms**." Choice (C) is correct because it avoids this redundancy.

19 **D** SEC "A part" refers to a piece of a larger whole, like how a tire is a part of a car and a button is a part of a shirt. "Apart" refers to separation, like how you might miss your friends when you and they are apart. This sentence is describing a portion of a program and so should use "a part." Choices (A) and (B) are incorrect for that reason. Choice (D) is correct because it uses the correct preposition "of" to go with "a part."

20 **B** SEC Choice (A) is incorrect because the introductory noun phrase ("Even those without a diagnosed anxiety or depression disorder") lacks a verb. Choices (C) and (D) are incorrect because you need a demonstrative plural third person pronoun here, not a nominative (or subject) or objective pronoun. "They" and "them" are nominative (subject) and objective pronouns respectively.

If the explanation above is confusing, just try listening to the entire sentence out loud. If you have read enough English, "they" and "them" should sound incorrect in this context.

21 B EOI Choice (B) is correct because it correctly presents specific information from the table in a way that is also relevant to the main point of the paragraph, that although many people are not aware, exercise does provide more than only physical benefits. Choice (A) fails to use any specific data from the table. Choice (C) fails to utilize information relevant to the main idea of the paragraph and claims that it is surprising that many respondents to a survey claimed physical fitness was a benefit of exercise, which is false because that fact is obvious to most people. Choice (D) is incorrect because it falsely equates the majority of respondents on the table stating that increased fitness is *a benefit* of exercise with that being the *main benefit* of exercise. Further, choice (D) fails to refer to the specific data in the table.

22 C EOI Paragraph 3 describes the physical benefits of exercise and begins with the transition word "First," which suggests that the paragraph should be placed early in the passage. Paragraph 1 provides an introduction to the passage, and paragraph 3 provides information on the psychological benefits of exercising. Paragraph 3 should be placed between paragraphs 1 and 2.

23 D EOI This question asks you to both use specific data in the graph and show how common the problem of not getting enough sleep is. Choice (D) accomplishes both goals and is correct. Choice (A) incorrectly summarizes the information in the graph by stating that almost 30% of American adults reported sleeping 6 hours or less per night, whereas the graph shows that this amount is actually 37.1% (23.0% 6 hours + 9.1% 5 hours + 5% less than 5 hours). Choice (B) includes a correct statement but does not cite any specific data in the graph. Choice (C) incorrectly rounds information from the graph and does not emphasize how common insufficient sleep is.

24 C EOI Underline the specific details that the question is asking: <u>...indicate that the majority of Americans are unaware of the health risks associated with a lack of sleep.</u>" Choice (C) is the only answer choice that suggests that many Americans are unaware of the health risks of sleep deprivation. The fact that the CDC has partnered "with other organizations in a widespread campaign to alert the public" indicates a widespread lack of awareness of the risks. None of the other choices indicate lack of public awareness.

25 D SEC   This question tests comma use. One way that commas are used is to separate a non-essential element at the end of a sentence. Choice (D) is correct because it uses a comma to separate a nonessential element "such as heart disease, etc." from the rest of the sentence.

Choice (A) is incorrect because it adds an unneeded additional comma between "as" and the list, which is the object of the verb "as." Choice (B) is incorrect because it uses a colon in such a way that it cuts a nonessential element in half rather than at the end of an independent clause before a list, quote, or another independent clause that explains or clarifies the previous one. To correctly use a colon to separate the independent clause from the list in this sentence, one would need to delete the words "such as" and place the colon after the word "problems," which is not an answer choice. Choice (C) is incorrect because it uses a semi-colon after an independent clause before a nonessential element. A semi-colon is used almost exclusively on the SAT in only the same places as where a period would also be correct.

Commas are generally used before the words "such as" and "including" when these words are introducing a list of items.

26 D EOI   For all "yes/yes/no/no" questions, start by answering the question yourself. Is this a good addition here? In this case the answer is no because the additional information represents an unnecessary deviation from the main point of the paragraph and the passage—that adults aren't getting enough sleep, which has various negative consequences. Choice (D) correctly answers the question while providing an appropriate reason. The rationale given in choice (A) is incorrect as the central topic of the following paragraph is unrelated to students. Choice (B) gives a rationale that is a true statement but does not provide a sufficient reason to justify making the addition. Choice (C) is incorrect because the reason it provides is incorrect—this statement would not actually contradict evidence provided earlier in the paragraph.

27 C SEC   This question tests comma use. The sentence contains a nonessential element, "many researchers have found," which should be set off with two commas or two dashes. Commas or dashes being used in this way should be paired, and so since there is already a comma after "found," there must be a comma added between "workforce" and "many," as in choice (C).

If you can remove a phrase or clause from a sentence without changing the meaning of the sentence (i.e. the sentence still makes sense), the phrase is considered nonessential and should be set off with commas.

28 C SEC   This is a misplaced modifier question. A modifier is a word or phrase that describes or modifies another word or phrase.

Modifiers must be placed immediately before or after the words they describe. Here, "Reviewing the results" at the start of the sentence is a modifier. That statement must be followed by the thing it is modifying. The researchers were the people who reviewed the results, so the term, "researchers," must immediately follow the modifying statement at the start of the sentence. Only choice (C) puts the right noun in the right place in this way.

29 B EOI This is a vocabulary in context question. The reason the nap stations described in the passage have been installed is to allow a location for workers to gain additional mental and physical energy through rest. "Recharge," as in choice (B), is the best word choice here because in this context recharge means reenergize.

30 A EOI This is a transition word question, and the transition word is beginning a new paragraph.

Read the full paragraph before deciding on the transition word and decide how/if it relates to the previous paragraph. The statement that follows the underlined portion refers to what would be the best way to go about integrating napping policies into a workplace culture. Choice (A) is correct because "ideally" means under the best possible (ideal) conditions. Choices (B) and (D) are incorrect because "Nevertheless" and "Consequently" are used to show a contrast and the ideas in this paragraph are not serving as a contrast to those in the previous paragraph. Choice (C) is incorrect because "Consequently" is used to show a direct causal relationship (i.e. because one thing is true, another thing is also true).

31 B SEC This is a pronoun question. The antecedent of the pronoun that should be used here is "overtired workers," which is plural. Choice (B), "their," is therefore correct, as "their" is the plural third person pronoun. "There" is used to refer to location (e.g. "I want to go there."), making choice (A) incorrect. Choices (C) and (D) are incorrect because they are both singular.

32 D SEC There is no need to insert a word here—the sentence is already complete and makes sense without an addition. Choice (D) is therefore correct.

33 A EOI This is a goal question. Remember to underline the goal in the question. In this case, it is "indicating that accommodating workplace napping is a trend among employers that will continue to increase in popularity." Only choice (A) meets this goal. Choice (B) is about students, not employers. Choice (C) focuses on employees rather than employers. Choice (D) describes reasons why workplace napping is beneficial but does not indicate that it will continue to increase in popularity.

34 B SEC This question tests verb tense. The underlined verb should be in the perfect tense, specifically the present perfect tense. Verbs in the perfect tense often focus on how a past action affects the present. For example, you can see in this sentence that a past action—the popularization of the automobile—has made the United States a nation of cars in the present. The perfect tense always takes the verb "to have" plus a past participle. Because we need the present perfect tense (as the United States continues to be a nation of cars), choice (B) is correct.

35 A SEC This question tests how to punctuate subordinate clauses. Choice (A) is correct because it separates a nonessential element at the end of the sentence using a comma. Choice (B) is incorrect because it pairs a semi-colon with "and." Remember you can only use a comma before a coordinating conjunction to separate two independent clauses, not a semi-colon. Choice (C) is incorrect because a colon can only be used before a list, quote, or something that could be a full sentence, none of which apply here. Choice (D) is incorrect because it changes the tense in a way that doesn't make sense in context.

36 C EOI This is a writer's intention or goal question. Make sure to underline the goal: "indicating that the car became symbolic of American values." Choice (C) is correct because it indicates that the car became symbolic of the American values of independence and individuality. The other choices all contain arguably true statements, but they do not meet the specific goal called for in the question.

37 B EOI This is a transition word question so you need to carefully read the sentence before and after the transition and determine the relationship between them. The sentence with the underlined portion is providing additional information about public transit, continuing on from the previous sentence. "Moreover" is correct because it means the same as "in addition." All of the other answer choices—however, even so, and regardless—are used to show contrasts.

You might notice that the three wrong answers all have the same general meaning, so it's unlikely that one of them could be correct. If one were correct, they would all be correct.

38 A EOI Choice (A) is correct because it most directly provides support for the claim that vehicle crashes are a significant cause of death in the US. The other choices all provide information that is either irrelevant or provides less direct support for the claim.

39 C SEC (C) is correct because we use a comma before "including" and "such as" when the phrases are followed by a non-essential phrase or clause. (A) and (B) are incorrect because you never put a colon or dash before the word including. (D) is incorrect because semi-colons are only used to separate two independent clauses, which are not present in this sentence.

40 D EOI This is a word choice question in which you must choose the best word for the context. We are looking for a word that means that the emissions are *responsible for* poor air quality, ozone depletion, etc. Of the answer choices provided, "implicated" is the closest in meaning to *responsible for*, so (D) is correct.

41 B EOI The main idea of this paragraph is that public transportation is good for the environment, so we are looking for an ending to this sentence that sticks with that main idea. Choice (B) is the only option that provides an additional reason why public transportation helps the environment—because it is more energy efficient than private vehicles. Choices (A) and (C) suggest that public transportation is the same or worse in terms of energy consumption, and choice (D) suggests that there is no way to know one way or the other, none of which fit in with the main idea of the paragraph.

42 **A** SEC This is a parallel structure question. When a sentence has two or more parts, such as items in a list or two or more things in a comparison, the different parts generally need to be in the same grammatical format. Here "use" and "investment" both need to be in the same form—either both need to be gerunds (words formed from verbs that end in "ing" and are used as nouns) or neither should be gerunds. Choice (A) is the only one that doesn't make one of the words a gerund but not the other.

43 **C** EOI The underlined sentence provides an introduction to the rest of the paragraph and serves as a topic sentence.

This question is a great example that when evaluating a yes or no question on the SAT, it is important to consider not just the yes or no part, but also whether the reason given is the reason that justifies saying yes or no. The reasoning in choice (A) is mistaken—this sentence does not contradict a claim made by the paragraph. Choice (B) offers a true rationale, but that rationale is not a good reason to delete the underlined sentence. Choice (D) offers a correct rationale, but we would not keep a sentence in this location only because it provides a true example of the impact of public transit. Choice (C) provides the best reasoning for why this is a helpful sentence in this spot.

44 **D** SEC This question tests the correct use of pronouns. The pronoun is replacing "millions of Americans." (D) is correct because the underlined word is the object of the verb "allowing," and so must be an object pronoun—"them." Answer (C), "these," and answer (D), "those," are the subject forms of the pronoun and are incorrect.

Math Test – No Calculator

Multiple-Choice Questions

1 D HOA The quickest way to find $8a + 5$ is to recognize that $8a$ is twice $4a$. Since $4a = 24$, $8a = 48$. Thus, $8a + 5 = 48 + 5 = 53$.

2 B PAM This question requires an understanding of function notation. $f(2x)$ means the function f evaluated at $2x$. To find $f(2x)$, substitute $2x$ for x everywhere x occurs in $f(x) = 3x^2 - 4x$:

$$f(2x) = 3(2x)^2 - 4(2x)$$
$$= 3(4x^2) - 8x$$
$$= 12x^2 - 8x$$

 A common error students make is forgetting to square 2 in $(2x)^2$. Recall that $(2x)^2$ is the same as $(2x)(2x)$ or $4x^2$.

3 B HOA One way to solve a proportion is by cross-multiplying. This will result in a linear equation in one variable, which can then be solved easily:

$$\frac{3}{x} = \frac{21}{x + 12}$$
$$3(x + 12) = 21x$$
$$3x + 36 = 21x$$
$$36 = 18x$$
$$x = 2$$

 Be careful because 2 is an answer choice, but the question asks for the value of $5x$. Multiply 2 by 5 to get 10.

 An alternate way to approach this proportion is to look for a relationship between the numerators. Notice that 3 times 7 is 21. Therefore, x times 7 is $x + 12$. You can then set up and solve the linear equation:

$$7x = x + 12$$
$$6x = 12$$
$$x = 2$$

Again, $5x = 10$.

4 **B** HOA You can solve this system of equations by solving the first equation for m.

$$\frac{m}{n} = 3$$

$$m = 3n$$

Then insert it into the second equation. This gives you one equation in one variable (n) to solve.

$$3n = 6(n-4)$$

$$3n = 6n - 24$$

$$-3n = -24$$

$$n = 8$$

5 **B** HOA This question is asking about a change of form. You are given a proportion and asked which proportion in the answer choices is correct if the given one is true. The best way to examine a proportion is to cross-multiply to get rid of the fractions.

$$\frac{y+2x}{x} = \frac{10}{3}$$

$$10x = 3(y+2x)$$

$$10x = 3y + 6x$$

At this point, look at the answer choices to see where you want to head. Notice that choices (A) and (B) include the ratio $\frac{x}{y}$. Try manipulating the equation so one side is $\frac{x}{y}$. To do so, move the x terms to one side of the equation and the y terms to the other. Then divide by $4y$.

$$10x = 3y + 6x$$

$$4x = 3y$$

$$\frac{4x}{4y} = \frac{3y}{4y}$$

$$\frac{x}{y} = \frac{3}{4}$$

Another form change that can assist you in this problem is splitting up the initial fraction on the left side: $\frac{y+2x}{x} = \frac{y}{x} + \frac{2x}{x} = \frac{y}{x} + 2$. Since this equals $\frac{10}{3}$, you can say $\frac{y}{x} = \frac{10}{3} - 2 = \frac{4}{3}$. Now just flip the fraction to get $\frac{x}{y} = \frac{3}{4}$.

If you are looking for opportunities to plug in numbers, this problem presents a cool one. Since the original proportion has x on the bottom of one side and 3 on the bottom of the other, see what happens when you make x equal 3. y would be forced to equal 4, leading you right to choice (B).

6   **A** HOA   Since (p,q) is on the line $y = mx + 3,$ it follows that $q = mp + 3.$ Next, solve for the slope. The slope of a linear function, like $y = mx + 3,$ is the coefficient of the x term, or $m.$ Simply solve $q = mp + 3$ for m:

$$q - 3 = mp$$
$$\frac{q - 3}{p} = m$$

7   **A** PAM   This is a radical equation because it has a square root. To avoid the possibility of extraneous solutions (answers that do not work when you plug them into the original equation), use the answer choices and back solve. Start by plugging in $x = 3$ since 3 is in two of the choices.

$$3 - 3 = \sqrt{2(3 - 3)}$$
$$0 = \sqrt{2(0)}$$
$$0 = \sqrt{0}$$

The statement $0 = \sqrt{0}$ is true, so 3 is a solution, and the answer can only be (A) or (B). Now try $x = 5.$

$$5 - 3 = \sqrt{2(5 - 3)}$$
$$2 = \sqrt{2(2)}$$
$$2 = \sqrt{4}$$

Again, you get a true statement, $2 = \sqrt{4},$ so 5 is a solution. Since 3 and 5 are solutions, the answer must be choice (A), and you do not even have to check $x = 1.$

8   **C** ATM   Perpendicular lines have slopes that are negative reciprocals. Therefore, you must first find the slope of the given line and then take the negative reciprocal. The easiest way to find the slope of a linear function is to put it in slope-intercept form, $y = mx + b,$ where m is the slope.

$$y = \frac{-6x + 9}{2}$$
$$y = -3x + \frac{9}{2}$$

The slope is –3, so the slope of a perpendicular line would be $\frac{1}{3}.$ Choice (C) is the only equation with that slope.

9 B HOA It may be easier to make sense of the equation by isolating p, the amount of money Katie profits in dollars.

$$44.50h = p + 2.20h$$
$$p = 44.50h - 2.20h$$

Since $2.20 is the average per-student travel expense, $2.20h$ is the travel cost for h hours of tutoring. Profit is usually determined by calculating revenue minus cost. Thus, $44.50h$ is the revenue, or amount of money Katie makes for h hours of tutoring. 44.50 must be the amount of money she charges per hour.

10 C PAM Do not be intimidated by the exponential functions in the answer choices. Start by figuring out how many players are left after each round. This is a form of plugging in numbers. After 0 rounds, there are 64 players. After 1 round, half are eliminated, so there are 32 players remaining. After 2 rounds, there are 16 players remaining, and so on. Now, use these combinations of r, the number of rounds, and $f(r)$, the number of players left after each round, to test the answer choices. Start with $r = 0$ and plug it into each choice:

A) $f(0) = 64(2)^0 = 64 \cdot 1 = 64$ B) $f(0) = \frac{1}{2}(64)^0 = \frac{1}{2} \cdot 1 = \frac{1}{2}$

C) $f(0) = 64\left(\frac{1}{2}\right)^0 = 64 \cdot 1 = 64$ D) $f(0) = 2\left(\frac{1}{2}\right)^{-0} = 2 \cdot 1 = 2$

Since only (A) and (C) give the correct number of players, eliminate (B) and (D).

Now try $r = 1$ in choices (A) and (C).

A) $f(1) = 64(2)^1 = 64 \cdot 2 = 128$ C) $f(1) = 64\left(\frac{1}{2}\right)^1 = 64 \cdot \frac{1}{2} = 32$

Choice (C) gives the correct number of players after one round.

11 C ATM To simplify a rational expression with complex numbers, multiply the numerator and denominator by the complex conjugate of the denominator. The complex conjugate of a complex number $a + bi$ is $a - bi$. The complex conjugate of $2 - 5i$ is $2 + 5i$. Multiply $\frac{6 + 3i}{2 - 5i}$ by $\frac{2 + 5i}{2 + 5i}$. This changes the form but not the value of the expression because $\frac{2 + 5i}{2 + 5i}$ is just a clever form of the number one. To multiply, double distribute, or FOIL. Also recall that since $i = \sqrt{-1}$, $i^2 = (\sqrt{-1})^2 = -1$.

$$\frac{6 + 3i}{2 - 5i} \cdot \frac{2 + 5i}{2 + 5i} = \frac{12 + 30i + 6i + 15i^2}{4 + 10i - 10i - 25i^2} = \frac{12 + 36i + 15(-1)}{4 - 25(-1)} = \frac{12 + 36i - 15}{4 + 25} = \frac{-3 + 36i}{29}$$

12 C HOA

The plants have equal heights when $A = B$. Set the equations equal to each other and solve for d. Since this is on the No Calculator section, you will have to do some arithmetic with decimals by hand, but the numbers work out fairly nicely.

$$14.6 + 2.35d = 6.9 + 3.45d$$
$$14.6 - 6.9 = 3.45d - 2.35d$$
$$7.7 = 1.10d$$
$$d = 7$$

Alternatively, you could use the answer choices to back solve. However, you would have to do decimal multiplication, which would be time-consuming without your calculator.

13 A PAM FOIL the left side of the equation to get it in standard form ($ax^2 + bx + c$), so it looks like the right side of the equation:

$(ax + 4)(3x + b) = 3ax^2 + abx + 12x + 4b = 3ax^2 + (ab + 12)x + 4b$. Now set this equal to the right side of the original equation.

$$3ax^2 + (ab + 12)x + 4b = 18x^2 + cx + 12$$

Since the trinomials are equal, the coefficients of the corresponding terms must be equal. For example, since $3a$ and 18 are the coefficients of x^2, they must be equal, and you can solve for $a = 6$.

Likewise, $ab + 12 = c$ and $4b = 12$. Solve for $b = 3$ and use it to find c: $ab + 12 = (6)(3) + 12 = 18 + 12 = 30$. Thus, $c = 30$.

14 A PAM The equation $3x + 4y = 20$ graphs as a straight line and the equation $y = x(-x - 4)$ graphs as a parabola since it is a quadratic function (this may be clearer if you re-write it as $y = -x^2 - 4x$). A straight line and a parabola can intersect at one point, two points, or not at all (0 points). To determine how many points of intersection exist, sketch the graphs of the line and the parabola.

To graph $3x + 4y = 20$, put it in slope-intercept form: $y = -\dfrac{3}{4}x + 5$. The y-intercept is 5 and the slope is $-\dfrac{3}{4}$.

The quadratic function $y = x(-x - 4)$ is already in factored form, so the x-intercepts are 0 and -4 (to find x-intercepts, set $y=0$ and solve for x). The equation $y = x(-x - 4)$ can be re-written as $y = -x^2 - 4x$. The parabola opens down since the coefficient of x^2 is negative. The x-coordinate of the vertex is -2 because that is halfway between the x-intercepts 0 and -4. You can find the y-coordinate of the vertex by plugging $x = -2$ in either $y = x(-x - 4)$ or $y = -x^2 - 4x$.

$$y = x(-x - 4) = -2(-(-2) - 4) = -2(2 - 4) = -2(-2) = 4$$

Thus, the vertex is $(-2, 4)$. Sketch the graphs of the line and parabola, and notice they do not intersect, so there are 0 solutions.

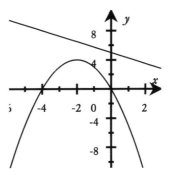

15 C PAM Use exponent rules to simplify $\dfrac{9^a}{3^b}$. First, get the same base in the numerator and denominator by re-writing 9 as 3^2. By the power rule, $\dfrac{(3^2)^a}{3^b} = \dfrac{3^{2a}}{3^b}$. Then, by the quotient rule, $\dfrac{3^{2a}}{3^b} = 3^{2a-b}$. Remember, you are given the equation $4a - 2b = 10$.

Notice that half of $4a - 2b$ is $2a - b$, so $2a - b = \dfrac{1}{2}(10) = 5$. Therefore,

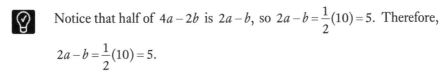

$$2a - b = \dfrac{1}{2}(10) = 5.$$

Student-Produced Response Questions

16   PAM   **2**

Solve for k by isolating the variable and taking the fourth root.

$$k^4 + 5 = 21$$
$$k^4 = 16$$
$$k = 16^{1/4}$$
$$k = 2 \text{ or } -2$$

Since $k > 0$, $k = 2$.

17   HOA   **0**

Sometimes when a question asks for an expression, such as $j + k$, there is a shortcut so you do not have to solve for j and k individually. Unfortunately, there is not an obvious shortcut in this problem. You must solve the system of equations for each variable and add the answers. A quick way to solve the system is by using elimination.

$$5(3j - k = -4) \rightarrow \qquad 15j - 5k \qquad = -20$$
$$2j + 5k = 3 \quad \rightarrow + \qquad \underline{(2j + 5k = 3)}$$
$$17j \qquad = -17$$
$$j = -1$$

Once you have $j = -1$, plug that into either original equation to solve for k:

$$3j - k = -4$$
$$3(-1) - k = -4$$
$$-3 - k = -4$$
$$-k = -1$$
$$k = 1$$

So $j + k = -1 + 1 = 0$.

18   ATM   **0.8 or $\frac{4}{5}$**

Recall from SOH-CAH-TOA that cosine is the ratio $\dfrac{\text{adjacent}}{\text{hypotenuse}}$. Since cosine of $b°$ is

0.8 (or equivalently $\dfrac{0.8}{1}$), you can label the leg adjacent to the $b°$ angle as 0.8 and the

hypotenuse as 1. Sine is the ratio $\dfrac{\text{opposite}}{\text{hypotenuse}}$, so using your labeled figure, sine of the $a°$

angle is $\dfrac{0.8}{1}$ or 0.8.

Sine of $a°$ equals cosine of $b°$ because a and b are complementary (their sum is $90°$) and sine and cosine are co-functions, that is $\sin a = \cos(90 - a)$.

19   HOA   **28**

This is a rate of change question. As the depth increases from 2,530 meters to 3,030 meters, the dissolved oxygen decreases from 205 ppm to 65ppm. The depth, therefore, increases by 500 meters, and the dissolved oxygen decreases by 140ppm. You can think of this as a rate of change.

$$\frac{\text{change in dissolved oxygen}}{\text{change in depth}} = \frac{140 \text{ ppm}}{500 \text{ meters}} = \frac{140 \text{ ppm}}{5 \text{ hundred meters}}$$

Since you are asked for the change per hundred meters, the answer is the quotient $140 \div 5$ or 28.

20   PAM   **144**

Substitute $b = 3\sqrt{5}$ into $4b = \sqrt{5x}$ and solve for x:

$$4b = \sqrt{5x}$$
$$4(3\sqrt{5}) = \sqrt{5x}$$
$$12\sqrt{5} = \sqrt{5x}$$
$$12\sqrt{5} = \sqrt{5} \cdot \sqrt{x}$$
$$12 = \sqrt{x}$$
$$x = 144$$

Math Test – Calculator

Multiple-Choice Questions

1 A HOA The cost of installing carpeting is the cost of labor plus the cost of the carpeting. If Luis spends $710 and the labor for the installation costs $160, then the cost of the carpeting is $550 (710 – 160). Since each square yard of carpeting costs $50, the area of Luis' living room is 11 square yards ($550 \div 50$).

2 C PSD You can solve this problem by writing a proportion using the ratio of cups of coffee to ounces of coffee beans. Notice that you must convert the 1 lb to ounces, but the conversion is given (1 lb = 16 oz).

$$\frac{40 \text{ cups}}{16 \text{ oz}} = \frac{x \text{ cups}}{20 \text{ oz}}$$

Now solve by cross-multiplying.

$$\frac{40}{16} = \frac{x}{20}$$
$$16x = 800$$
$$x = 50$$

Alternatively, you could find use conversion ratios:

$$20 \text{ o\!z} \times \frac{1 \text{ lb}}{16 \text{ o\!z}} \times \frac{40 \text{ cups}}{1 \text{ lb}} = 50 \text{ cups}$$

3 C HOA The amount of money the museum makes is the sum of the amount it makes from child tickets, adult tickets, and senior tickets. The museum makes $10c$ from child tickets (cost of child ticket × number of child tickets), $15a$ from adult tickets, and $12s$ from senior tickets. The sum is $10c + 15a + 12s$. Take your time selecting the correct answer choice since many look similar. Only choice (C) is the same sum.

4 A HOA Use the given equation, $v = 27 + 6t$, and solve for t when $v = 66$.

$$66 = 27 + 6t$$
$$39 = 6t$$
$$6.5 = t$$

When the car's velocity is 66 miles per hour, it has been accelerating for 6.5 seconds.

5 **A** HOA   To isolate the variable z, multiply both sides by the reciprocal of $\frac{28}{9}$, which is $\frac{9}{28}$.

$$\frac{9}{28} \cdot \frac{28}{9} z = \frac{9}{28} \cdot \frac{35}{3}$$

$$z = \frac{15}{4}$$

◇   You can also back solve by plugging in each answer choice for z to see which one makes the equation true.

6 **D** PSD   In this unit conversion problem, you must convert 3 dekaliters into milliliters:

$$3 \text{ dekaliters} \times \frac{10 \text{ liters}}{1 \text{ dekaliter}} \times \frac{1000 \text{ milliliters}}{1 \text{ liter}} = 30{,}000 \text{ milliliters}$$

7 **D** PSD   Sonny sold 14 computers in May and 14 computers in June for a total of 28 computers in the two months. The entire staff sold 109 computers in the three-month period (see the cell at the bottom of the "Total" column). Therefore, Sonny's May and June computer sales make up $\frac{28}{109}$ of all computers sold.

8 **C** PAM   If two variables are directly proportional, when one increases, the other also increases. This is typically represented by the equation $y = kx$, where k is a constant. In this problem, you are told that an object's momentum is directly proportional to its velocity, v, so the relationship can be expressed as $y = mv$, where m is a constant mass. You can find m by using the information about the bowling ball: $v = 2$ and $y = 12$, where y represents momentum. $12 = m(2)$, so $m = 6$. Since m is constant, the ball's momentum can be expressed as $y = 6v$. The question asks for the ball's momentum if it has a velocity of 10 meters per second. The momentum is $6 \cdot 10 = 60$ kg•m/s.

9 **B** PSD   You must first determine the velocity of the bowling ball when it hits the pins. The velocity is initially 4 meters per second but decreases by 27%. To find the new velocity, multiply the original by (1 – percent change).

$$\text{new velocity } = 4(1 - 0.27) = 4(0.73) = 2.92$$

Now, you must use the momentum equation from question 8, $y = 6v$. Plug in the new velocity: $6(2.92) = 17.52$ kg•m/s.

10 A PAM Since the function $f(x)$ has zeros at $x = 5$, $x = 2$, and $x = -3$, it has the factors $(x - 5)$, $(x - 2)$, and $(x + 3)$. You can write the function as $f(x) = (x - 5)(x - 2)(x + 3)$. Now look at the answer choices. Choice (B) is incorrect because it has the factor $(x + 2)$. The other three choices have $(x - 2)$, so to decide between them, you must multiply $(x - 5)(x + 3)$ to see which trinomial it matches. Using FOIL, $(x - 5)(x + 3) = x^2 - 2x - 15$, so $f(x) = (x^2 - 2x - 15)(x - 2)$, which is choice (A).

Always be aware that when you are on the Calculator section of the SAT, using the graphing element of your calculator can often be a way to check, or even do, a problem. Here you could set y equal to each of the choices and look to see which graph hits 5, 2, and –3 on the x-axis.

11 B PSD Kate is correct because one cannot make conclusions about an <u>exact</u> percentage of a population based on a sample of it. One can only use a sample to <u>estimate</u> a percentage of a population. Elizabeth is also correct: Eddy's conclusions are unreliable because of a bias in his chosen sample. Eddy wanted to make a generalization about the entire student body, but he only surveyed students who were waiting in line to buy lunch in his school's cafeteria. These students would more likely prefer the school lunch to the local fast food restaurant since they had already chosen, for whatever reason, to eat the school lunch rather than fast food. Thus the sample is biased. Ian is incorrect in saying that no whole number is exactly 90 percent of 330. 90% of 330 is $(0.9)(330) = 297$. The answer is choice (B) because only Kate and Elizabeth are correct.

12 C PSD In most data sets, if an outlier is removed the range will be most affected. The initial range is 65 (100 – 35), but after 35 is removed, the range becomes 29 (100 – 71). The mode (most common score) and the median (middle score) do not change in this case when 35 is removed. The mode remains 87, and the median stays at 88. The mean, or average, does change from 85.7 to 87.9, but this is a much smaller change than the change in the range.

Knowing that the range is much more drastically affected than the other statistics in this problem should allow you to answer it quickly without having to even bother with the calculations above.

13 C PAM In the exponential growth function given, 80,000 represents the principal, or initial, price. If the value of the boat decreases by 25%, it will be worth 80,000(1 – 0.25) = 60,000 dollars. In an exponential growth model, $A = P(1 \pm r)^t$, A is the price after t years. To determine the number of years it would take for the value of the boat to become 60,000 dollars while depreciating at 12% per year, use the equation $60,000 = 80,000(1 - .12)^t$ or

$$60,000 = 80,000\left(1 - \frac{12}{100}\right)^t.$$

14 **A** PSD Start by sketching a best-fit curve for the data on the scatterplot. It should be a curved line that decreases from left to right.

 If you are unfamiliar with what types of equations produce such a line, a great strategy is to plug in a value for m and graph each equation in the answer choices on your calculator.

Since $0 < m < 1$, try $m = \dfrac{1}{2}$. The equations become:

A) $y = m^x = \left(\dfrac{1}{2}\right)^x$

B) $y = x^m = x^{1/2}$

C) $y = -mx = -\dfrac{1}{2}x$

D) $y = \dfrac{x}{m} = \dfrac{x}{1/2} = 2x$

Graph each equation in your calculator to see which most closely matches your line of best fit on the scatterplot. It should be choice (A).

15 **D** ATM First, you must find how much jam is in one batch by finding the volume of the vat. The volume of the vat is the volume of the cone plus the volume of the cylinder. Note that the radii of the cone and cylinder are the same, but the heights differ. Also, be careful about the units. The measures of the vat are in feet, but the volume of the jar is in inches. It is easiest to convert everything to inches at the beginning. Since 12 in = 1 ft, 6 ft = 72 in, 4 ft = 48 in, and 8 ft = 96 in.

$$\text{Volume of cylinder } = \pi r^2 h = \pi (72)^2 (48) = 781{,}728.8$$

$$\text{Volume of cone } = \frac{1}{3}\pi r^2 h = \frac{1}{3}\pi (72)^2 (96) = 521{,}152.5$$

$$\text{Total volume of vat } = 721{,}728.8 + 521{,}512.5 = 1{,}302{,}881.3$$

To find the number of jars Vladimir can fill from one vat of jam, divide the volume of the vat by the volume of one jar: $1{,}302{,}881.3 \div 18 = 72{,}382.3$. He can fill approximately 72,000 jars.

16 **D** PSD The average (mean) is higher than the median due to a few extreme values. Several students must have scored much higher than the rest, and those scores are inflating the average. In any data set, the average is more affected by outliers than the median since the median is the middle value and relies less on the value of extremes.

17 **D** HOA Let's use x to represent the length of the first piece of the pipe. Since the second piece is 50 percent longer, it is $1.5x$. The third piece is twice as long as the second piece or $2(1.5x) = 3x$. The sum of the three pieces is 66 inches, so you can write and solve the following equation.

$$x + 1.5x + 3x = 66$$

$$5.5x = 66$$

$$x = 12$$

 Be careful because choice (A) is 12, but the question asks for the length of the longest piece. The correct answer is $3x = 3(12) = 36$ inches.

18 **B** PSD   This is a good time to plug in numbers since all of the answer choices include the variable x, which represents the amount of candy Sheila has now. However, rather than picking a value for x, it is easier to pick a value for the original amount of candy. A good number to pick is 100 because it is easy to find percentages of 100.

If Sheila started with 100 candies and gave away 70 percent, she gave away 70 candies. At that point, she had 30 remaining. Then, her friend gave Sheila 20 percent of the remaining amount, so 20% of 30 or 6 candies. Sheila now has 36 candies. Since x represents the amount of candy Sheila has now, $x = 36$. Plug $x = 36$ in each of the answer choices to see which gives you the correct original amount of candy, 100. Choice (B) is correct because

$$\frac{36}{(0.3)(1.2)} = \frac{36}{0.36} = 100.$$

19 **B** HOA You can write and solve a system of equations to find the value of B. If Mrs. Brennan buys x computers today, the total cost will be $1000x$. Her budget is less than the cost, and she will have to raise an extra $2,000. Therefore, $1000x = B + 2000$ or $B = 1000x - 2000$. If she waits two months, the total cost will be $900x$ and she will have $400 left over. This can be represented by $B = 900x + 400$. To find B, first find x by setting the equations equal and solving.

$$1000x - 2000 = 900x + 400$$
$$100x - 2000 = 400$$
$$100x = 2400$$
$$x = 24$$

You can substitute 24 in either of the original equations to find B:
$B = 1000(24) - 2000 = 24,000 - 2000 = 22,000.$

20 **C** PSD The first step is to find the percent of international tourists in 2012 who visited the United States. In 2012, 66,657,000 tourists visited the United States out of 457,179,000 total tourists. To find the measure of the central angle in a pie chart, multiply this ratio $\left(\dfrac{66,657,000}{457,179,000} = 0.1458\right)$ by the number of degrees in a circle, 360. The product is 52.488, which rounds to 52.

21 **B** PSD Percent increase can be calculated as $\dfrac{\text{new} - \text{original}}{\text{original}} \cdot 100$. Since 22,354,000 tourists visited Thailand in 2012, and 26,547,000 visited in 2013, the percent increase is $\dfrac{26,547,000 - 22,354,000}{22,354,000} \cdot 100 = 0.1876 \cdot 100 = 18.76\%$. This rounds to 19%.

22   C PSD   For this question, you must calculate the average yearly increase for Germany and compare that to the average yearly increase of each of the answer choices: the United Kingdom, China, France, and Spain. Average yearly increase is a rate of change and can be calculated for Germany as

$$\frac{\text{tourists in 2013} \ - \ \text{tourists in 2011}}{2013 - 2011} = \frac{31,545,000 - 28,374,000}{2} = \frac{3,171,000}{2} = 1,585,500.$$

Now, perform the same calculations for the four answer choices. The average yearly increase for the United Kingdom is 931,500. The number of tourists visiting China actually decreases by 947,500 per year. The average yearly increase is 1,588,000 for France and 2,242,000 for Spain. France has the closest average yearly increase to Germany.

23   B PSD   Standard deviation is a measure of spread. A low standard deviation indicates that the data points tend to be close to the mean while a high standard deviation indicates that the data points are more spread out. A quick look at the table should tell you that the mean is around 80. Therefore, adding three numbers that are clustered closely around 80 will change the standard deviation the least. Choice (B) is correct because 70, 80, and 85 are fairly close to the mean compared to the values in the other answer choices.

24   B PAM   This is an example of a literal equation where you are given an equation with only variables and are asked to solve for one of the variables in terms of the others. Start with the given equation and solve for r^2.

$$F = \frac{Gm_1m_2}{r^2}$$
$$Fr^2 = Gm_1m_2$$
$$r^2 = \frac{Gm_1m_2}{F}$$

25 B PAM The trickiest part of this question is understanding what g represents in relation to the given equation, $F = \dfrac{Gm_1 m_2}{r^2}$. It says g is the gravitational attraction between the planet and the star. This is another way of saying the force of gravity between two objects (the planet and the star), so g represents F. You must find g at the aphelion and at the perihelion. At both locations in the orbit, G, m_1, and m_2 are the same. The only difference is r, the distance between the planet and the star. At the aphelion, the planet is three times farther from the star than it is at the perihelion. Let 1 represent the distance at the perihelion and 3 represent the distance at the aphelion.

$$\text{Aphelion: } g = \frac{Gm_1 m_2}{(3)^2} = \frac{Gm_1 m_2}{9} = \frac{1}{9} Gm_1 m_2$$

$$\text{Perihelion: } g = \frac{Gm_1 m_2}{(1)^2} = \frac{Gm_1 m_2}{1} = Gm_1 m_2$$

The ratio of g at the aphelion to g at the perihelion is $\dfrac{1}{9}$.

26 C ATM Since $\triangle ABC$ is equilateral, $\overline{AB} \cong \overline{BC} \cong \overline{CA}$. If chords in a circle are congruent, then the arcs they intercept are also congruent, so $\overset{\frown}{AB} \cong \overset{\frown}{BC} \cong \overset{\frown}{CA}$. Each arc is one third of the circumference of the circle. It is given that the length of $\overset{\frown}{ABC}$ (the major arc from A to C including point B) is 18π.

$\overset{\frown}{ABC}$ is two-thirds of the circumference since it is the sum of $\overset{\frown}{AB}$ and $\overset{\frown}{BC}$. Therefore, $18\pi = \dfrac{2}{3}(2\pi r)$. Solve for r: $r = \dfrac{18\pi}{\frac{4}{3}\pi} = 13.5$.

27 **B** HOA The surest way to get the correct answer is to pick several values of h and see if they satisfy each inequality. The height of a child, h, must be between 34 and 56 inches, inclusive. Use the minimum 34, maximum 56, and one value in between, like 40.

I. $34 \geq h \geq 56$ This says h is less than or equal to 34 and greater than or equal to 56. If $h = 34$, this inequality is false because 34 is not greater than or equal to 56. Cross it out.

II. $|h - 45| \leq 11$ This says that that the absolute value of the difference between h and 45 is less than or equal to 11. In other words, h is less than or equal to 11 units away from 45. If $h = 34$, this inequality is true because $|34 - 45| = |-11| = 11$. It is also true for $h = 40$ since $|40 - 45| = |-5| = 5 \leq 11$. Finally, it holds for $h = 56$ since $|56 - 45| = |11| = 11$. It is a correct expression.

III. $56 - h > 22$ This says the difference between 56 and h is greater than 22. If $h = 34$, it is false because $56 - 34 = 22 \not> 22$. Cross it out.

The answer is (B) since only II is an expression that represents the correct range of heights.

28 **C** PSD This is an exponential relationship because the population of the ant colony is expected to increase by 34 percent each month. In an exponential growth relationship, the dependent variable increases by a percent of its current value. The rate of change is not constant, unlike in a linear relationship.

29 **B** PAM This question tests whether you know the polynomial remainder theorem, which says that when a polynomial $f(x)$ is divided by $x - a$, the remainder is $f(a)$. In this case, since $f(4) = 5$, the remainder when $f(x)$ is divided by $(x - 4)$ is 5.

30 **C** PSD There are a total of 48 students who studied at most six hours (14 students studied less than 3 hours plus 34 students studied 3 to 6 hours). Of those 48, 25 were from Class 1 (6 who studied less than 3 hours plus 19 who studied 3 to 6 hours).

If a student is chosen from those that studied at most six hours, the probability the student is from Class 1 is $\frac{25}{48}$.

Student-Produced Response Questions

31 HOA **15**

Since the tree grows at a constant rate, the tree's height can be represented by a linear equation. The average rate of change, also known as the slope, is 1.2 meters per year, and the initial height is 1 meter. The y-intercept is 1 because when time equals 0, the tree is 1 meter tall. The relationship can be expressed as $h = 1.2t + 1$, where h is the height and t is the number of years that have passed. To find how many years it will take for the tree to reach a height of 19 meters, set $h = 19$ and solve for t.

$$19 = 1.2t + 1$$
$$18 = 1.2t$$
$$t = \frac{18}{1.2} = 15$$

32 HOA **24**

A full tank can hold 14 gallons of gas, and the tank already contains 2 gallons. Therefore, it needs 12 more gallons to reach maximum capacity. The fuel pump can pump at 0.5 gallons per second, which is equivalent to 1 gallon every 2 seconds. To pump 12 gallons, it will take $12 \cdot 2 = 24$ seconds.

33 PAM **9**

If the point (2, 5) is on the graph of the function $g(x) = 2x^2 - 6x + c$, then $g(2) = 5$. Plug in 2 for x and solve for c.

$$5 = 2(2)^2 - 6(2) + c$$
$$5 = 2(4) - 12 + c$$
$$5 = 8 - 12 + c$$
$$5 = -4 + c$$
$$c = 9$$

⚠️ A common mistake that students make is forgetting PEMDAS. For $2(2)^2$, first raise 2 to the second power and then multiply the result by the first 2. Exponents come before multiplication!

34   HOA   **1020**

The most efficient way to solve this problem is by setting up a system of equations. Let A equal the amount of money Andy contributes each month and J equal the amount Jen contributes each month:

$$A + J = 420$$
$$J = A + 80$$

You can solve this system of equations either by elimination or substitution, but it is set up nicely for substitution since the variable J is already isolated in the second equation.

$$A + J = 420$$
$$A + A + 80 = 420$$
$$2A = 340$$
$$A = 170$$

 You may be tempted to stop here, but A represents the amount Andy contributes each month and the question asks how much will he have contributed after six months. Multiply 170 by 6 to get 1020. Remember, there is no safety net of choices in the Student-Produced Response section, so always read very carefully to make sure you've answered the "ask."

35   ATM   **3**

To find the radius of the circle, convert the equation of the circle to standard form, $(x - h)^2 + (y - k)^2 = r^2$, where (h, k) represents the center and r represents the radius. To do so, you must "complete the square" for both x and y. First, rearrange the equation so the terms with x are together and the terms with y are together. To complete the square for $x^2 - 6x$, take half the second term ($-6 \div 2 = -3$), square it ($(-3)^2 = 9$), and add it to the expression ($x^2 - 6x + 9$). Remember to add 9 to the other side of the equation as well to keep it balanced. Repeat this procedure with $y^2 - 8y$. You can then write each trinomial in factored form as a perfect square.

$$x^2 - 6x + \quad y^2 - 8y \quad = -16$$
$$x^2 - 6x + 9 + y^2 - 8y + 16 = -16 + 9 + 16$$
$$(x - 3)^2 + (y - 4)^2 = 9$$

In this form, it is clear that $r^2 = 9$, so $r = 3$.

36   PSD   **.333 or $\dfrac{1}{3}$**

Seven lawnmowers were sold in 2001, and 21 lawnmowers were sold in 2004. As a fraction, this is $\dfrac{7}{21}$ or $\dfrac{1}{3}$. If you choose to write the answer as a decimal, $0.\overline{3}$ should be rounded to .333.

37   PAM   **3**

The function $h(x)$ is undefined when the denominator equals zero. To find a value of x where the function is undefined, set the denominator equal to zero and solve for x.

$$(x+3)^2 + (x+3) - 42 = 0$$
$$x^2 + 6x + 9 + x + 3 - 42 = 0$$
$$x^2 + 7x - 30 = 0$$
$$(x+10)(x-3) = 0$$
$$x = -10 \text{ or } x = 3$$

Since the questions specifies $x > 0$, 3 is the only correct answer.

The SAT loves cute problems that can be solved with shortcuts. Rather than expanding $(x+3)^2 + (x+3) - 42$ and then factoring, you can factor it from its original form. Notice that it is written as a quadratic trinomial in the form $ax^2 + bx + c$ where x is replaced with $(x+3)$. This can be factored as $\left((x+3)-6\right)\left((x+3)+7\right)$.

$$\left((x+3)-6\right)\left((x+3)+7\right) = 0$$
$$(x+3)-6 = 0 \text{ or } (x+3)+7 = 0$$
$$x - 3 = 0 \qquad\qquad x + 10 = 0$$
$$x = 3 \qquad\qquad x = -10$$

38   PAM   **49**

This is an example of exponential growth where the amount of money deposited into a bank account increases annually by a percentage of its current value. The formula $A(t) = P(1+r)^t$ represents exponential growth where A is the final amount, P is the principal (initial) amount, r is the rate as a decimal, and t is the number of times the rate is compounded. The amount Anthony has after 10 years can be expressed as $1200(1+0.015)^{10} = 1200(1.015)^{10} = 1392.65$. Shaun's balance is $1000(1+0.03)^{10} = 1000(1.03)^{10} = 1343.92$. Anthony has 48.73 dollars more than Shaun. Be sure to follow the directions and round your answer to the nearest dollar to get 49 even.

Notes Regarding Score Improvements Reported on the Back Cover

1. SAT score improvements are calculated by subtracting the baseline score from the super-scored SAT score. Most tutoring students come to us in the summer before 11th grade. We thus use either an actual baseline SAT or the 10th grade PSAT as the baseline test. Students who came to us after taking the 11th grade PSAT improved almost as much, and their improvements are available on our website, marksprep.com.

2. In 2016, the SAT changed from a 2400-point scale to a 1600-point scale. Improvements on both tests are included on the graph.

3. In the class of 2017, because of the changes to the SAT, very few of our students took the SAT. Most of our students took the ACT, so we have not shown SAT data for that class.

4. Full score improvements are available on marksprep.com. Calculations include data from students who saw us for six or more tutoring sessions and include approximately 99 percent of students who have worked with us. The data have been verified by parents of the students seen.

5. On average, students see us for 10–11 tutoring sessions before a first administration of an SAT or ACT and 5–6 tutoring sessions before a second administration, for a total of 15–17 50-minute tutoring sessions.

6. The years in the graph refer to the graduating class year of the students, not the year in which we tutored them.

Thank you for purchasing *Four Realistic SAT Practice Tests*.
Our company, Marks Prep, is a small business of expert tutors with a passion for education. If you liked our book and found it helpful, we'd love an honest review on our Amazon page.

Made in the USA
Middletown, DE
04 September 2020